goddess of love incarnate

GODDESS OF LOVE INCARNATE

the LIFE *of* STRIPTEUSE LILI ST. CYR

LESLIE ZEMECKIS

COUNTERPOINT
BERKELEY

Quotes from the Mike Wallace TV show – Mike Wallace Collection, Harry Ransom Center, The University of Texas at Austin. A Photo Eleanor Roosevelt – courtesy of UNLV Special Collections. A Photo Lili – courtesy of PatrickMcGilligan, Robert Altman: Jumping off The Cliff, photographer Dan Fitgerald. (Ohio State University) From the Charles H. McCaghy Collection of Exotic Dance from Burlesque to Clubs, The Jerome Lawrence and Robert E. Lee Theatre Research Institute, The Ohio State University. Honeymooners: Use of dialogue from THE HONEYMOONERS – Courtesy of CBS Broadcasting Inc. Photos of Lili's Jerry Giesler trial: USC "Courtesy of the University of Southern California, on behalf of USC Libraries."

Library of Congress Cataloging-in-Publication Data

Zemeckis, Leslie
 Goddess of love incarnate : the life of stripteuse Lili St. Cyr / Leslie Zemeckis.
   pages cm
1. St. Cyr, Lili, 1917-1999. 2. Stripteasers--United States--Biography. I. Title.

PN1949.S7Z46 2015
792.78092--dc23

                          2015023035

ISBN 978-1-61902-568-4

Cover design by Natalya Balnova
Interior design by Domini Dragoone

Counterpoint Press
2560 Ninth Street, Suite 318
Berkeley, CA 94710
www.counterpointpress.com

Printed in the United States of America
Distributed by Publishers Group West

10 9 8 7 6 5 4 3 2 1

To my daughter Zsa Zsa Rose,
another incomparable beauty

For happiness I long have sought
And pleasure dearly I have bought
For happiness I long have sought
And pleasure dearly I have bought
I missed of all but now I see
'Tis found in Christ the apple tree.

I'm weary with my former toil
Here I will sit and rest a while
I'm weary with my former toil
Here I will sit and rest a while
Under the shadow I will be
Of Jesus Christ the apple tree . . .

Jesus Christ the Apple Tree

Miss Lili St. Cyr

TABLE OF CONTENTS

INTRODUCTION

It started with a dance.

Curtains part. Out unfolds a strong tan leg. A shapely calf begins to kick to the beat of the music. A woman emerges, a tall blonde goddess whose slender arms lift over a golden halo of curls. Tapered fingers pinch together, wrists softly begin to circle. Her slim hips undulate. She is small-waisted, not overly bosomy. From the sounds of the music and the look of her costume there is more than the hint of the Orient. She neither acknowledges the audience nor seeks their approval. She moves in a fantasy world of her own making, ebbing and flowing with the soar of violins. Her skin is flushed by a cool violet light that spills across her perfect skin, a lustrous pearl.

The corners of the sheer panel of her skirt are raised between her hands. She twirls. The music accelerates. She turns faster. She is utter perfection to look upon. She is the Unobtainable One. Her bra of gold rope shimmies back and forth, shoulders seesaw up and down as the music crashes. Enticing. One leg thrusts to the side, then the other. She rises on her toes. Her chest heaves. The flat of her stomach swells.

Her body is on display, her thoughts hidden under yards of cherry red chiffon. She covers herself—her *real* self—with the illusions of the stage. She barely glances at the audience. She is so expert a performer that each man believes she dances solely for him.

The music rises. Her chest lifts, bangles shake, a slight sheen appears at her hairline, the only evidence she is working hard. The dance is not as effortless as it appears, as she makes it. Her act is art, finely crafted, labored over for hours. Her moves flow seamlessly. A stretch of the leg, a twist of the rib cage, the reach of an arm. Her neck is slim and long and delicate and often compared to a swan's or a queen's. She arches backward. The movement says *take me, take me.* Her mind moves with her body; she doesn't censor herself. Her whole body snaps forward, then back again in movements that echo the beast inside.

Sex. It is the writhing movement of copulation at its most powerful. Rising. Her body lifts. She is about to reel in the audience as the music dips quietly. A tease of a pause.

It started with a beautiful girl, long of leg, graceful and lithe with green cat eyes, a dimpled chin, soaring dark brows. She is six feet tall in her gold-sandaled heels. Firm, muscled legs, elegant fingers and feet. A cool gaze to melt the hearts of many.

It started with a dance.

Heat pours from her skin. Platinum curls swing. She arches, uninhibited, overtaken by the music of desire. She dives to the stage, floor leg outstretched while the other points above her head. She is triumphant. Longing and sex—pure sex— rises from her skin like perfume.

She reaches up, her arms moving through the air, hands grabbing, hips swinging. She is off the floor and revolving upstage, stretching toward the break in the curtains. A pause. A look. A finger to the red of her glossy, swollen red lips. Hesitation. Then, as if she had been a mirage, she vanishes.

It started with a dance.

It started with desire.

It started with a beautiful girl.

It started with the dance.

LILI ST. CYR WAS BORN WITH THE CONVENTIONAL AND SOMEWHAT uninspired name of Marie Frances Van Schaack. Eighty-one years later her death certificate would identify her as Willis Marie Van Schaack. No matter. The world knew her as Lili St. Cyr; the Blonde Venus, the Form Divine, La Belle Lili, the Anatomic Bomb, Goddess of Love Incarnate. Of course no one really knew Lili St. Cyr. Obsessively private, shy to the point of rudeness, she would seek confidence in romance, pills, and, later, memory-dulling drugs. A thoroughbred filly, high strung, unpredictable, and hypersensitive. Ulcers and stage fright would plague her. The discomfort of her physical ailments was noth- ing compared to overwhelming insecurity and foreboding, a dread of aging. Death would take her in obscurity, once she had become the thing she had most feared, irrelevant.

The face Lili St. Cyr presented to the world was that of a confident, aloof strip- per. She was recognized for her tempestuous and numerous marriages, for rumor and innuendo, for headline-grabbing suicide attempts, for arrests, for wealth and a lifestyle of extravagance.

The private side of Lili was artist, dancer, and craftsman. She had been a savvy director of her career and life. "She was entirely self-controlled, aware every moment of exactly what she was doing."[1]

She explained there was purposely "a certain stand-offishness between myself and the audience. The further away and in awe I can keep them, the better."[2] She withheld, mysterious like her idol Garbo. Called both icy and untouchable, Lili masked herself as such, knowing what she was doing. "The more mysterious the act the more intrigued the audience becomes."[3]

Like Liberace whose image was synonymous with candelabras (Lili used them too) or Elvis with his blue suede shoes, Lili's signature piece was her bathtub. Or tubs, as she would use many; elaborate, transparent, antique, gilded, Styrofoam, even wood. The audience would thrill as pink and lavender bubbles floated over their heads while Lili bathed for them.

The world in which Lili pirouetted, the world of burlesque, was considered a second-rate entertainment bordering on sleaze. Burlesque was as misunderstood as the lady herself. Critics were outraged by the multitude of scantily clad women disrobing onstage. Lili shocked even further. She created a boudoir onstage and entered the scene nearly nude. She bathed, dressed, and caressed herself in front of curious eyes as if in the privacy of her own room. The act was erotically intimate, a personal ritual not performed so publicly before.

She danced in diamonds and pearls, designer gowns and mink coats. She had a uniformed maid onstage. She was like no other.

Lili St. Cyr burst into stardom in 1944. She had been working her way through the ranks of chorus girls since 1939, when she was hired at a Los Angeles nightclub. Lili's beauty, regal bearing, and five-foot-nine physique were said to have dazzled the owner who offered Lili a job on the spot.

Lili revolutionized stripping and redefined what a stripper could be. Lili's audience held their breaths, mesmerized by her queenly carriage. She was classy. She would surpass Gypsy Rose Lee in terms of fame, though hers would not be as lasting. Lili didn't write books, host a televised talk show, or have her life made into a musical that has become a theatrical perennial for fifty years. But Lili had a better body and a sexier act than the "Gyp," as she was known to her friends. Lili didn't just strip. She acted in silent "pantomimes," creating stories that sought a clever way to incorporate losing her clothes.

Her stories were personal. Whether a damsel in distress over the loss of a love ("Suicide"), or a sensuous game between matador and bull ("Carmen"), the audience got to peek into what they thought was the intimate world of Lili St. Cyr.

At the height of her notoriety Lili never showed too much, though it seemed as if she showed it all. Lili didn't bump and grind and fling herself around the stage like the big-bosomed Tempest Storm or the feisty Blaze Starr—both Lili's contemporaries, though they came on the scene a decade behind her. Lili wasn't a Margie Hart or a Rose la Rose, who were known to pull a G-string aside and "flash" pubic hair. Lili thought Rose la Rose "vulgar" and Hart got burlesque banned in New York the year Lili was starting out.[4] Lili would bring her act into swank Hollywood nightclubs. She was the first exotic dancer brought to a Las Vegas resort. She played there well into her fifties.

Lili did much to legitimatize burlesque and turn stripping and herself into a first-class entertainment. But Lili was never a snob and she never forsook her roots, returning repeatedly to dingy theatres and tiny clubs where leering men were at her feet—literally and figuratively—aroused over her glowing flesh.

Stripper, ecdysiast, exotic dancer, peeler, whatever one called her, Lili St. Cyr topped the marquee, gliding across stages in Balenciaga and Dior. She danced to the music of Gershwin and Rimsky-Korsakov. Her props were genuine antiques, costing thousands of dollars. She made a fortune in the thirty years she teased and tantalized.

Much of her story is shrouded in myth and lies, half-truths that she never bothered to correct, many of the deceptions her own.

Journalist James Bacon, who saw Lili perform many times, wrote, "Her sexy beauty surpassed anything Hollywood had to offer."[5] Hollywood had little to offer Lili, who much preferred the details she lavished on her act in the theatre. And it was profitable. She once figured she worked a total of seventeen minutes for a couple thousand dollars. She didn't like getting up early and she loved staying up late. Nightclubs and the theatre were her world, not the chill of early-morning sound stages.

She scorned the movie-making process because she had no control over the end result. On *her* stage she was in charge of how the audience reacted. And by meticulous attention to detail and nonstop work she felt "necessary."[6]

She infused her performances with a level of artistry not often seen in burlesque, though oftentimes denying what she did had anything to do with art. *No*, she wasn't an artist, when asked. *No*, she wasn't proud of what she did. Never let them see the real Lili St. Cyr.

Graceful, breathtakingly beautiful, flamboyant, selfish, narcissistic, extravagant, haughty, there were many sides to Lili.

Lili professed to live for love. She had to be "obsessed with a man." Men were her drug of choice. "I like to spoil men. That's my hobby. I always make a fuss over whoever's around me."[7]

Her string of famous lovers included Orson Welles, Yul Brynner, Vic Damone, Artie Shaw, Jack Dempsey, José Ferrer, just to name a few. Limousines were sent for her, champagne corks popped, jewels draped around her neck. There were many professions of love whispered in her ear. She fell in love often and hard.

She could be predatory and went after a man if she wanted him, not caring if he was married. She searched for someone to fill the emptiness inside. Seldom would she stay with one relationship for long. She wasn't often faithful. She would claim she hated being married because it made her "responsible" for the other person. The longer she stayed with someone, the more trapped she felt.[8] Freedom and the quest for it ruled her like the moon ruled the tides, like the planet Mercury ruled her sign of Gemini.

The twin. The Gemini personality is characterized by duality, described as quick-witted, clever, fickle, restless, easily bored, sometimes lacking in loyalty. Lili spent a lifetime flitting and fleeing, constantly on the move, the life of a gypsy. She detested any sort of restrictions. Like others of her sign, she didn't like to verbalize deep emotion. She was not introspective. Either supremely selfish or fiercely independent, she did what she wanted to do and damn the consequences.

She believed in making money, and if men wanted to spend time with her, it came with a price. She charged for "dates," which by no means included sex. She married for love. None of her husbands were rich. She would support most of them. Money was to be spent, not saved for a rainy day. As she was always working, she assumed there would always be money. Her lack of savings would bring terror and worry to her later years. But she remained a generous tipper, even when she had nothing. She would reach in the pocket of her robe to pay for her dinner and hand a twenty to the kid who had just jimmied open her apartment door with a credit card.

There were two Lilis: the private and the public. The public one, expertly coiffed and wearing pearls, long tanned limbs gracefully stepping in and out of a glass tub, who was defended by Hollywood's most notorious attorney during a trial that would make her infamous. The public Lili would be rushed to the hospital numerous times to have her stomach pumped; men brawled over her; and there were the divorces, six in all.

But there was the private Lili, who lived quietly, loving nothing better than to sit in her elaborately decorated home in complete silence, reading and sewing and cooking in perfect tranquility.

In the end, the misconceptions were long. Lili was a slut who would sleep with anyone, a cold-hearted bitch who used men. She was a feral Amazonian hunter. She was Wolf Gal (quite literally, Al Capp created the character after meeting Lili). She was devastated by drugs and poverty. She was fat. She was skin and bones. Her apartment was a Hollywood time capsule where she was living like Norma Desmond. She lived in filth in a dangerous neighborhood. She was *Sunset Blvd.* and *Grey Gardens* combined.

After her first transatlantic crossing, still in her teens, she vowed to travel first class through life. She did. Enjoying life on a lavish scale. She saw and accomplished things few women of her era did. A poor girl from Minneapolis raised with a secret by relatives who weren't who they said they were. Her family carried a multitude of lies. She learned from those closest to her.

Her life was filled with joy and laughter and much adventure. Heartache too. A deep despondency that sometimes overwhelmed her ran in her blood. It would often bring her to her knees. But time and again Lili would rise out of the ashes of despair and emerge once again to hear the roar of adoration and acclaim.

She had few, if any, long-standing friendships and claimed to despise women. In the end she shunned contact with what remained of her splintered family.

For a woman who made a career of her astounding Nordic beauty, the loss of it affected her most. When her spectacular looks vanished she felt she had nothing to offer. She was used to a great commotion being made over her every whim. People "bowed down to her."[9] When it was gone she decided to go "Garboesque" and retire from public—and private—view. She would close the door for nearly twenty years.

The woman who collected handsome men, antiques, minks, and jewels would in the end have nothing but stacks of photos that she sold for a few dollars to keep a roof over her head.

This then is the story of an extraordinary, private, complex, witty, misunderstood woman. Sex symbol, icon, enigma. This is the story of Lili St. Cyr.

PART ONE

CINDERELLA LOVE LESSONS

"When executed with deftness and shyness, disrobing becomes an artistic achievement."

—LILI ST. CYR

CHAPTER ONE

1994

A SEPTEMBER DAY IN LOS ANGELES. NOXIOUS, SMOG-FILLED WAVES OF brownish heat bear down on the desert city, smothering everything under a grimy cloud. Sprinklers shut off as the city feared another water shortage. Grass turned yellow, bleached of life. Everything is brown. The air. The land. It is an ugly time of year. It is nine months past the Northridge earthquake, when the San Fernando Valley shook, hardly felt in Hollywood. Where she lives.

The apartment is within walking distance of Paramount Studios where the greats such as Dietrich, Swanson, and Pickford used to pull their chauffeur-driven Bugattis and Duesenbergs and Mercedeses through the tall iron gates immortalized in movies such as *Sunset Blvd*. She too has been driven through the legendary gates to work. If she had known then how her life would end, would she have glanced down the treelined street and warned her younger self, or would she have continued down the path she was on?

The apartment is placed well back from the street, an old 1920s Spanish triplex. Built by Paramount Studios for the starlets and quite possibly studio executives' trysts with the same. It was rumored Gloria Swanson once kept an apartment there. W. C. Fields's mistress had another. The front room, though not large, is comfortable and would have been sunny if she ever opened her tattered curtains. It is a lower-floor unit with a thick wooden door. Quiet blankets the interior. A place of retreat. Cats roamed inside and out. A few mewed at the back door off the tiny kitchen that was never used. Most people thought the stray cats her only companions.

In the living room facing the expanse of green lawn and tall trees rising outside the French windows, she lies in bed. She had always had a bed in unconventional places. Her bed had been her stage. It still was. This time for the last act of her life.

As a child her bed had been tucked into a corner of the sun porch because there had been no space for her own room. They had been so poor back then, even before the Depression devastated the rest of the country.

And what a bed she had lounged on in her beloved home at the end of a wide twisting boulevard dotted with charming Craftsman cottages—oh! The remembered torment of having given that up—a big hand-carved wooden bed positioned smack in the living room. She had entertained lounging across it like Cleopatra sailing down the Nile, the banks of the river strewn with the carcasses of her lovers. She had played the Egyptian queen onstage, so why not in her home? That life long over now.

The bed, like so much else, was gone. Sold? She doesn't remember.

She avoids the other residents of the apartment building. She assumed they knew she had once been the infamous . . . the notorious . . . the legendary stripper. *Once*. Thirty, forty years prior when Los Angeles still had some semblance of glamour. When one dressed to attend the nightclubs and she drank gin fizz and listened to jazz, though admittedly not her favorite music. Life had been more bearable. Or had it? She had certainly had her share of drama and heartache back then. Rushed to the hospital. Stomach pumped. Another divorce. Romance. Another terrible headline. Robbery. Pills. Always the pills.

She was seventy-seven years old. She had been terrified to grow old and ugly. The thought depressed her. As much as her spine was stiff and she experienced difficulty in bending, she wasn't yet bed-bound. The arthritis hadn't yet racked her body constantly. She had never been a person not moving. She had been a restless soul traversing from nightclub to theatre, from husband to lover, always on the move. A gypsy dancing her way through life, the wreckage of others left behind. Was it relief or torture to now be confined to a single place, nowhere to go?

Her wings have long been grounded. Flight no longer possible. Except in her mind. Her dreams are the only thing that take her away, that transport her crippled body away and above this modest apartment and the pain in her limbs and her heart and her desperate fear. A dread that has always been there, a terror that she had kept at bay until now.

Her mind could still travel where her body could not.

She lay across the bedspread that had once been fashionable and new. She looked at her arm hanging over the bed. Scarred. It was too damn hot to move. She had always liked the colder climates. "I'm a northern girl," she would say.[10] She should have retired to New York, but here she was, stuck in this suffocating putrid city, wilting and irritable. She had always enjoyed remarkably good health. She had rarely been sick. Rarely been without money either.

Now the only way she didn't feel—pain or memory or regret—was with a system full of junk. A thick, heavy feeling would wash over her, taking away her apprehension. She would drift in pleasant nothingness, which was preferable to the here and now.

So much to worry about. Her bank was the cash in the pocket of her robe. A thin stack folded against her breast.

Wasn't she the one who had flippantly told some reporter she always supposed there would be someone around to buy her a burger? She had made *baskets* full of money. Oh, how she had loved those baskets, decorated with pink ribbon, filled with crisp green bills.

She looked around the nicotine-stained walls that protected and imprisoned her. A dim light shone through her worn curtains, shutting out prying eyes. She didn't want people to see her. She didn't want a camera to capture who she was now. It pained her worse than the ache in her joints. She had never wanted to be forgotten and insignificant. But she was.

From the small table next to her bed incense burned, a constant, thin trail of smoke spiraling upward, mixing with the white cloud from her Salem cigarettes. From outside her apartment the smell was pungent. One of her fans joked, "Lili, people are going to think you burn incense to cover the smell of pot." She thought that funny. "Good," she said, "give them something to talk about."[11] People had always thought the worst about her. With her help. She had loved the headlines.

LILI ST. CYR IS ONE OF THE WORLD'S MOST EXCITING WOMEN.

'I CAN'T SING OR DANCE,' ADMITS STRIPPER LILI ST. CYR. BUT HER SHAPELY FIGURE IS TALENT ENOUGH!

"SHE EARNS $10,000 A WEEK FOR HER DARING WEDDING NIGHT ROUTINE AT THE SWANKIEST NIGHTCLUBS IN LAS VEGAS, HOLLYWOOD, AND NEW YORK."

She had toiled in dozens of heat-filled rooms. There were the clubs and the old burlesque houses with vermin crawling backstage—and not just the baggy pants comedians. Always the dust and the peeling paint and smell of beer and Limburger cheese, the comedians' favorite.

She missed traveling. Like she had told Mike Wallace almost forty years earlier, she believed in UFOs. It was really quite arrogant to think humans were alone in the universe. How she wished a spaceship would swoop down and carry her away, which is what the drugs did. Her own unidentified flying opiate.

She was a dot. An infinitesimal insignificant blip in the universe. She could sense the junk moving through her. It made her heavy. Her breathing slowed. Floating. She was drowsy. She was coming down. The walls felt as if they were pushing in on her. Each breath an effort. She was pinned and had no escape.

She dozed. No memories, the reason she embraced the drug. Thoughts washed away and relief danced through her. No more pain. No more regret or shame. No more fear. All magically washed away. The crash was coming and would hurt. Stabbing sensation, vomiting, diarrhea. Until she injected herself again.

She woke with a parched throat. The skin loose and crepe-like around her neck. The once beautiful neck caressed by diamonds and pearls and expensive perfume and kisses from an endless variety of handsome suitors.

A cat mewed in the kitchen playing with the leaky faucet that she didn't want the landlord to fix. It would mean he would have to come in and there would be too many questions. He would see too much. Needles, though she tried to be careful. But most of all she feared he would see her. Ten years she had been here. Before that the previous apartment had been miserable. One room and Lorenzo had brought too many of his friends in. The middle-class neighborhood had swirled with rumors because of the traffic in and out of their dark apartment on the narrow path crammed beside other cottages. Squalid, admittedly. A comedown in the world. From her big house to that. Thank God she had the prescience to put her name on a waiting list for this apartment. Most assuredly her last residence. Besides the neighbors' parking right next to her window that disturbed her sleep and the sounds of the laundry room banging around the corner, she managed. Not enough privacy, but she could always make the best of whatever life threw at her.

She mustn't let anyone see her.

She remembered how they used to steal the most appalling pictures of Garbo, head down, thick glasses, a black turtleneck pulled up to her chin, baggy pants and flat shoes walking the streets of Manhattan. The old sex symbol gone four years now. It didn't seem possible. The steel-haired, flat-footed Swede captured trying to outwalk her past.

She had patterned herself after Garbo, seeking to emulate her allure, her mystery. She had been great friends with Garbo's dear friend Virginia, yet she had never asked Virginia to introduce them. She, like Garbo, hid from the world. She had been so terribly insecure about her looks.

There would be no more adventures for her. She had lived her life in pursuit of adventure, getting everything out of life she could; fame, money, romance, sex, fun. She knew there were those that pitied the life she lived now. But they didn't understand the life she had led. She had done *everything* she had wanted to do. And more. There were no more adventures in store for her, but she could remember the past ones.

She had been the stripper who had them lined up around the block in Chicago. Men had filled her hotels with flowers, showered her with jewels, furs; a few had punched her. She had lived her life in screaming headlines. And now this. A darkened room with thick red curtains, infused with dust. Old red curtains the color of the walls of her Canyon Drive bar. The curtains had come with her move; so little had.

She was the woman who created beautiful, memorable acts such as "Carmen," "Afternoon of a Fawn," "Chinese Virgin," not to mention a dozen others. A "Salome" act that had gotten her thrown out of Montreal was now a yellowing photograph accompanying an article in a long-defunct girlie magazine. But she had been in them all. All the *Confidentials* and *Gazettes* and *Night and Days*.

That woman had filled her beautiful home with exquisite objets d'art. She had led a beautiful life. She had been a beauty. On the inside too. No one ever said a bad thing about her except to say she was "aloof."

Where was Lorenzo? She vaguely recalled something about a hospital but couldn't remember if he was in one or if she had been.

She heard Betty Rowland, the old bird, still bothered gluing false eyelashes on every day. She didn't wear makeup any more. Hadn't for years and years. She didn't dress up, didn't brush her hair that was as fragile as spun sugar from all the years of peroxide. Her vanity was long gone. Exhausted. She no longer spent hours in front of the mirror getting her "look" just right, oiling her hair and powdering her cheeks, inventing a fuller lip with red pencil, rubbing oil into her long legs, polishing her nails. Oh, the hours and years of attention she had lavished on herself. Now when she ventured out she threw on a worn long skirt, scarf, and hat. She had become like the women Colette wrote about in *Chéri*, "women past their prime, who abandon first their stays, then their hair-dye."[12]

She remembered being a teenager and reading how to bleach hair in one of her movie magazines. Peroxide, ammonia, and Lux soap flakes. First she tried it on herself and then her sisters. No, Dardy hadn't let her, until later. But Barbara had. And suddenly she and Barbara were platinum blondes. That turned a lot of heads. The boys had tripped over themselves to get to the sisters.

The silence in the apartment was eerie. Where were her "touches"?[13] Her fans she corresponded with and whom she sent pictures of her younger self and they sent cash and kept her alive. If one of them would call, she would mention she could use a carton of cigarettes and some stationery. People had always done things for her.

A gnarled hand rubbed her perspiring forehead. It was sweltering. The breath in her head scratched at her brain. Years and years of smoking. She wondered if she would get cancer, hell, if she *had* cancer, if she would die from that. She didn't want to go to doctors. Her body wasn't worth preserving any longer.

She never had children. Her body was her temple. And a lot of others'.

Leaning toward the television next to her bed she turned it on and dozed, the noise filling her head with memories of a time she could understand.

Applause swelled. Always at the end of her act. No one had shouted, "Take it off! Take it off!" while *she* performed. Unlike the other strippers of her day, she commanded a certain amount of respect, just by the way she held herself as she stepped onstage. "You could hear a pin drop while I was on," she said.[14]

One magazine noted, "With the audience now fretful in anticipation, Lili breaks the hushed atmosphere."[15]

Another noted, "Lili is always the heroine in an exotic and sensual story. . . . Each guy can't believe himself up there with her alone and so he's silent, attentive, and respectful until the end of the story and the curtain brings him back to reality."[16]

The applause had sustained her. She had lived off it. She had been an artist. She had always had to defend herself. Arrests, divorces, accusations in the papers. Questions regarding her "private parts," testimony from "experts." Countless humiliations.

As far back as 1948, after her first arrest, she had defended her performance as being art. To the judge she attempted to explain "anyone who doesn't understand the story I dance probably would think the dance is suggestive. The story is about the lonely wife of a sultan who is unfaithful with a slave. My dance didn't go that far, however."[17] Always she tried to inject humor in a situation. Her little acts always had a backstory, a beginning, middle, and end, she explained.

She took pride in her work. She was the first to produce little mini plays. "Pantomimes," her great friend Tom Douglas had called them. She had changed the business of stripping forever. She had been the first stripteaser to play Vegas, for *years*. When Vegas had been a handful of quaint hotels scattered randomly in the middle of hot sand she had earned thousands there. A charming western town. Remote, outcast, trying to be something it wasn't. Inventing itself.

She had been a star. She had worked hard to remain one. She learned where to place a light, what color gel to put over that light. She didn't skimp on her costumes, one of a kind from Bergdorf Goodman, and jewels from Cartier. She created elaborate sets decorated with antiques. She gave everything of herself on the stage. Ironically, reviewers said her popularity was due to the fact that she was unattainable. "She had this wonderful haughtiness. After she'd taken a few things off, she'd half cover herself with the curtain and say, 'That's it, boys. You're not getting any more from me.'"[18]

She didn't play *to* the audience as the majority of strippers did. She danced as if she were alone. Reporters were wrong. She gave *everything*. She was a savvy, calculating entertainer. She knew who could help her and what the audience wanted.

She regularly decried any sense of ambition, saying she preferred to stay at home, that she worked only for the money. She always "needed" it, true, but she lived and breathed her work. It is what would kept her alive and on top. It was the only thing that made her feel substantial, the only thing that meant something.

There weren't many regrets. She had lived her life as she wanted to. Yes, she had lost her house, her looks, her health, and her family. She had nothing. But she had had *it all*. Every single damn thing. The men had come to see her because they wanted her. The women came because they wanted to be like her.

When her act ended and the audience applauded, she smiled, satisfied, and slipped between the curtains and off the stage. The show was over. And Lili St. Cyr would vanish.

CHAPTER TWO

Lili was named after her mother, Mariah Marie Curry Klarquist, or "Maud" as she was known in the family.[19]

Pasadena was a fashionable winter destination for the well-heeled in the 1930s, catering to a bustling tourist industry. With its wide boulevards and temperate weather the city was the ideal place for middle-class families to put down roots.

By at least 1929, fifty-four-year-old Maud Klarquist had rented a modest one-bedroom cottage on the pleasant treelined South Oak Street at 215.[20] Lili slept on a cot on the porch. Maud procured a job, working long hours in the alteration department of Peterson's, the woman's store for "Those not slender,"[21] hemming and fixing dresses for an upscale clientele for owner Chester W. Peterson. With older parents and after years of a nomadic existence, no doubt daughter Lili was a solitary, shy child.

It had been a long, circuitous road from a quaint village in central Wisconsin to the citrus groves of Southern California.

Maud had been born in or about 1874 in Port Edwards, Wisconsin.[22] The village was built around a sawmill and her Canadian-born father, Daniel, was a foreman/partner in a lumber mill. Mother Emily Jerome was New York born. Maud was one of seven sisters and a brother.

She would grandly claim to have been "a showgirl back in the day when Diamond Jim Brady" was about and had "traveled with a road company of 'Uncle Tom's Cabin'" some sixty years prior. If that wasn't enough yarn for the reporter, Lili's grandmother Maud went on to claim, "I used to do a special dance to a song called 'There's a Longing in My Heart.'"[23]

At twenty Maud married Francis Cedric Peeso in Monroe County, Wisconsin, on September 4, 1895. A year later she gave birth to the first of what would be three children: Idella; a baby, who died at birth in 1898; and son William, born in 1899. By 1900 the family was living in South Dakota renting a farm and taking in

a boarder. In the census Francis was listed as a "stock raiser." One would assume of cattle. By 1910 the family had settled in Hennepin, Minnesota.

Hennepin lies among numerous lakes and hills. Originally home to the Dakota Indians, it was largely settled by Germans, Norwegians, and Swedes. The area was another town built around sawmills and that was presumably why the family settled there.

However, the marriage between Maud and Francis did not last. By 1916 Francis Peeso was listed in the Hennepin directory living with "Cecilia," possibly his sister. Peeso then drops out of the picture and by 1918 Maud was divorced and remarried to a forty-one-year-old carpenter by the name of Ben Klarquist.[24] Ben had been an aging bachelor, moving often, living as a boarder in Hennepin, whose parents were Swedish born. Ben, probably born with the name Bryoguin, had blue eyes, light hair, and was of medium build. He too came from a large family with a sister and three brothers, all carpenters. There was a large contingency of Swedes by the name of Klarquist who settled in Minnesota and worked construction.

ON OCTOBER 25, 1916, MAUD'S TWENTY-YEAR-OLD DAUGHTER IDELLA wed twenty-seven-year-old Edward Van Schaack, a South Dakota–born traveling "land salesman."[25] The two probably met in Hennepin where they would live for the next several years while Edward worked for the First National Bank.

Edward himself was from a divorced home and had been living with his father, Frank, a proprietor of a grocery store, while his mother, Rebecca, moved in with her daughter Mabel. Edward was handsome, stood five ten and a half, with brown hair and gray eyes.

Idella soon became pregnant, giving birth to a daughter in 1917. A year later, on June 28, Van Schaack enlisted.

Idella was by all accounts a beautiful, temperamental young lady. At some point she contracted polio, either as a child (though photos show no effects) or probably around 1916, when the United States was experiencing an outbreak, and indeed President Roosevelt himself contracted it as an adult.

With a husband in the army, Idella moved on. By 1919 she married brown-eyed, dark-haired Louis Sherman Cornett Jr., born in 1896 in Crawley, Louisiana. They had a child, Bettie Lue or Bettalee ("Betty"), born (probably) in Nova Scotia in 1919. A son, Louis Cornett (Jack), followed in 1921.

In the 1919 Hennepin directory, Louis is listed as a chauffeur for an undertaker.

LEFT: *Baby Lili*

Lili with Maud and Ben Klarquist

In 1920 the Cornett family was living in Louisiana with Louis's brother; both were listed as rice farmers. By 1923 the family had settled in Texas.

Not surprisingly for the ambitious Idella, that marriage didn't last either. By 1925 Cornett was living in Nebraska and had remarried. He would have three more children, becoming a real estate salesman. With Cornett gone, the pretty Idella took her third husband, John Alfred "Ian" Blackadder, a charming "black-Scotsman" from an impoverished yet noble background who resembled Errol Flynn and had lovely "aristocratic manners."[26]

Ian had sailed to Canada at the age of nineteen with $65 in his pocket, crossing into Minneapolis (where he listed his age as twenty-two and claimed no living relatives).

Idella and Ian were married in Grand Rapids, Wisconsin, on May 2, 1923, at age twenty-six and twenty, respectively. They were a gorgeous couple. Ian stood six feet tall, brown-haired with gray-blue eyes. He had a scar (possibly from a motorcycle accident years earlier) behind his right ear. Idella was petite and copper-haired. By the following year the two had a daughter, Idella Ruth (hereinafter "Barbara"). Fourteen months later Rosemary (hereafter "Dardy"), named after Ian's favorite sister, was born.*

---

*   For simplicity I will refer to Barbara, Dardy, and Lili by those names

Sisters Barbara and Dardy (front) in Minneapolis

From 1924 to at least 1927, Ian was listed as a "helper" for the Minnesota Linseed Oil Co., residing at least once in Minneapolis.[27] The company was the major producer of flax and linseed oil in the state.

Ian struggled financially, and with four children—Betty, Jack, Barbara, and Dardy—in tow he moved his family to Pasadena, hoping to find permanent employment in the Golden State.

MEANWHILE, MAUD'S SECOND HUSBAND, BEN KLARQUIST, HAD BEEN working for J. P. Klarquist and Bro., general contractors and presumably a relation. One afternoon Ben fell two stories and, while miraculously nothing broke, he damaged his optic nerve. Lili, their daughter, was four at the time. Gradually Ben began to lose his sight and was no longer able to work. It wasn't a time in the country to be injured and unemployed. Maud, Ben, (son William was by now an adult and does not seem to have made the move[28]) and Lili moved to a farm in Webster, Wisconsin, where the grueling poverty soon drove them on to Seattle, Washington, where Maud's older sister, Katherine Willis Deem, had settled with her family.[29]

A young Marie Van Schaack

It seems after Katherine died of a heart attack in 1930 the desperate family descended south to follow Ian and Idella to Pasadena, hoping life would get easier. Lili was around twelve or thirteen, a difficult age for a girl both sensitive and awkward who hadn't grown into her looks nor made lasting friendships due to—she claimed—attending seventeen schools in all the years the family tried to find a permanent home.

BOTH FAMILIES SETTLED NEAR EACH OTHER. IAN HAD PROCURED A JOB as a garage mechanic (Barbara was now five, Dardy four). Shortly thereafter Ian moved his family out of Pasadena to the more rural Eagle Rock, a twenty-minute car drive from Maud, Ben, and Lili. It was like leaving the city altogether. Coyotes howled at night; rabbits bounded across the dirt roads. It was perfect for Ian, who loved horses. His father had been a championship horseman, supposed "three-time winner of the Royal Military Tournament."[30] With plenty of open land, Ian taught his young daughters how to ride while they were still toddlers.

The Blackadder clan was a sprawling, rambunctious family and Lili bounced

Idella in happier times sitting on Ian's lap while Idella's mother Maud sews

between her home and Eagle Rock, occasionally sleeping upstairs in a small bedroom. Ian encouraged the children to fill the home with friends. It boomeranged with the sounds of laugher and racing feet; dogs barked and horses neighed. He proudly nailed a sign to the house: "Bedlam Manner." Among the chaos the affable and outgoing Ian sought to escape Idella's foul moods that often turned to dish throwing. Idella hadn't always been so religiously unhappy. But after eight years of marriage with too many children and too little money she had hardened into a cranky despot. By the time Dardy was born, she was tired of caring for a house full of children. She was also tired of poverty, stuck at home with a leg stricken by polio. She sometimes used a cane and was self-conscious of her limp. She also wore "some sort of devices on her legs."[31]

There were too many dishes and loads of laundry and beds to make. It was not a happy marriage. Perhaps too she was resentful of the beautiful girls she was raising who would soon tower over her.

A PORTLY WOMAN WHO WORE GLASSES AND DRESSED IN CONSERVA-tive flowered dresses, gray hair tied back in a bun, Maud was the matriarch of the

From Lili's scrapbook, 1931, Lili at age 14

disjointed family. Not a physically affectionate woman, she nonetheless professed a deep love for Lili. Maud was also overly protective, relaxing only when Lili was safely under her roof. Just shy of the age where she would get in serious trouble with boys and not yet chaffing at the reins, Lili was content to stay close to home.

Maud was a remarkable caretaker to Ben, now a semi-invalid whose eyesight had vanished within two years of his accident.

Maud would remain one of the only constants in Lili's life. A strong-minded woman, generous, upbeat, and a hard worker. She was Lili's world.

Though for a moment it all seemed to fall apart.

FOURTEEN-YEAR-OLD LILI HAD COME HOME FROM THE LOCAL LIBRARY with an armload of books. Not a serious student by any means, they weren't studious tomes, but fashion books with sketches of dresses that Lili wanted Maud to show her how to make. Maud was a seamstress of remarkable talent and expertise. She made all Lili's clothes and was patient enough to teach Lili how to sew with equal skill, as what remains of Lili's costumes today is confirmed by the sturdy and precise stitching.

Lili might not have been thinking solely about dresses this day. She had received her first kiss from Jimmy Nichols, a cute older boy and a friend of Jack's who spent hours at Bedlam Manner underneath abandoned old cars, barely mumbling to her, covered in grease next to Jack.

It was her first romance and it sent her emotions soaring. She would become giddy by love, transported. Not knowing what to do, she pretended she was Garbo to Jimmy's John Gilbert. She was swept up in a surge of ecstasy and experienced a previously unknown feeling of confidence and power. Jimmy looked at her completely smitten and obliging when their lips parted, like at the end of a movie when the camera closed in on the satiated faces of the two movie stars as the fade-out began to happily ever after. Lili wanted to live in that feeling forever.

As Lili stepped into her house on Oak Street, her heart was pounding and her head was in the clouds. She was quickly brought down to earth. The atmosphere in the house was heavy and electric. Briefly Lili paused at the door, troubled, trying to discern what the dark essence was. She would recall the atmosphere as "grueling."[32] Dusk had fallen and it took a minute for her eyes to adjust. On the sofa her sister, Idella, faint traces of the beauty she had once been, sat clasping her hands in her lap. Maud sat stiff-backed, her brow creased anxiously. Lili stared at the two, suddenly wishing she was elsewhere.

Lili could tell Maud was tense by the muscles in her jaw.

For a moment the three generations said nothing.

Daddy Ben wasn't home. Unusual, as he was always in his room or on the porch.

Maud began. She admitted there was "something we should have told you years ago." But at the time it had seemed "unnecessary."

Idella spoke. "The time had come." She and Maud would tell Lili the truth. Why that day is anyone's guess.

"It was done because we love you," Maud interjected. "What was done as it was meant to be, because we love you. We did the best we could for you. Don't make any of this matter."

Lili might not be so sure there was much love coming from Idella, but Maud she would never doubt.

Maud looked at Idella sternly. "Idella, you know it was done because we loved you. We *love* you. And you too, Lili. Me and Daddy Ben love you. Idella loves you."

Lili was thin, hadn't yet grown into herself, still somewhat awkward and feeling too tall, unaware of her beauty that was about to burst forth.

"*Everything*," Maud emphasized, "was done because we love you. Remember that, honey. We love you."

"We all did the best we could," Idella said, nearly hysterical.

Maud told of a charming handsome Dutchman who had come into Idella's life and had "whispered words of love."

Idella explained they had met at a dance. Lili couldn't picture that. The Idella she knew was self-conscious about her pronounced limp. So there was an Idella before the ill-tempered woman sitting before her. Lili glimpsed a different Idella, a girl who might have been carefree, maybe a girl like her who yearned to flirt and go to dances, a beauty with her pick of boys.

The two women told Lili the Dutchman disappeared "in a fog" from Milwaukee, leaving Idella "in the family way."

Idella was very sick in the hospital and had a beautiful baby, but the baby was sick and born early and unable to leave the hospital. Idella was in agony—possibly because of the polio—and couldn't begin to take care of the baby girl.

Maud, her face anguished, explained that Daddy Ben had wanted to marry her.

Maud said she would marry Ben if they could bring up Lili, providing a "real home" for one daughter and a second chance for the other. Maud assured Lili she was wanted.

"I was so scared for you when you were little. You needed so much protection," Maud explained. She thought Lili was going to "die," tiny and helpless in the incubator. The doctors predicted she would be there for months.

"I knew it was the right thing for you," Idella whispered.

Lili was shaken. She needed to think. She stood up and walked out of the cottage, the truth whirling inside her head.

She walked up the wide boulevard where a streetcar ran down the middle, past imposing banks, a post office, Jordan's dry goods store. All the while her thoughts a jumble. Dardy and Barbara and Jack and Betty were half-siblings, not nieces and a nephew. Idella her mother? It seemed so preposterous.

Slowly her mind began to quiet. She decided she didn't feel deceived, she felt strangely liberated. And whether this happened over time or that night, Lili would realize that though she wasn't who she thought she was (Marie Klarquist), she would be who she wanted to be.

Somewhere in her walking she decided that none of it mattered. This information didn't need to alter anything. She wasn't all of a sudden going to call Idella "mother" and move in with her. She had always loved Maud and Daddy Ben. What did it really change?

It explained so many things, like why Maud, with her stoutly figure, wrinkles, and gray hair, was so much older than most mothers, the age span between the "sisters," Idella and Lili, so great.

She knew if she scratched beneath the thin layer of feelings and probed she would experience something decidedly not uplifting. But Lili, as she would always do, chose not to go beneath the surface. Fantasy was bearable. Truth was so often not. She would "not let it affect" her.[33] She would make her own reality. She set out to orchestrate her life as she wanted to live it, and work and romance and one day drugs would sustain the illusion.

This was a new chapter in her life. She liked new beginnings, always would. She claimed not to mind the constant moving of homes. She welcomed change that meant escape. Nothing would tie her to a place, not friends, family, or a man. Each new city held possibility, a chance for "adventure." Pasadena bored her. She longed for something. She would reinvent herself as she went along, a new name, a new place. She would remain an itinerant gypsy most of her life.

She would also turn Maud's and Idella's guilt into something she could manage to her advantage. Until the end of her days, Lili would become a master manipulator.

When Lili finally crawled into her bed with an old *Vogue*, Maud came with dinner on a tray. Maud would always be there for her *granddaughter*.

"We don't manifest our love," Lili would one day tell a reporter, "with hugs and kisses." It was a family that didn't talk about their feelings. There were few outward signs of affection. "But I knew I was loved."[34]

Daddy Ben, equally reserved, was a minor character. He played a benign role and would quickly fade from the narrative. It was women who ruled Lili's world. It was strong women who made the decisions. She learned from the women in her family to take care of herself and to do as she pleased. She also learned not to trust them.

Momentarily, Lili felt in peril. She was no longer Marie Klarquist. She felt as though something—she didn't know what—had been taken from her.

She compared the two names and thought Van Schaack was more exotic, different. "I'm going to call myself Marie *Van Schaack*," she declared. And indeed that would be the name she would sign for most legal papers for the rest of her years on earth.[35]

Maud agreed. Lili wrote in her French Canadian biography *Ma Vie de Stripteaseuse* that Maud then dropped another bombshell. Her real name wasn't Marie, it was Willis. But even that was not the truth. Either Lili or Maud made up the story. Clearly on Lili's birth certificate her given name is Marie.[36] Perhaps Lili remembered Aunt Katherine in Seattle whose middle name was Willis and she thought that different enough to appropriate as her own. Lili would vacillate between Marie and Willis for the rest of her life.

It wasn't enough that she was a different person, but those around her had to transform also. She could no longer call Maud "mother."

Maud must have been devastated. She had lived for this little girl and wanted nothing more than to be her mother. Lili had been named after her. *Marie.*

But Lili didn't want to punish or hurt her beloved Maud. She knew all the

Lili's mother Idella

sacrifices Maud had made for her. She knew Maud's life revolved around *her*. Maud would hold the deepest part of Lili's heart.

Lili had decided that to live the life *she* wanted, to deal with the shock that nothing was as it seemed, she would make them all change. (She would spend a lifetime reinventing and renaming people.) She wanted everyone to be different, not just her. Maud would now be "Alice." Where the name came from is anyone's guess. But it was accepted and immediately incorporated by the entire family.[37]

Lili decided Idella was now "Adelaide."** It was no time for arguments and Lili got her way.

Alice knew everything would be all right with her imaginative, clever, and always *adaptable* Lili. It was one of Lili's most dominant traits; she was versatile to whatever came her way. Lili would always be a survivor.

Alice stroked Lili's forehead and left her in the dark of her room, names pinging around her head like popcorn on the stove. Marie. Van Schaack. Grandmother. Sister. Mother. She smiled.

Now Lili had something in common with her idol. After all, Garbo had been born Gustafsson.

What should have been, and probably was, seismic news, Lili quickly filed

---

** For simplicity the author will continue to refer to Idella as such, because that is how Dardy and others referred to her. But Lili did call her mother Adelaide from that day forward.

away. Or so she claimed. But what a shift it must have made. The truth of it would do nothing to instill a sense of honesty in relationships. It was okay to say and do what you wanted no matter how it might affect others. Lili would become almost pathologically incapable of telling the truth about her past.

One sure result of this revelation was that Lili began to compartmentalize people. Few knew of, let alone met, Idella or Alice or any of Lili's half-siblings. Later, husbands would be told parents were dead. Half-truths. It was easier than explaining the abandonment, half-siblings, the messy, chaotic lies. There was underlying shame in the secrets. Lili distorted the truth and told outright fabrications. Marriages and relationships were not explained. One created the reality they wanted.

As strange as the story of Lili's "adoption" by Alice and Ben was, it is only part of the story. Whether she was told *another* lie by Idella and Alice, or Lili chose to dismiss her father outright by having him conveniently go AWOL with her birth, it is fantasy. It was lies on top of lies and secrets that remained buried.

Lili's parents were married eight months prior to her birth. How premature she was at birth is anyone guess, maybe quite premature, as she remained in the hospital and gave them all pause that she might not live.

Lili was born at 8 a.m. on June 3, 1917, in Hennepin County at Abbott Hospital. Two days later Edward Van Schaack did register, but according to the application for his military headstone he did not go into the army until June 28, 1918, a year after Lili's birth, possibly because US troops had started landing in France by the end of June. (He would be honorably discharged as a corporal on March 7, 1919.)

Alice admitted she was desperate for another baby. If Edward remained in the picture, Lili must have lived with her parents at least in the beginning. But records show that as of 1920 Lili (or as she's listed in the census, Birnee or Binee) was living with Alice as her daughter in Hennepin, Minneapolis, Minnesota.

Either to discredit or dismiss Edward, Idella did the unthinkable and implied that Lili was "illegitimate." Idella was capable of such cruelties, or maybe Lili thought it a better story. Lili liked stories of seduction and betrayal and she would dance them on the stage, but Idella and Edward had been married.

Was a young, excitable, and sick Idella incapable of taking care of a baby? The pair blamed Edward for abandoning Idella. It would taint Lili's feelings about her father and men forever.

FROM THAT DAY FORWARD SHE WOULD FANATICALLY GUARD HER PRIvacy and her secrets. She seemed to want to be Lili St. Cyr, fully formed and sprouted from nothing to be presented on the stage with the seven veils of mystery protecting her true identity. No one was interested in little Marie. She wasn't either.

CHAPTER THREE

It was 1932. The three girls stood in the glassed-enclosed porch that ran along one side of the big rambling house. By spring the green jacaranda trees would explode in a generous veil of trumpet-shaped purple blossoms. Clusters of orange trees threw off heavy fragrance in the yard near the tall eucalyptus with gray bark peeling down the skinny trunks. The sweet and pungent scent mingled with the sharp smell of frost on this early morning.

The glass walls insulated the girls from the cold morning. Their heated breaths clung to the dusty glass. The house was surrounded by acres of sage and scrub oak and open land. The big rock that loomed nearby from which the area got its name—Eagle Rock—was just ten miles from the bustle of downtown Los Angeles yet seemed further in terms of sophistication. This was rural land with skinny horses roaming and coyotes howling after dark. At night the sky was lit by a canopy of stars, not by the klieg lights of Hollywood. According to fifteen-year-old Lili, it was the sticks.

Lili often took a bus from Pasadena to visit Barbara and Dardy and teach them ballet. She didn't have many friends at school, preferring the company of her younger siblings, both long-legged, wide-cheeked, and dimpled like herself. In fact all three bore a striking resemblance to each other.

Barbara, ten, and Dardy, eight, stood behind their sister, their hands on a ballet bar that ran the length of the wall.

LILI STOOD IN FIRST POSITION. AT FIFTEEN, SHE WAS ALREADY HER FULL height of five nine and instructed the younger girls to follow her, ordering another set of pliés and jetés in a soft voice that would never change, never dominate, squeaky and high pitched, a startling Minnie Mouse sound. "No, no. Back straight, heels down, soften your wrists. Turn your feet out. Tuck your bottom under," Lili ordered.[38]

Ballerina Lili

Lili didn't yet carry herself with the noble bearing she would become famous for. Taller than most boys, she slouched. Alice was constantly encouraging, "You look like a queen, stand like one."[39]

Lili was clearly the more experienced dancer, having taken ballet classes for years from Madame Henderson for $1 a week. Madame H. had taken a particular interest in the pretty girl. It was one of the only luxuries in a spartan childhood lacking many indulgences. The ballet lessons would prove to be prescient; it would be a skill that would bring her fame and fortune and set her apart in her future profession.

The girls acted like frisky young colts, skittish and exuberant in their youth, long-maned and carefree. Spoiled by Alice and Ian, the girls did as they chose. Barbara and Dardy would tear through the scrubby hills around Eagle Rock on their horses while Lili closeted herself inside, doing nothing more than reading her movie and fashion magazines while daydreaming of living a glamorous life. She thought about designing clothes. She loved beautiful things and would spend hours arranging her drawers of colorful ribbon and lace.

Lili's beloved grandmother Alice

The girls wore pink satin toe shoes, a recent extravagance from Alice. Alice was always encouraging the girls, perhaps to make up for Idella's lacerating tongue. Lili was no closer to Idella after learning the truth, nor would she ever be.

WITH HER HAND ON THE BARRE, DARDY, SEVEN YEARS YOUNGER THAN Lili, looked up at her with awe. As Idella's last child she knew she was her least favorite. "I never remember her telling me she loved me."[40] Idella had run out of patience by the time Dardy was born. Idella blatantly doted on the more beautiful Barbara, a mere fourteen months older.

Idella struggled with loads of laundry, limping through the house, dragging a leg that had been damaged. Bitter and ill-tempered, the once beautiful woman whose life hadn't turned out as planned must have felt diminished in her family's eyes. This wasn't what she had wanted for herself. She didn't know how to care for this big, chaotic family. "None of us liked her," Dardy said. They adored Ian. He spoiled the children. He wouldn't let them lift a finger to help clean or cook. "Not my daughters," he would say. Neither Barbara nor Dardy would learn to cook or do

Barbara in Eagle Rock taking care of her horses

much of anything domestic. But they were fearless on their horses. And that was more important than domesticity.

Ian had rescued a half dozen skinny nags from the glue factory. He could barely afford to feed them but offered them to Barbara and Dardy with the stipulation they were to groom, feed, and ride them daily. With no money for saddles, Ian taught the girls to ride bareback, clinging to the animals with the strength of their knees. Madly passionate about their horses, they became expert riders.

Lili wanted nothing to do with pets. She had no desire to tear around the countryside kicking up dust and dirt in her face, burning her fair skin under the hot sun. "She was the least athletic person I knew," Dardy said.

FREQUENTLY LILI HOPPED BUSES AND STREETCARS TO DOWNTOWN Los Angeles. She loved nothing better than to spend hours in the palatial movie houses with hand-carved banisters, giant crystal chandeliers, thick red velvet curtains, plush seats, the lobby a sea of marble. She fell in love with movies—and theatres—when she had lived in Seattle. It was relief from worry as she sank into a darkened theatre. She was no longer a lonely and isolated girl. She was anything she imagined herself to be. Life on the silver screen was glamorous and she felt life should imitate the movies. It was everything Lili, sitting in a narrow bed in a cramped cottage on a quiet street, wanted.

Fifty years later she could recall in minute detail a scene in *Shanghai Express* starring Marlene Dietrich as Shanghai Lily (Lili's future moniker, if not the exact spelling): A train steams slowly through a Chinese slum. As with so many others at the time, movies and the stars were a heavy influence.

In the 1930s Greta Garbo was "the biggest money making machine" and at the height of her fame.[41] Lili became fascinated by Garbo. She wanted not only to look like her but also to seduce men as her characters often did. She had seen *Mata Hari* repeatedly, swooning over the costumes. At the opening of *Mata Hari* in New York, mobs had caused near riots, with dozens of adoring fans hysterical over their idol. Lili loved Garbo's sphinx-like expression, her mysterious manner and how it drove the men wild. From Garbo Lili learned the power behind being inscrutable. Everything was about cloaking, hiding, obscuring, protecting. She would invoke an alter ego when she went on the stage, most likely that of the actress.

John Gilbert, Garbo's leading man on and off the screen, was dark, good-looking, and rugged. He would become the epitome of the type of man Lili would fall for.

Clark Gable was another Lili developed a crush on. Her type, but elegant. Paired with Harlow and Crawford and Lombard, Gable was the crystallization of Lili's desires.

With her long dancer legs sprawled across her bed, Lili spent hours flicking through movie magazines. She tacked pictures of Garbo on the walls. She had begun her quest to reinvent herself.

A movie Lili would have enjoyed was *Dinner at Eight* starring that slinky Jean Harlow, who famously wore silky gowns that clung to her perfect body, leaving nothing to the imagination. She was laughter and light and beauty. In the film she plays Kitty, a gold digger with social aspirations to better herself by marrying a tycoon whom she is unfaithful to. Lili longed to be desirable enough to be a gold digger.[42] Lili's hair color would eventually match the star's distinctive shade after she discovered a recipe on the back of a box of Lux soap flakes, which consisted of adding Clorox, peroxide, and ammonia.

In Pasadena Lili would walk down Colorado Boulevard to the library and sit for hours flipping through *Photoplay*. She loved fashion and would buy *Vogue*, reading it until the pages were worn. Her dream was to be on a "best dressed" list.

Lili had begun waitressing at a Chinese restaurant owned by a family named Fong. It was there Lili developed a lifelong love of Asian food (that and the fact that

Lili at fifteen

most burlesque theatres seemed to have a Chinese joint nearby for inexpensive meals between shows). Sundays she spent at the movies with the Fongs in Chinatown watching Charlie Chan movies. She claimed she searched for opium—but never found it. Maybe she had a romantic idea of what taking drugs was like.

Having a job meant Lili soon quit school. She never regretted it, saying, "I wanted to have money to buy things." She turned her nose up at attempting to learn "a lot of dates in history."[43] She was more interested in making history.

While at the restaurant Lili was "discovered" by a photographer named Jack Powell, a local Pasadena resident who begged her to pose for professional photographs, promising it wouldn't cost her a thing. Powell developed a crush on the tall skinny girl with the wide smile who served him pan-fried noodles. Lili loved the camera. She appears fearless in front of it.

LIKE MANY MODELS WHO MADE UP SCENARIOS IN THEIR HEADS TO get into the mood, Lili was adroit at make-believe. Draped in exotic fabrics Lili could let her imagination run rampant. Lili would have many insecurities about her looks but it never showed in pictures.[44]

Lili and Jack could laugh over the awful photos of her with her head swathed in a striped bandana. They both hoped the pictures would lead to a modeling career. It did not, despite later claims she worked steady for two years. Her first disappointment.

If Lili showed the photos to her family, Idella would have made a snide remark, Alice would have exclaimed she looked beautiful, and Dardy and Barbara would have wanted their pictures taken too. Her entire life Lili freely gave out advice to family and friends about decorating, work, relationships. She would counsel Barbara and Dardy on how to get men to do things for them. She, after all, would become expert at it. Perhaps it had started with Jack Powell and his free photographs.

"DADDY DOESN'T FEEL WELL" BARBARA AND DARDY WOULD OFTEN whisper.[45] In his youth, Ian had fallen off a motorbike in Scotland and suffered migraines that over time would intensify in frequency and strength. When they struck, the girls were ushered outside. The house would be shuttered, and silence would blanket the normally boisterous household. The girls had to tiptoe when they were allowed back in. It was another accommodation of bad luck for the family.

No one had gotten over the horrible accident that Betty had suffered. In 1925, when Betty was six and still living in Minnesota, a reckless driver in a Model T hit the little girl while she played in the street. The running board sliced through her face, leaving her with an ugly scar from the top of her head across her nose, through her mouth, and down to her chin. Never as pretty as her sisters, Betty suffered both emotionally and physically. The sisters didn't talk about Betty much. Dardy would refer to Betty only as the "smart" one. Betty and what happened to her would become a tale the family rewrote, oftentimes denying her very existence. She was never mentioned in any of the sisters' later press.

RIGHT: *A very rare photo taken by Jack Powell of a ravishing Lili*

CHAPTER FOUR

During the worst year of the Depression, 1933, unemployment was as high as 25 percent. A loaf of bread was 7 cents and a fancy women's hat cost upwards of $1.60. Then came the repeal of Prohibition. Audiences lined up to see Fay Wray wriggling in King Kong's hairy palm while the country swooned to Duke Ellington's "Sophisticated Lady" and sultry Ethel Water sang about "Stormy Weather" in Harlem's Cotton Club. FDR had just become president and food lines stretched across America.

Pasadena would see its economy fall dramatically. The city with the idyllic climate—this was years before the smog infestation of the late 1950s—was home to around seventy-seven thousand. The city would never recover its pre-Depression splendor.

Ian Blackadder was thirty-one years old. He had a hard time finding and keeping work. From garage mechanic he became a salesman for Crown City Dairy based in Pasadena. Money had never been easy to come by and things were tight for both the Blackadder and the Klarquist families. Alice sewed from dusk to dawn at Peterson's. What beauty Alice might have had had long since worn away from hard work and squinting over piles of stitching.

That year Lili would have seen Joan Crawford shimmy with Gable in *Dancing Lady*. Lili loved to dance, loved her hours at the barre and in class, but barely dared hope she would end up on the stage. But the longing burned inside her.

Alice was fun-loving yet strict when it came to Lili and her safety. She didn't like Lili out of her sight and rarely approved of the few friends Lili had made. Maybe it was because the lanky teen was turning into an extraordinary beauty.

Marriage hadn't tamed Alice's independent streak. She didn't ask Daddy Ben his opinion or permission. When she decided to move to Pasadena she simply announced to Ben that was what they were doing. She was warm and generous and single-minded, all things Lili would inherit from her. Alice would give a meal to

Lili never shied away from nudity

a starving soul or the last coin from the bottom of her purse. Lili loved to relate a story, whether truth or exaggeration, of Alice giving a homeless woman, crumpled in tears on the streets, a sum of money almost equal to her week's worth of work. Lili would loathe those who were cheap.

Alice, though not a religious person and didn't attend church, was spiritual and installed in Lili the Golden Rule. Alice's generosity of heart was a trait Lili never regretted emulating. Alice never seemed to judge Idella nor said a harsh word about the divorces. She loved her large unconventional family. They made her feel useful. They were her pride and joy.

Alice did without many things so Lili could have her much loved dance lessons. She would sneak an extra coin in Lili's purse when she went off by herself to the movies. Alice knew the daily deprivations affected Lili, who longed for a richer life. Lili bought yards of colored ribbons that she obsessively organized, stringing them through her hair, a small luxury.

Lili was well aware she didn't come from a good family in one of the fancier homes in Pasadena. If other families looked down on them, she thought them hypocrites. She spent hours daydreaming about escape from Pasadena. There was nothing for her to do. She longed for grand passion.

At some point Lili posed topless (probably for Powell), except for a wreath of necklaces. She was never inhibited about her body; comfortable from dance lessons, she thought nothing of displaying her breasts.

THOUGH SHE FANTASIZED ABOUT BEING THE NEXT GARBO, SHE TOOK no steps, no training, no sending of photos to theatrical producers or agents, nothing to get her closer to Hollywood. She didn't believe she had the talent to act, or, quite frankly, for anything. But like a girl in an orphanage named Norma Jean, she knew she could dream bigger than most. Lili was not going to spend her life like Idella, breeding too many kids, with men that left, days a constant struggle of housework. Nor would she be like Alice who sacrificed her young-girl, hoped-for adventures to care for others. Lili vowed that her life would be about her.

With the family's peripatetic existence Lili was never afraid of new places; in fact she embraced them. Moving would prepare her for a life on the road working theatres from coast to coast, comfortable in hotel rooms, rarely in one place long. She thrived in the gypsy's life. "It gives me an opportunity to be someone else. To start anew," she said. "I always made the best of it."[46] Moving also allowed Lili freedom from herself and her past.

By cutting her life into sections, like a pie, Lili maintained her secrets. They were a family of secrets, maybe ashamed of Idella's many relationships, or the poverty, or Ian's headaches and Idella's limp and Betty's scar. Survival was something Lili would become very good at. And survival, she learned, meant keeping secrets.

LILI SAT FOR HOURS GAZING CRITICALLY AT HER IMAGE IN THE MIRror. It would remain a habit with her, later assumed to be vanity. Others didn't understand she could not perceive her beauty—or her identity—without seeing herself. Like children who search for their being in their reflection, so did Lili. As Diana Vreeland surmised, "To look into a mirror . . . I consider it an identification of self."[47] Lili was looking for who she was. Without seeing she couldn't feel who she was, who she was becoming. Was she attempting to make her face expressionless like Garbo? Garbo seemed impenetrable. Incapable of being hurt.

Lili described Jimmy Nichols as "fragile." After they shared their first kiss she pressed a finger to her lips. "From now on you belong to me." He was worshipful and they spent hours walking in the park.

One weekend, after a morning sewing and stitching, Alice shuffled home exhausted, hauling a bag of groceries. From the front porch an unexpected site greeted her.

"Alice," Lili and Dardy yelled. "Look what we got."[48] Next to them stood a serious and dignified border collie. It was a seeing-eye dog for Ben and would be named Barry.

Lili would claim it came from a Ms. Mable, a wealthy client of Peterson's. Ms. Mable had struck up a friendship, or rather took an interest in the kind, big-hipped woman often at her feet with pins in her mouth and a measuring tape between her chapped fingers. Ms. Mable knew where the Klarquists lived and their difficult circumstances.

Lili would write in her biography how Ms. Mable's charitable contributions would include buying Alice a tiny cottage, hardly credible as the census records continue to list Alice at South Oak Street. It was just the sort of fairy tale Lili was hoping would transform her life.

When Alice became too restrictive, Lili would hop over to Idella's. When Idella belittled her she would slink back to Pasadena. She learned to make the most of the two homes. And the most of her freedom. In her biography she would claim Bedlam Manner held little charm for her. She "couldn't stand the noise and confusion."[49]

Idella had a "huge chip on her shoulder." It must have been mental agony for the former beauty with a "disfiguring disease" to watch her beauty fade.[50] Emotionally distant and unaffectionate, she had a "vicious tongue" and was unafraid to use it on anyone.[51]

Dardy would claim Idella never learned social skills because she was isolated as a child, either because of infantile paralysis or circumstances of how she was raised, with a mother who moved often and ultimately divorced. Idella was woefully unprepared or unwilling to nurture any of her five children. Lili would be equally ill-equipped to cultivate a healthy mature relationship of almost any kind.

BEFORE DROPPING OUT OF SCHOOL LILI HALFHEARTEDLY ATTENDED the John Muir Technical High School on Walnut Street in Pasadena. She was no scholar. One of the few things she enjoyed participating in was an art class project competing in the Rose Bowl Parade. The class designed a float that was a salute to Iceland. The behemoth float of various-sized paper-mache icebergs ended up taking first prize. The students were rewarded with tickets to the usually sold-out Rose Bowl football game. Lili couldn't have cared less about some stupid game and sold her two tickets for five bucks apiece.

On Saturday nights Ian cooked hot dogs on the grill for the strapping young football players who wanted to impress the girls. With "car-loads of suitors"[52] the sisters good-naturedly competed to see who could get the most boys to show up. One wonders where Betty was and what she thought about the activity that didn't involve her. Perhaps she had already moved out. Or did she sit alone in her room hiding her scarred face?

It was a carefree time for Lili and her sisters. Still the football players didn't do much for Lili, who flirted while she dated Jimmy Nichols, her first kiss. The dissatisfaction she felt was palpable. Lili wanted more. Then she suffered through one of the most traumatic events of her life.

Lili found herself pregnant.

She was devastated, too ashamed to confide in anyone. And really, who was there? Her sisters were too young. She couldn't face Alice or the wrath of Idella. Jimmy was naive. She didn't want his reaction to confuse her.

Lili had a horror of being a young mother. She was determined to have a life of "adventure" like "Garbo." She was meant to be rich and have affairs. To achieve it she felt she would "need a man to liberate herself."[53] She felt trapped by the awful circumstance.

Determination was a key ingredient in Lili's makeup. Without a word to anyone she found a doctor on Third Street in downtown Los Angeles. Going alone she paid the $50 for an abortion. She was frightened. Not that she wasn't making the right decision; she knew she was. She didn't want, then—or ever—the life of a mother or "obedient" housewife. [54] She was worried the doctor would botch the job and she would become ill or die.

It would have been a long stomach-cramping ride from Third Street back to Pasadena on her own, changing buses and trams. But as Lili would continually show, she was made of steel and grit, absolutely focused when she set a course to see it through. She allowed nothing to get in her way.

Abortions, though commonplace, were both illegal and dangerous in the 1930s. It would have been much worse to be saddled with a squalling baby and Jimmy. She was by now disillusioned with their childish romance. There was more beyond the cottages of South Oak Street and she was going to get it.

Afterward she didn't feel well, mentally or physically. Trembling and insecure, needing assurance from someone that she would be okay, she admitted to Jimmy what she had done.

"You should have told me."[55]

She felt it was her responsibility, not his.

They held hands in silence, each alone with their own thoughts, knowing something between them had irretrievably changed. It was the end of the relationship. Jimmy looked at her differently. She felt a million years more mature than him.

A short time later, Lili, still feeling unwell, was forced to tell Alice what she had done. Alice swallowed her shock and tucked her into bed, saying she would call a doctor. Lili would say Alice showed marvelous understanding despite holding back the anger that Lili read on her face.

Lili refused. No more doctors. Inside the pit of her stomach Lili felt a burning anger grow. She felt betrayed—by her body?—and she was ashamed and didn't like feeling that way.

When Idella found out about the sex—not the pregnancy—she lectured Lili on how difficult it would now be to find the right husband. Lili's "value" had decreased from this "episode." Lili was shocked. She had never equated her "value" to the husband she would marry. Idella told Lili she was "spoiled merchandise."[56]

Idella spoke with Jimmy's family, who forbade Lili to see Jimmy anymore. There was a fight among the families about who corrupted whom. Lili felt as if everyone was judging her. "Ruined" was continually being thrown at her. *Ruined for what?* she wondered. She would harden herself against the screaming judgmental women around her. Lili was more determined than ever to get out of Pasadena and away from the disapproving faces. She was going to show her family exactly what she was worth. It was around this time Lili dropped out of school.

She had discovered love wasn't like a Hollywood movie. Love wasn't giving her a happy-ever-after ending. Love was something that had a consequence. Love would never be as innocent and pure for her again.

For the first time, she decided that if she was going to be told she was a "bad" girl, then she would become one. All the way. She would be a femme fatale that wouldn't disappoint. Bad was coming, she thought, just you all wait.

CHAPTER FIVE

Cordy Milne was a slim, nineteen-year-old motorcycle speedway rider when he met sixteen-year-old Marie Van Schaack in 1933. Born in 1914 in Detroit, Michigan, Corydon Clark Milne attended John Muir and the two probably at least knew of each other before they started dating. He lived on Winona Avenue four miles from Alice's bungalow.[57]

If there was something Lili knew nothing about—and cared not a whit for—it was motorcycle racing. Cordy Milne and his older brother Jack raced, he explained when he visited Lili, who was still working at the Chinese restaurant slinging chow mein and ripping open fortune cookies looking for something to change her destiny. As a now ardent fan of Charlie Chan movies, Lili would part the bamboo curtain separating the kitchen and dining room with red manicured nails and "enter" her set dramatically.

She never bothered to read the papers—nor would she—or she would have known about Cordy's growing fan base. Cordy Milne was a hugely successful scratch rider. Scratch riders competed in races that lasted no more than a blink of an eye, four laps that were typically won in a minute. Cordy was winning big "flat track" races in front of crowds that held thousands.[58] In the seconds they flew over the dirt, it looked as if they were clinging to their bikes for dear life.

A sports paper favorite with his blond tousled hair, a shock of which fell over his forehead, and rugged good looks, Cordy was, despite his small size, attractive, and Lili was interested. She could see the girls sniffing around yet had no interest in becoming one more notch on his well-tooled belt.

CORDY PERSISTED IN WOOING LILI, COMING AROUND EVERY FEW DAYS and asking her out. Finally she relented. She didn't plan it, but she began to see this older, seemingly financially set boy as her ticket out of Pasadena.

From Lili's scrapbook

Nothing had become of the professional photos Jack Powell had taken, despite his wild promises that she would soon be "discovered." She was still practicing barre, running to the restaurant, flipping through *Vogue* magazine, and watching endless double matinees, immersed in the tap-dancing *Gold Diggers of 1933* humming along to "We're in the Money." There was Mae West's *I'm No Angel* with a dreamy and sophisticated Cary Grant. And of course Garbo shone in *Queen Christina*, swaggering around in men's clothes, a style Lili would one day adopt.

But not even the movies could soothe her restlessness, her desire to *be* something. She needed a diversion and Cordy Milne seemed to be the perfect one.

She experienced her first taste of having her person in print. A local paper wrote that Cordy and a rival rider, Bo Lisman, were competing for Lili's affections as she sat in the stands.

Alice didn't approve of Cordy—probably because he engaged in a dangerous sport—and she worried for Lili, as she always did.

He didn't push himself on Lili, believing her to still be a virgin. They spent time in the safety of a group of his friends. She avoided being alone with him though he persuaded her to call in sick to work and join him at meets, sometimes as far away as San Diego.

She was shocked by the screaming fans who shouted his name. She sat among four *thousand* hyper men and women who whooped and hollered as Cordy tore his motorcycle around the oval-shaped track. His brother Jack stayed in the lead as his "blocker," clinging to the handles as he drove at a sharp angle, the bikes sliding sideways around the track, the rumble of the engines, mud shooting off the wheels, feet scraping along the ground. Cordy explained they raced without brakes and in only one gear. For Lili it was thrilling and jarring. She was a nervous wreck watching him.

Lili couldn't believe it when the race ended at one minute and 7.4 seconds. Before she was barely settled in her seat with her *Vogue* it was over. And Cordy had won. Though it seemed somehow common to her, the sport and the people, she was impressed by his celebrity. Fans tore at Cordy, asking for his autograph, pushing her aside to get to him. In her eyes his stature grew.

Cordy would hold her to his side, making it clear she was with him. She liked his possessiveness. At first. That didn't mean she wasn't above trying to improve him.

She complained about the tight riding breeches that the entire motorcycle club wore. She thought they were ridiculous. And they were filthy postrace.

What did the team name "Short Snorters" mean? She didn't like it. She tried to class him up, as she would with all her working-class men. She would attend to their details, while they attended to her.

Cordy wasn't interested in changing. He loved the intense competitiveness of his sport. He loved having his beautiful Marie waiting for him after a race. He liked his uniform and he liked it dirty and no one was closer to him than his team, a boisterous, close-knit crowd of thrill seekers who experienced a rush as they raced for their lives. Cordy and Jack were constantly in the papers, though not always positively.

In 1934 a competitor claimed Cordy, the national champion, "deliberately attempted to kick him off his machine." The competitor also accused Jack of illegal blocking. A rematch was called and Cordy lost.[59]

Though satisfied with his career, Cordy was ready to add a beautiful girl who would watch him from the stand and start a family. Cordy told her he wanted lots of babies. Lili smiled and didn't tell him what she wanted was "adventure" and "limousines." There was no room for babies in her future.[60]

She loyally stood by Cordy during various injuries. The following year he would be thrown fifteen feet in the air, his bike landing square on his face, knocking out his front teeth, which gave his already charming smile—his best feature, Lili thought—a sweet vulnerability. Truthfully, the ruggedness and the danger of the sport was what excited her and she felt a growing respect for her boyfriend. Soon she too was screaming in the stands as the riders dragged their feet behind to slow down and stop. The Milne brothers revolutionized the sport by riding "foot forward." Cordy would badly burn his legs on an exhaust pipe and the following year Jack would get hit by another rider and break his back.

Idella complained to Lili that staying with Cordy provided no "financial stability." She thought Lili was "wasting her time."[61]

The more Idella complained, the more Lili wanted him. She was attracted to the "forbidden," turned on by his bad-boy image. Idella would gripe and Lili would shrug her shoulders and throw up a wall of impenetrable silence. She learned that not saying anything was a powerful tool. It put her in control by not allowing someone to get to her. Of course it was an isolating tactic, one that would cost her dearly.

The relationship wasn't progressing where Lili thought it should despite trips to Big Bear and Palm Springs at high speeds, clinging to Cordy's waist, arms around his red jacket with the Short Snorters' emblem on the back.

One New Year's Eve, Lili, Cordy, his brother, and their race buddies spent the festivities in San Bernardino drinking cheap wine. Sometime after midnight, Lili persuaded Cordy to drive her home. She clung precariously to his back as they raced toward Pasadena at speeds that whipped her hair and caused her eyes to sting. She was terrified. Cordy decided to detour out into the desert. Over a bump Cordy felt Lili lose her grip and he lost her. She felt a tremendous pain in her shoulder. With scrapes on her arms and legs she was badly shaken up.

She got up furious, swearing at him, hitting him mildly on his back and telling him she wasn't getting back on *that machine*. She insisted they walk the entire way back to Pasadena.

Alice was waiting on the porch when they arrived. When she saw Lili in tears she rushed forward.

Lili was immediately taken to the hospital. She had broken her collarbone. She would always say how that night was the turning point. She used Cordy's guilt to her advantage.

She decided no more traveling on the back of bikes to save a buck. Cordy was thrifty and she couldn't stand it. To her money was to be enjoyed. It would be one of many differences that would drive a wedge between them.

CHAPTER SIX

In 1934 Ian's sister (and Dardy's namesake) Rosemary von Urach arrived from Europe. She was hoping to make it an extended stay. According to her sister, Frederika (Erica), Rosemary wanted to get into the movies.

Lili was taken by the blonde and glamorous woman with the "expressive purple eyes."[62] Rosemary was witty and clever, wore a fur coat, and traveled with enormous trunks, her manners gracious and elegant. She was a beautiful, enchanting woman, a genuine princess, and, as yet undiagnosed, schizophrenic.

ROSEMARY BLACKADDER VON URACH HAD BEEN BORN THE MIDDLE child of Anne Wilson and John Blackadder in Scotland. She was high-strung and extremely intelligent. She had studied at Girton, "degrading" for a couple terms, meaning one had permission to have the term disregarded, in Rosemary's case, due to health reasons.[63] She studied English and modern and medieval language Tripos.[64]

What remains of Rosemary's school records is a slim file that notes she toured "over Europe with a puppet show" after leaving Girton and then became a journalist writing "middle" articles for the *Saturday Review* and *Evening Standard*.[65] For the *Daily Express* she was hired to interview famous people for the Manchester edition. She often illustrated her own articles.

Conversant in a multitude of languages, Rosemary was well-traveled, studied art and Italian in Florence. In Paris she studied painting and roomed with composer Gustav's daughter Anna Mahler.

Close with her mother throughout her life, Rosemary relied heavily on Anna, often writing for money. She was accused by her sister Erica of being frivolous and manipulative, the same charges later leveled at Lili by others.

At a party at the German embassy in Paris, Rosemary met her prince—a real

Lili's step-aunt Rosemary

live prince—whom she fell in love with. They married in Oslo, Norway, in 1931. The two-years-younger German Prince Albrecht von Urach came from an impressive—albeit impoverished—background.

Born in 1903, the sixth of nine children, young Albrecht spent his days at the family's fabled Lichtenstein castle outside of Stuttgart.

Albrecht was handsome, tall, and light-haired. He was an expressionist painter, photographer, war correspondent, and diplomat. His princess mother was aunt to Prince Albert I of Monaco, for whom he was named (and at one time stood next in the line of succession). Albrecht joined the Nazi party in 1934. Interrogated for war crimes at the end of the war, he would suffer no ill repercussions for his Nazi association and began a successful career with Mercedes-Benz.

Rosemary and Albrecht's marriage might have lacked money but there was no shortage of adventure. Albrecht continued painting, though they sold poorly.

In 1932 Rosemary gave birth to daughter Marie-Gabrielle "Mariga," who would one day marry Hon. Desmond Guinness, son of the gorgeous and glamorous Diana Mitford, one of the famous Mitford sisters.

Having a child did little to settle the relentlessly traveling couple. They lived in Germany but left for Venice and Mahler's apartment in 1934 where they both continued as freelance journalists.

According to her sister, Rosemary had an idea to get into the movies and thus planned a trip to California to stay with brother Ian. When nothing panned out she lay around on Ian's and Idella's sofa shooing her curious nieces (Barbara and Dardy) away. "Go away, little girls. Go away."[66] She wasn't interested in her own child, let alone someone else's.

Lili thought this fragile, eccentric, glamorously made-up woman was wonderful. She envied the princess's title, travels, and clothes. Though Rosemary had obligations of husband and daughter they didn't hamper the ethereal young woman collapsed in languor on Idella's couch. One can only imagine what Idella thought. And though they weren't related by blood Lili was greatly influenced and infatuated by Rosemary, the most exotic creature to cross her path. Here was a woman, practically a relative, who had managed to escape her provincial family to lead an adventurous life trotting around the globe, draped in chic clothing. Rosemary was the epitome of the independence—and glamour—Lili dreamed of.

Rosemary was soon gone, continuing her travels with her big trunks to the Far East and then Berlin where her husband and daughter waited.

In 1934 the von Urach family set up home in Japan, where Albrecht worked in the German press office as a journalist. He was sent to China to cover the Chinese-Japanese war. For unhappy Rosemary, being left behind was lonely and increasingly difficult. Daughter Mariga weathered her mother's mercurial manners and "impulsive behavior." The isolated child would write her father a letter saying she was "terrified" of Rosemary's "wild unreasonable temper." To her father the girl noted he was "sane" as opposed to Rosemary, but admitted she still adored her charismatic mother. [67]

In Japan Rosemary suffered a concussion (her third) after falling from her horse.

One day an agitated Rosemary took her young daughter by her five-year-old hand and managed to make her way into the Royal Palace, intent on warning the Japanese emperor that his generals were plotting against him. Erica claimed Rosemary attempted to drown the crown prince along with daughter Mariga. The emperor's guards seized and arrested Rosemary. After being given enough morphine to knock her out, Rosemary was entrusted to the care of two nurses who transferred her to a ship bound for Europe. Albrecht was deeply embarrassed by his wife's erratic and criminal behavior that put him in an awkward and dangerous position with the Japanese. There must have been other episodes to cause Rosemary's drastic banishment. Mariga stayed in Japan with her father.

In Hong Kong Rosemary ditched the nurses. Again according to Erica, Rosemary went from London to Berlin intent on meeting Hitler. While staying at the swank Hotel Adlon she slit her wrists. She supposedly lost part of her nose due to jumping out of a glass window. Rosemary was put into an asylum back in Scotland where she had made her way to be with her mother, Anna.

At Morningside Mental Home she was officially diagnosed with schizophrenia. In 1941 the troubled young woman was given one of the early experimental procedures to cure an assortment of mental disorders. Into her confused brain doctors bore holes in either the top or side of the skull and a sharp instrument was then inserted. The instrument was then jiggled back and forth cutting the nerves and the offensive behavior. The two- to five-minute procedure was widely popular, with thousands being performed. The British neurosurgeon Sir Wylie McKissock was said to be responsible for three thousand operations during his days of practice, roughly the same time Rosemary underwent hers.[68] McKissock admitted that very often the lobotomies killed the patient or left them, in his words, in a "harmless vegetable state."[69]

Ian's sister was left nearly catatonic and "incarcerated" in Craig House, a sixteenth-century house turned into a psychiatric hospital for "paying" customers. The memory of "bolts and bars" traumatized daughter Mariga when she visited as an adult.[70] Rosemary denied having an adult daughter; she insisted her daughter was five. Rosemary would remain at the home for the next twenty-seven years until she died in 1975 at age seventy-four.

Though not related by blood, Lili and her exotic step-aunt would share eerie similarities: Both loved traipsing from one exciting locale to another. They expected—demanded—life to be fascinating and adventurous. Lili was impressed by Rosemary's courtship and marriage to a real prince, regardless of the character of the man himself. For Lili a man's good looks—a cleft chin and dark chest hair— would be more important than the substance underneath.

What no one saw coming was that Rosemary's outgoing, eccentric, and prone-to-depression personality would increasingly echo in her niece, Barbara. That tragedy was many years in the future.[71]

CHAPTER SEVEN

By 1935 Cordy was racing up and down the coast of California. He was so popular that he was asked to endorse many products.

Cordy spent a season in Camden in New South Wales, Australia, winning and making large sums of money.

A British racing scout recruited Cordy and his team to join the English motorcycle circuit, promising him an increase in prize money. Cordy was excited and assumed Lili would be too.

She wasn't. She was tired of being left behind. She busied herself at the restaurant and went on a few dates, spent hours at the movies and in the library reading *Screenplay*.

She missed Cordy and the excitement. She longed to escape the dusty roads and wide boulevards of her sleepy town. Then Cordy called from England.

He asked her to marry him.

She didn't need to think twice. She was going to marry a semifamous—at least locally—man who would show her the glamorous life. She would escape Pasadena and the restaurant and Alice's worry and Idella's criticism, who had taken to declaring that Lili was a bad influence on her sisters. Lili's head filled with thoughts of transforming herself into Mrs. Cordy Milne.

Surprisingly the entire family was thrilled for Lili.

Cordy wired money for a first-class ticket on the luxury liner the SS *Manhattan*.

Alice organized Idella and the girls to get together in the evenings and sew beautiful gowns for Lili's trousseau. Alice paid for the material and they made chic suits, dresses, and ball gowns. They sat on the porch evenings and weekends and laughed while Ben slept in the bedroom. Even Idella lightened up. She complimented all her girls on their excellent sewing skills. Lili had bought yards of tulle. She was making a Venus de Milo–type dress. Also a white jersey dress to get married in. There would be hats, gloves, matching shoes, shorts, and sweaters. She needed so many things.

Lili was ecstatic. At eighteen she felt as if she was embarking on a life-changing adventure. Finally.

Lili packed a trunk in a whirlwind of nerves and terror. She wouldn't know anyone on the voyage. A mixed blessing. She could be someone other than Marie Van Schaack. Soon she would be Marie Milne (though she supposedly also used Willis) She was about to set her slim foot into a new life and she couldn't wait to see where it would lead her.

Would they continue to live in England? Would Cordy expect her to work? To follow him from meet to meet? There were a million questions she should have been asking, but didn't. Nothing was going to hold her back from living the life she had dreamed of.

LILI FLEW TO NEW YORK—HER FIRST FLIGHT—ARRIVING TIRED AND hot, not to mention wiped out after the utter terror of flying. She would never like flying, preferring trains, but because her new passport arrived late she had no choice.

Cordy had reserved Lili a room at the San Moritz Hotel. Not yet six years old, the luxurious hotel sat directly across from Central Park at 50 Central Park South. Taxis and cars bustled by. The noise and the lights of the city lit up her mood.

Beautifully dressed men and women walked arm in arm, some swinging packages from Bergdorf's department store. Others were walking silly little dogs on dainty chains. She had to feel all the country bumpkin. She had bleached her hair to its brightest incarnation to date, which drew attention from men in the streets.

The spacious lobby of the San Moritz was sumptuously furnished. On one wall hung a large painting of the resort town in the Swiss Alps, for which the very metropolitan hotel was named. The various guest rooms, suites, and especially the penthouse rooms had open windows where cooling breezes blew in from the park. The décor was opulent and designed to impress. And Lili was impressed.

On the thirty-first floor was a salon for dancing and dinner. Lili peeked her head in, admiring more oversized murals on the walls.

If she ran a bath in her room's tub, it would be the biggest bath she had ever sunk into. She had never experienced such a luxury before. She was overwhelmed with feelings of—love? appreciation?—for Cordy. It was because of him that she was here. She opened her window and listened to the sounds below. Horses and carriages clomped by. Shouts and laughter floated up. The city was alive. She was headed toward something.

The next morning was a crisp, cool May day. She slept in—she would never be an early riser—ate, and walked in Central Park. In the afternoon, with trunks in tow, she hailed a cab for the port where she would board the SS *Manhattan* along with throngs of "rich people" anticipating the voyage on one of the most magnificent ships sailing the Atlantic.[72]

In 1936 the SS *Manhattan* was one of the country's most luxurious ocean liners. Passenger No. 568 was left speechless at the grandeur. The liner had the capacity to hold twelve hundred. There was a full orchestra playing somewhere. Lili would explore the many decks where couples, exquisitely dressed, strolled. Cabin waiters in white blazers rushed to and fro. Someone offered her a glass of champagne.

A siren blew, signaling it was time for visitors to come off before the ship sailed. Ribbons of multicolored confetti shot out over Lili and her glass of champagne as the great ship slowly pulled out of New York's harbor. Dusk was falling as lights of the city begin to turn on. It was magical, like standing on a many-layered wedding cake. With the cool breeze lifting her hair and the tang of salt water in her nose she felt a sudden passion for life, joy overtaking her. She silently vowed she was going to live among luxury like this. This was the world she wanted. Always.

Up on the first-class desk she watched New York shrink as she said good-bye to everything; Pasadena, Jimmy, Third Street, it was all behind her. In the bar she ordered a very dry gin martini. A young woman on the brink of all life had to offer. "A passion for the joy of life overtook" her.[73]

Because of a mix-up involving a senator that needed her cabin, Lili was forced to share a cabin with a woman "surly" and "green" who didn't take to the ocean as well as Lili.[74]

Lili was determined to stand out and it didn't take long for the crew and guests to notice the lone gorgeous blonde who always had a ready smile to share. She was taller than most, prettier than most. Everyone was friendly, asking her if there was anything they could do for her. The first night she was given a message that the captain wanted her to dine at his table the following night. She had no idea this was a privilege not accorded to everyone. She casually accepted.

Lili couldn't reach for a cigarette without someone appearing at her elbow to light it. She collected photographs of herself; seated at a bar, on the deck; laughing and drinking champagne. It was everything she had seen in the movies—and more.

FOR A GIRL UNTRAVELED YET RIPE FOR MAGIC, LILI REVELED IN HER newfound freedom. There was the sheer joy of not having to report to anyone. Alice had been a vigilant caregiver, walking her everywhere or having her sit with her at work. Lili hadn't realized how much anger she had built up; she adored Alice, though she resented being suppressed.

Lili rose when she wanted. She didn't have to tell anyone where she was going

Lili looking very Jean Harlow on board her first luxury liner

or what she was doing. If she wanted to smoke instead of eat, that was fine. If she wanted a dry gin martini, she ordered it.

She took long walks on all eight passenger decks, past the swimming pool, around the full-sized tennis court, pausing in front of the kennels for the dogs on the sundeck. Two large smoke stacks painted blue and white with red stripes jutted up into the clear blue sky. All around midnight-blue waters surrounded like a skirt of velvet. Lili turned her face toward the sun.

The SS *Manhattan* was known to be so luxurious that competing liners renamed their first-class cabins "cabin class." Lili was awed by the riches surrounding her. There was a smoking lounge with a fireplace. There was a library where she curled up with beautiful leather-bound books.

She was ensconced in a Louis XVI decorated cabin—with her roommate. The wood was polished hardwood paneling, a tiny but beautiful room with a window.

In the afternoon one could pop into the beauty parlor for a shampoo and set, or a manicure if a beautician was free.

She ate in the main dining room also decorated in the Louis XVI style with large murals. She wafted into the room beautifully made up in one of her homemade gowns. Perhaps she had to battle her innate shyness, or maybe she was feeling bold, already pretending to be someone else. Did she imagine herself as Garbo playing Queen Christina and this was *her* yacht? She would continually measure her actions against Garbo's, wondering what Garbo would think, what Garbo would do in the same circumstances.

Lili sat at a table with an older couple. A steward poured her a glass of wine. Within minutes another steward brought over a cold bottle of Mumm champagne and a note. "With compliments, an admirer."

"Give my thanks to the gentleman."[75] (She noted Garbo would be proud of how calm she was.)

Five minutes later a tall man with slicked-back hair sauntered over and introduced himself.

In his fancy British accent he introduced himself as Maxwell Croft. The striking dark-haired and dark-eyed Croft made sure she knew he was a furrier, having a shop on London's Bond Street.[76] Lili had no idea of the exclusivity of the street until later. Bond Street in central London was loaded with art dealers, antique shops, and expensive boutiques. Croft was twenty-two, London born, and came from a Jewish family. At six two, he towered over the image of her fiancé Cordy. She was enchanted.[77]

Lili and her dinner companions dined on chicken gumbo, filet of sole, corned brisket of beef, and steamed savoy cabbage, food Lili most likely never had tasted before.

After dinner Maxwell took her arm and the couple strolled the deck. The air smelled sharp and tangy mixed with the musk of his cologne. At one of the bars they slipped in for coffee. They moved around the grand salon two-decks high. An orchestra was set up at one end of the cavernous room. There was "Sing, Sing, Sing," Louis Prima's new song, and "Ridin' High" by Cole Porter.

Couples swirled arm and arm under a shallow dome in the center of the room. Ladies dressed in pretty pastel colors moved around them. But no two cut as dashing a pair as the tall blonde and her even taller escort. They proceeded to dance until the orchestra stopped, then another walk to her cabin, "star gazing."[78]

They parted late in the night. By the time Maxwell walked her to the door of her cabin, as he bent to kiss her, she knew she was in love.

They were inseparable after that. They drank coffees in the Veranda café decorated like Venice. It was a large room with more polished wood; waiters carried silver trays past windows clad in iron grill and painted columns. The café opened onto a game deck where passengers played shuffleboard.

For the first time she was reaping the benefits of her extraordinary beauty. She turned heads. It was the first time she would feel the full force of what good

Celebration on the SS Manhattan

looks—what her kind of attractiveness, regal, reserved, tall, and sunny—could do. Lies came "easily" to Lili, though she thought of herself as an "inventor."[79] She deliberately did not tell Maxwell she was engaged.

Afternoons she would lay in a skirt pulled above her knees, a short-sleeved sweater and round sunglasses on a chaise flirting with men until Maxwell showed up. She sat in a white bathing suit by the pool and accepted attention from the lifeguards. There was no shortage of someones wanting to buy her a drink or a coffee.

Lili and Maxwell stayed up late into the night with a young crowd sipping drinks and laughing. They would meet for cocktails at the bar, walk the decks smoking, and then dance the remainder of the night away. There was a nightcap as the sun rose out of the flat horizon. The group rarely slept.

Lili's heart and head was filled with "romance, like from a novel or movie."[80] The talk on everyone's lips—as it was on two continents—was whether King Edward would marry that *dreadful* Wallis Simpson. To many, the American Wallis Simpson was a dreadful gold digger, to others; admirably stylish. One can assume Lili was on the side of style.

Maxwell invited Lili back to his cabin where they made love. Afterward they both saw blood staining the sheets. Possibly she'd just gotten her period, but Maxwell assumed he had just deflowered a virgin and immediately proposed.

She was thunderstruck by his honor. She realized she couldn't live with Cordy after sleeping with Maxwell, who was a "man" and not a boy. She had fallen in love with the dashing and handsome Englishman—whom, like the advertisements for his shop, was good at "making women feel good—and looking good." He was attentive and elegant, everything Cordy was not.

Lili took Maxwell's hand and told him "Tomorrow's my birthday." Which it certainly was not, though it was only two weeks away. The next night was the "Captain's gala" but it was Lili who would be celebrated.[81]

As Lili entered the dining room on Sunday, May 24, the band struck up "Happy Birthday." She was wearing a dress she had made. The bust was tight and the skirt full, barely brushing the floor in layers of sky blue, purple, deep maroon, and shell pink tulle. She smiled, delighted to have stolen the captain's party.

EVERYONE RAISED THEIR GLASSES OF CHAMPAGNE TO TOAST HER NINE-teenth birthday. Guests wore party hats, Lili a pillbox. The menu read, "Special Dinner Given to Miss Marie Van Schaack on the occasion of her Birthday." Her guests at her table were Mrs. Walter M. Holdstein, Miss Bettie Maranteete, Mr. Erwin Schaefer, Mr. M. Luizzi, Mr. J. L. Lindner. There was no mention of Maxwell, no doubt assigned to a different table.[82]

The meal began with beluga *malossol* caviar, followed by consommé, frog legs, duck with an apple and raisin dressing accompanied by green peas and potatoes, followed by an avocado pear salad, and finally a chocolate soufflé birthday cake. Lili would keep the menu carefully pressed into her scrapbook for years until finally ripping the page out and sending it to a fan.

When the cake was wheeled out, another rousing "Happy Birthday" rose from the room.

"Beautiful Cheri." Maxwell handed her a beautifully wrapped gift. The card read, "In memory of the pleasant and amusing evenings with infinite love to continue." It was a delicate gold bracelet, presumably her first piece of jewelry from an admirer.

She ached to continue to live in this "grand setting." [83]

But reality was fast encroaching. As tug boats slowly pulled the boat toward the English coast and a waiting fiancé, twinges of "old loyalty" pinched at Lili.[84] She didn't want to hurt Cordy, but she wanted Maxwell. Lili gathered her things, wrapped her coat around her shoulders, and hopped on the transporter boat that would take her to her unsuspecting fiancé, unsure if she would ever see Maxwell again.

CHAPTER EIGHT

While she missed the aquiline-nosed Maxwell, it was exciting to again be with Cordy. The newspapers snapped photos of the young couple everywhere they went. Piled together with two of his new teammates from the Hackney Chiefs in the back of an open landau, Lili beamed as fans cheered.

"Willis Van Schaak [sic—she seemed to vacillate between "Marie" and "Willis," maybe unsure of who she was or else to hide from Maxwell, who was still unaware of her engagement to Cordy] is now in London to marry U.S. Speedway champion Cordy Milne . . . wedding next Saturday. Miss Van Schaak flew from Los Angeles to New York to catch liner for London."[85]

Cordy treated her well and it was a turn-on for Lili to be in the spotlight that spilled onto her. She liked knowing other women wanted her fiancé. However, her heart remained elsewhere. Lili would honor her commitment, yet her intention was to return to California, divorce Cordy, and then return to England to marry Maxwell. For some reason she felt honor bound to go through with the marriage and then break it off, instead of letting Cordy down beforehand.

She spent the next few months following Cordy to various speedways as he raced with the Hackney Chiefs. She also spent equal amounts of time alone and bored while Cordy hung at pubs with his teammates reliving their victorious seconds on the track.

Quickly she tired of the routine. She wanted to go dancing at night, but Cordy was too tired or wanted to hang with his friends.

Lili found her own place to be alone. The Lyons Corner House was a chain of upscale art deco tea shops with a live band. She could sit for as long as she liked, eating rich cream puffs. Idle, with no friends and no work, panicking as the wedding day approached and missing Maxwell, conflicted about Cordy, whom she no longer even wanted to kiss, she found herself eating dozens of cream puffs as she devoured British *Vogue*. She gained twenty pounds.

Lili at her marriage to Cordy

While the press was still speculating about whether Edward would make Mrs. Simpson his queen, Lili prepared to wed. The white wedding gown she had sewn was forsaken and instead she opted for a black silk dress, claiming she wanted "to be different."[86] It could have easily been a reflection on her nuptials or the fact she had gained too much weight to fit into her intended wedding gown.

On a warm, rainy afternoon, Saturday, July 25, 1936, Lili stood next to Cordy in Hackney Wicke Stadium and exchanged rings.[87] It had been Cordy's manager's idea to "stage" the wedding at the site of his impending race. The papers back home showed Lili's picture and acknowledged that "Mrs. B. Clark" (Alice) had to write her approval as Lili was considered a minor.[88] A reception for five hundred was held at the Hackney Wick Club.

It would not be the last time a wedding and headlines fused together for Lili.

AFTER THE CEREMONY THE NEWLYWEDS POSED FOR PHOTOGRAPHS IN front of a borrowed limousine while fans pelted them with rice. Lili held a long spray of flowers. She looked like a young, happy bride. She was all of that, except for happy.

In her French biography, Lili claimed to beg off sleeping with Cordy on their wedding night with the excuse that it was her time of the month. She didn't want sex with him, despite Cordy threatening he would have to find another woman as the days of abstinence turned into weeks.

Lili hoped marriage would change Cordy and they could move to a more private apartment, one that didn't have her sharing a communal bathroom in the hall with strangers. She longed to be back on the SS *Manhattan*. They began to argue over little things. Cordy kept to his routine of races and hanging with teammates. He didn't want to take her to shows and plays and ballets. And he didn't want her going on her own. She didn't have her own money and depended on Cordy for everything. He insisted on paying for things directly. She resented it. Was this her adventure? There was a whole exciting world in London and she was missing all of it.

Lili began to see Maxwell while she continued to beg off sleeping with Cordy (she might have started seeing Maxwell prior to the wedding). She reveled in how Maxwell thought her "mysterious" because of the game she played with him, disappearing and reappearing days later. She recalled how she pushed the "role" of an enigmatic woman as far as she could with him.[89]

Cordy, never immune to a pretty face, took care of his sexual needs through the willing fans that appeared at the tracks. Women loved his boyish charm and daredevil ways packaged in an unassuming manner. Cordy must have been mystified by his bride. She wasn't like the sunny Marie from Pasadena, the sweet girl he had fallen for. This girl moping around the apartment had changed. She was moody and secretive.

During Cordy's out-of-town competitions Lili stayed behind and met with Maxwell for lunches.

Whether he eventually found out about Maxwell or not, Cordy was fed up with Lili and plotted his revenge.

One morning when Lili was out he invited a pretty young thing—probably a fan—back to the apartment. He delayed getting the girl into bed until he was sure Lili would be returning. They were in the midst of making love when Lili blithely walked in, shopping bags in hand.

Cordy jumped up. The girl screamed and dived under the sheets.

They waited for Lili's explosion.

Lili turned around and closed the door behind her. Presently they heard quiet banging coming from the other room. A teapot whistled as the naked girl reached for her bra and slip. She stayed under the covers wiggling into them.

"Some tea?" Lili breezed through the door, a tray filled with scones, jam and cream, a pot, and cups.[90] She placed the tray on the foot of the bed as the two stared at her astonished. Without so much as another word Lili left the apartment. She didn't care what Cordy did. For Lili, when a romance was over sexually, it was over. She couldn't stand the thought of someone she was no longer head-over-heels in love with touching her. It was only a matter of time before the marriage would end.

LILI MADE AT LEAST ONE FRIEND IN ENGLAND, A SHOWGIRL WHO worked at the Windmill and had admired Lili's body as she sat around a pool one afternoon. At her friend's suggestion, Lili made her way to Piccadilly Circus. At Archer and Great Windmill Streets stood the Windmill Theatre. This would be the first of two important places in Lili's life that would have a windmill as a beacon. Perhaps this first windmill, though briefly enjoyed, would be why she had such a huge affection and loyalty for the second, in Las Vegas, years later.

The Windmill was built in the exact spot where, in the eighteenth century, an actual windmill had stood during the reign of King Charles II. It was a small theatre with only one tier that hosted a variety of acts. Despite losing money the theatre manager boasted continuous entertainment from dancers, singers, and showgirls for nearly twelve hours every afternoon into the evening. After World War II the theatre would claim never to have closed during the war, not even at the height of bombing. In 2005 a movie about the manager and theatre would be made, starring Dame Judi Dench and Bob Hoskins and titled *Mrs. Henderson Presents*.

Lili met the forty-nine-year-old producer Vivian Van Damm, known simply as "VD," who copied the format of the Folies Bergère and Moulin Rouge in Paris by *displaying* nude girls, which was completely legal as long as the girls did not move, holding a pose without so much as wiggling a toe. Lili's girlfriend was one of the "Windmill Girls" and Lili hoped to become one too. Girls in the shows posed in costumes as everything from Annie Oakley to mermaids to Indians. The numbers were theme-oriented, an important element that later influenced Lili. She would use themes throughout her career, dressing as a cowgirl and Indian, even a mermaid, as first seen at the Windmill.

One production at the Windmill featured a fan dancer, a girl who concealed her complete nudity behind a giant ostrich fan until the final moment. The prop-heavy ingredient of the show seemed to cement itself inside the ever-curious and clever mind of Lili. She quietly observed what was going on around her and would take from productions and performers to create her own iconic numbers.

The Windmill boasted a glass stage and an even more daring act as a nude girl held on to a spinning rope. The rope moved but not the girl, so no laws were broken. Lili delighted in technicalities that bent and twisted around the rules. There was always a streak of rebelliousness in Lili, who despised authority and being told what she could or could not do.

"I've got just the spot for you," VD declared, taking one look at Lili.

"But I've no training. What do I have to do?"

"All you have to do is stand at a big stake, burning . . . nude of course." Lili was to be Joan of Arc.[91]

Lili learned, when VD took over management of the theatre, that he had started a nonstop run of shows. Despite this, the theatre was still losing money. VD was hoping to change that and the prettier the girls he added, the better.

Lili would always claim Cordy stopped her before she had a chance to appear. But it is more than possible, even probable, by looking at what she did later in her shows, that Lili worked a night or two before she confessed to her preoccupied husband, who indeed would have told her to quit. There was much from the Windmill she would incorporate in her future onstage.

LILI AND CORDY'S CRAMPED RENTED ROOMS WERE TOO SMALL TO contain their opposing wills. Cordy came home one afternoon and told her the team was moving to Australia for six months. In his hands he held two *second*-class tickets. She was horrified. She told him she wasn't going.

To Cordy, Lili was a wild thing he couldn't control. He had better luck with his motorbikes than with his wife. He was forced to admit defeat. The relationship was over.

With Cordy out of the picture Maxwell should have taken his place, but when Maxwell didn't come through on a marriage proposal or a plan for their future together, a despondent Lili decided it was time to return home.

By September of 1936, just four months since her maiden voyage, she was back on another luxury liner, this time the SS *Ile de France*, which was even grander than the *Manhattan*. It did much to lift her spirits. She would spend the rest of her life trying to recapture the experience of these crossings, free, feted, and fussed over, as if nothing could touch her while in the great ritzy cocoon on the sea.

For dinners Lili made her grand entrance down a sweeping staircase rising three decks high. The rooms were modern in décor. There was a grand foyer four decks high, a sun deck, merry-go-round, gymnasium, shooting gallery, and chapel. She felt at home enjoying the attention from crew and passengers. She was wined and dined at every turn. Men scribbled notes on dinner menus that she glued into a scrapbook. In them she refers to herself as "WVS" or "Willis," never Marie, though she was called that by others.

There was no need to tell any of the attentive gentlemen she was heading for a divorce. She was simply a dancer leaving England after a season in London. She quickly got over any guilt she might have felt about Cordy and her affair with Maxwell. She wasn't one to look back.

On board were members of the Ballets Jooss and it wasn't long until a handsome young dancer by the name of Otto Struller won her attention. Feeling quite the woman of the world, Lili had a brief and passionate affair with Struller, who was twenty-five years old. His hair was short in back but with a long blond shock that fell over his eyes down to the middle of his aristocratic nose. He was muscular and graceful. Lili and Otto made a stunning and elegant pair on the dance floor, equally matched in beauty and grace.

OTTO TOO HAD BEEN DANCING IN LONDON. LILI HAD TO THINK, IF only Cordy had taken her to the show, or any shows, she might not be lying in Otto's arms in his room on the *Ile de France* surrounded by art deco opulence. If only he hadn't wanted to hold her back, she fooled herself into thinking, not for once admitting her desire for Cordy had already waned before she had set a heel on London soil. Lili was young and inexperienced in romance. She needed and wanted her head turned. She admitted she was immature, fickle, and easily believed the grass was greener elsewhere. There would be something about all of Lili's subsequent romances, and even most of her marriages, that remained impulsive, and, as she admitted, "it was immaturity that doomed them to failure."[92] She discarded men after she outgrew them. She needed constant stimulation. The gypsy in her always longed to pack and go.

Alone in her room outfitted with a real bed, Lili dreaded the end of her voyage. She had hoped to return in triumph instead of with a short-lived marriage and dull Pasadena facing her.

On South Oak Avenue Lili settled back in among her family. Lili didn't know how to put into words the hopelessness she felt.

Alice, who understood Lili and "had a gypsy soul," told her "for the first and not the last time that life was too short to stay with a man unless she was crazy in love with him."[93] Alice told her that if something made Lili unhappy or stood in her way, to get rid of it as quickly as possible. This no doubt led to a sense of entitlement that Lili (and Barbara) had. Lili would callously disregard relationships when she no longer wanted them. No matter her actions, Lili was taught to believe it was okay. If someone opposed Lili, Alice let it be known she was against them. She would remain fiercely loyal to her granddaughter.

Idella was quite another matter and launched into many a stormy scene. "You are supposed to be an example for your sisters," Idella screeched. Lili had tossed away *stability*. Lili didn't need stability; what she needed was romance. Lili tried blocking out Idella's ranting and ravings about her "wicked ways."[94]

After the altercations, Lili admitted, "I kept away from my mother."[95]

Lili had to feel as though she had failed. At night her heart pounded while she fought for sleep on the porch, right back where she had started. Except for blonder hair, tweezed eyebrows, and a thinner waist, she was the same, no closer to living an exotic life than before. It wasn't long before she would begin waltzing to a very different dance step.

According to Dardy, Lili had a brief romance with a young Pasadena boy, setting off on a road trip by car as he dragged his horse trailer behind. Dardy wasn't surprised that it did not last.

Perhaps not wanting to admit how passionately she had fallen for Maxwell or how much she had hoped they would wed, Lili would claim she spent the next several years traveling back and forth on luxury liners, paid for by various lovers. At the time of her biography she was well into maintaining her image of a hard-boiled sophisticate. The truth is Lili did sail the Atlantic several times. However, it was usually *with* Maxwell, or on the way to visit him. For Lili, her relationship with Maxwell was serious. Serious enough to span three years.[96]

On the sea she lived in a kind of a suspended reality. Lili (and Maxwell) traveled first class, dining on sturgeon and shrimp salad and "Matie Herring on Ice," "Artichoke a la Grecque," soups of potage essau, consommé ecossaise, chicken gumbo, and delicious cold beef broth. There were platters of boiled fresh codfish, sole a l'orly, soft-shell crab, halibut, poached eggs, shirred eggs, omelet, veal, lamb, chicken, pork, brisket, and on and on.

Lili was registering as Miss Willis Marie Van Schaak [sic].

From 1937 through 1939 Lili was often in the company of Maxwell, perhaps while she waited for her divorce to come through.[97] She experienced the best of the best, the SS *Washington,* the SS *American Banker* and *Antonia* and *Queen Mary.* She saved menus, itineraries, photos, and notes that she glued into her scrapbook: "Good morning, we have searched the ship over a dozen times for you. . . . Have your dessert over here," and, "Sweet!!!! Do come and talk to us. Mac has asked you to dine this evening."[98]

By July of 1938 Lili and Maxwell sailed from New York to England, arriving August 2. She is listed in the manifest as Willis Van Schaak [sic] and Maxwell lists himself as a "farmer" (perhaps meant to be "furrier"). Later in the month they sailed from New York to the UK, returning to New York by September 26. Maxwell spent Thanksgiving in America with Lili. By December she was finally divorced and no doubt hoped things would progress to matrimony with Maxwell.

IN HER CANADIAN BIOGRAPHY, WRITTEN WHEN SHE WAS SIXTY-FIVE years old, Lili writes that sometime in 1939 she received her first telegram:

CAN'T LIVE WITHOUT YOU (STOP) MARRY ME (STOP)
COMING TO AMERICA (STOP) LOVE MAXWELL[99]

A happy Lili with—presumably—Maxwell in America

Instead of excitement she was frantic and sent a return telegram telling him it was best to meet in San Francisco (to keep her family away). She had implied she was a rich young American and was afraid he would see the reality.

Sometime possibly in April of 1938 Ben died, and Alice moved in with Ian and Idella. Lili makes no mention of Ben's passing.

She met Maxwell in the lobby of the Saint Francis Hotel in the heart of San Francisco on a balmy day. The St. Francis, on Powell and Geary on Union Square, was a simple square façade that belied its fabled and fashionable reputation. In 1921 Fatty Arbuckle held his infamous party after which starlet Virginia Rappe tragically died of a ruptured bladder, not raped by Arbuckle, as he would be put on trial for. Celebrities and heads of state regularly stayed at the St. Francis.

With a blue sky overhead and a mild breeze blowing off the Pacific, Lili had dressed carefully.

They would naturally have had separate rooms, but she spent the entire two days before the boat set sail in his suite. If he poured champagne and ordered caviar, they could dance effortlessly together as if it was their first night on the SS *Manhattan,* or cuddle in the Rose Room of the hotel and listen to jazz late into the night. She would have found herself swept up again. This is how she wanted to always feel. She later admitted she agreed to marry Maxwell because of the style of life he offered.

Lili would recall that her feelings were a mess. What would Garbo do, she wondered. Did she love Maxwell? She had pursued and wanted him for so long she was no longer sure. Would she be giving up her independence? Since leaving Cordy she had made no advancement in her life and future beyond aimless travel. Alice reassured her the best she could: "You're young, Willis. It's the time to enjoy everything."

Days after Valentine's Day, on February 17, Lili boarded the ocean liner with Maxwell and together they watched the Golden Gate Bridge fade in a swirl of fog. Arriving in New York on March 6, they sailed on the *Antonia* to the UK, arriving back on Maxwell's turf April 4. In the ship's manifest Lili lists Maxwell's Bond Street shop as her proposed destination.

On the boat there was tension between Maxwell and Lili due partially to her continuous flirting—so much so she thought the two were finished. Maxwell instead surprised her by presenting her with a diamond ring.

Now that she was free to marry she was filled with doubts. She dreaded arriving back in London and the trial of meeting Maxwell's family. She had told him she was the niece of Rosemary, Princess von Urach, desperately wishing she came from that sort of a royal family.

Maxwell booked her a room at the Dorchester House overlooking Hyde Park. The Dorchester had a long history with burlesque. Roz Elle Rowland had danced there nude except for a costume of gold paint. At the Dorchester Roz Elle met the suave and sophisticated Baron Empain of the famous Paris subway family, eventually marrying him. Coincidentally, Lili would end up friends with Roz Elle's sister, Betty Rowland, who held the moniker the "Ball of Fire" for her flaming red hair and her hot style of stripping.

Lili was full of second and third doubts about meeting Maxwell's family. Did she really want to go through another marriage? Would she have to beg for money as she had with Cordy? And after the numerous flirtations with other eligible handsome men on board the *Ile de France* she wasn't sure she could stop herself. Or if she wanted to be faithful.

In a panic she locked herself in the bathroom.

What Maxwell's perplexed family must have thought. Surely it was uncomfortable not just for Maxwell and his parents but also his brother, the future playwright Neville who would go on to write *All the Year Round* (a dismal failure), become a part owner in a chocolate shop—along with Maxwell—called Prestat (the chocolate was named top three in the world by 2003 and the company thrives today).

For two hours Lili read a book and did her nails while the family waited. Eventually they left.

There was no question. The relationship was over.

She tried pulling off her engagement ring but Maxwell insisted she keep it.

She left England with her four-carat ring and her heart still intact. She was sorry he was heartbroken but realized with a little kindness she didn't have to *stay* with a man just because he wanted her to. They could part and remain friends. And she could keep the jewels and the gifts. Maxwell paid her first-class passage home. She didn't feel upset this time. Maybe her adventures had begun after all.[100]

CHAPTER NINE

In 1939 Lili found herself crowded into the chaotic Bedlam Manner in Eagle Rock. Lili got a job waitressing at Carson's Blue Casino in Los Angeles. Lili had blossomed in the two years since the end of her marriage to Cordy. Her hair fell below her shoulders in platinum blonde curls that she labored over. Her legs were long and fit. She always wore a smile with her makeup. As the beautiful new girl at the restaurant, she wrote, the boys poured in hoping to get a date with her.

AT CARSON'S SHE MET A WEALTHY YOUNG POLO PLAYER BY THE NAME of Maury Morrison. He was suave, good looking, and hung with a fast crowd of rich young things. Morrison, or his father, owned a yacht that he would cruise to Catalina Island along with half a dozen friends, including Lili, living it up under the sun with free-flowing cocktails and rich food. Lili tried her best to fit in but felt she didn't. She marveled that Maury's friends didn't *do* anything. Just a bunch of spoiled rich kids idling their days away. No one had a job. Except her.

Maury was mercurial, hard to get close to. Lili was hoping for her next serious romance but felt she was a mere dalliance for the shallow young man. The girls on the yacht were polite to Lili but offered no real friendship.

Lili was dissatisfied with everything. She complained about the people in Pasadena. The women had no panache. They were amateurs compared to the women in London. She was a fish out of water, postmarriage and post–multiple affairs, having seen and experienced things other girls her age had not even dreamed about. More than ever she was determined to make her mark on the world.

When not at the movies, Lili and her sisters went to tea at the Biltmore Hotel and danced with young men. The trio felt "powerful." Though this would put Barbara and Dardy at only fifteen and fourteen, they had grown into nearly six-foot-tall beauties. When the girls walked into a room they turned heads. The three felt "enchanted"

to be in the "adult world."[101] Lili felt confident with her gorgeous posse flanking her. Afternoons and evenings were filled with laughter as they readied for dates.

Half-brother Jack was still fixing up old cars that hung in the yard like ship-wrecked vessels. He was crazy for sports. Lili was most uncomfortable with Betty, that wicked scar cutting down her face. Lili would say she thought Betty was a "little crazy," having suffered "brain damage" from the accident. Betty was eccentric, to say the least, taking on "causes" and befriending strange people, at least once ending up in jail for defending someone.[102] Betty would never be a big influence on Lili, nor would Jack. Both would drift out of Lili's life.

Despite Lili's unease around Betty, Lili would be a witness at the second of Betty's three marriages.[103] In 1937, seventeen-year-old Bettalee Cornett married forty-one-year-old German-born Fred Schwarz. Then, in August of 1939, she married another older German gentleman. The last record of Betty marrying is in 1955 to thirty-one-year-old Angel Hernandez.

It was Barbara and Dardy who remained closest to Lili. Just fourteen months apart, Dardy and Barbara were so bonded that Lili nicknamed them Tweedle Dee and Tweedle Dum (often spelled "Teedle" in letters). Like most sisters they shared clothes and stories and gossiped over boys and had their dis-agreements. They were experimenting as young women did. It had to seem as if they would remain close forever.

Sleeping at Bedlam Manner the sisters would chatter late into the night, ignoring Idella hollering up the stairs, "Girls! Go to bed. It's late."[104]

The year 1939 was a banner one for movies with the release of *Gone with the Wind*, *The Wizard of Oz*, and the romantic *Wuthering Heights*. Audiences flocked to the picture shows. The radio was filled with Glenn Miller's band playing "Moonlight Serenade." The highlight for the Blackadder girls that year would be the Saugus Rodeo, held just northwest of Pasadena. Nuts about horses, Barbara and Dardy couldn't wait to attend. They had become expert riders at a young age, addicted to rodeo shows, which they entered every chance they could. Both learned dressage.[105] Out of the arena, Dardy in particular thrilled at the speed with which she pushed her favorite horse Snoopy through the paths of Eagle Rock. She was invited to ride before the football games in the Los Angeles Memorial Coliseum.

Lili wasn't the least bit interested in getting on a horse. She would stay inside doing her nails and reading her "bible"—*Vogue*—dreaming of life beyond Eagle Rock.[106] "She wasn't outdoorsy," Dardy explained.[107]

Dardy recalled a time she and Lili had gotten into an argument and Dardy stormed off up the hill in anger.

LEFT: *It was easy to see why the boys were swarming around Lili*

Bedlam Manner was remote, with only one neighbor close and a confection-ary store at the end of the road. It was beautiful and wild. But not the place for lace and satin shoes.

After Dardy had been gone awhile, Ian asked Lili to go find her and bring her home.

Mad as a hell, Lili ran out wearing a pair of delicate shoes calling, "Rosemary! Where are you? Oh! My shoes! Oh, my shoes are being ruined. Come out now. My shoes! Rosemary! Come out now! If I ruin these shoes you are in so much trouble."[108]

IDELLA WAS RESENTFUL OF HER GIRLS' FREEDOM AND WATCHED AS they rode their horses away from all responsibility. The whole family had a rever-ence for freedom and unconventionality. Alice and Ian had ingrained into the children at a young age to seek independence, to do what they wanted. *You can do anything.*

Ian's family had lived for centuries along the Blackadder River in Scotland. His father John had been an avid horseman who would joust for fun wearing full armor. In Germany he met the Scottish Norwegian beauty Anna Wilson. Both Barbara and Dardy would look strikingly similar to Anna.

JOHN AND ANNA MARRIED AND SETTLED ON HIS FATHER'S FARM (HIS father was now deceased) at Chirnside, Scotland. The Blackadder family prided themselves on the mix of languages spoken in the home: English, French, German, and Norwegian. The couple would have three children: Frederika (later known as "Erica Hunt"), born in 1898; Rosemary, born in 1901; and Ian, born a year later. According to Frederika, on coming to America Ian spoke with a broader Scottish accent. When Frederika asked him why, he told her, "It's good business.'"[109]

Barbara and Dardy were beautiful to watch astride their mounts, hair stream-ing behind them. One brunette, the other blonde. They were happiest riding.

The Saugus show was filled with bareback riders, clowns, and steer wrestling. One hot and dusty afternoon, Dardy and Barbara were lounging on a fence sipping lemonades. They were wearing cute white-fringed short skirts, vests, and hats. At their full height they stood out in the bright hot sun. Their hats were slung down their backs, and their long hair shone. They looked several years older than the teenagers they were.

A roar from the crowd rose above the hot and dusty hills.

"Hello," a fortysomething man said. He had a funny accent and was smartly dressed in a dark suit, not an ounce of sweat marring him.

The dark-haired man introduced himself as "NTG," or Nils Theodore Granlund. He said he produced a show at the Florentine Gardens in Hollywood and he could always use a couple of beautiful girls like them. Would they be interested in trying out as showgirls?

The girls giggled. They had no idea what or where the Florentine Gardens was, but it sounded exotic. Sure, they said.

"How tall are you?"[110] He asked.

Both girls stood up, and though he was tall himself he was impressed. "Six feet," Dardy said, and in heels she was.

"Here's my card. Here's my address. Day after tomorrow we're having auditions. You girls come on down." He could just about guarantee he would hire them. He tipped his hat and left. NTG often sponsored rodeo beauty contests and most likely that is why he was in Saugus, scouting for girls.

The girls told Ian when he came back with hot dogs in hand what had happened. Ian promised to personally call this Granlund.

Mr. Granlund assured Ian that indeed he was auditioning for girls and wanted the sisters to come down. It was a swanky nightclub and he meant no funny business. It was a class joint. Errol Flynn came nearly every night, enjoying the $1.50 fee that got a decent meal and an eyeful of beautiful showgirls parading by.

NTG, a former reporter, press agent, producer, and host, would be credited as being the "creator of modern nightlife." [111]

Ian decided that if Lili, now twenty-three, chaperoned her sisters, they could go. Lili had been adrift since returning from London. She was no longer seeing Maury and his snobbish friends.

Things seemed to come easier for her half-sisters; Miss California, ribbons and titles in horse shows, now an offer of work in a club. Though she would act disingenuous, most likely Lili—an avid movie magazine reader—knew all about the glitzy club in the heart of Hollywood frequented by John Barrymore, Rudy Vallee, and many other movie stars. Live radio shows were broadcast from the Gardens. Unlike other clubs on Sunset Boulevard, the Florentine catered to the "meat and potatoes" crowd, compared to the caviar set over at Earl Carroll's, a nightclub west on Hollywood Boulevard.

The Gardens was a spacious supper club with floor shows featuring beautiful girls. There was a revolving stage and seating for 1,160.

The three girls arrived at the appointment, a little wrinkled and dusty after transferring buses from Eagle Rock. One can imagine the scene that confronted them: a vast club where they would be swallowed up by its current emptiness, dimly lit, a couple of boys sweeping the outer edges of the floor, sticky with spilled drinks. Various long-limbed girls sitting around the unadorned square tables. And

Interior of the Florentine Gardens. Barbara's nude is prominently displayed.

the tangy smell of all nightclubs, old smoke, sour fruit, liquor, and sweat. The smell the girls would grow to love. It would be the smell of work and good times and carefree nights of their youth.

SINCE LILI WAS NOT THERE TO AUDITION SHE SAT IN THE AUDIENCE and opened her *Vogue* while a stage manager assembled Dardy and Barbara among the other girls. Lili had to be feeling turbulent, no matter how cool she acted. She was between boyfriends and jobs, drifting aimlessly, wasting afternoons doodling costumes and outfits in a notebook, listening to Sergei Prokofiev's *Alexander Nevsky* or Tommy Dorsey and Judy Garland on the radio. She toyed with the idea of designing clothes. She was excellent at sewing and loved pretty things. She would later claim that something told her—on this very day—to pay attention to what was going on around her. She felt luck was in the air.

NTG was scrutinizing the lineup of girls. He stopped and gave the *Vogue*-reading, long-legged blonde a look up and down, wanting to know why she wasn't on the stage.

Barbara, on the left, easily outshone Lili—at the Florentine Gardens

Though elegant, he was hardly handsome, with a sagging chin, receding hairline, and large nose. But NTG was very good at producing live entertainment.

Did he ask if she could dance? Did he care? With her almond-shaped eyes, wide cheekbones, and statuesque body, she was made for the stage. He could hire three sisters as easily as two. No one else was as tall as the trio.

He insisted they call him Granny.

It looked as if all three sisters had a job until someone asked Dardy her age.

"Well, I was wearing my school outfit," she later admitted, apparently including skirt and ankle socks. They needed to fill out some paperwork and though she lied and said she was fifteen, it was obvious Dardy was underage.

"Get off the stage," someone yelled at her. Dardy was devastated, possibly jealous. Her time onstage would have to wait.

At the time, hiring girls under eighteen was prevalent in the clubs. However, the Board of Equalization was stepping in and preventing the practice. Though Barbara was only sixteen she was deemed safe to hire. By the following year both NTG and nightclub king Earl Carroll were "stripped of" the practice of hiring underage girls. Carroll was forced to fire a fifteen- and a seventeen-year-old.[112]

Lili and Barbara were exactly what NTG had been looking for. He positioned each one on either side of the ponies—chorus girls—who were shorter. They would be his bookends.

AT LEAST THAT IS THE BASIC STORY LILI TOLD OF THE BEGINNINGS OF her show business career. There would be variations over the years as if she was embarrassed to have wanted a career. In her telling it would always happen accidentally.

But according to Dardy, all three sisters took four buses to arrive at their mutual audition for a Harry Howard–produced show. The Blackadder/Klarquist girls were literally heads above the others. As in Lili's version, Dardy was shouted off the stage and Barbara and Lili were hired.[113]

Barbara and Lili were now officially in show business. They signed contracts for a whopping $25 a week.

The girls began rehearsals. Barbara and Lili shimmied into skimpy outfits wearing tall gossamer headdresses, net pants, and rhinestone-covered bras across their nearly flat bosoms.

If anyone worried what Alice would think about the girls parading about nearly nude, it didn't seem to be a concern. None of the girls were self-conscious about their bodies. Idella, of course, would thrill that her girls—especially Barbara—were in the spotlight. And in fact, Alice loved it too. She thought her granddaughters were spectacular and they should enjoy the adventure, the attention, and the paychecks.

The money seemed to go a long way toward soothing any concerns.

The reality of making money—*real* money—during the Depression was slim. Especially for young, not especially well-educated women. There were teaching jobs and secretarial jobs. Both mundane and not suited for girls who wanted adventure.

Burlesque, an outgrowth of (or stepchild of) vaudeville, could and did afford single young women the chance to travel, earn decent—if not *really* good—money. And if they weren't quite "stars," they did make fans and generate publicity and were for a while "someone" in that circle. They, like Lili, felt "necessary."[114]

And though strictly speaking the Florentine Gardens was not a burlesque house, the acts were similar and would have played both vaudeville and burlesque.

In the beginning Lili didn't move anywhere near as gracefully as she would in the coming years, but she had a sparkle and a beautiful body, not to mention stunning features with a cleft chin, wide jutted cheekbones, and green eyes that were both mischievous and wholesome. She was fresh and nervous, occasionally tripping over her own feet, not exactly sure what to do with her hands. But she was endearing and delightful, eager to please, anxious to be liked. Barbara was equally stunning with an easy smile and enthusiasm for everything.

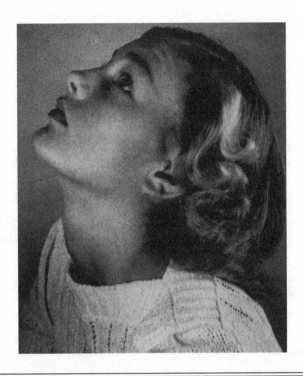

Barbara

LILI WOULD FOREVER REMEMBER HER FIRST NIGHT AT THE FLOREN-
tine, the smell of tomatoes and garlic and sweet cocktails. The sounds of the band
and laughter. It seemed to be the happiest place on earth. Barbara and Lili were
deliriously nervous, stomachs in knots, but also electrified too.

Backstage was chaos; girls running around in various stages of undress, stagehands lugging props, lifting furniture. Music soared through the club along with
the tinkling of glass and silverware. There were many dressing rooms for a show that
included an enormous cast of twenty chorus girls, jugglers, dance teams, and more.

For her first bit Granny had Lili walk around in net panties and bra. Years later
she recalled the terror. She couldn't feel her feet and hands. Her lips stuck to her
teeth. The audience scared her. All those eyes on her.

To assure the girls didn't get into trouble, Ian drove them to and from the club
each evening, a thirty-minute car ride that any number of new admirers would have
been willing to do. And soon were offering. Dardy was left at home to cry at the
injustice of it. After all, NTG had spotted Barbara and *her*, not Lili.[115]

The shows at the Gardens were "built around NTG," who meandered
from table to table between the shows, bantering with the audience, sometimes

telling crude double entendres and ribbing his celebrity friends like actor John Barrymore, a notorious drunk who often fell over.[116] Movie stars such as Judy Garland, Robert Taylor, and Barbara Stanwyck packed the place.[117] The show had comedians and chorines, dozens of scantily clad girls who slithered and slinked across the wide stage or gathered on the dance floor for spectacular and elaborate dance numbers. NTG was big on audience participation, sometimes asking soldiers up, inviting patrons to hula-hoop. Between 1940 and 1942 an astounding two million patrons enjoyed Granlund's show at the Florentine.[118] For Lili and her sister it was a huge opportunity.

The Florentine employed dozens of pretty girls who came and went. Lili gathered that if she wanted to stand apart from the ambitious showgirls clogging backstage, it was advantageous to be as naked as the law allowed. She was determined to get noticed and was bare-bosomed often. Ironically, as her career progressed, Lili would learn the value of clothing and cloaking, becoming less nude as she danced up the ladder of success. But for now she needed the attention of an audience jaded by the plethora of beautiful girls shaking across the floor. Competition was fierce.

Just west on Sunset Boulevard loomed the cavernous Earl Carroll Theatre, a supper club that showcased the same type of starlets as the Florentine, billed as having "the most beautiful girls in the world." Not a unique claim. In Hollywood there was the Trocadero, Mocambo (opened in 1941), and Ciro's (opened in 1940), all snazzy clubs vying for the attendance of movie stars. There was the Coconut Grove downtown and Sebastian's Cotton Club. La Conga on Vine was a dance club that featured the recent Rumba craze. Clara Bow's "It" Café was lush, with an elegant art deco interior. Hollywood nightlife was at its finest.

NTG treated the beauties with respect. Many of the girls lived with Granny in his big house on Fountain Avenue. "And never any hanky panky," the girls swore, since he had a beautiful showgirl girlfriend, Sylvia McKaye.[119]

Lili watched and wondered and wanted the audience to single her out. She had bleached her hair about as white-blonde as it would go, and she wore thick Max Factor foundation that made her break out. She had even darkened her arched eyebrows. Along with Barbara, she had nude photographs taken. They were beautiful and artistically shot. Barbara sat modestly on the floor, Lili standing behind her, arching her slender torso, brazenly bare-breasted, her arm in the air.

RIGHT: *This rare photo of Lili at the Florentine Gardens*
clearly shows she hadn't yet chosen a stage name

Marie Van Shaack, of the Los An- geles Florentine Gardens.

BARBARA DANCED UNDER A PSEUDONYM, BILLED AS BARBARA Moffett.[3]*** Granny took credit for naming her after his two dear friends, heiress Barbara Hutton and Adelaide Moffett Brooks, a "society songstress" who was the daughter of a former vice president of Standard Oil and the widow of David "Winkie" Brooks, who "fell" out of his fourteenth-floor apartment in 1936.[120]

Undecided as to her perfect name, Lili remained Marie Van Schaack (and occasionally Mary Van Schacht). Possibly she wanted people to know of her success and didn't yet want to hide behind a pseudonym.

WHETHER FROM SHYNESS OR SNOBBISHNESS, LILI WOULD NEVER become chummy with the other showgirls backstage. In return most would feel threatened by her. Many of the girls were younger than Lili. There was competition for boyfriends and prominent positions in the show.

Barbara and Lili were moderately friendly with "Dingbat," a tall, raven-haired girl who had renamed herself from the ordinary Margaret Middleton to the more exotic Yvonne de Carlo. Barbara and Yvonne had much in common, such as ruthlessly ambitious mothers. Dingbat's mother made Idella look modest in her plans for *her* daughter.

Yvonne, who would go on to become a star in both film and television, was pushed by a stage mother who showed up regularly at the club. They lived together in a small apartment downtown. Yvonne's mother had always wanted to be a ballerina and forced her daughter into dance, though Yvonne lacked the ballerina's body, with too long a trunk and too-short legs.

"She had a screwy figure," Dardy recalled. "But she was sweet and charming." Yvonne's father had left home when she was three. For a while she too had lived with her grandparents. Like Lili she had dropped out of high school. It was unfortunate they never became friends. Yvonne too longed to escape her past and become a sophisticate. Her path would cross with Dardy's one day at Earl Carroll's. Lili, however, remained—not yet aloof as she would become—separate from the other girls. Women were and would remain a threat.

By March of 1940 Barbara and Lili were enjoying a variety of numbers in the show. "The 'Bookends'," Granny teased.[121]

DARDY MARVELED AT THE TRANSFORMATION OF HER SISTERS INTO glamorous "showgirls." They learned to bead their eyelashes, which was an

---

*** Remember her real name was Ruth

GORGEOUS and GLAMOROUS The alluring N. T. G. Revue performing one of its elaborate specialties at the . . . . . FLORENTINE GARDENS

elaborate process of melting black makeup from a round metal tube in a spoon and then carefully glopping little balls onto the end of each eyelash with an orange stick. There is a famous photo by Man Ray, a close-up of a woman's eyes with both rows of lashes holding tear-like dots on the end of the lashes. The effect is, though dated today, stunning. "It made the eye pop," Dardy explained. The showgirls wore thick red lipstick. They attached falls to their hair for volume and length. The girls wore platform shoes. Dardy viewed them as exotic creatures and she couldn't wait to become one.

Lili, who still pined for her traveling days, declared working in the club to be the next best thing. She was becoming entranced by this show business life. Yet the girl who wore black on her wedding day to be "different" still searched for an opportunity to stand out. She wasn't meant to be one of a dozen. She felt stymied in her personal and professional life. She studied lighting and dressing. She looked for an opportunity.

IAN CONTINUED TO ARRIVE PROMPTLY AFTER THE LAST SHOW TO escort the girls home. They would bundle up against the cold night and ride home drained, though excited, usually falling asleep before they reached Eagle Rock.

In the beginning Grandma and Idella stayed up wanting to hear all the details

RIGHT: *"Queen of the Orient"*
ABOVE: *Barbara and Lili (on the right) as bookends*

Lili St. Cyr

of the night. Barbara and Lili relayed stories about the other showgirls and the famous faces in the audience, singer Rudy Vallee, restauranter Steve Crane, producer Pat de Cicco. Errol Flynn would stagger in with an even more inebriated John Barrymore.

The two sisters spent the better part of the next eight or nine months performing nightly. They were eager to do anything Granny asked of them. One night Lili was a "Southern Peach," another a "Chinese queen" held aloft by a flank of girls. Her high moment came crashing to the floor as she was accidently tipped over. Another night Lili wore a green wig, which she occasionally wore out "as long as her dates didn't protest."[122]

BARBARA STARRED IN THE ANNUAL COLORADO RODEO, WINNING THE title of California's Loveliest Cowgirl and in 1941 she would have several pictures published in *Life* magazine. Barbara, who others called "buoyant," seemed to be the sister with the most promising future, much to Idella's delight.[123] Barbara was more nervous than her sisters. Barbara had a fragile personality. A brilliant girl who took her varied interests to extremes. Barbara was sensitive and delicate, easily hurt and easily influenced by others. In 1942 *Billboard* would call her a "rodeo performer of note."[124] Riding was and would remain an important means of escape.

Lili seemed to be making no more headway at the club than a secret romance with the headwaiter, a thirtysomething man named Dick Hubert of "Belgian descent."[125] He was tall, charming, and dark haired with a sculpted physique. Dick was enchanted with Lili but it was forbidden for coworkers to date. They were "nuts about each other."[126] The pair would bide their time.

LILI WATCHED FROM BACKSTAGE AS A LITHE COUPLE SPUN AROUND the dance floor. The evening's program announced the novelty dance act of Corinne and Tito Valdez, who danced to Chopin's nocturens.

Billboard applauded Corinne and Tito for titillating with their "cobra dance" and their "slinky castanet dance." The audience went crazy for the "sexy, smart" lovely Corinne as she was scooped up in Tito's strong arms.[127] They performed from coast to coast, often choreographing other acts. Their work was flashy and they sprinkled their show with a hint of the exotic.

One of the "favorites" of the Florentine Gardens, they would travel the circuit as dancers and dance directors from Miami to New York in everything, including Mike Todd's *Peep Show* starring Gypsy Rose Lee in 1950.[128]

Young, muscular, and dark-haired Tito wound his arm around the lithe

Corinne and Tito helped propel Lili to the front of the line

Corinne, who was blonde with perfectly shaped ballerina legs. Lili admired not only their flawless figures but also their gorgeously choreographed dances. Both performed a "near nude, weaving, sexy dance in smart style."[129]

Corinne asked Lili to appear in a number with them. The trio performed a seminude number about Adam and Eve and the serpent in the Garden of Eden. Corrine, as the snake, stalked Adam, slithering suggestively, attempting to crush Tito/Adam. Finally Lili/Eve, wearing a knee-length blonde wig and G-string, appeared onstage, swaying between the pair, attempting to ward off the serpent, until she too fell under its spell. It was a smashing success, an imaginative and highly erotic dance.

Lili had been knocked out by her participation in the number. It was energetic, sexy, and creative. It was also an opportunity to be noticed. "Taking off your clothes doesn't take much nerve,"[130] Lili would always say. She was never shy or embarrassed with the human figure. As long as it wasn't vulgar.

If nudity—and it wasn't yet technically stripping, that would come later—meant

GET
FOR
TONIGH

Marie Van Shaa
gorgeous eyeful
NTG's Florenti
Gardens, suggests
"Spirit of Aviatio
quite vivacious

a higher salary and rising above the chorus, Lili was all for it. But she would be con-flicted. Stripping was thought of as low-rent. She never liked the word "stripper."

After much searching and experimentation she would find a way to strip on her terms. Elegant and classy. "Always the lady," they would say about Lili.[131]

LIFE WAS GOOD FOR MARIE. AS MARIE, LILI WORKED HARD. SHE WAS ecstatic when Granny singled her out for any special bits. After shows she was reg-ularly feted by customers eager to get to know her. She sipped champagne, never having too much, then moved on to the next admirer's table. There was always some-one who would buy a pretty girl dinner. Lili and Barbara often received invitations between the shows. When one sister received a dinner invitation she would convince the man to bring a buddy along for the other. It was one for all and all for one.

Barbara had her share of romance, going on dates with many eligible men like actor Franchot Tone, recently divorced from Joan Crawford and not yet moved on to the disastrous Barbara Payton. Idella carefully monitored the level of the man's fame to see if she approved of her daughter's choices.

Headliner Faith Bacon would make a huge impact on Lili when she joined the show. A dancer who garnered acclaim holding two giant ostrich feathers nearly the size of her petite figure, Faith claimed to be the "original" fan dancer, though both she and Sally Rand danced at the 1933 World's Fair with their fans. By the 1939 New York World's Fair in NTG's "Congress of Beauties," the popular Faith was making $450 a week.

In May of 1940 Faith joined the cast at the Florentine for an "indefinite" stay.[132] She would temporarily be sidelined in a Santa Monica hospital for an opera-tion in July but was back onstage at the Paramount by August. The show had been preceded by a spectacular publicity stunt. Bacon as "Lady Godiva" led a parade on horseback through the streets of Los Angeles where curious onlookers were treated to the fan dancer in the near—if not total—nude followed by dozens of chorus girls. It is conceivable, as an expert horsewoman and Florentine regular, that Barbara was one of them. *Variety* reported the parade left the "yokels to gap in wonder."

As just one of the chorus, Lili would have had little contact with Faith. But one afternoon Lili slipped downtown to see Bacon perform. The show would have a seismic shift in how Lili went about trying to get noticed, turning what she did into an artistic performance.

Lili would credit Bacon as changing her whole perception about a career stripping. Technically, Lili wasn't yet a stripper. She did not *remove* clothes at the

LEFT: *At the Florentine Gardens*

Florentine. She hadn't performed a tease, which is the defining element of burlesque. Lili realized she needed something that would identify her, something that audiences would want to see because she—and no one else—performed it. Also, "If I was going to do nudes, I might as well get paid well for it."[133]

"Faith Bacon was the greatest artist in the business," Lili would declare.[134] She was thunderstruck by what the petite beauty who looked like a blonde Clara Bow, with thin, arched black eyebrows and big blue mischievous eyes did. She was an extraordinarily graceful dancer, performing sensuous ballet-like moves without shoes. Bacon held a pair of creamy ostrich feather fans that were quite heavy, requiring strength and skill to (mostly) cover her body. Faith twirled them with gusto and elegance. Though she made it look easy, it was not.

LILI WAS INSPIRED BY FAITH'S DANCING, NOT ONLY BECAUSE OF THE movements—obviously more than parading, as Lili had been doing—but also by Bacon's elaborate props and scenery. She worked to classical music that soared and mimicked her story. In one number Faith rapturously portrayed a bird, wearing gorgeous, vibrant colored feathers. At the end of the number she died, her chest penetrated by an arrow.[135]

Bacon did not just dance, she told a story. Bacon was using herself as art; her body was her tool. "This is the kind of thing to strive for," Lili said, feeling as if she'd been struck by an arrow herself.[136] Lili watched Bacon create illusion on the stage: "The stage was haunted by the appearance of beauty." [137]

Faith defiantly reveled in her nudity. Lili thought she was beautiful and recognized her performance as a "big moment" in her life.[138] She would try to live up to her new idol's artistry.

Lili threw herself into work. She was determined more than ever to be a solo performer. She would be the creator of her destiny. She was through waiting for Granny or Corinne and Tito or anyone else to give her an act. She would design her own.

Years later a starting-to-be-well-known Lili crossed paths backstage with a down-and-out Faith Bacon. Lili had been misquoted as saying that if Faith could dance, so could she, as if Faith's talent was small and dismissive. At this point many had copied Faith's act, Sally Rand being the biggest name who claimed she was the original fan dancer. Faith had turned bitter and "aggressive."[139] Lili's idol, hardened and aging, turned away from Lili backstage.Faith didn't want anything to do with the young upstart criticizing her.

Lili, shivering backstage (at the Follies in Los Angeles) tried to explain she hadn't meant it like that, she admired Faith.

RIGHT: *Lili's bird act*

Faith, with her big blue eyes and white hair, still young but disillusioned, perhaps on drugs, having lived some desperately unproductive years, her salary slipping, injuries to her beautiful body tearing at her, snarled her lip and flounced away.

Later still, Lili made a special trip to Texas to see Faith perform. The aging stripper had a palpable smell of desperation about her by then. After a horrific accident onstage she had scars and pain in her legs. She was coming to the end of the road, unsure where her next $100 or her next job was coming from. She had lost the inner beauty that had driven her dance. She was just another down-and-out stripper.

Not long after, Faith would sail—possibly in a cloud of drugs—out her hotel window seeking relief from her life. Without work, without admirers, without money, the former "inventor of the fan dance" who was once billed as "the most beautiful woman in the world" had nothing left to keep her on the ground.[140] It was a story that terrified Lili. She thought, "This is how we push great artists" to tragedy.[141] Lili too would dance to the highest peak of a career that depended on her beauty. When her looks faded, what would become of her?

Faith's death would not be an easy one. Her body wrecked and broken when retrieved from a second-story awning that broke her fall, she expired after a few agonizing hours. Faith's lungs were punctured, her ribs broken, her face mangled. Lili couldn't imagine it.

ANOTHER SEMINAL MOMENT IN LILI'S LIFE WAS ATTENDING A PERformance of the Ballet Russe de Monte Carlo at the Philharmonic Auditorium in Los Angeles. The Monte Carlo was a famous offshoot of the Ballets Russes, which had performed under the genius leadership of Sergei Diaghilev. After Diaghilev's death in 1929 several companies formed, one being the Monte Carlo Ballet. The Monte Carlo toured mostly in the United States, debuting in Los Angeles in January of 1935.

In her Canadian biography Lili would claim she was seventeen and it was 1934 and Ian took her alone as a special treat. This was pure fiction. Maybe it was something the kindhearted Ian *would* have done. But the particular show she saw wasn't until 1945 (dates would never be important to or remembered accurately by Lili). By then Lili was a twice-divorced woman, not a schoolgirl who needed an escort.

Lili thought the performance magnificent. The troupe danced to Debussy's "Prélude à l'après-midi d'un faun." (She would later create her own version of "Prelude to the Afternoon of a Faun.")

The choreographer and lead dancer that profoundly impressed her was twenty-four-year-old David Lichine, a handsome Russian "poet-choreographer."

Performing at the Florentine Garden

He danced to *Scheherazade* (Lili too would include this in her repertoire), which incorporated a "protracted orgy" scene.[142]

Lili was mesmerized by the graceful ballerinas in "sensuously skimpy" costumes, with their elegant arm movements, their haughty manner as they danced as if there was no audience.[143] The male dancers were strong and sensual. It was a thrilling, artistic experience that deeply moved her. The dance (though it did not include Nijinsky's infamous and controversial masturbatory scene) opened Lili's eyes to the possibility that dance could be not only erotic or lustful but also artistic, despite the half-nude costumes. And more importantly Lili had been dancing to and for the audience. She had been seeking their approval and their eyes. This would soon change. She noticed most of the acts at the Florentine sought approval from the audience. Something about that bothered her. Later she equated it with dating. She felt once a man thought a woman was interested in him, the less interested he became. She would learn the same was true of audiences. *They* had to want *her* and not the other way around. Lili would make the audience seek her. She would perform privately as if there were no one to please but herself.

When Nijinsky had originated "Prélude à l'après-midi d'un faun" in the 1920s he had been roundly condemned because of the subject matter, shocking the audience by rubbing himself. No matter when or where Lili saw the performance and Lichine, it would change her ideas about dance and give her a taste of emotion through movement. She would often deny it but Lili did strive to elevate her work to be on par with the highest level of the artists of her day.

CHAPTER TEN

The girls never feared misbehaving at the nightclub because Alice had sternly instructed them on how to behave. She told the girls to not do anything they couldn't tell her about.[144]

Idella, who once had her own aspirations for the stage, sidetracked either by polio or children, perhaps tried to dissuade the girls from mingling with other show-girls, because Lili did not make friends. Maybe it was part of the conflict she felt about the career. Dardy later would complain about the strippers and burlesque performers, "They weren't necessarily the people you *wanted* to hang out with."[145] Other chorus girls couldn't help Lili's career, so she would feel no need to make friends with any of them. By now she had taken a small apartment in Hollywood and was enjoying her space and privacy away from Idella's nagging and Alice's worry.

EVERY NIGHT LILI WALTZED INTO THE NIGHTCLUB, PAST A SWEEPING staircase winding up to the second floor. She would stroll past the bar looking for Dick to say hello. In a short time the place was packed with mink-clad women in jewels, men in tuxedos. Everyone was laughing, drinking champagne, and watching a terrific night of entertainment.

Errol Flynn and John Barrymore were regulars. Lana Turner was spotted wearing a dress of beige crepe and a white fox. Texan Rex St. Cyr impressed Lili, sweeping in regularly with Lady Furness (the former Thelma Morgan), the Prince of Wales's former paramour before her friend Wallis Simpson stole him. Furness's identical twin, Gloria Vanderbilt (mother of fashion designer Gloria Vanderbilt), clung to St. Cyr's other arm. He threw $100 bills around as if they were confetti.

The self-styled Texan had been born Jack Thomas. He was a generous supporter of the Hollywood Canteen and made sure his name was in the entertainment trades lauded for his efforts. St. Cyr hosted numerous parties attended by celebrities, despite

Lili at the Florentine; Barbara is in the background

the fact that no one knew exactly who he was. When hosting the 13th Academy Awards, Bob Hope opened his monologue with, "Who is Rex St. Cyr?"[146]

In June of 1942, St. Cyr's name was important enough to be included as one of the guests at Errol Flynn's birthday party (which got out of hand when a butler was injured) along with Jack Warner, Ava Gardner, Tyrone Power, and Dinah Shore.

Lili was fascinated by him. His name would stay tucked in her head, associated with grandeur, flamboyance, and wealth; it sounded French and Lili loved all things French. She admired—and later emulated—anyone who was generous, mysterious, and glamorous.

Barbara's sometime beau was the tall and handsome Hearst columnist Harry Crocker who invited her swimming at San Simeon. As a regular part of the newspaper magnate's circle (he had done a film with Hearst's mistress Marion Davies, *Tillie the Toiler,* in 1927), Crocker had a distinguished pedigree. His father was an oil tycoon, his grandfather a railroad builder, and his uncle an important banker in San Francisco.

Crocker snapped a picture of Barbara in the San Simeon Grecian pool and inscribed it to Idella.

Barbara at San Simeon—Inscribed by Harry Crocker "For the nicest mother in the world"

BARBARA ALSO HAD DATES WITH THE FRENCH-SOUNDING FRANCHOT
Tone, who in reality had been born in New York as Stanislaus Pascal Franchot Tone.
The thirty-five-year-old movie star would send his limousine to wait for Barbara at
the Florentine's artists' entrance and drive her back to his house in Beverly Hills
for dinner. If Lili didn't have plans, she would show up too. All three would sit
at one end, "dwarfed by the table." He was a good sport and would have his uniformed houseman serve the hungry girls a sumptuous meal under a chandelier lit
with candles.

He had a large English-style home, with formal dining room as "big as a ship"
that looked out on beautiful gardens, the windows swathed in sheer lace curtains.[147]
Tone's butler would serve lavish seven-course meals. The sisters could eat; they
weren't dainty, nor did they pick at their dishes, despite being rail thin. Franchot
would tell the butler to call the driver and made sure the sisters were returned to the
Florentine in plenty of time so as not to miss the next show. He didn't want them
fired on account of him.

One night a handsome, round-faced actor with a deeply dramatic way of pon-
tificating asked the twenty-four-year-old Lili out.

His name was Orson Welles, theatre director, actor, and current Hollywood boy wonder, hot off his controversial production of *War of the Worlds* that for a short time sent radio waves of panic across America with his faux invasion of aliens taking over the earth. Hollywood came calling with a contract offering him almost (this would later be debated) complete artistic control. Welles was fully enamored of himself and his enormous talents.

Backstage at the Florentine, Granny interrupted Lili. He watched her dip a damp cloth in a jar of Ponds and rub it over her face to remove the heavy pancake. Other girls in the crowded dressing room were doing the same.

"Someone wants to meet Miss Champagne. Hurry up. I'll wait to introduce you."[148]

Granny had nicknamed Lili because of all the bottles purchased on her behalf.

Lili favored masculine-looking pants and button-down shirts offstage and slipped into a pantsuit. Granny complained, "Why do you wear that, Lili?" And he left her to finish getting dressed.

Dressed, Lili entered the front of the club and found Granny waiting for her. He led her to a small table.

"Marie, this is Mr. Orson Welles," Granny said, wearing a satisfied grin on his face. The place was packed and even among the many celebrities all eyes turned to Welles's table where the striking dancer stood in her very unshowgirl-like outfit.

Welles stood and took her hand. "Pleased," he said in his deep-timbered voice and bowed. He was conservatively dressed in a dark suit and tie. His voice was distinctive, but Lili thought it "domineering." "Join me?"

Lili, knowing he was the "important man of the year," slid into the banquette.

"Champagne?" he asked.

Welles poured a bottle of Piper-Heidsieck that sat in a silver ice bucket at his table.

"Mr. Welles—"

"Orson."

In the middle of the table was a small vase of fresh flowers. He plucked a rose from the arrangement and put it in his buttonhole. Then he did the same for her.

They made idle chatter but didn't stay long, not even to finish the bottle.

"Do you drive?" Orson asked.

She smiled sheepishly. "I do . . . but not well," she admitted. Driving made her nervous. She found it a difficult task and had a hard time concentrating behind the wheel.

Orson stood up. Lili stood nearly as tall as the director. They were two distinct figures as they strolled arm and arm across the crowded club and out the front doors. Lili could feel jealous eyes boring into her, which made her stand even taller,

Lili and her first car

basking in the glow of envy. It was a different kind of attention, and one she didn't mind. She had stopped caring that women sent daggers her way. Recognition of any kind was paramount for Lili.

Welles slid into the big Pontiac that another admirer of Lili's had lent her. It was a beautiful black convertible, big enough for her to feel safe behind the wheel. Lili took the steering wheel in hand.

WELLES WANTED TO TAKE HER "SOME PLACE SPECIAL" AND INSTRUCTED her to head east on Sunset Boulevard, then west toward Watts, south of downtown, which was at the time only just becoming a predominantly black neighborhood.[149]

Lili nervously parked on what she thought was a rather dodgy street, hoping nothing would happen to her borrowed car.

They got out of the convertible and walked to a nondescript one-story building. Welles knocked on the door.

The door opened a crack and a man's narrow face poked out. There was an exchange Lili didn't hear but immediately the door was hinged open.

It was a big room, grand, yet dark, with many tables filled with laughing and drinking couples and heat. There was a tiny stage with a black pianist playing jazz. They were ushered to a table near the piano. The black man acknowledged Orson and continued playing with a big grin on his face.

Interestingly, Lili's fifth husband, Ted Jordan, would make note of a "Brothers Club" that Orson liked to go to about this time, which was surely the same club he took Lili to. One knocked on the door and a "mean-looking man glared at you through a porthole" until you said the password, "Brother, let me in."[150]

To Orson the place was hip. They ordered sloe gins. Orson ordered BBQ chicken and ribs. They didn't speak much, just listened to the loud music as it filled the room. Orson liked it more than Lili. But she was enjoying herself. Jazz would never be her favorite music nor places like this her thing. Still she loved the illicit feeling of it, the hipsters in their bright clothes. *Hepcats.* The men wore shiny high-waisted, tight-cuffed zoot suits, pinstriped or brightly colored. Others wore shiny tuxedos with opera scarves trailing off them. Watches dangled on chains down to baggy-panted knees.

It was nearly 4 a.m. when Lili dropped Orson at the Garden of Allah, the hotel where he was staying at the corner of Sunset Boulevard and Crescent Heights. He chastely kissed her goodnight.

"Tomorrow?"[151]

They agreed and she drove to her tiny apartment in Hollywood. Still not tired, she undressed, washed her face, and leaned her head against the window sill looking down on the side of the opulent Grauman's Chinese Theatre. A cool breeze lifted her hair.

The next night she met Orson at his hotel. He had been renting an apartment at the former residence of silent-screen actress Alla Nazimova. And, in fact, he'd broadcast several live episodes of his radio series *Campbell Playhouse* from the Garden of Allah.

The Allah was the place where a multitude of celebrities found refuge, both short-term and long. Writer F. Scott Fitzgerald lived there, as would Dietrich, Garbo, and writer Robert Benchley. There was the main hotel, Nazimova's former mansion, with twenty-five individual villas built around the three and a half acres of gardens. It was Spanish Moorish and exotic like the former actress herself. There was a central pool where many recovered from hangovers. The parties flowed endlessly. It was charmingly decadent, just what Lili approved of.

Lili thought the setting incredibly romantic and ideal for a rendezvous.

For the next week she would drive to the Garden after her show or meet Orson at the Florentine and they would go together for a late dinner at any of the illegal bars in Watts that he loved. Orson seemed to know them all. One night her tires were slashed outside a club while they drank inside. He offered to pay for new ones. They would end their nights in the early-morning hours at his bungalow listening to the sounds of others partying nearby.

One morning when she woke, it was early afternoon and she discovered a note on the pillow next to her. "I am at the pool."[152]

She put on her sunglasses and the pair of shorts she had brought and wound her way over to the pool where she was surprised to see Orson in a sport coat and open shirt, scripts scattered about, surrounded by a bevy of sycophants hanging on to the his every order. She thought he acted like a king.

She stretched out on a lounge in the sun. He made sure one of the hotel's staff brought her a steaming cup of coffee, which she savored as she watched him, amused by how his minions fluttered nervously, worshipfully around him.

Orson had a two-picture deal at RKO and acted like royalty, a script in his hand and one at his feet. A cigarette was lit, and he constantly ran a hand through his hair.

A young secretary was taking notes. He was planning his next film, what would become the now classic *Citizen Kane*.

Tired and bored, Lili fell asleep. She was rarely impressed with the stature of others, much preferring to have attention center on herself.

One weekend Lili decided to stay out in Eagle Rock and asked Orson to catch a ride out to fetch her. This way he could meet Alice and the rest of the family.

He arrived at Bedlam Manor, hat in hand, carrying a large wooden staff, something Moses might have shook at the heavens, and wearing a wool burnoose. There was even a hooded cloak dramatically thrown across his wide shoulders. He claimed to be preparing for a part.

Dardy and Barbara couldn't help but giggle.

The entire family gathered around to listen to him pontificate about New York and the film he was writing. A film that was going to *change movies forever*. As he talked, the women sized him up. True, he was a movie star, but he sure liked to go on about himself. This was a houseful of women who each thought they were the center of life.

Lili kept her date waiting while she curled her hair, applied makeup, and dressed meticulously. The family's eyes started glazing over as Orson kept talking, not allowing anyone to get a word in.

They were grateful when Lili finally descend the staircase. She towered over most people, except her sisters and Orson. The director with his thinning hairline, which he was most sensitive about, appreciated Lili's fine beauty and her statuesque figure.

She smiled and Orson dramatically rose; bowing formally, he took her arm. She was amused. Out into the night they went. It would be one of their last dates. He was too wrapped up in himself for her taste. His preoccupation frustrated her.

Dardy raced over to the chair Orson had sat in, intending to mimic the "great" actor stooping down into his throne.

"Stop," Alice shouted, raising up her hand. "Don't sit in that chair. His royal ass sat there." Everyone burst out laughing.[153]

Lili felt lost around Welles. He took up so much air. She compared him to Napoleon. He never listened to her, his mind clearly elsewhere. Lili was equally frustrated at work. She was trying to figure out how to get out of the Florentine. She felt as if she were playing a game waiting for a career to take off. She was unhappy and bored. Her nerves were on edge.

Another reason she didn't care for Orson was he was a cheapskate. He ordered the least expensive thing on the menu, never asked if she'd like a second drink, and tipped horribly. Lili, who never had money, was free with hers. She bought endless gifts for her siblings and Alice. Like her grandmother, Lili couldn't stand to see someone in dire straits. A lot of the girls at the club, though they weren't close with Lili, were always asking for small loans. She would lend a few bucks if a girl needed it. After all, it was only money. She could always make more (though she complained regularly how she barely had enough to spend going out to a club).

THE DAYS TURNED WARM AS SUMMER APPROACHED. LILI AT LONG LAST started an overdue romance with Dick Hubert, the handsome headwaiter at the Florentine. Hubert must have seen her sweep by on the arms of Orson and other attentive males.

Despite the fact that she was enormously popular at the club with customers who asked after her and came back often, or cheered enthusiastically, Lili knew she wasn't any closer to being a headliner. She was just one of a dozen. In Dick's eyes she stood out.

Both sisters were getting mentioned in the gossip columns, even if their names were usually spelled incorrectly. Men bought presents, drinks, and flowers.

Lili would claim Dick asked her to marry him on their second date, though surely they had known each other for months.

She was "lonely" and agreed, eager to set up house with someone who adored her. True, they really didn't know each other but she liked having a man to take care of. It made her feel complete. She would dote on Dick, buy him things, attempt to cook. She vowed to be a wonderful wife and sex partner. And Dick already knew about her work; he wasn't likely to make her quit as Cordy had. It seemed an ideal arrangement. She had developed a cavalier philosophy when it came to marriage; if it didn't work, there was always divorce.

Lili and second husband Dick Hubert

LITTLE IS KNOWN ABOUT DICK HUBERT OR WHERE LILI AND HE LIVED. *Billboard* listed him as the headwaiter through early 1942 when he became the maître d' after his divorce from Lili.[154]

They drove the three hours to Tijuana and were married. "In those days you had to wait three days in California," Dardy said about the popular Mexican weddings both she and Lili enjoyed. "Tijuana was easy."

Dick, a beautiful dresser, spent hours grooming. He wore tails to work, bought Lili a fur, and drank "a lot," a turnoff for Lili, which lead to arguments, which she didn't care for.[155] They spent days sleeping and nights separated by a stage. No doubt Dick drove Lili to the club every late afternoon. She had never liked driving, and besides, Lili *liked* being driven. She *liked* having things done for her. It was a habit that would become an expectation that people would drop whatever else they were doing to attend to her.

"We were strangers who slept together," Lili later explained.[156] She would admit it should have been a weekend love affair, but in those days—and she would claim this into the 1950s—women didn't shack up. They got married. And Lili was no different. It is what Alice had taught her. Lili would always want the fireworks and drama and passion of a courtship. But she did not like the routine of marriage. Dick asked at the opportune time, when she was "waiting for men, waiting for a career."[157]

A source of friction must have been the fact they had to keep the marriage a secret. Granny would expect her to continue to sit at customers' tables. Perhaps Dick became jealous, as so many of her husbands would. Maybe he scoffed at her ambition to be a headliner. Either way, Lili was too young to settle down for long. With Dick she began a lifelong habit of leaving someone midsentence if she didn't like what they were talking about or if she grew bored. She didn't apologize, never realizing—or caring—how rude it was. She gave the impression they had offended her. She would simply get up and leave. No explanation. It was what she would do with this marriage.

ONE NIGHT LILI OVERHEARD DINGBAT AND A FEW GIRLS CHATTING after the show about how a couple of big producers had caught the performance.

Lili would learn Lou Walters was an important director, producer, and owner of the Latin Quarter Club in Miami. Eventually he would have a string of clubs in New York and Boston. It was the top of the top spots to play.

A child of a Polish Jewish refugee, Louis Walters was, despite being unattract-ive with a glass eye, "dapper, slim," and a man who spoke in slogans with a British accent, having been born in London. One of his catchphrases was "Never get a suntan that leaves lines." [158]

Lili would take it to heart. Another was never get fat and to always do your best even if it was just a rehearsal.[159]

Walters had caught the show along with talent agent Miles Ingalls, who booked burlesque comedians and dancers. He maintained offices in the Astor Hotel in New York.

Lili found out the high-powered duo were staying at the Roosevelt Hotel on Hollywood Boulevard.

Lili grabbed some of the publicity photos she had recently shot with John Reed, the big photographer on Hollywood Boulevard with the gigantic picture of Dietrich hanging in the window. She wrote a note on the pictures and stuck them in an envelope.

Lili made her way to the Roosevelt, a twelve-story Spanish-style hotel financed partially by Douglas Fairbanks and Mary Pickford, which stood across the street from the massive Grauman's Chinese Theatre. The hotel had opened in the twenties and was frequented by a slew of movie stars. It was the epitome of glamour.

Inside the beautiful lobby were big potted palms; the walls were painted a muted yellow. At the front desk she told the receptionist she had a package to deliver to Mr. Ingalls. The receptionist told her the room. Lili sprinted toward the staircase. She was claustrophobic and avoided elevators when she could.

She slid her envelope under the agent's door.

The next day the phone rang. It was Ingalls looking for Marie Van Schaack.

He would have remembered Lili from the lineup and the club's brochure. He asked her if she wanted to dance in the Latin Quarter in Miami. He had already showed the owner—Walters—her picture and he offered to book her.

Of course Lili agreed. Miles told her it would be a while before she would start and in the meantime she should get all the experience she could.

Lili told her husband she was quitting the Florentine, moving out, and divorcing him. She wanted to "be discreet" in the way she left both her "elegant husband" and the Florentine, which she considered "her second home."[160] She would tell no one about Miles Ingalls.

Was Dick surprised? When Lili turned off to someone it was obvious and uncomfortable. Maybe he thought his wife sheltered, too immature, a pretty young girl looking for a bigger fish that could make her career. All things that were true. Hubert didn't fight her decision and that was the end of marriage number two.

Lili made a clean break. She headed for the cool air of San Francisco.

RIGHT: *Lili at the Florentine—easy to see what Miles Ingalls saw*

CHAPTER ELEVEN

1987

The Whittier earthquake had shaken the ground in October. Unsettling to have the terra firma not so firm under one's feet. She was alone with her thoughts. The fact the holidays were approaching didn't help. Her mind was filled with memory. The Duncan Sisters. The Music Box. A gorgeous club. The most beautiful one she had ever worked.

Writing to fans kept her thoughts in the past. Visions of faces she hadn't seen or thought of in ages. It was a *different world*.[161] Oh, how her world was different now.

She had been uprooted in December, the landlord kicking everyone out to tent the building. So inconvenient to move out, holing up in a hotel with Lorenzo, having to vacate every day to let someone clean. Scoring difficult.

She was glad to be back home. Lorenzo was in the bedroom with his memories while she watched the smoke from her incense pirouette toward the beams above her head. Wasting time.

She wrote a fan, apologizing for being out of touch. The lined yellow pad she used to keep track of her money showed a small amount from Armando.

Armando, tall and elegant like Dick, husband number two. Was Armando still handsome? Above her head the sound of feet shuffling, chairs scraping. The lack of privacy pricked at her.

The bustle of the Florentine Gardens, the smell of perfume and flowers and smoke. Days when she had been young and eager. Those big headpieces. She'd been a giant onstage. So much laughter backstage with Barbara and the other girls. Parading across the stage, pasties on. Oh, how they hurt if the glue was on too thick.

Picking up an old photo she saw what Dardy marveled at, her "pigeon breast."[162] A jutting chest and a narrow waist. So slim. Once. Long ago. Now she was bloated.

Stiff. And *depressed*. She stuffed a couple of extra photos *from Santa* for her friend in Maryland. *It's so beautiful there this time of year.*

To another she started the letter as she always did: *Thanks so much for getting in touch—it's nice to be remembered* . . .

Was she remembered now? As what? Dancer. Arrests. Slut. Too many men. Never enough of that for her. Lovers slipped through her fingers like jewels. The eyes she had gazed into.

Need roared over her. Anxiety pinged. Time was warped inside her brain. Were her pupils horribly retracted? "Pinned" they called it. Tiny black dots in the middle of her fading blue orbs that saw so little. Her throat was sore, as it often was as the drug wore off.

From Lorenzo she would need relief. The weather had turned cool, bringing rain. She longed for a fireplace; she wrote a fan. She must have meant a working one because there was a fireplace in her front room. But she had always liked the sympathy of others.

It wasn't like before when she could wrap herself in fur in front of a fireplace on Canyon Drive and listen to the crackle of a roaring fire.

SHE HAD DISCARDED PEOPLE EASILY. FAMILY. HUSBANDS. NOW SHE WAS saddled with Lorenzo for as long as he, or she, remained alive. *There are strange turns in this road of life.*

Independence and privacy is not all that bad! was her motto, a joke now. She had neither.

Her obligation was Lorenzo. She had to make sure the rent, the gas, and phone bills were paid. He just had to keep them supplied with juice, drugs, escape.

The past.

Impossible for people to understand her gowns onstage had been by the best designers in her day. "As a schoolgirl I wanted to become a designer. Ironic that I should become a strip tease queen with a career taking off my clothes."[163] Now she—the queen—was dressed simply. She hated that term "burlesque queen." Some "queen." In need of a carriage. Her neighbor still drove her to get groceries, the odd errand. Foolish young man had tried to flirt with her—actually flirt with her— she'd been courted by the best bullshitters, Paul, Ted, Jimmy even. What did this young kid think? Her head would be turned by his smooth lines? "No, I never really danced much," she had told him.

She had a package of bills she needed to get to Dardy to pay. Good old reliable Teedle Dee.

A phone call from a fan. A welcome respite in her day. This one usually called late afternoon or early evening. To check in on her. She asked him about the "dot coms" that were mentioned on TV. Interesting. She told him she thought the advertising aspect of it brilliant.

There were marvels still to discover. She heard about bifocal contact lenses. And Apple computers? Imagine. She didn't understand how—essentially—a TV had information in it and spewed it out. In just a year she would learn about the new wonder drug Prozac.

Yes, she could still marvel at things. She liked learning things. She had a long conversation with Pat until "the light bulb . . . is getting hot," so it was time to hang up.

CHAPTER TWELVE

It cost 25 cents to cross the Bay Bridge into San Francisco in 1941, the year Lili arrived alone in November. She found a room in a boarding house that looked clean and decent. Before she even undressed she perused the phone book for local theatrical agents. She found one not far away and set out to conquer San Francisco.

Showing up unannounced she threw her nude picture on the desk and told him she was a dancer from the world-famous Florentine Gardens and she would soon be working with Lou Walters, but . . . she needed work now.

The woman standing before the agent was stunning, with a wide smile, a face that could stop traffic, slim, seemingly as tall as the tallest building. He called the Music Box and sent his new client over for an interview.

Twenty-three-year-old Lili got the job.

The Music Box Theatre was the most dazzling theatre Lili had ever seen. It would remain a loving memory for her among dozens of venues. Smaller than the Florentine, it had a capacity for only six hundred on its two tiers. There were three bars painted blue and gold with a band at one end and a dance floor in the middle of the ground floor. Tall marble columns held a balcony that wrapped around the second floor. To Lili it was like pictures she had seen of European opera houses. It was a luxurious, bejeweled candy box.

The burlesque theatre located at 859 O'Farrell Street was not an "ideal location for a club."[164] It had opened in October 16, 1940, backed by Frank and Clarence Herman. After a year it shuttered while the Duncan Sisters, who took over management, ran the nearby Lido. It was small and ornate, like its operators.

The once-famous Duncan Sisters had triumphed in a winning act that had wowed the country in the twenties. Rosetta and her younger sibling Vivian were two petite veterans of vaudeville. They had been performing since they were kids. Vivian played the pretty dumb blonde. Rosetta had performed for years in blackface

Lili's employers, The Duncan Sisters

in their $1-million-making act "Topsy and Eva," an *Uncle Tom's Cabin*–ish musical written specifically for them. The music was a "riot of success" and had been enormously popular.[165] It was an act they would regularly regurgitate well into the 1950s.

The two women, no longer charming young ingenues, were now in their forties, standing a mere five two. Once vivacious and popular, they were now irrelevant with their antiquated act, yet they valiantly trooped on, oblivious to the changing times. They refused to believe the world was moving on from their dated form of entertainment where it was acceptable for a beautiful young white girl to sing and act in blackface.

THE VETERAN TROOPERS TREATED THE SHOWGIRLS THAT WORKED for them like daughters. Where Vivian was sweet and resembled Barbara Cartland, Rosette was completely different, "rude" and a "lesbian."[166]

Lili loved San Francisco. She loved the Chinese restaurants, pork noodles for 35 cents. Great carts parked along Powell Street; with a riot of fresh flowers for sale. Fisherman's Wharf was crowded with boats, most of the Italian sailors sat mending nets, singing in their native language. What Lili loved most was the cool temperatures. She walked around the city, jumping into restaurants or bars. Without Dick and her family, Lili had no one to answer to. San Francisco was freedom and would hold fond memories for her. She would return time and again throughout her career, appreciating the invigorating breezes.

The Music Box had a revue-type show much like the Florentine Gardens. Vivian played the piano, though one reviewer complained the sisters "seemed tired."[167] A hot dance team called Harger and Maye appeared to much applause. It was one of the Duncan's idea for Lili to be the "Girl of the Hour."

Lili was to come out every hour wearing something spectacular and walk among the crowd. She could smile or chat briefly. Then she was to remove a piece of clothing. Her first proper tease to date. Lili would exit and leave the audience waiting until the next hour, when she would return to remove another item of clothing.

Presumably it would keep the men in the club buying more drinks throughout the night, waiting to see the nubile blonde until she was revealed in all her glory.

At the top Lili removed a fur, revealing her beautiful white shoulders in a strapless gown. Smile. Turn. Leave them wanting more.

The next hour she peeled off a glove. She left them wanting more.

By the end of the night she was naked except for a tiny sequined G-string, satin pumps, and a gardenia behind one ear. She looks wildly happy and in her element. Experiencing her first taste of success.

LILI LIKED THE SPECIAL ATTENTION. TERRIFIED AND EXCITED AT THE same time, she would hold her head high and smile. All eyes were on her.

Stage fright is a paralyzing feeling. The stomach cramps, the mouth dries, hands become numb, and the heart races. It can be sheer terror. Yet there is no better reminder that one is fully alive, fully in the moment. There is no conquering the feeling. There is only the stepping into it and walking through it. For some performers they cannot endure the terror; for others it is intoxicating. Despite the agony she felt, Lili always managed to go on. Always.

Lili said she worked with an alter ego. Was it Greta Garbo she hid behind? She mentions her constantly in her Canadian biography, asking herself what Garbo would do to help her make a decision.

The nights were long but fruitful. Lili would slowly glide down the staircase to the main part of the room, her fur dragging elegantly behind her. Underneath the crystal chandeliers Lili glittered among the patrons. She felt beautiful and powerful and she knew she had them in the palm of her hand.

As a final tease she would unpin the gardenia behind her ear and toss it into the audience. She was irresistible. Yet with her attitude she created a barrier between herself and the audience. She was an "untouchable beauty."[168] Maybe her alter ego allowed her distance yet desirability, à la Garbo. Lili's version of Garbo was far more lush and feminine, her body more inviting.

Lili was supremely comfortable with her body. It was exhilarating being naked in front of applauding strangers who oohed and awed at her mere presence. NTG wrote that for Lili, "clothes were unimportant." And "she had an aversion to wearing anything" on the stage.[169]

Vivian chided Lili for not mingling with the guests. Lili wanted to remain mysterious. Vivian continued to protest until reporters called wanting to know the Girl of the Hour's name. Lili got her way.

Lili was an unpolished performer, winning kudos for her sheer beauty. She had something, but it was largely unproven. In fact the whole Music Box show was rough. The sisters hired a new choreographer by the end of November.

Ivan Fehnova had previously worked with Mike Todd at the New York World's Fair. He stepped in to whip the show into shape.[170]

In his midforties, Ivan was a flamboyant, homosexual Russian who wore black silk shirts with high upturned collars. His thinning black hair was parted in the middle and slicked back. He carried large white handkerchiefs. He was chubby yet elegant, impossibly glamorous and rigidly disciplined, prone to whacking dancers on the back of their legs with his six-foot staff made out of polished wood. Of course, not too hard. He didn't want to inflict damage.

FEHNOVA WOULD BECOME A GREAT FRIEND TO LILI. HE SAW HER potential though he declared her hopeless as a dancer. "She had absolutely nothing," he declared.[171] But Lili was willing to follow his every direction. She would always warm to having a mentor, eager to improve herself.

The Russian had an idea that would cause a sensation. He had her change into her G-string and stand on the empty stage. He hooked a fishing wire onto the side of her panties. The wire was attached to a fishing rod that was held by a stagehand standing up in the rafters. Before Lili knew what was happening she felt a tug and her G-string went flying off into the balcony.

Next Fehnova had the G-string coated with radium paint, used mostly on watches that glowed in the dark.[172]

At the evening show Lili stripped down to her G-string, the stagehand pulled

---

LEFT: *Down to the bare essentials*

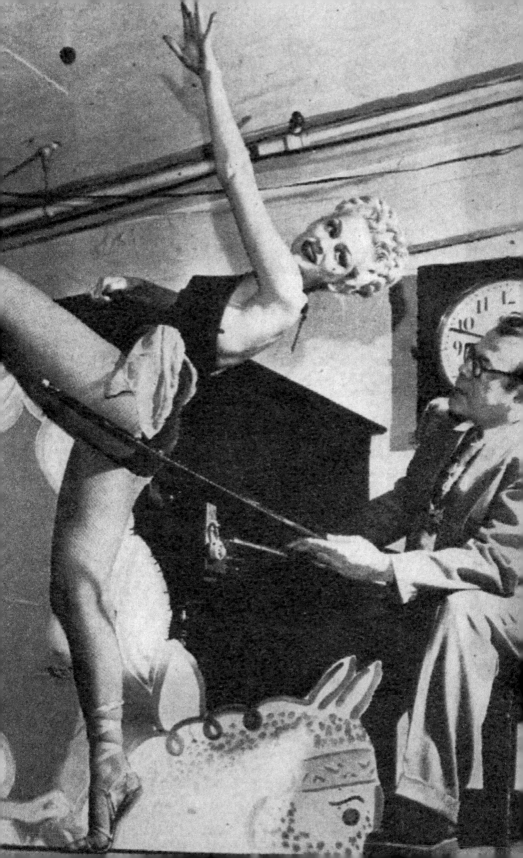

on the wire as the lights were hit, and the phosphorescent G-string flew through the air, landing in one lucky man's lap. The audience went crazy.

Lili might tremble backstage, yet once she stepped in front of the audience she had a confidence that was unflappable. If she stumbled, and she did in the beginning, she would spend more time rehearsing with Fehnova, who drilled her hard.

"It was the presence of the women in the audience that gave me butterflies in my stomach."[173] Where she felt confident and took "pleasure in tantalizing and intriguing" her male audience, she felt the women judging her and they terrified her.[174] Preshow jitters would plague her for the rest of her professional life. "I hate the audiences," she would explain. "Anyone hates anything that frightens them."[175]

Under Ivan's tough and persistent tutelage she mastered a fluid gait. "I walked her until I thought she would drop but before we were through Lili knew how to walk across a stage, believe me."[176] She dance-walked across the stage, her head held high, shoulders back. She appeared sensuous and inviting, enticing from the sway of her hips to the arch of her back, her uniquely "pigeon breast" jutting forward. Lili became calm and confident. Fehnova was proud of her, declaring her "intrinsically graceful." He had spotted her "natural grace and poise that many ballet dancers work years to get. . . . She radiated personality."[177]

Under Fehnova's tutelage she danced for hours. They developed acts she would repeat for years, such as "The Love Bird" and "The Chinese Chastity Belt." With each new daring invention she received more notice in the papers. The demand for her grew. San Franciscans wanted to see the new sensation.

Since the Florentine, Lili had begun experimenting with pseudonyms. Often she was Marie Van Schaack, which few seemed to know how to pronounce or spell. Ivan suggested "Fehnova" and then "Lili." She remembered Marlene Dietrich's character Shanghai Lily. Alternatively she tried Lili Marie. Ivan informed the publicity manager at the Music Box that from now on she would be known as Lili Fehnova should any members of the press ask who the tall cool blonde was. And they were asking.

Fehnova began shaping the show. There was a ten-girl lineup, a dance duo, singer, Vivian Duncan on the piano. During the December 3 show Lili had the good fortune to have her flying G-string land in a reporter's receptive lap. *Variety* singled out Lili, noting her "G-string takes the air."[178]

Lili made friends with the dance duo Harger and Maye. Burt Harger and Charlotte Maye were café dancers and "one of the strongest teams" working.[179] "Their varied sets arrest attention" and Lili was impressed.[180] Of course she would

---

LEFT: *Fehnova "disciplining" Dardy*

have observed and taken from the dancers as she did with others.[181] She was close enough to sleep on the couch of Harger, whose life would have a tragic end.

Lili said she was "infatuated" by the handsome Burt but he did not reciprocate her advances. Finally he set Lili down and explained he was gay.[182]

Puzzling that Lili misnames the duo in her biography (as she would so many), but just the mere mention of them means they had an influence on her (she mentioned so few). Lili wrote they went on to enjoy a "long friendship."[183]

Burt Harger's career was cut short in 1945 at age thirty-nine. His dismembered torso was found washed ashore in New York, while an arm and leg were found in the Hudson River. Maye had become worried when her dance partner missed a rehearsal. Police would discover Harger had been murdered with multiple blows from a hammer, then cut in pieces with a razor by his lover and roommate of fourteen months, who was upset over the news that the dancer was set to marry. The murderer took multiple trips on ferries dumping body parts wrapped in sheets into the water.[184]

Newspapers at the time called it the "Torso Murder Case." Lili had to have known about it, as she was in New York herself, but she makes no mention of her murdered ex-crush.

Back in Los Angeles, Barbara was working hard-to-conquer Hollywood, still dancing at the Florentine. Signed with RKO, she was pursuing an acting career with Idella's encouragement.

Dardy was finally allowed to work and landed a job dancing for vaudeville producer Harry Howard.[185] The show would take her to San Francisco.

At the LA train station Ian helped his youngest daughter with her suitcase while she wrung her gloved hands, nervous, prepared to head north. At sixteen she had never been away from her family.

Gray streaked Ian's auburn hair. He still suffered debilitating headaches and was particularly close with his youngest daughter. She was brave and fearless on the horses, high-spirited and saucy. Organized, capable, sharp-tongued when she had to be. Dardy adored her dad.

In San Francisco, Dardy and the rest of the dancers in the show were put up at the Grand Hotel, directly across from the Golden Gate Theatre where she would be performing. She had begun the oftentimes harsh life of a showgirl. It was a noon curtain; four shows, bed by three, up and at the theatre again by ten.

Contrary to what most believed, the grind in a showgirl's life was in the travel, not on the stage.

Exhausted from the pace, Dardy would fall asleep backstage, fully and elaborately dressed, to awaken to the sounds of her overture being played by the orchestra and she would dash to make her curtain.

Stripper Betty Rowland with gas mask

DECEMBER 7, 1941. WAS A COLD DAY IN SAN FRANCISCO. ARRIVING AT the theatre early, Lili busied herself getting ready. The dressing room was eerily quiet. Girls and crew began showing up walking around in tears, somber faced.

The Duncan Sisters were even whiter under their ghost-like pancake. Vivian stood onstage and in great theatrical style told the cast that the Japanese had dropped bombs on Hawaii.

In the coming days there was palpable fear in the air as police patrolled the waters off San Francisco bay. The city was dark by sunset. The mayor declared a state of emergency. Attendance dropped. Just as she had been garnering good press, Lili's dreams would have to be postponed.

Lili was at her dressing table pulling bottles from a beautiful white leather makeup case. As soon as she started earning money Lili began to spend it on beautiful things. Things she had dreamed of owning. She had great taste; expensive taste.

Dardy trawled through Lili's treasure trove of liquid and powder and lipsticks, bleach and perfume.

"What's this?" Dardy held up a scary green mask with a long tube that ran down to the ground.

"It's a gas mask and you better get yourself one, babe."[186] Lili was perfectly serious as she penciled in her eyebrows. One never knew when the bomb was going to be dropped and "we had to look our best."[187]

HYSTERIA WAS IN THE AIR. ROSETTA ANNOUNCED TO CAST AND CREW that they were moving to the River House in Reno.

With the Latin Quarter temporarily shut due to the war Lili was grateful for the Reno engagement. With several weeks to fill Lili returned to Los Angeles to help Alice pack an emergency kit in case the Japanese attacked.

Unable to remain idle Lili booked gigs dancing at both the Merry-Go-Round and Sugar Hill clubs on Vine between Sunset and Hollywood Boulevard.

In general the Mafia had a hand both directly and indirectly in many burlesque clubs. They watched the customers, made sure the girls stayed in line, and themselves were often loyal customers. At the Florentine Gardens, if they didn't actually run the club, many Mafioso certainly attended. Bugsy Siegel was a regular. Lili would, as would Dardy and Barbara, make friends with many over the years. They "loved gangsters."[188]

Lili arranged through her friend Jack Dragna, the "Capone of Los Angeles," for Alice to have enough ration coupons.[189] Dragna was the boss of the LA crime family from 1931 until his death from a heart attack in 1956. Lili probably met him in one of the clubs after a show and was familiar enough to telephone him for a favor.

Lili packed emergency luggage for Alice, who was living in Long Beach before boarding a train to Nevada for the January 1942 debut.

The River House was located five minutes outside of Reno in Lawton's Hot Springs. The casino and restaurant boasted a large outdoor pool conveniently located on Highway 40, the main route from Sacramento to Salt Lake City.

Nearby was a granite outcropping where warm mineral water sprang and the tourists soaked, hoping to cure everything from serious diseases to natural ailments caused by aging.

Sam Lawton had built his railway station and home for himself next to the spring in the late 1800s. Eventually the station was enlarged and an inn added. In early 1930 a bar faced the river with a large sitting area, fireplace, and dining room for weary travelers who either stopped to bathe and imbibe or settled in for the six-week divorces available in Nevada. Because of the latter the River House was always packed.

Lili, ripe for romance, fell in love with another tall, dark, and handsome man, the bartender, Eddie.

RIGHT: *Lili before her dramatic transformation*

To Lili, Eddie appeared sophisticated with a seemingly endless array of Cadillacs at the snap of his fingers. He spent money freely and lavishly. She didn't think to question where his free-flowing income stemmed from.

Lili found the desert's remoteness charming. The sunsets in particular were spectacular. It was a cool time of year and the weather was bracing in the late-night hours.

Lili once again wowed the audiences with her "Girl of the Hour" number, though attendance was poor.

After about a month in the desert her romance looked to be going well. She was happy and tranquil, confident in herself.

Cuddling with Eddie, who was rubbing her shoulders late one night after her last show, she rested her head on his chest. She wondered if tonight was the night he was going to propose. She had decided she was going to ask him if he didn't bring it up. At this stage of her life marriage still meant she was wanted.

Quietly Eddie suggested Lili could make a lot of money for the both of them. If she joined his stable of call girls. Lili was shocked. Devastated.

"How dare you?" she squeaked.

"I've had offers for you. You can start tonight. Now."[190]

She left him and his offer and cried for hours in her room.

In her Canadian biography she would admit she knew what prostitutes were but before Eddie's offer she had never thought about the "reality" of them. Forty years later she would still feel the sting of humiliation.

She went to Vivian and quit that night. Vivian admitted she knew about Eddie but couldn't tell Lili.

Lili left for Los Angeles, running again. Perhaps in her mind she was determined to create someone—an image—no one would ever again mistake for a prostitute. She was determined to outclass them all.

CHAPTER THIRTEEN

W ith still no word from the Latin Quarter, it was probably Miles Ingalls that
came to her rescue and quickly booked Lili another job. From Los Angeles
Lili hopped a train to San Diego. She would appear at the only burlesque theatre in
the beautiful city on the water. For $35 a week she was going to start over. Again.[191]

The Duncan Sisters weren't as lucky. They would close their show in early
August of 1942, leaving behind "local creditors" filing suit for unpaid bills.[192]

The Hollywood Theatre was located in sunny downtown San Diego on F
Street between Fourth and Fifth, operated by Robert "Bob" Johnston, a Belfast-
born family man whose wife, Fanny, a former showgirl, choreographed the shows.
Johnston, an ex-vaudeville performer, candy butcher, and singer, had taken over the
Liberty Theatre in the 1920s and renamed it the Hollywood. The theatre was doing
poor business despite the fact that famed stripper Sally Rand had performed there.
Her dance of "Leda and the Swan" had been a big hit. The Hollywood sat five hun-
dred, but audiences had dropped since the crowded days of World War I. Johnston
held on. When World War II broke out "you couldn't get a seat weekends," recalled
DeeAnn, Bob and Fanny's daughter.[193] The servicemen "gave it life."[194]

Lili found Bob Johnston friendly and fatherly. She liked the family atmosphere, similar to what the Duncan Sisters had created. She started out billing herself as Marie Fehnova. There were six shows on Saturday, five on Sunday.

Still reeling from her rejection from Eddie, depressed and insecure, Lili's dancing suffered. The Johnstons considered letting her go, but based on her extraordinary looks she was instead given a solo strip number. Fanny judged her performance
poor. An older stripper named Irish told Fanny it didn't matter what Lili did on the
stage; she was so beautiful the men would go crazy. Fanny agreed and put off firing
the young girl. Even a dejected and unsure Lili clearly had something.

Lili hated life backstage crammed in with people she didn't care for. Many of
the women were older relics grinding out a living week after week for drunks and

gamblers and hustlers at the noonday shows. She wrote Miles Ingalls to complain. "Get me out," she pled.[195]

He told her it was "experience."[196]

Both Irish and Fanny saved Lili from despair by taking her under their wing. Irish in particular became close with Lili, refocusing her maternal instincts on the now twenty-five-year-old. Irish, born Janne Cafara, would claim to be the one who taught Lili how to strip. She signed a picture to Lili, "your strip teacher."[197]

The thirty-three-year-old Irish seemed much more than eight years older than Lili. Her son had been killed by a drunk driver and grief paralyzed her. She immersed herself in the Hollywood Theatre where she would remain for eighteen years headlining and doing bits with the comics. She would marry the house singer, content to stay in San Diego.

The days were hard for Lili. She was living in a tiny room in a crappy hotel where she strung a rope over her bed to dry her clothes. There was no place to hang her costumes except for the walls of the room. But she would make due while she waited for her chance.

Fanny pulled Lili aside and told her that although she was beautiful she didn't "have a sense of spectacle." She didn't have what another stripper, a tassel twirler, had.

Lili was disgusted. Twirling tassels was vulgar. She didn't want to be the "best stripper." She wanted to be the best "specialty" dancer. When Fanny referred to her as "stripper" she demurred; she would rather be called "exotic dancer." Lili would always distinguish herself as a dancer who wanted to "amuse" and "attract" an audience.[198]

At the Hollywood Theater Lili took the stage with what would become a fixture for her onstage: a vanity.

IT IS QUITE POSSIBLY THE FIRST MINI SCENARIO SHE EVER PERFORMED. It was a defining step in the future success of Lili St. Cyr.

Many performers attest to the use of props and furniture as having a grounding effect. It can help steady nerves to have something literally to hold on to. Lili would need props and action and a fantasy to soothe jitters.

As proof of her newfound stage presence, the Johnstons asked Lili to extend her stay.

At the end of her extension a redheaded headliner by the name of Betty Rowland suggested Lili try the Follies in Los Angeles.

Rowland was petite and buxom, a live-and-let-live type. She had been performing since she was a young girl along with her two sisters, Roz Elle and Dian. They started out tap-dancing in vaudeville. Eventually, like Lili and her sisters, all three became headliners.

Lili at vanity

LIKE MANY STRIPPERS BETTY HAD HER PARTICULAR WAY OF DRESSING. Two pieces. Skirt and tops. Slit up to the fastener. There was a vivaciousness about Betty that made her hugely popular. Her moniker was "the Ball of Fire" because of her fiery hair and hot strip.

Either on her own or with Betty's help, Lili secured a spot at the Follies where she met Lillian Hunt, who would become another mentor.

Born Lily Izen, Lillian Hunt was a former tap dancer who ran away from home as a teen and married an actor in a show she was dancing in. They had a daughter before he deserted her and she moved into the chorus. There she met comedian Leon DeVoe whom she would marry and spend the rest of her life with, eventually moving to California to do choreography at the Follies, a burlesque house in the heart of downtown Los Angeles.

Hunt was redheaded, big-bosomed, and managed, directed, and produced the shows. She worked seven days a week marshalling a bevy of beauties across the stage, and up and down the many staircases backstage with her perennial bark rising from her "shabby office backstage." In her suits and gloves she was very much the lady, something Lili could appreciate. Hunt would share with Lili a love of Daché hats.

Sept 7, 1943

Sisters Dardy and Barbara

Lillian took dozens of girls under her wing over many decades, turning them into fine strippers. She insisted they conduct themselves as ladies, dressing properly outside the theatre. Hunt did not like vulgarity on or off the stage, telling one stripper when she performed, "You don't have to be vulgar, keep your tongue in your mouth."[199]

Hunt too would help Lili perfect her act and hire her year after year.[200]

The former Belasco Theatre, which had opened in 1904, was renamed the Follies, with generous seating for nine hundred that belied its modest exterior. Inside was a lovely, ornate theatre with balcony and box seats. The generous backstage could easily fit dressing rooms to accommodate eighty showgirls. A runway thrust into the audience, placing the girls within arm's length. Yet the lobby was surprisingly small and dingy. Between shows Hunt played the Charlie Chan movies Lili loved.

Sandwiched between a shoe store and a pawnshop, the Follies ran four shows a day, with a new show weekly. Strippers high and low graced the stage, from Rose la Rose to Patti Wagon. It would be the last burlesque house standing in Los Angeles, meeting the wrecking ball in 1974.[201]

Lili reunited with Dardy, now seventeen, who was sharing the stage with Barbara at Earl Carroll's on Sunset Boulevard. Thin, tall, and brunette, Dardy was striking. Being on the road had matured her.

THERE HAD BEEN A FAMILY UPSET RECENTLY. IAN HAD LEFT IDELLA. IT couldn't have been much of a surprise after years of volatile fights.

Ian, still handsome, now worked for or owned his own detective agency. Investigating Idella he found some disturbing news relating to Lili's father. And it was a bombshell.

To Ian (and possibly others) Idella had claimed her first husband had been killed in World War I. However, Ian found a letter from the very-much-alive Mr. Edward Van Schaack, who had written to Idella just the previous year. He was living in Spokane, Washington. It seemed Ian could find no record of Edward Van Schaack and Idella's divorce, because there hadn't been one, which meant Ian and Idella were never legally married.[202]

What did Lili, who had never received any contact from her father, think? A father she was told was either dead or had abandoned her mother? Had he tried to make contact and Idella kept the two apart? He must have wanted some news about his daughter, or why would he have kept in touch with Idella?

To add humiliation to Idella's presumed embarrassment, Barbara and Dardy testified in court they wanted Ian to have custody of them.

When contacted, Lili's father clammed up. "I don't want to talk about it."[203] To everyone's relief the judge ruled the sisters legitimate.

Did this mean that Idella's marriage to Cornett was also invalid? No one seems to have brought it up.[204]

It was another monumental secret to be kept.

LILI'S SALARY HAD BEEN STEADILY RISING. BY 1943 SHE WAS MAKING $75 a week at the Sugar Hill nightclub in Hollywood. Mentioned in the paper as the tall, cool blonde with the name of Lili, she would vacillate between Lili Fehnova (or "Finova"), "Lili LaSeur," and the unimaginable "Lili Wanamaker," hoping the right one would stick. With still no word from Lou Walters, whom she hoped would rescue her from burlesque, Lili returned to the Florentine Gardens and billed herself as "Lili LaBang" and "Lili Le Bang." (Lili always had a great sense of humor. She claimed she lived near Le Bang Place.[205])

She was popular enough that *Variety* mentioned when she missed work due to the flu.[206]

Into the Florentine one night walked that old regular Rex St. Cyr with an heiress on one arm and a movie star on the other. People leaned together and whispered, as they always did when the mysterious millionaire appeared. Hollywood remained curious. "Who *is* he?" they wondered. He wasn't handsome, but he was rich and he had European manners. Lili adored his last name.

In writing, "St. Cyr" looked sexy and elegant. It was pronounced not *saint cyr*, but *sin-cere*. The double entendre wasn't bad either. Lili decided to make it her own.

Barbara and Dardy performed as Moffett (or Moffet or Moffatt). They were on the road with Earl Carroll earning $65 a week. All three sisters could consider themselves doing very well.

On trains and in dressing rooms Dardy wrote letters to her father recording life on the road. She wrote how difficult train travel was becoming as all the good trains were used for soldiers. Very often they were late to engagements. The food was unmentionable.

Dardy told one story involving the pettiness that often arose backstage among the showgirls. Mascara in those days came in cakes and girls had their own because they spit on them to moisten the makeup before applying it. It wasn't something anyone wanted to share.

Dardy caught one girl as she picked up Dardy's tin and spit in it. Dardy was furious, especially as it happened more than once. "I didn't have money to waste on extras," not to mention she wasn't interested in some stranger's germs.

Shortly thereafter a stagehand caught a mouse, typical theatre inhabitants. "Could I please have that?" Dardy asked the stagehand.

The stagehand looked at her as if she was crazy but handed over the dead mouse by its ropey gray tail.

Dardy carried it in a towel back to the empty dressing room. Carefully scooping out half the contents of the spit-swapping girl's jar of Albolene makeup remover, she plopped the dead mouse in and covered it with cream.

About a week later, the girl dashed into the theatre with an itchy red and swollen face. She was in tears.

"Look at me!" the girl screamed. "What am I gonna do?" All the girls gathered around and exclaimed at her puffy cheeks. "I don't know what the hell happened."

"I do," Dardy said calmly.

"What is it?"

"Here." Dardy reached over and grabbed the girl's makeup remover jar. "Dig in."[207]

The girl screamed when a pair of gray feet protruded.

CHAPTER FOURTEEN

Lili St. Cyr was making her long-anticipated debut at Lou Walter's Latin Quarter in Miami. She was officially announced in the papers as Lili St. Cyr.

The Latin Quarter had been built in the 1920s as the Palm Island Club, a private club for the posh set during Prohibition. Located at 159 Palm Island Drive, it was smack in the center of Palm Island, accessible only via car along a narrow sand causeway that passed through a security gate.[208]

It was December 1943. A warm tropical breeze blew. The grand marble entrance was impressive and elegant, exhilarating for Lili after the nondescript entrances of the Follies and Hollywood Theatre. She was moving up in the world.

HOWARD HUGHES—WHO YEARS LATER WOULD PUT LILI IN A FILM— sat around a booth with his buddies. Joseph P. Kennedy drank whiskey with his Palm Beach cronies, listening to the band play the club's theme song, "So This Is Gay Paree." All of Florida came to gamble and enjoy the opulent, sophisticated shows.

The type of extravagant showgirl-filled entertainment that was proliferating from coast to coast in high-class joints had began in the 1930s when Broadway impresario Earl Carroll produced a show at the Palm Island Club. In 1940 Lou Walters bought the club and gave it a Latin flavor. There was a "state-of-the-art kitchen" along with housing for the dancers, where possibly Lili bunked. The show was two hours long, lush, and filled with a bevy of cancan girls who "not only did splits, but defied gravity and anatomy by . . . landing *in* the splits."[209] In its first year of operation Walters claimed the club made $1,250,000.[210]

Walters had started out booking talent in vaudeville. His first club in Boston was a former Greek Orthodox church. He took over the lease with "sixty-three cents" in his pocket.[211]

Walters's idea was to offer dinner and a show for a reasonable fee, keeping it naughty enough for adults but not enough so that mom and dad couldn't take the kids. He transformed the church into a Parisian club, painting the walls with "murals of Parisian café scenes."[212]

It was a huge success and by the time he opened in Florida he moved his wife and daughter Barbara into a fifteen-room mansion on five acres of lush tropical plants across from the club and down the street from Al Capone. More disturbing was the tenant that came with their rented home.

Bill Dwyer and his "chauffer or bodyguard" lived in one of the rooms. Named "The Fixer," he was a Mob man who would live with Walters's family their first year in Miami.

Backstage Lili prepared among thirty-six gorgeous chorus girls, "more than any Broadway musical today."[213]

The entertainment at the club was first-class, with Milton Berle and Martha Raye headlining. Sinatra would croon there. The music pumped out a sultry Latin beat. It was crowded with seats for six hundred. Sexy and glamorous, it was a huge leap above the burlesque houses Lili had been toiling in. Lili would always say burlesque was her stepping-stone.

Lili had persuaded Corinne and Tito to choreograph a routine for her debut.

THE PAIR DESIGNED A SOLO "EVE" FOR THE ENCHANTRESS THAT SHE was becoming.

It was a perfect balmy Miami night. With the war on, and men enlisting by the droves, over eighteen million women would join the workforce, patriotic and proud to do their bit. Everyone was in a mood to live life fully. The popular films were *Lassie Come Home* and *Heaven Can Wait*. *Oklahoma* opened on Broadway. A bottle of Coke cost a nickel, the average car $900.

Thirsty soldiers crowded the booths and tables in clubs throughout Miami, but in particular the Latin Quarter where they enjoyed the extravagant show. Buddy Mary, a juggler, tossed dumbbells up on the stage. A chorus did a boudoir routine. There were skating dolls and chorus girls. It was filled to capacity and this was only the ten fifteen show, one of three nightly.

About to go on, Lili was a nervous wreck. She hadn't been assigned the first show because one of the feature dancers had a last appearance before her contract expired. She didn't mind; the club was bursting to capacity by the midnight show.

One reviewer singled Lili out, calling her act vulgar and offensive. Perhaps

LEFT: *A radiant Lili*

eager to get noticed, Lili was far more obvious in the beginning of her career, stripping to "the brassy blare of trumpets and the beat of drums," as all strippers did using the "stiff-legged strut" seen across every burlesque house and probably learned in San Diego.[214] She was accused of leaving "nothing to the imagination."[215] Her belief that nudity would catapult her into the big time wasn't working. It was time to rethink her plan.

LILI WAS A LATE RISER. AFTER THE LAST PERFORMANCE AND A DRINK with a date it took time to come down. Probably about now Lili started to experience insomnia. She was lucky to fall asleep as the sun came up. Someone provided Lili with sleeping pills. Her "helpers," she would call them, and she would delightfully sleep until afternoon.[216]

Lili began to pore over books looking for another Joan of Arc or Eve, historical women to up her game. She admired "sophisticated women."[217] As she discovered, "alone onstage, more was expected of me."[218] She needed something like the flying G-string to rise above the other girls. She spent countless hours in dressing rooms and hotel rooms sewing costumes. She was on a mission to be the most well-known exotic in the business. Unlike many showgirls, Lili wasn't waiting to marry a wealthy man and get out of the clubs. She claimed she didn't want to ask a sugar daddy for money. Most of the girls wanted husbands and babies. That life didn't interest her in the slightest. Her body was everything. She couldn't imagine it swollen and distended by pregnancy.

When she had the time, Lili walked along Lincoln Road, lined with chic boutiques loaded with gorgeous clothes and accessories. She bought outfits for her numerous dates. Men in Miami shepherded her around to drinks at Club Bali or the Clover Club restaurant.

Business was brisk as the Latin Quarter packed with couples dressed to the nines sharing steaks and drinks and smokes. The music was loud and strong.

She finished her contract and moved to Walters's club in Boston and then the big time—New York City.

If Lili wasn't yet the star she wanted to be, that was about to change.

LEFT: "*Signing my first autographs—I wasn't famous yet but the boys didn't seem to give a hoot—later when they were released from the hospital they would come, crutches and all, to see me dance at the Old Howard Theater—some of them still write after all this time.*"—*Lili St. Cyr*

CHAPTER FIFTEEN

In 1944 Lili turned twenty-seven (though she lied by a year on her newly applied Social Security application, claiming 1918 as her date of birth. Either an oversight on the part of some clerk or a small lie on her part, her Social Security card was issued to Willis Marie Van Schaack [sic]).

In the news Prince Rainier took over the throne of Monaco. In America Bing Crosby climbed the charts with "I Love You" and "I'll Be Seeing You." It was a romantic moment in time. The Oscar would go to *Casablanca* for best picture, one Lili was too busy to see.

American troops were still fighting in Europe. Just months away on June 6, three days after her birthday, the D-day invasion would commence.

Lili was making a couple hundred dollars a week, not bad considering the average yearly wage was $2,400. A loaf of bread was up to 10 cents. Commercial sunscreen was developed by Benjamin Green, who had been trying to come up with something to protect soldiers from sunburn. FDR was elected to a fourth term, not that Lili noticed. Politics was not for her. "It bores me."[219] She was preoccupied with the business of Lili. She would ignore news and politics and issues around her, things she could not control. She would concentrate on her career. She worked tirelessly to improve her dance skills.

After jumping between Lou Walters's various clubs she again returned to Miami in January. This time Lou Walters built the show around Lili, who was "streamlined as a P-38."[220]

In the Big Apple Lili St. Cyr began to merit a steady mention in *Variety* and *Billboard*, both for whom she dated and for her revealing act. People were suddenly interested in the tall stripper. She was a draw. *Variety* proclaimed she "has personality and knows how to use it."[221] They were right. She was radiant.

She became the "outstanding stripteause of the nation" and reached a level of work that garnered more praise than criticism due to her "grace and beauty."[222] Her

Lili backstage

circle of notoriety was expanding. She thrived on the attention. Occasionally she showed up in someone's gossip column being escorted around town by this million-aire or that. There were rumors of an impending marriage with twenty-one-year-old Pedro Serramalera, her Argentinian polo-playing boyfriend who kept her in a fabulous suite at the Ambassador Hotel stocked with fresh flowers and buckets of champagne.

As swiftly as she'd fallen for her dark-haired lover she soon felt imprisoned by his temper and jealousy. Besides, there was a line of men interested.

Barbara was going through a particularly low period. Having signed a contract with RKO in 1941, she had an uncredited part in the film *Mexican Spitfire Sees a Ghost* starring Lupe Velez and Mary Pickford's husband, Buddy Rogers. Another unbilled role was in *This Land Is Mine* starring Charles Laughton and Maureen O'Hara. It wasn't much, nor was it fulfilling.[223]

Idella and Barbara had moved from Eagle Rock into an apartment in Hollywood. Idella would have overwhelmed the fragile and compliant girl by attempting to run her personal life and her career.

Barbara, an expert rider

Barbara posed often, usually on her horse or beside one, even on Roy Rogers's Trigger. She took speech classes and dance classes and posed for mountains of publicity stills. She was throwing herself into being an actress with everything she had.

IT HAD BEEN SEVERAL YEARS SINCE BARBARA'S PICTURE HAD GRACED *Life* magazine and a year since she had landed a part in the film *Red River Robin Hood* starring Tim Holt, a B actor in a B western. The film would fail to generate further interest in Barbara. Part of the problem, according to Dardy, was RKO had a difficult time finding leading men tall enough to star with her. But neither had Barbara proven herself to be an exceptionally talented actress. After six months the studio failed to renew her option. It had to be a blow to both Barbara and Idella.

It would be typical for Barbara to care more about her mother's disappointment than her own. She didn't like to let others down. Where Lili was the rebel and Dardy the pragmatic, Barbara was the accommodator.

A further blow to her self-esteem occurred when Errol Flynn, whom she had been dating, dumped her for another starlet. She began dating Lt. Bob Gregor, an ex-wrestler.

Barbara returned to Earl Carroll for "Vanities," performing in San Francisco along with Dardy. Written up as "Glamazons," they earned $45 and were billed as Dardy and Barbara Moffett, though their legal names on contracts remained Ruth and Rosemarie Blackadder.[224]

When "Vanities" ended, Barbara joined a USO show, and eighteen-year-old Dardy headed to Hollywood for another Carroll production.

Lili learned that it was easier to get hired after club owners saw her name in the paper. The more popular she was, the more she made.

She continued polishing her sophisticated image, teasing reporters, now that they were interviewing and not just reviewing her. She gave reporters what she thought they wanted, a sexpot, someone interested only in money and sex. As brilliant and sharp as the diamonds she was beginning to wear onstage, gifts from boyfriends. She would appear untouchable so they wouldn't see her shaking hands as she sashayed across the stage. She would craft behavior and exploits that would get her name mentioned over and over again. Usually the tidbits involved her treatment of men, which could be seen as callous. She was the cold, hard-hearted goddess that could pick men up and dump them on a whim, unbound by the constraints of loyalty. Lili St. Cyr was becoming crystallized. She would eventually freeze into this regal persona, an untouchable goddess secure in her "cool, emotionless mastery."[225]

She was mastering the ability to manipulate press, audience, and boyfriends. She was painting the iconic image that would forever define her.

FIFTY-SECOND STREET IN NEW YORK HAD BEEN KNOWN AS "SWING Street" because of the jazz clubs that cranked out a beat between Fifth and Sixth Avenues. Billie Holiday could be heard moaning about her right to sing the blues; Fats Waller's fingers flew across the keyboard. At the height of the jazz scene, clubs such as Jimmy Ryan's, the Spotlight Club, 21 Club, Leon & Eddie's, and the Famous Door all burst with the sounds of Charlie Parker, Thelonious Monk, and Dizzy Gillespie.

But by 1943 there was little jazz left, burlesque having bumped out the musicians. The street became known as "Stripty Second Street" with its neon signs advertising 3 Deuces, Onyx, and the Moulin Rouge. The Famous Door now boasted stripper Zorita who terrified customers not only by her healthy size, but also by swinging a live boa constrictor she wore like a stole over their heads.

Lili found herself in a tiny club at 62 West Fifty-Second Street named Club

Samoa. She would settle in and work the South Seas–themed club almost exclusively, except for a couple of stints at Leon & Eddie's at 33 West Fifty-Second Street.

Club Samoa, with its jaunty yellow canopy out front, was tiny and tacky with maybe fifty tables. Stools sat in front of the bamboo bar; a couple of lanterns cast a dim light. Two sad faux palm trees leaned against the walls.

Though Lili would refer to Club Samoa in later years as "that dump," its appearance was improved with pills. Dardy claimed (though the timing of the years doesn't quite work out as she related it) she helped Lili's trepidation at playing the club by giving her pills to take the edge off. As the pills took effect, the place suddenly became "delightful" and her objections vanished.[226]

Though she hadn't gotten out of burlesque as she'd hoped after the Latin Quarter, Lili would enjoy great success and become the reigning queen at the Samoa. She would meet husbands, lovers, and future boyfriends there. She would be admired by celebrities and columnists who kept her name in the paper as she danced on the tiny stage. She would bring class and sophistication to the club and the owner thrilled with the results. Cash flowed when Lili played the house.

AT THIS TIME DARDY WAS ALSO IN NEW YORK WITH EARL CARROLL, and Barbara's USO tour had ended and she was staying at Lili's tiny but lovely furnished apartment.

Barbara, out of uniform, was eager to wear pretty dresses again and Lili was the perfect sister to shop with. Barbara had saved all her money from the tour and it was piling up in the bank.

The sisters—who would never again spend such time together—tried on makeup, stopped in bars for cocktails, and had a ball in each other's company. It was like old times in Eagle Rock, only better. They were adults with spending money and no curfew. When they walked into a room the three statuesque beauties with their tight-fitting dresses, gloves, hats, and fur stoles stopped conversation. Men sent flowers, bottles of champagne, stopped by their table and begged for dates. It was a heady time full of romance and possibility. They were glitzy, gorgeous, and model-thin.

Barbara, caught up in the excitement of postwar New York and being with her sisters, bought herself beautiful things, including a lapel pin that was exquisite and expensive; Dardy thought it was of a horse's head. Lili approved. It was nice to have a man buy you beautiful things, but why wait? When Lili wanted something she got it herself.

Dardy surprised the two. "I've got us tickets to *Annie Get Your Gun.*" The musical had recently opened starring Ethel Merman singing Irving Berlin's "There's

No Business Like Show Business" and "Doin' What Comes Natur'lly" to sold-out houses at the Imperial Theatre. It was one of the hottest tickets in town.

Heads swiveled as the girls took their seats. Barbara scooted in first and sat next to a balding older man, who was himself seated next to an older gentleman. She didn't give the man a second thought but clutched her program waiting for the curtain to open.

"Excuse me," the man cleared his throat. "That is a beautiful pin," he said to Barbara.

"Thank you, I designed it myself," she lied.

"That gives me an idea for my business."

"Hmmm. What business are you in?"

"I make toys."

"Really?"[227]

Soon the lights dimmed and everyone turned their attention to the stage.

Ethel Merman gave it her all, dressed in outfits similar to the ones Barbara and Dardy had worn in their horse show days, which seemed like eons ago: white fringed skirts, boots, and cowboy hats.

Was it only six years since they had been kicking up dust in rodeos without a couple of nickels to rub together, and now here they all were in New York City wearing furs at a Broadway show?

At intermission the older man handed Barbara his card and asked her to call.

After the show the girls went to the Diamond Horseshoe, Billy Rose's impressive club in the basement of the Paramount Hotel in Times Square. The place was jammed with men in tuxedos and women in silk gowns. Lili seemed to know everyone. Miles Ingalls met her there, spending the better part of the night escorting her from one table to the next, introducing her to important people.

When asked if she would be giving up her career for her fiancé, Lili laughed. No, she wasn't engaged, "and I'm not giving my career up for anyone. Any man will have to take me as I am." Despite a gift of a magnificent necklace with rubies the size of her nails, Lili gave Pedro Serramalera good reason to be jealous, with any number of multiple suitors escorting her.

One of the men pursuing her was former world heavyweight boxer Jack Dempsy. Long retired from the ring, he ran Jack Dempsey's Broadway Restaurant in Time Squares. When a friend commented that Dempsey looked like an "Irishman," Lili replied, "Really, I thought he looked like an Indian!" Dempsey was part Cherokee.[228]

BARBARA HAD BEEN THINKING ABOUT CALLING LOUIS MARX, THE MAN who had thrust his business card on her at *Annie Get Your Gun.*

Sherry Britton at Leon & Eddie's

Louis Marx was a "millionaire toymaker," whose fortune the papers estimated was worth thirty to forty million, recently widowed when his wife René succumbed to breast cancer at thirty-seven, leaving him with four kids. Marx was twenty-eight years older than Barbara and a foot shorter. A millionaire before he was thirty, Marx started in the toy business with his brother David. They were wildly successful, counting among their greatest inventions the yo-yo. Marx lived with his children at 990 Fifth Avenue and drove around in several Rolls-Royces.

Barbara, though she did finally call Louis Marx, continued, like Lili, to play the field. One suitor was millionaire Jay Gould of the railroad "robber baron" family. Gould was closer to her age.

Life was good. New York was thriving with returning servicemen. The economy was on the verge of exploding with postwar growth. The city was filled with an array of men at the sisters' beck and call.

Lili filled in for stripper Sherry Britton at Leon & Eddie's, a club on the same street as Club Samoa.

Leon & Eddie's claimed better food, better service, and larger drinks than the Samoa. Unlike the other joints on the street, Leon & Eddie's was "family oriented," billed as a restaurant and cabaret, not just a strip club, though Britton regularly peeled down to bare bosoms. Their clientele was often rowdy and bawdy with many tourists crowding in between the businessmen and repeat customers.[229] They cultivated loyal clients by sending annual birthday cards to one and all. It was a much bigger operation than Club Samoa with more than 150 employees. It could accommodate more than three hundred. On hot steamy nights the roof opened for ventilation. Sunday was celebrity night. Over the years Bob Hope, Alan King, Harry Belafonte, Milton Berle, and Danny Kaye dropped by for impromptu performances.

Leon was expert at making customers feel welcome. He was the opposite of his partner Eddie. Leon drank; Eddie did not. Eddie, going deaf, sang four times a night, with a huge repertoire of songs. Their shows were packed with at least seven acts including comedians, strippers, harmonica players, dance teams, and two big production numbers.

WHILE 1944 WOULD BE A BANNER YEAR FOR LILI, IT WOULD BE A TUMULtuous one for the world. There was a failed assassination attempt on Hitler. Paris was finally liberated from the Nazis. Glenn Miller was reported missing. And a 5.9 earthquake hit New York that was barely felt in Manhattan. While Lili was getting used to regular gifts of diamonds and rubies, gas went for 15 cents. She stayed in a deluxe suite while rent for the average house was $50 a month.

Pulling back the drapes of her room at the Ambassador, Lili looked down on Manhattan, the city that bustled at all hours. She loved it, far from Pasadena, two exhusbands, and Marie. Dardy had returned to the West Coast and Lili promised to see Teedle at Earl Carroll's soon. Lili advised her sister to make sure the men she dated paid for everything. She also warned Dardy to not date "bartenders, actors, or musicians."[230] It would be better to be like Roz Elle Rowland, stripper Betty Rowland's sister. Roz Elle had married a French baron (shades of Step-Aunt Rosemary) and retired from stripping. Lili declared if she didn't have romance she would just die.

Lili's shows were selling out. She calculated that if an owner wanted to add a performance beyond her contract to accommodate the demand, she would insist on cash before she would move one pink-polished nail.

Stripping was a mostly cash business, and Lili loved the look and feel and smell of it. She had a specially made garter belt that she stuffed with $100 bills. The daughter of the Depression didn't trust banks.

"I always knew when she had a lot of money," Dardy laughed. Because Lili would suddenly have a belly. "And she didn't have a belly."[231]

NEXT PAGE: *Becoming a star*

E. Reed

CHAPTER SIXTEEN

1988

She wrapped a soft black scarf around her head. Darkness. She moved spider-like. Out her door. Across the path. Her ballet slippers were as worn as the feet they encased. She stopped inches from the lip of the curb.

Quiet. Cars rushed by at the end of the block. She looked around. Inhaled the pungent city air.

She turned. A car slid past. She remembered what she used to spend on limousines. She would not regret her choices, though the days of hiring a car to idle at the curb were long behind her.

Someday, when I'm awfully low . . .

Limousines waited. She liked them standing by. She needed to know she could leave. Escape at a moment's notice.

Her legs returned her to the apartment as if on autopilot.

Tired by the time she got inside.

Door closed. The world gone. She could be Lili again. With a uniformed chauffer waiting. Champagne on ice. A gorgeous man in her bed.

When the world is cold . . .

Inside she sliced open her mail.

A fan had sent her a poster of *Rocky*. A fan whom she had grown close to and called a friend. Decades apart in age and experience. But he took an interest in her. Not just her past, though she tried to entertain him with stories of her glory days.

He sent her a tape of Sinatra. *Had she listened to it?* She admitted she didn't own anything to listen to it on.

He sent her the poster after she mentioned how she admired the actor. Just her type. Dark-haired, rugged, rough around the edges. She put it next to a cache of small gifts she had received. *All things I never would have been able to get myself.*

I will feel a glow just thinking of you . . .

She didn't feel well. Her spine ached. Her feet were swollen. She was arthritic and cranky and needed drugs. But the drug was betraying her. She had another blood infection that almost did her in. Ravaged. She was becoming an utter ruin, like the coliseum in Rome that she had visited decades ago. A lifetime ago. With a handsome "prince."

She wasn't feeling strong. She wrote a fan asking if he wanted a particular framed portrait. *If you can scare up $17.50.* Such a small amount, but it would save her. *I need the loot at the moment.* Which was a lie. She always needed the loot.

She fingered the Sinatra tape. It reminded her of how Francis Albert used to come into the Samoa with Ava. Gorgeous Ava. He was never really her type. Too short and wiry. A bully. She liked muscles and chest hair and height. She didn't care about brains as long as he was sexy and generous and fun.

She sent a photo and quick letter to a friend of Pat's.

And the way you look tonight . . .

SHE WAS BROKE. DESPERATE. SHE LONGED FOR ICE CREAM. SILLY THAT. As kids the sisters used to enjoy ice-cream sundaes. Then when she was older she'd had them at Schwabs where Barbara bought all her makeup.

Once again—as she had for years, she thought: *I'll just wing it with what I have and hope for the best.*

She knew she would not—could not, physically could not—go to the movies to see Stallone in his boxing shorts. Reminded her of Ted Jordan. Nice physiques, both. Occasionally she still heard from Ted. He was rude enough to show up at her apartment. Scoundrel. He was writing his biography. He went on about Marilyn and how he knew her death was accidental dispite all the rumors because she loved her drugs. He was going to expose all of Marilyn's secrets. Marilyn had given him her diary.[232]

She had never kept a diary. Who had the time to write it down when they were living their adventures? No one would believe her life anyway.

'Cause I love you . . .

She inhaled her Salem and thought of all the betrayals. Some her own. To herself. To others.

A line of disloyalty. With Jimmy. By Jimmy. Ted cheating on her. She cheated on him. The betrayal of time.

Betrayals ran through her mind.

Disloyalty.

Lovely, never, ever change . . .

CHAPTER SEVENTEEN

The romance between Barbara and Louis Marx moved forward. He appeared besotted and offered her a job in his office. Her lapel pin had inspired him to put into production jewel-encrusted lipstick and compact cases.

Lili negotiated the details. "She needs an office,"[233] Lili told Marx. Lili liked to insert herself into the midst of others' relationships.

"Can she type?" he wanted to know.

"What does it matter?" Lili knew it wasn't about having a skill. "What are you paying?"

"A hundred a week." Marx had broached the idea of working for him when Barbara declared she needed something to do. She was no longer working the night-clubs and needed direction. Barbara was like his first wife, who was "gentle, loving, submissive."[234]

Marx was an extremely disciplined man whose motto was "Do your best." Though he might have found her frivolous, he was in love.[235]

"Two hundred," Lili told Marx. Marx agreed, possibly choking back the beginnings of a grudge he would maintain about Lili and eventually the rest of Barbara's family.

Marx believed "material security was the purpose of work."[236] Growing up poor he never again wanted to go without. An agnostic of Jewish origins, he never told his children they were Jewish.

Barbara started working for Marx, as both a secretary in his offices at 200 Fifth Avenue and as a hostess entertaining business associates. Smoking his cigars every night, Marx regaled out-of-town clients with dinners at "21" where a center table was reserved for him downstairs. Next it would be on to El Morocco for dancing and Singapore Slings. He was generous, sending potential clients tickets to the best Broadway shows. Marx fed off his power, both having it and obtaining it. Others in Marx's circle of acquaintances were politicians and movie people. As his secretary,

Barbara sent boxes of toys to his friends. He was a charitable man who for forty years would distribute toys to children in his neighborhood of Scarsdale at Halloween.

The toycoon was generous and attentive to Barbara, studiously wooing and dining the twenty-one-year-old with a singular determination. He was equally resolute to change her. He suggested outfits to wear, what to read, how to improve her vocabulary.[237] He wanted her showgirl past erased.

Marx "was in love with power"[238] and would use his wealth to hook Barbara. He took her to the best restaurants. He wore her down with presents and flowers and opened charge accounts at all the best stores. The young lady from Eagle Rock was swept off her feet. Other beaus fell by the wayside.[239]

While courting Barbara, Marx stayed in a suite at the Waldorf and they shared romantic evenings dining on caviar and beef Bourguignon and drinking French wine.

Marx proposed.

Lili, once again meddling, told Marx that if Barbara married him, she would need her own money. Lili detested asking a man for money. Gifts were fine, explaining purchases such as a sable coat were not.[240] Lili was cutting herself into her sister's love life like only Lili knew how, speaking up for Barbara, who wouldn't dare.

Maybe as much as to be rid of Lili as to land his intended, Marx agreed with Lili's demands, bestowing on Barbara a car, chauffer, and a check for 150,000 dollars, ostensibly to use as she chose.

Yet Marx was growing uncomfortable around Lili. He thought her flashy and conniving. Lili liked him no better. Most likely Marx didn't approve of his beloved's sister being a very public stripper with a prolific love life. Not that he was a prude by any means. His daughter Barbara Marx Hubbard remembered sitting in the front row at Gypsy Rose Lee's show, brought there by her father who was a "good friend."[241] Barbara Hubbard claimed her father wasn't judgmental in that way. He wanted his very privileged children exposed to things. The children were blasé about Lee's strip. They "didn't see anything wrong with it."

Marx's daughter, only a year older than her father's fiancé, thought, "I don't know if this is going to work."[242] She believed Barbara was "not totally appropriate"[243] and doubted it would last.

Check in hand, a triumphant Lili and Barbara went to the Colony at Sixty-First and Madison for lunch. With the rest of café society the sisters dined on light French fare in the white wood-paneled room in upholstered banquettes. Dardy would say Marx was afraid of Lili's influence on Barbara and didn't want her around. Lili wrote of the same thing. He might have felt his fortune was at risk, as Lili could come across as mercenary. She enjoyed playing the role of dominating woman who punished men.[244]

In any event, Marx's five years as a bachelor were about to end. He and Barbara announced their engagement.

Barbara loved his marvelous, opulent estate in Scarsdale reminiscent of *Gone with the Wind*, complete with tennis courts and swimming pool spread over twenty acres, with thirteen servants to care for Marx and his four children (when they weren't in boarding school) and a multitude of dogs.[245] It was a white-pillared, red-brick, Georgian-styled mansion with twenty-five rooms, nine fireplaces, and fourteen bathrooms. There was even a seven-room caretaker's cottage. He had built it for his wife René, but she died before ever moving out of their magnificent Fifth Avenue home. At least Barbara wouldn't feel as if she was moving into another woman's home. Barbara had no idea of the mountain she was about to climb.

There wasn't much Barbara had to do. The staff and routine were strictly regimented by Marx. There was a plethora of tutors for the children. Instructions in judo, French, piano, and singing.[246] The "children stood on chairs to recite new words for dinner guests."[247] When his daughter Jacqueline went off to boarding school he wrote her a note telling her to "work, work, work. Diet diet diet!"[248]

Often Marx played his children against each other, saying this one was "the best" or that one was "smarter than all the others," his attention and "his favor moving arbitrarily" among his children.[249]

It was an ordered world Barbara was walking into. And though she was "brilliant" enough to keep up with her older husband, she would, in her usual fashion, take things to extremes.[250] A symptom of a deeper problem not yet diagnosed.

According to Dardy, Barbara would feel as if she was intruding on their family territory and Marx did nothing to incorporate her ideas into their daily pattern. It was hard to teach an old dog new tricks. His oldest daughter had bridled at her father's treatment of her mother, left alone "night after night" while Marx entertained at "21."[251]

The impressive home, grand enough to entertain his five-star-general friends, had a portrait of Marx done by Eisenhower and eventually a "regal" portrait of Barbara on the sitting room walls. A tulip garden would be given as a gift from Prince Bernard of the Netherlands.[252]

Though Marx's friends thought his fiancée was "flighty" and a "gold digger" from a "dubious background," he had set his mind on making Barbara his next wife.[253] She had the perfect look and the malleable temperament to be molded into his dream mate. Outwardly, her show business background didn't seem to bother him. But it did. Hugely.

CHAPTER EIGHTEEN

I n burlesque theatres, rules were strictly enforced as to what the strippers could and could not wear. There were rules that pasties—which covered the areola—must be worn at all times. Pasties were adhered with glue (Lili watered hers down to make it less painful to remove at the end of the night). Some theatres allowed only panties with wide opaque seams up the rear.

In some theatres strippers could not leave the stage with anything less than what they entered in.

It was food for thought. Lili was twenty-seven years old. She had been dancing for five years. At the time, many dancers and strippers started out as young as fourteen or fifteen, some even thirteen. Time was tapping on Lili's shoulder. Soon she would be thirty.

Lili's polo-playing Pedro returned to Argentina for business and she took the opportunity to call off the relationship. Pretending to nurse a broken heart she finished her engagement at Club Samoa. Yet Lili was preparing a trip of her own. She had been booked into the Gayety Theatre in Montreal. For Lili it was just another gig. She had no idea how much her life was about to change.

MONTREAL IN 1944 WAS THE LARGEST CITY IN CANADA WITH MORE than one million people. Though 65 percent of the population spoke French, tourist guides assured that the city catered to English-speaking tourists and businessmen, offering entertainment geared toward their "amusement." Lili's type of entertainment was one of the foremost pleasures offered.

Postwar Montreal was experiencing rapid growth in "population, economy, and size."[254] With wages on the rise, construction exploded. Prosperity saw an upshot in nightclubs, bars, and casinos that catered to a dizzying array of gambling from blackjack and chemin de fer, to baccarat and craps, all multiplying at a

Montreal's Sweetheart

dazzling pace. There was said to be "two hundred major gambling establishments operating in the city and the suburbs."[255]

Illegal gambling generated millions of dollars of revenue for the city.

Not only did Montreal teem with theatres, cabarets, and restaurants, but also dozens of underground bars. There was a renowned red-light district where gambling, whorehouses, and prostitution were prevalent. It was an exciting "wide-open town where the police looked the other way as they pocketed an envelope of cash.[256] Lili would drop into the center of this sexy, seedy, completely unknown world.

The Gayety Theatre was situated among bars, smoke-filled nightclubs, and illegal "gambling dens" on rue Sainte Catherine. It was an unimposing building of red brick, with supposedly an underground tunnel that led to a brothel across the street. Billed as a "vaudeville house," its shows consisted of song-and-dance men, strippers, ventriloquists, an emcee, jugglers, an orchestra in the pit, comedians, and novelty acts. The shows were naughty, entertaining, and "fast moving."[257]

Arriving at the train station Lili caught a cab to the Mont-Royal Hotel, west of downtown. The gorgeous beaux arts hotel held more than a thousand rooms on, amusingly, Peel Street.[258]

Never a light traveler, Lili would unpack sheet music (dancers traveled with their own arrangements), elaborate costumes, and props (nothing near as unwieldy as years to come) from her numerous trunks.

She was nervous, but it was no different than any opening in any other city.

Lili telephoned the theatre and asked for the manager of the Gayety.

"Conway here." The voice was gruff.

"It's Lili St. Cyr. I've just arrived."[259]

Conway asked if her room was comfortable and let her know some of the artists were meeting, then abruptly hung up.

The next day being Sunday, and Montreal being a very Catholic city, burlesque shows were not allowed to perform on that holy day. One way the theatres circumvented the law was to start the evening show at five minutes past midnight.

In person Lili found the middle-aged Tommy Conway to be friendly. He had probably been put off by her "weird demands" including a request for incense and a giant gold Buddha.[260] He showed her to her private dressing room, little bigger than a walk-in closet. There was a scratched makeup table with light bulbs around the mirror and a tiny rusted sink attached to the wall that dripped. She had been in worse.

He let her know the bathroom was at the end of the hall.

Lili liked the theatre with its old brick walls and exposed ceilings, pipes crossing overhead. Though dilapidated—it looked as if it would fall apart at any minute—she thought it charming. A part of Lili enjoyed the seedier side of life, including dive bars and rundown theatres. It was one of the many contradictions about Lili. When she became famous she liked seeing the expressions on faces when she was recognized in some dark hole in the wall. *No, that couldn't be her.*

Lili had less than twelve hours to prepare for her opening. Time to quell nerves, organize, familiarize herself with the stage, meet the musicians. Lili needn't have worried.

In less than twelve hours Lili would become an immediate "sin sation."

AS THE RED CURTAINS PARTED, ORIENTAL MUSIC FLOATED OVER THE crowd, transporting them back in time to ancient China. A huge golden Buddha loomed over the stage. Incense burned, sending ribbons of smoke wafting toward the ceiling. Though no one in the theatre (probably including the management) expected much from the newcomer, the audience held its breath as they experienced something entirely different than anything they had ever seen at the Gayety before.

They were about to be treated to Lili's "Chinese Pavilion."

The Len Howard orchestra played the unusual score they had been given.[261]

It was "languorous and melancholy."[262] On her cue, Lili, clothed in a gold robe, her hair elaborately curled into two buns on either side of her head, her eyebrows darkened and swept outward like the wings of birds above her green eyes, slowly slunk and slithered across the stage, her movements and gestures heavy with sadness and despair.

The story in her head played through her body. She was wife and slave. Her master, a Chinese warrior, had imprisoned her in a huge heart-shaped chastity belt, which she revealed as she parted her robe. She wore panties underneath. She would never again be as blatantly nude as she had in her Music Box days.

The tempo of the music accelerated Lili's movements. The undulations of her hips, the turn of her mouth, expressed love for another. Lili's body arched. She made grand sweeping gestures with her arms. Her bends and kicks were erotic. She swiveled and danced with pent-up passion for her lover. Leaning forward she seemed to cave in on herself, hoping to convey her sexual desire for her man. She poured her frustration into her legs, up her back, through the crown of her head, looking down at the damn belt that restricted her. She wanted freedom. Her dancing was fluid and fierce yet restrained by her movements and the belt.

Lili fell to her knees in front of the Buddha, imploring him to help. She wept; her body collapsed. *Liberate me.* She slipped from her golden robe. The tempo increased. She was a woman in the throes of ecstasy. Passion propelled her. She tried but could not get rid of the belt. She tried again. Clothes began to melt off her. She flailed; the gods struck her with lightning as lights flashed in the theatre. She thrashed. In a joyous gesture she indicates the gods have given her a key and she begins to unlock herself. *She is free.* The music ends. Lili runs offstage.

The audience gasped then burst into thunderous applause.

Quickly the set was dismounted as she scampered down the stairs to her tiny dressing room to prepare for her second number. She dressed as the audience went wild, shouting, applauding. There had been utter silence while she was performing, enough that "you could hear a pin drop."[263] Now they were screaming. She had felt—perhaps for the first time—completely and totally in charge of the audience and their emotions. Lili St. Cyr now knew what she was doing.

"BIRD OF LOVE" WAS A MORE SUBDUED DANCE. SHE REENTERS WITH A fake parrot on her shoulder, a colorful spray of long feathers falling to the floor. Lili's costume is birdlike, feathers bursting like a bustle from her panties. She has copied from Faith Bacon's memorable dance. Lili begins to twirl, a silk scarf flying above her head. The dance is between her and the bird; the bird an extension of her long, thin arm. The music changes. The lighting becomes "mysterious."[264] A blue spot follows her like a tunnel of light. She wears gold gladiator sandals that wind around her strong ankles. The dance ends just as the "bird" plucks her bra off with its beak. Again the theatre erupts with hand claps and whistles. The audience has never seen anything like it. The sets, the costumes, the story. The tall blonde American. She holds herself beautifully and differently. There is distinction and class about her. She is in her own world, not there to beg for approval. Something has hit Montreal and burlesque like nothing before. "Who is she?" is shouted through the theatre. "When does she go on again?"

IN HER DRESSING ROOM LILI COULD RELAX. MR. CONWAY SHOWED UP with a bouquet of flowers and congratulated her. She looked at the clock. Two thirty in the morning.

As Mr. Conway left there was a knock on her door.

It was Len Howard, the conductor of the orchestra. He asked if she wanted to see something of the town. Are places still open? Boy, are they.

She finished dressing. It was not for Lili to go back to a cold empty hotel room and savor her victory. She was of the night and wanted to celebrate.

Lenny took her to the "French" part of town where the illegal bars—called blind pigs—stayed open until dawn. They ordered drinks. Standing nearby was a handsome man that instantly caught Lili's eye. The "brutal magnetism" she felt irresistibly pulled him to her.

Lenny warned her, "You don't want that, Lili. *That* is trouble. The wrong kind of man for you." She raised an eyebrow and didn't ask, *How do you know he's the wrong kind of man for me?* He seemed perfectly right to her. Lili didn't like being told what to do. Tell her not to do something and it became a challenge.[265] She decided the dangerous-looking stranger was *exactly* what she needed. Now. Rugged and dangerous in his masculinity, dark curly hair, dark eyes under thick black brows. The opposite of the cool whiteness of her.

To Lenny's disgust Lili left the bar with her forbidden fruit. His name was Maurice and he was charming and at first did not seem to be as lethal as he would turn out to be. Maurice introduced her to another blind pig. She would remain enchanted by these illegal establishments, as she would anything exclusive and forbidden. The Canadian speakeasies were often little more than dives that served booze without a license.[266]

It was a triumphant night. She had conquered the management and the hearts of the audience. And now there was the possibility of new romance in the arms of a beautiful stranger in a new city. Years of hard work had paid off. Lili would forever recall and attempt to recapture the intoxicating high she experienced that spectacular night.[267]

Lili on stage

In her mind she envisioned herself as a famous woman of the stage, scandalous, a femme fatale—like Garbo at her best. She felt as if she were standing on a precipice ready to take off on a new adventure.

And thus began the seven-year reign of Lili St. Cyr over a French-speaking city. Montreal would have long and lasting memories of a "Blonde Venus" that took the town by storm. She would be dubbed "Montreal's Sweetheart." It was a place she would consider home. It was a city that worshiped her yet would, in time, betray her.

PART TWO

ENCHANTRESS

". . . Every young man's fantasy. If you hadn't seen Lili, you had seen nothin'. . ."
—FROM THE DOCUMENTARY *LILI ST. CYR*

CHAPTER ONE

Recollections of that magical summer when Lili glided across the minds and fantasies of Canadians would be recalled decades later in *Commerce Montreal* "She executes the most fantastic dances of eternal theme. . . . She gives a wake-up to adolescence, a stimulant to the young man, comfort to the middle-aged man, sweet memory to the old man. . . . Lili is the goddess of love reincarnate."

Lili never expected such adoration from the Canadian audiences. She was just presenting what she had figured out: that working-class folks—predominantly the core of a burlesque audience—wanted the same elegance and refinement of the swanky nightclubs. She had made herself into a class act. Lili wouldn't change her performance whether she was at the chic Latin Quarter or a dilapidated old theatre with drunks in the audience. Wherever she was Lili gave her all. She wouldn't use fewer props, or dress differently, but instead swept onstage wrapped not only in fur but also in a cloud of elegance that she draped around her audience. She would elevate them through a first-rate show that lifted her out of the disreputable business she was in and made it bearable for her. She would write how most strippers didn't even consider her one of them. All those years she had kept herself apart from the backstage melee had worked. She was something else. She would do everything she could to lift her act and her life out of the stigma attached to stripping.

It could be argued that her shyness and inherent standoffishness were why she was touted as "classy" and "elegant." But she went out of her way to cultivate the image in both dress and dance. She was carefully and systematically crafting her image and it would never change.

Montreal exploded with "Lilimania." The Gayety saw an increase in repeat business with Lili's name on the marquee.

After shows Lili would see thirty-four-year-old Mario Maurice Bresciano, brother-in-law to Vic Cotroni, a Calabrian criminal, who among other things sold illegal booze. By the 1940s Cotroni was heavily involved in the running of nightclubs in Quebec and today is considered to have been the founder of the Mafia in Montreal.

Lili also learned Maurice had a wife at home. She merely shrugged. A wife was never a deterrent for Lili. She wasn't looking to break up his marriage. She rationalized that if the man was interested in her, then his marriage must not be so great. *She* wasn't the problem. A man's marital woes were the problem. [268]

Maurice wined and dined the jaw-droppingly beautiful Lili. Their favorite haunt was the Samovar. Lili was written up as the cool blonde packing them in on Saint Catherine Street and wowing the men after hours. She was garnering attention wherever she went. She made a splash in furs and jewels when she walked into a joint, lushly dressed in expensive gowns, drenched in White Shoulders perfume. She enjoyed the recognition.

One night Maurice took her to a blind pig on the second floor of a building that was decorated like a bedroom. It was a small room with a door that locked.

The city lay under inches of snow. It was a frosty March night and Maurice pinched her check.

Not too long after, the couple was startled by screams of "Maurice! Maurice!" from outside the door. Lili looked questioningly at Maurice, whose face clouded with anger.[269]

The shouting continued, then there was a splintering crash. Quiet followed. It was 8:00 a.m. before they felt safe enough to leave. Lili noticed a woman outside as they left. Maurice dropped Lili off at the Mont-Royal. She was exhausted and scared. Maurice would tell her nothing though she asked if the shouting came from his wife.

From her room a depleted Lili rang room service for tea and eggs while she ran a steaming tub. All she wanted to do was soak the night away.

Keeping the door to her suite slightly ajar, Lili slid into the tub and submerged herself. She was certain someone was going to get hurt. Whether it would be her or Maurice she didn't know, but she detested physical violence.

Presently she heard room service enter. She quickly dried herself and emerged in her robe and was surprised by two women blocking her doorway. She recognized one of them from outside the blind pig earlier.

One woman asked her what she wanted with Maurice. Lili observed the woman vibrating with anger. She had images of them cutting her to pieces.

Lili deflected, as she always would; there was nothing serious with Maurice, she relayed. And she knew it was true. She knew he was a passing thing, one she nevertheless enjoyed.

The two women spoke in French to themselves; Lili didn't understand a word.

Earlier in the evening a photographer in a club had taken a photo of her and Maurice. The women spied it on her bureau.

One snarled, yes, it didn't look serious.

Lili shrugged. There was nothing to say. Words were not her weapon.

One of the women informed Lili *she* was the mistress of Maurice and pointed to the other woman, the wife. They didn't want "someone like her" interfering.[270]

Later Lili would recall a disquieting out-of-body experience. She observed herself from the corner of the room watching the ridiculous scene play itself out.

One of the women told Lili not to see Maurice again and they left.

Maurice, Lili claimed, quickly rented her rooms in an old residence to the east of the city. If he wasn't at the Gayety, he waited for her at her new rooms to begin their nightly crawl around town. Very quickly Lili was becoming the talk of the town. She saw her name in big letters on the marquee of the Gayety and wondered why she was living in miserable rooms with Maurice. Maurice either worked at a gambling establishment or spent his time playing "barbotte," perhaps both.[271]

Barbotte, "a game of unknown origin," was an extremely popular game with the Canadians.[272] The fast-paced dice game, similar to craps, involved players playing against each other with bets as low as $1 and as high as thousands.

Lili added two new characters to her Canadian repertoire: Carmen (fiery) and Eve (original seductress). She also appeared in stunning full Indian headdress. Clearly with her success she grew in confidence. She was in command of her winning acts, constantly surprising her audience with their sheer inventiveness.

THE GAYETY CONTINUED TO SELL OUT FOR HER PERFORMANCES AS men *and* women lined up in front of the theatre. All of Montreal wanted to feast their eyes upon the much-gossiped-about stripper who was raising temperatures. Lili felt like a star. Her name was as prominent in the papers as it was on the marquee. Her dressing room overflowed with flowers and gifts.

Maurice continued to escort her, waiting for her after her shows. One night, busy either gambling or working he told her he would meet her at the apartment late. In his absence Eddie Quinn, the owner of the El Morocco, invited himself backstage at the Gayety. After introducing himself Lili found herself being driven to Quinn's club.

Where Quinn was rough, the El Morocco was elegant. She found herself attracted to Eddie, possibly by the power he exuded. Quinn managed wrestlers, and Lili thought he looked like the actor Broderick Crawford. He dressed in silk suits and made tons of money. She thought he believed her to be the perfect decoration

One never knew what Lili would dream up next

for his club. It would become another second home to her. The El "attracted visiting celebrities in such numbers that the place became famous."[273]

Lili stayed out till dawn. When she returned to her rooms Maurice was in a lather, accusing her of being with another man.

Like a panther Maurice jumped Lili, knocking them both to the floor where he began to viciously punch her in the ribs. She managed to extract herself as he grabbed a hanger. Again he knocked her to the floor, hitting her ruthlessly. Fortunately he was drunk and she was not. She used it to her advantage, managing to make a quick escape to the street where she hailed a cab, terrified as she heard his footsteps and screams following.

At the Mont-Royal she entered through a side door, surprised to find the lobby empty, though it was late at night. Down a corridor she ran until she heard the ringing of phones and machines behind a wooden door. Pushing open the door Lili was confronted with fifty typists aghast at her disheveled appearance.[274] She was a mess, clothes ripped, her hair loose.

She was also in excruciating pain from the beating she had received at her lover's hands.

Earlier in the night a man, not handsome but elegant and gallant, had given her his card in case she ever needed anything. Unsure what to do she asked someone to call him. They did. Harry Ship was a familiar name.

Billboard called Harry Ship the "wealthy and fabulous owner of the Tic-Toc, night clubs, restaurants, and dance palaces."[275] Arrested numerous times, Ship began his criminal career as a bookmaker's clerk. He had set up his operation from many Saint Catherine Street apartments. When called before an inquiry for the Caron Commission in the 1950s, Ship would admit to making more than $1 million off his bookmaking operation. In 1948, when he met Lili, Ship was thirty-three. He would become known as "the King of the Montreal Gamblers."[276]

Ship immediately sent two men to get a doctor to attend to Lili. She had several sprained ribs. The two men helped retrieve her belongings from her crappy suite of rooms.

Lili was certain once Maurice found out about Ship and his men she would have no further trouble, hinting that what they carried under the coat and overcoats would blast Maurice to kingdom come. And though she was in pain she would not miss her show.[277]

ONE NIGHT AFTER THE SHOW A JOURNALIST WITH THE *HERALD* knocked on her door and asked if she would be available for an interview.

"If you buy me a drink somewhere," she told the man, who introduced himself as Al Palmer.[278]

The tall man with thick brown hair was known to be a fair and affable journalist. His columns were filled with the nightlife of his beloved adopted city of Montreal.

Palmer escorted Lili to a loud sweaty bar where they ordered food, drank sloe gin, and became great friends. Palmer let her know he had been at her first show at the Gayety and he, like the entire audience, was a fan. They were both tickled by whispers of "That's her. That's Lili St. Cyr!" echoing through the bar around them. Lili sat tall, a diamond necklace around her neck. She casually let her fur drape over the chair onto the ground.

Palmer would fill his "Man About Town" column in the *Herald* with her nightly goings-on for years, even if it was no more than a "Lili St. Cyr set to return to Gayety. . . . Sizzler Lili St. Cyr moved into the Laurentien Hotel. . . . Montreal's favorite visitor . . ." He kept his ladylove in print. He would become a touchstone every time she visited the city, always catching up over drinks at various bars. They clearly adored each other and oftentimes ended up in bed together, though Palmer too was married.

LILI'S CANADIAN FAME WOULD GROW TO SUCH PROPORTIONS THAT she could not walk down the streets, despite later claims she was seen sashaying from her hotel to the Gayety, hips out, fur coat to the floor, haughty and halting traffic. And much later were the absurd rumors that she walked with a tame leopard on a leash.

"Don't believe everything people tell you," Dardy warned decades later. "Lili *never* walked down the street with a leopard. First of all, she couldn't even walk down the street. She was mobbed in Montreal. I had never seen anything like it. She was a *star* there."

Lili quickly became savvy about publicity, essential to any performer's career. She played up an image of the much-dated girl about town on the arm of wealthy, handsome, or dangerous men, often seen in the company of shady characters. Both Dardy and Lili were drawn to gangsters and Mafia types who proliferated in the clubs and bars. Many gangsters in the forties were themselves celebrities and made good press.

Lili was seen laughing and having a good time. Because she was. She knew how to work the adulation and flattery to her advantage and have fun while doing it. She kept the "real" part of herself hidden. "Ice Queen" they called her, not knowing how hot and passionate she boiled inside.

Lili would be linked with dozens of men; politicians, sports heroes, actors, millionaire businessmen, and local Mafioso. She was constantly on the arm of one attractive man after another. It didn't matter if the man was married or not. She was portrayed as "heartbreaker," "home wrecker," a cold goddess of the striptease. A fantasy. A phantom image she would have to live up to for the rest of her days. That Lili, part myth, part imagination, part real, wouldn't be allowed to grow old, change, or be anything other than a star stripper, a man-eater, at the top of her game with the perfection of face and figure frozen for all time in glossy photos.

"If I had had affairs with them all, I never would have had time to be on the stage," she would later tell reporters, who didn't believe her denials. Someone that beautiful and unattached making a living taking off her clothes had to be promiscuous. It was an accusation—or rather a presumption—most strippers endured. And especially one who lived so boldly in the public eye.

To the general audience she was a woman interested only in diamonds and love affairs. She played it up, tossing off big tips. She would give a cabbie a twenty; the same with a busboy. She started hiring a limo and chauffer to drive her places. She trolled the local antique shops on Saint Catherine Street looking for beautiful things to buy. She spent hours on her routine and on her looks. She could never look less than perfect when she was out. The mask was becoming firmly fixed. It was not a burden to her—at the time—it was in fact liberating. Marie was buried underneath. Lili spent her money as she liked, slept with whomever she liked. She was calling the shots and loving it.

The more ink she received and the more popular she became, the more money she could demand of theatre owners. Her philosophy was to let them write anything. She wasn't interested in playing the puritan. She was intrigued by her growing "bad girl" reputation. It would take nearly two decades after her death to separate myth from the woman.

It was as if Lili was a complete fabrication—and she was.

In a few short years the newspapers would accuse Lili of corrupting the public morals—an indictment frequently leveled at strippers, usually from a judge's bench in a courtroom. The allegation was behind arrests of many dancers and theatre owners. For the time being Lili escaped, landing on the wrong side of the law, perhaps protected by influential mobsters in Montreal who ran things.

"If I do demoralize an audience, as some people say, then I'm glad I do it," Lili was quoted as saying. "People need a loosening up. Most of the people in this country [she spoke about Americans at the time] are hypocritical, too many put on a front of being shocked at certain kinds of behavior. It's a joke to think I could demoralize anyone with this little act."[279]

And furthermore, she felt, "If one has morals, then they can't be taken away by me or anyone else."[280]

Her burgeoning image, real or false, sold tickets. And Lili was about making money.

"I make a living off my looks, boys," she told the newspapermen. "And why not? What's the use of being beautiful if you can't profit from it?"[281] What's the use of having money if you don't spend it?" She would toss her blonde curls back, laugh, and caress her pearl chocker, wearing ladylike gloves and a modest suit.

The *Gazette, Montreal Star, La Press,* and the rest of the daily Canadian newspapers constantly mentioned "class" and "Lili" in the same sentence. They were unaccustomed to her haughty attitude and her "high-hat" routine.[282]

Lili put into action the idea she had about the rule against leaving the stage with anything less than what she appeared in.

She came onstage barely dressed and then "put on a chic wardrobe."[283] Though it wasn't a completely original idea, she was given much credit for the way she did it and the little scenarios she built around it. She was utter perfection to look at, and it was shocking in the sensuality she conveyed when her long limbs moved about the stage in sheer panties and pasties.

Her twist on the reverse strip would be not only to dress, but also to undress and dress again. Women admired her fancy gowns. "I don't just take off clothes onstage. I put them on and take them off."[284] All in the context of getting ready for a date. She pranced around a boudoir—that was growing more elaborate with time—on the stage.

Lili, after much thought, had "come to the belief a girl can look much sexier dressed than undressed."[285]

"The Goddess of the Gayety," the papers wrote. "Lili has them in the palm of her hand" with her "plays," as she called them. She had hit on the right gimmick. Her shows from now on would tell a story. They would have a beginning, middle, and end. She had found her element. She poured herself into her work, often as historical figures such as Cleopatra or Salome. Her fans couldn't wait to see what she would come up with next. It was a beautiful surprise every time.

She was deliriously happy. She loved going out after the shows, more than she would in any other city. To Lili Montreal throbbed with excitement and glamour. It was "cosmopolitan."[286] She adored the uniquely French character. And it felt like *her* city. She was welcomed and doted on everywhere she went.

She partied nightly after her last show, unable to sleep, thankful for the blind pigs that stayed open until the wee hours of the morning. She reveled in seeing and being seen. She never lacked for dates to chaperone her to one of her favorites like Café Martin and the Indian Room. She slept little and played hard, often waking with a hangover that she cured by eating watermelon.

She began to rely even more on her "sleepers" that brought her relief when she collapsed at her hotel as dawn lit up the sky. Lili would be lucky to catch a few hours of nothingness before rising much too soon in time to head to the theatre to prepare for the early show. It was grueling but she was strong, young, and healthy.

In their newsletter the Montreal Chamber of Commerce gave Lili the title of "Goddess of Love Incarnate." Montreal would be an integral part in creating the myth of Lili St. Cyr.

CHAPTER TWO

By now Lili's nudity was less aggressive. She instead veiled her appeal in sheer costumes.

Her captivating sets were filled with props that could include statutes, beds, chaise lounges, marble vanities, wooden hat racks, or full-length mirrors. Expensive furniture that she found and purchased from nearby antique stores. When not traveling, she would keep them stored at the theatre.

Lili teased the audience with her hands-off manner, dressed like a society lady in beautiful gowns, no longer accused of "romping" across the stage or her act "crude" and lacking "sophistication."[287] Her tease of getting made up and dressing was intimate. Lili showed the goings-on inside a woman's boudoir were mysterious, personal, and right where the nudity belonged, which made Lili and her act more "acceptable" than most strips. Her audience became silent voyeurs. They believed they were privy to her secret machinations. Men and women were titillated and intrigued.

Not that it didn't sometimes lead to misadventure. "There was one time I got as far as one shoe on and one shoe off," Lili said, when one ardent fan "swiped the shoe" and she was forced to finish the act "lopsidedly."[288]

She remained plagued by preshow nerves. With every triumph, with every increase in salary, the stakes were raised. How to remain there? Lili felt *responsible* for the audience's enjoyment. She strove for perfection, her stomach a tangle of knots. She cared so very much. As frivolous as she would like others to believe her to be, she worked hard to dazzle and bring art and elegance to the stage. Onstage she appeared ladylike and unattainable; offstage she seemed very much attainable, which set gossips buzzing.

After a season in Montreal her scandalous reputation was set.

Lili felt she was hitting a peak in her career—how much higher could she go? She had no idea.

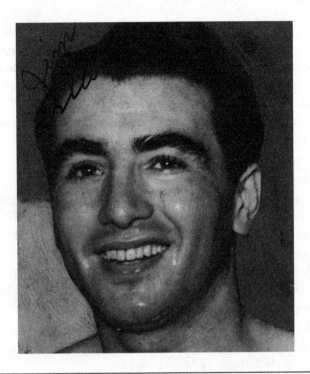

The love of Lili's life, Jimmy Orlando

BY THE MIDFORTIES LILI'S PATH BECOMES MORE DIFFICULT TO TRACE.
Like a hothouse plant spreading its vines, twisting and turning, Lili moved from one
end of the country to the other. She would remember some, forget others, dismiss
and return over again to smoke-filled clubs and raked stages. She danced in places
big and small. She had Montreal to thank for the demand.

Probably about a year after her debut, in 1945, she would meet one of the great
loves—if not *the* love—of her life: Jimmy Orlando. "They were mad about each
other," and in the coming years Lili would find any excuse to return to Montreal
and to Jimmy.[289]

James Vincent Orlando was a charming former ice hockey player for the
Detroit Red Wings who had been residing in Canada for several years. Two years
older than Lili, he was Italian and a notorious playboy cutting a wide swath through
showgirls, cigarette girls, anything hot and sexy in his path. When they met he was
retired from the game and managing the El Morocco nightclub for one of Lili's
beaus, American wrestling promoter Eddie Quinn.

During his career on the ice Orlando was what was referred to as an "enforcer,"
a term for a "tough guy," a fighter on the ice. His teammates referred to him as

"Little Caesar."[290] His job was to deter, *in any way* he saw fit, the opposing teams' dirty or oftentimes violent moves. The enforcer was expected to be aggressive and violent enough to stop the opposition. Hockey is the only "major team sport which tolerates fighting." Enforcers "fight with their bare knuckles" and are "rarely used for anything else."[291] They were to protect the more valuable players.

In the often-brutal world of the NHL the enforcer was a popular position. The men were considered "working-class superheroes—understated types with an alter ego willing to do the sport's most dangerous work to protect others . . ." They were clearly "underdogs."[292]

It was a perfect job for the hot-tempered Jimmy, who loved giving a good thrashing. Most enforcers lived with incredible pain due to injuries in fights. There is one particular well-publicized photo of Jimmy standing in gear, blood pouring from a cut in his forehead that would require twenty stitches and put him on the cover of *Life* magazine. That particular fight caused him to be suspended for three games and pay a $100 fine to the Red Cross, which he thought should be paid to him as he was the one who had given all the blood.

Many players become addicted to pain killers to dull the concussions, broken noses, aching shoulders, and disjointed knuckles from the relentless fighting on the ice. Perhaps Lili's love of pills was shared with Jimmy.

Lili loved both the dark horse and the black sheep in Jimmy, as she would in many of her romances. Outsiders. She stood by the scraper, the con man, the one who tried to live by his wits or his fists. They amused her. She saw through their bluster and boasts, but she never busted them on it. She let them tell their lies and spin their stories. Lili didn't sweat the small stuff; after all, her profession labeled her the ultimate outsider, going against what society expected of her.

As "easy-going off the ice" as the enforcer might be, Jimmy was constantly getting into fights off the field. He was said to be "fiery, exciting to watch and as tough as they come."[293] Lili found him fiery and exciting in bed. She would say they "lived furiously."[294]

Not all of Orlando's actions were heroic. Arrested in 1944 by the FBI for dodging the draft, he claimed to be working an "essential war effort job" as a machinist from 1936 to 1938, which he was not.[295] Found guilty on two counts, he was sentenced to four years in jail for each count.[296] Telling the court he was visiting a sick mother, Jimmy skipped out on his bail, returning to Canada, thus becoming a wanted man in the United States. He was forced to hang up his hockey skates.[297]

For years it would be rumored Jimmy was nothing more than a beard for the Catholic and very married Quinn, but Lili's affair with Quinn died as soon as Jimmy entered the picture. She continued to hold Quinn in sweet regard, but she fell madly in love with Jimmy. (Quinn trusted Lili so much that, in one of her frequent trips across the border to America, he would ask her to smuggle a large diamond in her bra. She did.[298])

Quinn had sent Jimmy to fetch Lili from the theatre and bring her to El Morocco. They started an affair that would span many tempestuous years of fights and recriminations, regrets and reconciliations. Lili would always love Jimmy. Always. They shared an affinity for their bad reputations. Both were stunningly gorgeous.

Though he would never treat Lili as well as she hoped, she became obsessed with him. He was a notorious ladies' man, and even Lili couldn't curtail his bed hopping. Like Lili he took what he wanted.

There would be rumors of Jimmy's ties—minor and major—to the Mafia. He would end up owning a nightclub, Aldo's (at least by 1958), and ran with a crowd that included gangsters, which was not off-putting to Lili. She loved the swagger and bravado of the gangsters she encountered and held no judgment about them.

That same year Lili met another man who would be instrumental in her career. Paul Valentine met Lili at Leon & Eddie's. Lili was once again filling in for the "good looking peeler" Sherry Britton who would reign at the club for over seven years, starting when she was seventeen (or so she claimed) in 1941.[299] Sherry was a class act with a sheet of brunette hair that fell down to an eighteen-inch waist. Despite a tough life of abandonment, abuse, and abortions, Sherry too had carved a niche for herself as an elegant stripper. She demanded the audience treat her like a lady. Lili was a natural substitute.

Paul Valentine was a minor dancer who performed under the names Val Valentinoff and Vladimir Valentinov, though he was born William Daixel. He had started dancing with the Ballet Russe de Monte Carlo when he was fourteen during the 1934–35 season.[300] His father was a writer and his mother a nurse. Valentine was a graceful and powerful dancer, formerly, briefly—if at all—with the American Ballet Company. Two years younger than Lili, he had the type of face, dark hair, and muscles that she swooned over. He had come to see her perform and, as he fervently told her, had immediately fallen in love.

Lili would claim she saw him in the audience and turned up the heat. "Her smoldering gaze never left Valentine's face."[301]

Harry Delmar, a former vaudeville dancer, wanted Lili to perform in a musical of *Beauty and the Beast*. Lili was enthusiastic. Not only did she love the fable of woman and animal, but also she continued to reach for ways to legitimize herself as a performer, to prove she was more than just a stripper.

Their first task was to find a male dance partner to play the beast. Delmar had staged *Follow the Girls* on Broadway with Valentinoff in 1944 and told her she

Paul Valentine and Lili

needed someone like him. So why not the real thing? He was considered a very good dancer, and as a bonus, he was taller than her. Lili told Harry to set up a meeting.

Paul Valentine knocked on Lili's dressing room door. Immediately, she found herself drawn to his smooth good looks and his energy. He looked like Argentine-born actor Fernando Lamas. He was confident, dynamic, and brash with a finely chiseled chin. He was full of himself in a wonderfully commanding way. His confidence balanced her insecurities and, away from the philandering Jimmy, Lili was ripe for another romance.

Paul asked her to dinner. There was undeniable chemistry between the two.

The next day she phoned Delmar to say they had found their beast.

It quickly became apparent Paul wasn't going to be just a dance partner. They began rehearsing immediately. Though they became lovers Paul found he was not the only one in her life. He waited patiently and persistently as Lili's other men began to fall by the wayside.

He was ballet-trained, and she no longer had a Fehnova or a Corinne and Tito choreographing her. She longed to collaborate with a partner for inspiration and guidance. She felt Paul understood her and could help develop her act. Here was a man who would finally enhance her artistic life, not try and pull her off the stage. They could be the Lunt and Fontaine of dance.

They made plans to perform together beyond *Beauty and the Beast*. Lili had high and surely unrealistic hopes for her new suitor. She would place boyfriends and husbands in more elevated esteem than they deserved. It would take a lot to disappoint Lili when she was in love.

PAUL LIVED WITH HIS MOTHER, WHO WAS NONE TO FRIENDLY TOWARD Lili. His mother was upset by the breakup between Paul and his former girlfriend, fan dancer Sally Rand (coincidentally Faith Bacon's rival).

Despite their hard work *Beauty and the Beast* never came to fruition. Lili was disappointed. She loved the story, thought it the ultimate in romance. An amusing side note that says much about Paul's rather healthy ego, Paul had assumed *he* would portray Beauty.

The two continued to work together, Paul skillfully choreographing Lili's next act. "You'll be the greatest," he told her.[302] He suggested she add him to her show. Lili thrived—as she always would—under a stern taskmaster. It was familiar to her, like Madame Henderson and later Fehnova. Paul's criticism could be harsh. With his help her act would grow in sophistication and scope. He thought her act "spoiled by the mechanical movements of the typical stripper." He admonished, "Frankly, I didn't like it, honey." He told her she should change her act; she was too much "like all the other strippers."[303]

In the beginning she was all ears: "Just show me what to do."[304]

The pair spent hours dancing, making love, and planning ways to enliven her act. They were inseparable. She was flattered by his desire to know everything about her routine. She added great detail. Her body and gestures would speak in place of words. A hand could convey sadness, a step ecstasy. The audience must be able to read what her body was feeling. When she picked up a gown she had to be thinking something, feeling something. He "taught her how to dramatize sex."[305]

He probably suggested she add his framed photo to her set. She would dance for him.

Paul wanted to manage her career and her life. She had found a creative soul mate. He worked her hard, running her through complicated routines, refining her wardrobe.

THEIR ONLY PROBLEM APPEARED TO BE FINANCES. PAUL WARNED HER he was not the man of means she was used to. Of course, it didn't matter. She bought him gifts, including a gold watch and engraved lighter. She was making *real* money. No doubt she picked up the tab wherever they went.

She convinced him to move out of his mother's and in with her. Unbeknownst to Paul, Lili turned to other men to help supplement what she was spending on him. Lili remained adept at getting money from a variety of admirers, or "sponsors" as she called them.[306] It didn't mean she wasn't in love with Paul. She gave freely. Despite being in a relationship, if someone asked her out, she went. She felt it was part of her job.

"It's expensive to take care of all the things I need to take care of," she told reporters, bragging how much she spent on her show and lifestyle. She had to accept generous gifts of money and presents from suitors. Most likely Paul knew some of what Lili was up to. To what degree he cared—in the beginning—is anyone's guess. He certainly benefited from her involvement with other men.

Lili was booked to do *The Windy City*, a musical about gangsters in Chicago. The Katherine Dunham–choreographed play was produced by journalist Dorothy Kilgallen's husband Richard Kollmar.

Many thought Lili should be a legit star. Miles Ingalls probably arranged a meeting with the producers. Lili was hired but quickly tired of the rehearsal process. She had trouble learning lines. Being told to walk for someone else didn't interest her. Her own show was easier. She wasn't a natural in the theatre; her voice wouldn't have carried. And the pay wasn't what she was becoming used to.

Miles no doubt urged his client to stay with the show as long as possible. She made it to Philadelphia before she quit. The New Haven tryouts in April were a disaster and reviews in Chicago labeled it a "flop." The musical was "overlong" and left the "audience cold as a clam."[307] Her name isn't listed in the credits and the play never made it to Broadway, though there is one review listing "Lili St. Cyr's dancing brings a warmer breeze to" the production.[308]

The one valuable thing Lili took from the show was Sadie, a young black maid who worked backstage helping the actors prepare, dress, and clean up. Sadie had a sly sense of humor and Lili offered her work. They would be together for at least the next decade, through marriages, clubs, arrests, and overdoses. Lili would write Sadie "earned her money."[309]

Either Lili or Paul had an extraordinary idea. There was not another stripper attended to onstage by a uniformed maid. What Sadie did for Lili offstage she could do for her *onstage*. Her job would be to help Lili in and out of her costumes, fix her

hair, and put on her jewels. It was outrageously glamorous, giving her yet another distinction far above the typical burlesque fare.

In Club Samoa the lone males in the audience often asked the girls to sit and drink with them after a show. Lili sent Sadie into the audience and let the wolves know, "She won't meet you if there is no champagne."[310] Sadie would often have six or seven tables lined up with silver buckets of overpriced bottles. Lili leisurely wound her way between the crowded tables. Then out of nowhere, boom. A bottle of champagne would be "accidentally" knocked over. The distressed men would order another. Then boom. Another man's bottle would crash to the ground. The owner split the take with Lili. He claimed sales quadrupled during Lili's run.

Lili's relationship with Sadie would be important and enduring. Sadie was smooth, calm, and spoke in a tender voice. She kept Lili from despair when a romance went south. "It's another bright sunny day ahead of us," she would say, trying to lighten Lili's mood. "Miss St. Cyr," she would say, "don't be upset." "Miss St. Cyr, you're too beautiful, don't be angry." Off the road Sadie worked in Lili's home, staying until Lili fell asleep and returning before she woke in the afternoons. She was always filled with joy. "We have another day ahead of us," she'd say, and begin to organize what Lili needed to do.[311]

With small children in New York, Sadie would periodically leave Lili, who would be desperate Sadie might never return.

One time Lili bought a beautiful fur coat in New York; leaving for Montreal she left the coat in storage. However, upon arriving in Canada Lili, typically, changed her mind and decided she wanted the coat with her. She sent Sadie to retrieve it. "Come right back," Lili warned.

Sadie returned several days late and Lili was furious.

"I just know you're gonna forgive me, Miss St. Cyr," she whined. "But it was a romance. A man. I met a man and I looked so good in your coat."

With her rapidly growing popularity Lili was besieged by men wanting to spend time with her. And they weren't always men she wanted to spend time with. "It was such a drag."[312] She decided to charge men for dates. She charged $150 for a breakfast date and as the day wore on the cost dropped. It was $125 for lunch and a mere $100 for dinner.

Lili felt she was being just. She would always dress with care. She applied her makeup and had to endure the often-arduous task of small talk. Her time was valuable. Onstage and off.

Reporters—and readers—that weren't already shocked by a beautiful woman earning a living taking off her clothes were aghast that she made men pay to escort her.

Lili raked in the dough and the publicity led to cries of "nymphomaniac" and "hooker."

Of course dates did not mean sex. She never charged for that. Sex meant love and she was willing to give that. Where Paul was in all this isn't known. As was often the case with Lili's romances, they ebbed and flowed. Perhaps they lived together for a while and separated and reunited. Lili still had her eye and heart in Montreal. She was a beautiful woman whose head was turned by the attention coming at her from all sides. Jimmy in Montreal, Paul in New York. And just because she gave her heart and body to both didn't mean she wasn't immune to the attentions of others. Love for Lili didn't necessarily mean monogamy. She was tempted by many and careless with her favors, drunk from the excess of attention cascading on her.

Lili became the headliner on the bill at the Gayety, this time with Dean Martin. Canadians once again embraced Lili, lining around the block to see her.

Ricocheting back to America she returned to familiar haunts—Lou Walters's in Miami, the Samoa in New York, the Old Howard in Boston (a former church), and the Follies in Los Angeles. Lili was on the move.

Up, up, up.

CHAPTER THREE

1989

She winds a scarf tight around her face. It catches in her hair and pulls. A web of white cotton is all her hair is anymore.

As much as she wants to return to the quiet of her apartment she is already headed north toward Melrose. She has not lost the determination of her youth. If she has to do something she does it. She no longer has anyone to run errands for her. No houseboy or Sadie.

Past her old apartment she shuffles. Bad memories there. Dark days. Days when she had been frightened, unsure what the future would hold.

Lorenzo is in worse shape than her. So much pain his body folds in on itself. His legs cannot bear his own weight.

At the market she hands the clerk a check. She picks up a few things, Salems, a little booze. They give her cash. She doesn't speak much. Lowers her head. What they must think, an ugly old lady who buys little and cashes small checks she has received from strangers.

Her sight isn't great. Cataracts. She negotiates the sidewalk carefully. She will not cry. She is tough. She wobbles forward. She is bent. Not L-shaped like Lorenzo, thankfully.

At the pawnshop the man looks at her. *Hello. Hello.* She unwraps a trinket, a nothing from her purse. *How much?* He will give her next to nothing. She will take it. And when she can find something else to scrounge from the disaster that is her apartment she will be back. *Hello. Hello. How much?* He will give her next to nothing. She will take it.

She returns. Just a few blocks more. She moves slowly. Past traffic. Blinding sun. Heat. She hates the heat. *Keep going,* she tells herself.

Just keep going.

Inside she dashes off a letter to Dardy. She hates asking for help, but what was she to do? She looks around the apartment, *a shambles.* There was nothing left to trade at the pawnshop.

She had traded her beauty for money and success. She had always been mercenary about money. Receiving it.

She lit a Salem and saw trouble in the smoke.

Lorenzo was unable to sell dope any more. He couldn't get it.

She lay in bed, a cigarette in her arthritic hand. She tried to sit up. Could barely lift herself. She was short of breath. Her hands once displayed beautiful rings on her fingers. Now she wore age spots. How had she gotten so old?

Out of the blue an old flame called. Why would the clarinet player want to see her? He was pleasant on the phone. Vaguely she wondered how he fared in the looks department. *He must be close to eighty!*

He had been handsome in his day. But an unpleasant man. Sadistic. He had dated and married all of them. Lana, Ava, Evelyn Keyes, even poor little Judy Garland, certainly no match for his caustic tongue. There was hardly a beauty in the forties and fifties Artie Shaw hadn't bedded. She had been one of them.

She remembered his unrelenting delving into the mind. He was obsessed with shrinks. Freud and all that crap. Stuff she wasn't interested in.

She knew why she took the drugs and that was enough. Escape.

Quiet. She didn't listen to music anymore. Nothing to play music on. She liked beautiful music like "Rhapsody in Blue." She had paid for her own special orchestration. Paul was right. Picking the right music was important. But living with Paul had felt like prison.

Ironic. Which was more restricting, a husband who never let you out of sight, relentlessly tried to improve you, or the constraints imposed by age and lack of money? She could never escape again. She could never pick up a pale cream-colored piece of luggage and head out the door into the limousine and float away.

CHAPTER FOUR

O ver the door hung a sign that might well have made Lili chuckle, a rip-off of
Mr. Carroll's: "Through these portals, the most beautiful girls in the world
pass." Eddie or Leon, with their sly sense of humor, had painted a sign: "Through
these portals, the most beautiful girls in the world pass out."

The ceiling was painted with big white letters: UNDER THIS ROOF STARS SHINE
ALL NIGHT. LEON & EDDIE'S.[313]

The vaudeville-style show ran three to four times nightly. A regular performer
at the club, Sherry Britton made the raucous audiences listen to her sing while
she danced with a stage full of beauties before she'd strip down to bare breasts.
Contradictorily, Sherry was considered "prudish" because, unlike the other girls, she
would cover up *backstage* with a robe.[314]

Sherry's introduction to stripping had been harsh. The petite brunette had
worked her way up from dingy burlesque theatres on the Bowery, where she could
see the "men's seed all over the theatre floor." Though she "despised burlesque" the
New Jersey native loved performing her strip to classical music, wearing beautiful
floor-length gowns and crowns pinned atop her lush mane of hair.[315]

It was a frigid February night in New York, 1946, but inside the club was
warm. Steamy even. Smoke settled low over customers' heads. They stood three and
four deep in front of the rectangular bar at the back of the club. Customers held
chartreuse-colored souvenir programs and waived the smoke away from their faces.

Men and women eagerly anticipated seeing Lili St. Cyr after the previous
week's review in *Billboard*. The papers couldn't get enough about her reverse
strip routine.

Upstairs in Eddie's office, with a rehearsal piano shoved to the side, a waiter
delivered a box of white roses.

Eddie Davis raised an eyebrow. Lili wasn't the kind of stripper that enjoyed
small talk before a show. She practically barricaded herself in her dressing room

until it was time to go on. After the show she was always friendlier, relaxed after the applause, ready to enjoy champagne.

Eddie pushed his way into Lili's dressing room with the long box under his arm.

Lili sat fastening a rhinestone necklace around her neck. She stood in black fishnet opera hose rolled to just below her buttocks. Her sparkly red pasties were covered by a net bra covered by another sequined bra. From a chair she picked up a lovely ice-blue gown with yards of tulle and silk. Delicately she stepped into it, unself-conscious of her nudity but nevertheless aware of its effect on others.

The room smelled like powder and perfume and Lili. All woman.

Music and the sounds of laughter, clanking glasses, the roar of a good time seeped under her door. Nightclubs sounded the same, smelled the same, smoke and booze and expensive perfume, sweat and garlic. Paradise to many.

Eddie scratched his bald head and looked around the dressing room. Flowers were squeezed onto every surface. She adored getting flowers. If an admirer was smart enough, he learned white roses where her favorite. Not red.

Prior to the midnight show Eddie entertained the room for an hour, doing gags, singing, even making a plea for the March of Dimes.

With the help of Sadie, Lili entered the stage in semiundress and began tearing through boxes and bags, pulling out evening dresses and trying them on. Not satisfied she would undress and try on a different outfit. She played the scenario deftly, without saying a word. It lasted about ten minutes. It was innovative. And it was a hit.

Raising "the blood temperature" of the men, Lili began "slow grinds and decorous bumps to Persian Market." And though they were called "bumps" and "grinds," they were—to be nitpicky—no more than undulations and pelvic circles.[316]

Lili's costumes looked expensive. Silk and satin floor-length gowns. She tossed fur stoles over her shoulders, looped pearls and diamonds around her swanlike neck. She strolled between real antiques on the stage, twirling around her "boudoir." A powerfully erotic setting.

Sadie hovered around Lili in a crisp uniform. Lili didn't play to the audience. She let the audience feel as if they were peeking through a window into her private administrations. It was shockingly intimate in its simplicity.

Lili used music by Gershwin, Rimsky-Korsakov, and other classic composers. She was spending a fortune on the act but it was paying off with standing-room-only crowds night after night, which meant a higher salary for her return engagements. She poured heart and soul and time and money into her act, making her the "most 'artistic' take-off routine of anybody in the business."[317]

Fans adored her, in part because of the class and elegance she brought to the clubs, but also because no matter how she took it off, or what she showed of her body, there was much about Lili that she withheld. She wasn't approachable and

"Oriental Fantasy"

friendly. Lili wasn't vulnerable and needy. She was in control; she gave only as much as she wanted, not what was asked of her.

Imitators began to crop up. On Fifty-Second Street the clubs were looking for more strippers like Lili—but Lili was the one Sinatra, Gene Kelly, and Jack Dempsey were showing up to see.

IN LOS ANGELES, LILI FOUND HER DREAM HOUSE. IT STOOD AT THE END of a wide slow-climbing avenue up Canyon Drive north of Franklin in Hollywood, the last house at the end of the street before Bronson Canyon.

Bronson Canyon was far north of busy Hollywood Boulevard and had the feel of being out of the city. It was situated in the southwesterly corner of Griffith Park. The area had been a former quarry that ceased operation in the late 1920s. It had become a popular spot for hiking and filming in the 1940s, as it still is today. Such serials as the *Lone Ranger, Zorro Rides Again*, and *I'm a Fugitive from a Chain Gang* had filmed there, just minutes from a faux Tudor house at the end of the street.

The two-story house was built in 1927. It was a manageable two thousand square feet. Situated next to an empty corner lot and directly across from an empty weedy hill. A quiet neighborhood. A perfect place for privacy. It would become first a respite, then a refuge for Lili.

It would be the only place where she would invite a small group of friends and entertain lavishly. It was where she would stage many publicity shoots, some on her bed, some on the white carpet in front of one of the fireplaces, or on a chaise in her sitting room, others outside in a private patio.

In the comfort of her home she could rest her feet, wipe an egg white facemask on, drink tea, and push away the demands of her work. The home would become her proud treasure.

HER DREAM HOME HAD FIVE ROOMS AND A WALLED COURTYARD. IT was within easy driving distance of the clubs where she worked. Having mostly given up driving, Lili would beg rides from Dardy when she was in Los Angeles, or from men, or she would catch cabs and rent limousines.

Sometime before 1945 Lili moved into the house, probably as a renter.[318] One of her husbands remembered living there as early as 1946. Lili wouldn't actually purchase the house until 1953. She would claim to see the house with Alice and a real estate agent and her eyes lit up. Alice told her to go ahead and buy it if she liked it so much.

In the beginning Lili would spend little time there, but even then it became her base. Lili was on the road from New York, Montreal, Philadelphia, Detroit. She lived like a gypsy, out of hotel rooms, sometimes only dressing rooms. Canyon Drive was a sanctuary from her frenetic life and her tempestuous and oftentimes complicated romances. She would come to rely on Canyon Drive for serenity. She envisioned herself retired there, tending to her garden. She imagined how she would fix it up once it was hers and walked through the house with Alice decorating in their minds.

In New York Lili continued to see Paul Valentine, very much in love and encouraged by their collaboration. Paul was pursuing his own career so was perhaps more tolerant of her disappearances to other cities than he would become.

Jimmy Orlando remained in the picture. She met cartoonist Al Capp when he rushed backstage at the Gayety to meet her, as did so many. The tall and robust man was eight years Lili's senior. He had lost a leg as a child in an accident. Capp had been raised by struggling, dirt-poor parents, which fostered the dark outlook on life he poured into his work. He had been writing *L'il Abner* for about ten years. His strip was sardonic, hilarious, full of suspense, and extremely popular. The characters he drew were outsized to go with their outlandish behavior.

Variously described as volatile, contentious, cynical, sarcastic, contradictory, misanthropic, curmudgeonly, controversial, and bitingly funny, Capp captivated Lili, who thought he was "charming." Capp liked the "Blonde Venus" of Montreal and soon after meeting her he created a character named Wolf Gal that was pure Lili.

Wolf Gal was untamed, an Amazonian raised by wolves who preferred to live among animals rather than people. She lured her unwary prey to their doom to feed her ravenous animal pack.

Wolf Gal's taste for the dangerous and her predatory ways mirrored Lili and her preference for bad boys to take to bed. Lili was greedy with her desires. She wanted Paul but was unwilling to give up Jimmy or others, hungry for the affection she had been denied as a child, swept up in being popular. Lili would say men thought her "demanding and vain."[319] Her point of view was that her vanity made her money.

Lili thought Capp's depiction of her delightful and added to her growing allure as a femme fatale, a "bad girl," the I-don't-give-a-damn-you-can't-hurt-me burlesque queen. "Burlesque queen" was a title Lili didn't like. She was doing everything possible to shatter the image of what a "burlesque queen" was.

In Montreal Lili spent enormous sums in antique stores. She would walk around the high-end department store, Ogilvy on Saint Catherine Street, buying things to be shipped home, now that she had one.

On Cherburge Street boutiques were loaded with sumptuous treasures. She spied a gorgeous satin, hand-carved Italian blond wood bedframe. Impulsively she purchased it for $750, a great sum at the time. The bed was several hundred years old and massive. With a big canopy and carved inlaid double headboard rising at least five feet above the frame, Lili thought it perfect for the stage.

LILI NOW—AND FOR DECADES TO COME—FOUND HERSELF BOOKED months in advance. Clubs called and requested her. She turned nothing down. Firmly on the road she would store the bed for a not-inconsiderable sum. The bed would remain in Canada in storage for nearly two years. Eventually she had it shipped to Los Angeles. (To ship it the bed had to be taken apart. She paid an enormous sum to have it disassembled.) When it arrived she called her friend and interior decorator Tom Douglas to have it reassembled in her bedroom on the second floor. She even had a special ten-inch platform built in anticipation. To her dismay the bed wouldn't fit. It was too tall. According to Dardy, Douglas suggested they raise the roof. Lili did.

Until then the bed sat in Lili's living room and wouldn't be moved upstairs for several years, not until after 1953 when Lili embarked on major renovations on the house.

She eventually traveled with the unwieldy prop, which meant it was constantly being put together and pulled apart. "And there were no nails," Dardy said. "Only wood dowels. It cost her a *fortune* to have it disassembled then reassembled again. But that was Lili."

"Before I spent a single night on it, the bed cost me nearly $10,000," Lili claimed.[320]

RIGHT: *Lili's magnificent new bed*

CHAPTER FIVE

"Bubbles," Paul declared. "That's what you need in the act." He dipped a stick into some liquid and waved a wand over her head saying, "We have to figure something for you to do where bubbles would look like they belonged."[321]

Naturally the perfect excuse for bubbles was for Lili to take a bath onstage. They worked out how she could turn bathing into a centerpiece of an act. It was the perfect excuse to disrobe. Sadie could draw a tub, help her undress, and help her towel off and dress. It was a tantalizing concept.

Together they mapped out the routine. One that would revolutionize her act.

PAUL CARVED A HOLE IN THE SIDE OF HER "MODERN LOOKING BATH-tub" from which he could blow bubbles from offstage.[322] The act, which debuted at the Samoa (or Follies; she claimed both) became an instant sensation, one she "never could eliminate."[323] Her one complaint in the beginning was whatever was making the bubbles left a sticky substance on her body and she had to shower between shows.

Lili had a return engagement in Los Angeles. She told Paul she didn't want to leave him. She stroked his black hair. She was not unaware of the splash they made together. Both had strong bodies; he was all dark, she all blonde. They walked as if stalking, graceful as cats.

Recently she had returned from Jimmy, who had wrecked her, once again confronted by his infidelity with another beauty. This one had gotten pregnant. They had fought. She returned to Paul.

Paul had just signed a contract with RKO, Barbara's old studio. He was going to California too. They wouldn't have to be apart.

Paul and Lili booked a train to California. First class with a private drawing room attached to the luxurious sleeper. Once again she was surrounded by mahogany

Lili possibly at the Follies

wood and polished brass, her preferred mode of travel, and one Paul would easily grow accustomed to. Lili never slept better than she did soothed by the sway of a speeding train. It was still very much the days of porters in crisp uniforms, silver sets and linen service at meals, flowers and crystal vases on tables, excellent service.

Trapped in the cocoon of opulence Lili told Paul she wanted to marry him. Usually once she agreed to marry someone it happened quickly, but other things (possibly Jimmy) must have gotten in the way because she and Paul wouldn't marry for months. It is also quite possible she got cold feet, as she often would, and hesitated to make another commitment until forced to.

In Los Angeles Lili had a mini reunion with Alice and Idella, whom she hadn't seen for three years. Idella was now divorced and living in Hanford, in central California, and presumably so was Alice. Lili would comment on Idella's frosty attitude toward not just herself but also Paul. Because he was a dancer he couldn't offer the security Idella felt Lili needed. Lili later claimed she didn't care about Paul's security; she knew she wouldn't be with him indefinitely.[324]

In California Paul spent days on the phone with his pal Howard Hughes, who owned RKO. He hoped Hughes would put him to work. Days turned into weeks and still Paul remained at odds, with a contract but no work. He seriously considered taking the name "St. Cyr." Then in July Hughes crashed his plane in Beverly Hills and all communication vanished. Paul became frantic.

But in October he started shooting *Out of the Past*, a noir film starring Robert Mitchum and Kirk Douglas. It was to be his screen debut. He played Joe, Douglas's "henchman." *Out of the Past* was based on the novel *Build My Gallows High*.

Paul and Lili

Hired as Val Valentinoff, though he would ultimately be credited as Paul Valentine, he holds his own in scenes opposite the leads, though it could not be said he was remotely a threat to Douglas and Mitchum, who clearly have more star wattage on the screen. Sharply dressed and smooth shaven he is supremely handsome. Though he was lauded by a couple of reviewers, the audience remained firmly focused on a cool and nuanced Douglas and a smoldering Mitchum.

Paul was in excellent physical shape and it shows in the film. He moves with a dancer's confidence, exuding cockiness. A bit of studio hyperbole advertised Paul as being the "best dancer since Nijinsky."[325]

The three female leads can't hold a candle to Lili's beauty and it remains a shame she was never given a suitable role in a film to immortalize her brand of cool sexy. Eyes would not have left her face. Her bone structure was made to be captured on film. But Lili remained in the nightclubs and burlesque houses where she thought she belonged.

Out of the Past was shot on location in Mexico, San Francisco, and Los Angeles. Shooting was completed by December and released in January of 1947. Lili and Paul spent an evening at Mitchum's house as his two sons roughhoused around them. The genial actor didn't seem to mind. Lili found them annoying. But then she found all children annoying.[326]

The film did well, though it would not be recognized as one of "the greatest of all film noirs" until decades later.[327]

One night Paul met Lili after her late show at the Follies. He surprised her by asking her to run to "Tia Juana" (as it was often spelled at the time) and get married.

The ceremony took place on December 29, 1946.[328] Harry Crocker, Barbara's old beau and the man who had introduced the pair, was Paul's best man.[329]

Lili was ecstatic. Marriage number three to another hunk. Perhaps it was a man's beauty that gave Lili reassurance of her worth. Time and again it was a cleft chin and strong pecs that drew her in. The men were usually not worthy of her. But Paul was different; he had artistic vision and discipline to offer. She credited him with filling her "with artistic inspiration."[330]

Lili wanted to make sure the quickie Mexican marriage was legal, so they had another in San Francisco. She signed the certificate as Marie Valentine.

INITIALLY SHE LISTENED TO NEARLY EVERY ONE OF PAUL'S SUGGES-tions, wanting to improve. She perfected her bathtub act by getting in and out of her tub. He instructed her on how to breathe, how to sit. A tireless teacher, he taught her about all the arts, music, sculpture, even architecture.

In the nascent stages of her bathtub routine Lili hired a chorus girl to lay down behind the tub out of sight of the audience and blow bubbles in the air. Lili was thrilled when the bubble machine was invented because she was tired of the girls complaining about crouching on cold floors. She would claim the man who leased her the device later sold the same to Lawrence Welk for his television show.

Most strippers, when they tossed their clothes offstage, paid a chorus girl standing in the wings to catch it. But Lili didn't throw her expensive clothes. She had Sadie place the gowns carefully on a table that had been covered with a clean sheet, as everything backstage was so dusty. Sadie was protective of Lili and her wardrobe. And one never knew what a jealous chorus girl might do with her delicate gowns.

Lili had to hire a pair of stagehands to guard her tub after someone filled it with buckets of ice prior to her entrance. Lili had to grit her teeth as she sank into the frigid water and leisurely perform her act. It wasn't atypical of backstage behavior. There were tales about girls putting itching powder in costumes. As Lili already knew she had no reason to trust women.

CHAPTER SIX

For a while they were happy, but Paul's contentment was short-lived once filming was over and *Out of the Past* moved into the theatres. Offers didn't pour in as he had expected. He was back in the shadow of his more famous wife, his name in the paper only when he escorted Lili.

Soon Paul's constant improving of Lili "was no fun."[331] Lili just wanted to enjoy herself and she begged him to give it a rest.

After being a married a year Lili returned to the Gayety and Jimmy Orlando, neither of which had lost their appeal.

The Gayety was paying her the astounding sum of $1,500 a week at a time when the median family income for 1947 was $3,000.[332] She worked several weeks and again her act sold out every night, wowing her Canadians fans. She would return three or four more times during the winter season alone. Her growing audiences watched in awed silence.

LILI WAS BOOKED SOLID FOR THE NEXT SIX MONTHS, AND THAT included several stints in Montreal, close to Jimmy—very close to Jimmy—while Paul filled his time in Los Angeles looking for an acting job.

Lili and Paul and Barbara and Albert Ostermaier (possibly a horse trainer who worked for Robert Young, among others, at MGM) spent a night at Earl Carroll's enjoying Dardy in the show.[333] Paul badgered Lili to include him in her show.

In January the papers were filled with shocking news that would spread like wildfire to the rest of the nation. The papers blasted lurid headlines as the country ate up the salacious details of the naked body, sawed in half and dumped in an empty lot in Los Angeles.

Her name was Elizabeth Short; grifter, wannabe actress, failed showgirl, possible prostitute. She was labeled everything as reporters scrambled to find out

anything about her. Short had frequented the Florentine Gardens back when Lili first started out. It's tantalizing to speculate that Lili remembered the raven-haired girl, not quite a beauty because of her crooked teeth, an air of desperation permeating her somewhat dirty and disheveled look.

Short's mutilated body was found spread-eagle in a dirt lot at South Norton in Leimert Park, a respectable upper-middle-class neighborhood. She would quickly become immortalized as the Black Dahlia, a moniker invented by sensationalistic reporters, based on a movie playing at the time, *The Blue Dahlia*.

Lili was shaken by the news. The association too close for comfort. The poor girl tossed in the weeds, nude, drained of blood. It was a haunting image. Paul began to complain about where Lili worked, that the joints were seedy and unsafe. Lili couldn't deny there was some truth in what he said but soon was distracted by happier news.

THAT SAME YEAR, THE SAME YEAR AS *LIFE WITH FATHER* STARRING William Powell, Irene Dunne, and a young Elizabeth Taylor, the same year *Miracle on 34th Street* debuted with the precocious Natalie Wood, Barbara was finally set to marry Louis Marx.

Lili boasted that three millionaires were in pursuit of Barbara at the time: Harry Crocker, Marx, and some unnamed other. Barbara chose Marx.[334]

It had taken several years playing the role of secretary/hostess/fiancée to Louis Marx, but in 1947 Barbara seemed to pass an unspoken test. A date was set.[335]

Lili was back in New York—*sans* Paul—and seemingly thrilled for her sister. Lili insisted on a meeting with her future brother-in-law. Lili told Barbara she was making sure Barbara would be taken care of and once again stepped in to negotiate.

Another not fantastical idea was that Lili didn't want to see the marriage happen and was hoping to scare Marx off, because she announced to the papers Barbara would marry Harry Crocker. In fact the year before, from the stage at Leon & Eddie's, she had announced Harry as "the man who is going to marry my little sister."[336] There continued to be little love lost between Marx and Lili.

Louis had to be wary of another encounter with the mercenary Lili, who perhaps thought it her job to substitute for Idella and protect Barbara. The last time she had negotiated Barbara's position as his secretary it had cost him thousands. She claimed to negotiate a substantial sum of dough for Barbara up front.

The more sensational Lili's act became and the more headlines she made, the more Louis seemed to cringe at having *that* kind of a sister-in-law in the papers. Now that Barbara was going to be his wife, he would find a way to push Barbara's sisters from their life. He didn't need his sisters-in-law prancing through the papers every time they took up with another man or dropped another G-string. He would bury Barbara's showgirl past by having her revert to using her birth name of Idella.

Quite simply, Barbara's family would have to go. It was a dictate that would tear the family apart forever.

When Lili returned to the Follies she introduced Los Angelinos to her "Chinese Virgin" act, recycled from Montreal, chastity belt and all. Though she would later claim to hate the Follies, she returned year after year to a loyal following. She would perform everything from her bathtub act to stripping from a champagne glass onstage.

With Lili headlining, the "throngs" came. Once again she was "breaking box office records."[337]

Lillian Hunt's granddaughter Pearl recalled the first time she saw Lili. Pearl was about six years old and stunned when a statuesque blonde walked out of her dressing room wearing a blue robe with a hood over her head. She was "unreal" with the "most beautiful features and body" the little girl would ever see. She was very sweet to Pearl, but talked with a "funny high voice."[338]

The Follies was now run-down and dingy. Hunt had two dressing rooms for Lili, appropriate for a star of her box office, one with a bed squeezed inside the tiny room so she could rest comfortably between shows.

Criss-crossing back and forth across the country, never turning down a job afforded Lili her money, her name in the paper, and a way to escape her out-of-work husband who was becoming cloying and kept demanding to be used in her show. They made an announcement to the trades that they were forming a dance team, which appealed to Lili—in theory; her fantasy was to be half of a Lunt-Fontane team. But the reality of the driven, desperate Paul Valentine was a whole other matter.

Because of her contract at Earl Carroll's, Dardy was unable to make Barbara's wedding. Dardy sent her congratulations via telegram, asking Barbara to come west with her groom after the honeymoon.

As maid of honor Lili slipped down to Miami. Walking down the aisle ahead of Barbara, who radiated happiness, Lili would never suspect that she and Barbara wouldn't continue to follow each other through life. Neither realized their days as fun-loving companions and confidants were numbered.

Barbara wore a "white brocade" dress "embroidered with seed pearls" and a "train length veil." Marx had bestowed a beautiful pearl necklace and an "eight carat Marquis cut diamond" on his beloved.[339]

Marx's best man was Hank Greenberg, the handsome Detroit Tigers' power hitter and first baseman. Greenberg would become a five-time All-Star. In 1946 he had married Caral Gimbel of the Gimbel department store fortune, whom he met through Marx.

Beautiful bride, proud groom, and a stunning maid of honor

AT 5:00 P.M. AT ALL SOULS EPISCOPAL CHURCH IN BELLE ISLE, SOUTH Beach, Miami, a happy and gorgeous Barbara strode down the aisle with her elegantly dressed and almost three-decades-older groom. She walked on the arm of Louis's brother David.

The church was in the former estate of Joseph H. Adams, author, inventor, and millionaire who built an eleven-bedroom, eight-bathroom mansion on the water. A massive music room that held three hundred was turned into a church where the couple exchanged their vows.[340]

Among the distinguished guests were the president of the National Geographic Society, Major General Emmet O'Connel, boxer Gene Tunney, and, as the papers misreported, "Lillian St. Cyr of the stage."[341] Perhaps Marx's misquote.

A reception was held afterward at the block-long Roney Plaza Hotel on the beach. Known as the "grande dame of Miami Beach" the hotel "was the place to see and be seen."[342] However, it was reported Marx and his new bride "had to rush back to N.Y.U's night classes" that they had been attending in "Logic, Classic Literature, Dominant Ideals of Western Civilization," so a honeymoon would have to wait.[343]

No one else from Barbara's family attended.

Barbara had "always wanted a husband and kids and she didn't really care about being a dancer."[344] Not the way Lili had. She just wanted someone to love her. Even though she'd been Idella's favorite, her mother's erratic love wasn't enough. She had—understandably—wanted things—they all did. They had grown up without anything. They wanted nice cars and clothes and a big house. Indeed Barbara got it all, but she hadn't known at the time what she would have to sacrifice to keep it.

As a wedding present Marx gave his beaming bride a check for $100,000.

Wanting to share her good fortune with her family—and likely assuming she didn't need it now—Barbara gave everyone $10,000—Idella, Dardy, Lili, and even according to Dardy absent siblings Jack and Betty.

"I bought a car," Dardy said. "Lili bought her house."

Lili might have told Dardy she bought the Canyon Drive home, but that purchase was still another six years away.

According to Dardy, when Marx found out how his bride disbursed the money with her family he exploded. Perhaps for the first time Barbara felt the full force of his temper. The "tyrannically" oppressive Marx often controlled through his checkbook. He would eventually block his daughter Barbara's "access to" her "inheritance" because he did not like how she was spending her money.[345]

Dardy was on hand to greet Barbara and the "Toy King" at the Santa Fe Station in Pasadena just weeks after the wedding. Barbara looked magnificent draped in a fur stole and hat. The newlyweds were in town for just two weeks before departing for Moscow to visit an ambassador friend of Marx. Marx had brought along at least some of his children to "meet Aunt Lili," as she was to be referred to.[346]

Marx's daughter Barbara observed "Aunt Lili" was "not interested in the children." It's intriguing to wonder why Marx wanted his grown children to meet Lili especially in light of what was to come. Perhaps Lili's fame still held currency for the celebrity-loving Marx who enjoyed surrounding himself with the rich and famous. Barbara Marx wasn't impressed with her new aunt and dismissed Lili as "flamboyant and flashy."[347]

There would be no other meeting between Lili and Marx's children.

CHAPTER SEVEN

By 1948 Lili was breaking records wherever she performed. Singled out for her elaborate wardrobe and her evolving and inventive acts, she was noted for her "unusual dance routines, such as 'Afternoon of a Faun,' 'Ballerina's Boudoir,' 'Bird Love Act,' and 'Dance of the Chinese Virgin.'"[348]

When she performed at Zucca's Opera house in Culver City the newspapers noted that though her costumes might be "abbreviated" they still required "two extra large wardrobe trunks for transporting."[349] The littlest thing about Lili became news.

At home she kept a select circle of friends and began to quietly entertain at her Canyon Drive home. Sadie would whip up delicious Southern dishes. Lili was accumulating expensive linens, crystal, silver sets with ornate candelabras. She lit everything with candles, much preferring how she looked in the subdued light.

Her dinner parties were a way to distract from an increasingly constricting marriage. Lili and Paul argued over everything. She chafed as he tried inserting himself further in her work. But no one was interested in Paul Valentine. His brilliant bathtub idea was now a fixture in her show and with his urging she even had her bubble bath act copyrighted. But there was no room for Paul in the tub.

Lili put him into a show to disastrous reviews. Paul might be a good dancer, but audiences wanted to see Lili.

Paul nagged and berated and *bugged* her to no end. With endless time to fixate on her he wanted her to change everything. Nothing she did was good enough. *Do more. Work harder.* He told her she "must learn to grow."[350]

He considered himself her teacher, father, manager. He only had to remind her the tub was his idea. He was genius. Didn't she see?

She would turn away with a slow burning in her stomach. It was *her* act, and people came to the theatre, flocked, lined up outside because of *her*. Yes, the bathtub was game changing; it also cost a fortune hauling an antique tub from

Paul rehearsing Lili

one end of the country to another. She kept asking for an increase in her rate. She was supporting them both.

His career in Hollywood hadn't taken off as he had envisioned. He wouldn't make his next film until *House of Strangers* in 1949. There was no work for him on Broadway. Nightclubs weren't calling. He was ambitious and bored, jealous of a wife whose career was soaring.

He resented her schedule, the demands made of her, the salary she brought in. The phone rang with offers for her. Never for him.

He complained she worked too much. But she needed to. She spent extravagantly. No expense was spared in the creation of her scenarios. The antiques and jewelry, clothes and props were costly, not to mention the extra musicians she hired, violinists and cellists to travel with her. Being Lili St. Cyr had become a complicated, costly business.

Paul wasn't without inspiration and continued to dream up dances for her, like one particularly sultry dance involving a painting of a matador that she danced for and sometimes the matador would come to life and dance with her. At least once Paul would be the matador.

PAUL "DOMINATED" HER "AND SHE WASN'T USED TO THAT. LILI WAS used to being spoiled. But Paul "didn't want to do that." When he managed work he was "impossible to work with." On movie sets he would arrogantly tell the director how to light a scene.[351]

Around the house he wanted the radio on. She wanted silence. Nothing but the sounds of the birds outside. Her nights were filled with noise—music, chorus girls chattering, comedians laughing, audiences shouting, and drinks clinking. She needed the quiet to revitalize herself.

Lili's existence was packing, traveling, rehearsing, performing, going out *constantly*. Couldn't he understand her desire for rest and silence? He certainly did not comprehend her silence toward him. She had nothing to say.

Marriage wasn't something she felt warranted a change, or a suppressing of her desires and wishes. Lili wanted to do what she wanted, when she wanted to. As with all her marriages, "the fun goes out of it for me."[352]

They fought over how they spent their time. He wanted to go out after her shows. She was tired and would rather go home. On her rare night off she didn't want to put on makeup and be Lili. She wanted to sit in her home.

Often she would barricade herself in the bathroom for hours, reading magazines, rubbing lotion on her face, painting her nails, dying her hair, conditioning it with oil so it wouldn't become straw-like from the bleach.[353] She ignored his pounding on the door. The door to *her* bathroom. She resented his big, loud, demanding presence in *her* home.

Most times, he'd grow impatient waiting for her and leave. She'd emerge, take some pills, and go to bed.

VIRGINIA BURROUGHS WOULD BE THE CLOSEST IF NOT THE *ONLY* REAL female friend Lili would ever have. Lili admired Virginia, twenty years older, and would emulate the stylish way she wore her clothes, the regal way she carried herself, and the older woman's good manners.

Burrows was a rich socialite who had married often, inherited great wealth, and had a son. She shared rooms with her elderly mother at the Chateau Marmont. The sharp-nosed woman was aristocratic looking, if not beautiful, impeccably put together. The two met at a party and hit it off immediately. Virginia was soon bringing Lili to the best Hollywood soirees. Even after Lili married Paul the habit continued without him. Though Lili tended to sit shyly off to the side listening, she enjoyed being with Virginia and observing her friend's ease and smooth manner. The talk tended to revolve around Hollywood and who was working on what film, what studio was making the next *The Best Years of Our Lives*, or what

One of Lili's only female friends, Virginia Burroughs

Rosalind Russell had been cast in. Lili in return enjoyed dragging Virginia to the dicey bars and dark dives she frequented.

"Let's go to the El Rancho," Lili would suggest to Virginia. The El Rancho Nitery in Los Angeles was a dump where Lili sometimes stripped.

"But *I* can't go there," Virginia would protest, waiving a bejeweled wrist. "Not with this jewelry on." Lili got a kick out of the way Virginia would chide her for some outrageous behavior.

LILI BELIEVED VIRGINIA DIDN'T REALLY APPROVE OF HER CHOICES, IN men and otherwise. But they were friends and saw each other often. There was a mutual fascination with the other. Virginia would never be a stripper and Lili would never be society. Virginia was proper and organized, elegant and worldly. Lili was flagrantly flamboyant.

Virginia was a great friend of Greta Garbo and often told Lili how much she resembled Garbo. Lili couldn't hope to believe it was true. "You are my friend. Trust me, you look like her more than anybody," Virginia said.[354] Lili was delighted.

Still Lili struggled. She was brought to a new low whenever Paul began attacking her: Her friends weren't good enough; the burlesque theatres weren't good enough. She should be on Broadway (which is perhaps why she'd agreed to be in *Windy City*). Stripping wasn't good enough. She felt beaten down. He heightened her insecurities, unsettled her nerves, increased her doubts. His "not good enoughs" mashed up against her own worries, making her feel "inferior." The noise in her head could be drowned only by more work and more pills.[355]

Paul complained that her friends excluded him from conversation. Her friends thought he was boastful and a bore. They tolerated him because of her.

In turn she would "refuse to allow his friends in their home."[356]

Lili wasn't a good fighter. She turned cold and quiet. She resented making an effort to defend herself. She didn't give away her power by screeching like Idella. Her power was in her steely silence.

In the throes of first love Lili inevitably plunged over the cliff, headlong into a man's needs and desires. She loved being in love and the all-consuming heat of it. She doted on her men, catered to them, showered them with gifts and affection and attention. Did she believe in love? Was there such a thing? "Of course there is. . . . I'd commit suicide if I didn't think so."[357]

Lili had no patience nor was she prepared for the day-to-day tedium of having someone interfering with her freedom. Another's presence grated on her. She escaped into work, her sole relief and sense of worth, and Paul was trying to strip it away.

Most of the men in Lili's life would question, interfere, suppress, and ultimately attempt to change her. It was a mistake to try to corral Lili. She was a woman who valued her autonomy. Compromise wasn't something she learned to do. She would return to her habits as a single woman when the marriages stalled.

Lili grew restless in marriage. She hated being bored. The roving gypsy and the Gemini in her sought change and stimuli and often drama.

"The first two years are wonderful," she confided to Dardy, "but after two years they are like your brother. And you don't want to sleep with your brother." And that would be that. "Until another tall good looking guy came along," said Dardy.

LILI SPENT A PRODIGIOUS AMOUNT OF TIME IN MONTREAL WHERE she was spotted attending a soapbox derby on Mont Royal. When recognized, she was driven out by cries of "Take it off" and she fled with some "flack"—probably Jimmy Orlando.[358]

In December Lili was back doing three shows a day at the Follies, except for Saturdays when there were five. The last show commenced at midnight.

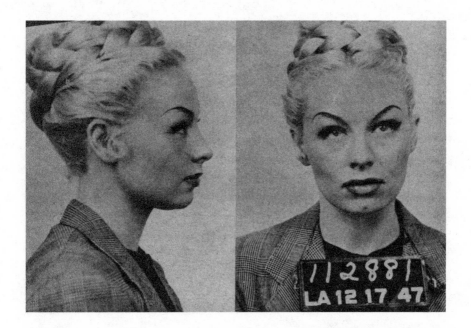

Lili's mug shots

It was December 17 and Lili had no time to think about the Christmas season fast approaching. She was working. She had bookings further into the future than she could see.

As usual, the shows—with her headlining—were sold out. On this particular night, after her act she glided offstage and into a young vice squad officer named Cletus O. Smith, who announced, "You're under arrest."[359]

She was allowed to change into a black top and plaid suit. She looked defiant and tired and disappointed in her mug shot. Her hair was piled on top of her head in a neat bun, thick eyebrows soaring. The heavy makeup made her look older and harsh. She only hoped her mug shot would never surface. She felt demoralized.[360]

PAUL GAVE HER NO END OF GRIEF AFTER MAKING BAIL, ACTING AS IF the arrest were her fault.

She didn't want to be busted. Paul should know; the cops would do this now and again. Make a couple of arrests because some ambitious politician was campaigning on a platform to clean up burlesque. Lili had luckily avoided the law until now.

In April Lili showed up at court with Follies owner Mrs. Anna Eva Biggs, formerly Louise Miller, in a conservative suit, shirt buttoned to her throat, hat, gloves, and fur stole.[361] She looked anything but a burlesque dancer. It would prove to be a humiliating two-day trial where Judge Byron J. Walters reprimanded Lili at every turn.

The police claimed Lili had entered the stage "carried on a table, removed the upper portion of her apparel, leaving a bare midriff up to her neck."[362]

Officer Smith testified Lili removed her black veil, net skirt, and beaded jacket and then "'shed practically everything' during an oriental dance." When she faced her fans, "only her hands kept her from being nude and she quickly dropped them."[363] This was not true.

The officer also accused her of lying back on silk pillows and grinding and bumping.

Lili boiled inside. *He wouldn't know what art or an interpretive dance was if it bit him in the ass.*

Eighty feet of a sixteen-milimeter film of Lili's dance (taken surreptitiously in the theatre) was shown to the judge and "overcrowded courtroom." Lili protested her innocence, saying her performance was "art" and she was merely doing "an interpretive dance."[364]

Prosecutor Walter Allen ("a bachelor," one paper had to note) claimed she was nude "except for shoes and net stockings."[365]

Lili countered that she wore a net bra.

Allen scoffed, "Then maybe it's[366] one of those new fangled things, made of liquid which goes on like glass or something."

The judge told the court Lili's act was a "serious menace to the morals of those who viewed it."

Lili had entered the courtroom confident in her innocence, as nothing she had done onstage was indecent. She said she was utterly "surprised" at the guilty verdict.[367] She was offered a choice by Judge Byron Walters of either doing time or paying a $350 fine. An easy decision. The fine was merely a third of her weekly salary. The judge leveled a final rebuke at the tall stripper polluting his court, that her act "corrupted public morals."[368] She took it, expressionless. Lili suffered in silence but decided to be even "badder."

CHAPTER EIGHT

When Lili booked her and Paul as a team at the Florentine Gardens the papers complained they "interpret independently."[369]

One patron praised Lili's figure but derided her for not knowing "what to do with it."[370] Others dismissed Lili as doing "the easy work" and praised Valentine for "the real work" with his "spectacular leaps, mid-air splits."[371]

In Oakland they performed to terrible reviews in "Varieties of 1948." The papers noted her blue hair but weren't impressed as "she dallies around with a papier-mâché head of St. John"; it was "dreadful." [372]

LILI'S FAMILY HAD MOVED IN DIFFERENT DIRECTIONS.

Alice had moved to Pismo Beach into one of the homes Idella's new husband owned. As a county clerk, George Beck could acquire homes for next to nothing when they went into foreclosure. George and Idella lived in Hanford, California, in the south central portion of the San Joaquin Valley. Idella would treat Beck, a World War II vet and widower, no better than "the help."[373]

According to Dardy, Beck would acquire five homes. Idella moved her mother into one of them and Alice bounced between it and Hollywood, looking after Lili's home when Lili was on the road, which was a majority of the time.

In fact, with Lili traveling, her first cousin Ellie Hiatt recalled spending weeks during the summers at Lili's home with Alice. She remembered Lili's house as being "beautiful" but "gilded," everything decorated with a lot of "scroll work." There were mirrors on the ceilings over her big round bed that sat on a dais in the middle of her bedroom. The bed was covered with a maroon velvet bedspread.

Still independent, Alice was unafraid to travel on her own and would visit her sister Dorothy ("Dode") in Portland, Oregon. Known interchangeably as "Aunt Maud" or "Aunt Alice" in the family, Alice was always "cheerful" and "had a great outlook on life."[374]

Salome

The busier Lili became and the more involved she was in refining and defining Lili St. Cyr, the less time she had for others. Likewise, now that Barbara was married to Marx, she too had less time for the family. Whether intentional or not, it has to be assumed she had partial responsibility in the rift among the sisters. Barbara, once married to Marx, reverted to her birth name of Ruth Idella (she would go by Idella), forever erasing Barbara Moffett, showgirl, from her resume.

At some point, and maybe it was gradual, there was categorically a pulling away from her old world, probably to fit better into Louis's world of politics and business. Barbara wanted to be a good wife for Louis. Without a career she threw herself into what interested him. Stepdaughter Barbara Marx Hubbard surmised she was creating a different life, one without burlesque clubs and strippers.

Barbara developed intense and varied interests. If physics caught her fancy, then for weeks the house would be covered with books and pamphlets on the subject and she'd have a scientist in the house for salons. When she discovered opera, opera records replaced physics books and that became her entire focus.

Marx had exacting standards and Barbara would have to accommodate him, as his children learned to do. Marx had instructed one of his daughters, "If you want to get married in white, be sure that you live morally. Otherwise, get married in Reno."[375]

Barbara became pregnant and lost twin girls. It was understandably very hard on her.

DARDY HAD BEEN TOURING WITH EARL CARROLL FOR YEARS BY NOW. She adored the producer, songwriter, director, and former World War I pilot who was like a father to his showgirls. Dardy was understudying for the beautiful and kind Beryl Wallace, Carroll's girlfriend, a lush, raven-haired woman some fifteen years younger than Carroll. No one was sure if Carroll still had a wife (French, some claimed)—as she hadn't been seen in years.

With Mr. Carroll's help Dardy earned a small role in the film *Love Happy*. Coincidentally Paul Valentine played a minor role along with Marilyn Monroe in her debut picture.[376] After working until one thirty at the club and then driving back to Eagle Rock, Dardy barely had time to fall asleep before rising for the thirty-minute drive to reach the set by 5:30 a.m. She frequently fell asleep. "When it was time to be on the set," Dardy explained, "no one could find me and it held up production while they looked for me. When they found me I was fired."

At the nightclub Dardy was wined and dined by various VIPs: the president of Mexico, President Alaman (who presented her with a oversize bottle of Schiaparelli perfume), West Coast Mafia boss Jack Dragna, Benny Siegel and his beautiful girlfriend Virginia Hill. It was at Virginia's house that Dardy met handsome actor George Raft and started dating him.

Another mobster Dardy fell for was the Russian-born Alan Smiley, a close friend of Bugsy Siegel's. He had delivered to her at Earl Carroll's giant tubs of ice cream from Schwab's drugstore. On the night of June 20, 1947, Smiley was out to dinner with Bugsy and Virginia Hill. After dinner they returned to Hill's sumptuous Beverly Hills mansion where the "white-haired" Smiley sat "side by side on the davenport" next to Siegel reading the newspapers. At 10:45 p.m. shots burst through the windows. When silence descended, Virginia's beau was decidedly dead. Smiley went into hiding for the next year.[377]

BUT THEN DARDY FELL IN LOVE. JIMMY GREENLEAF WAS A BARTENDER at Rounders, a bar near the Earl Carroll Theatre where the girls would go between shows for cheap hamburgers and a soda.[378] A few months later Dardy and Jimmy drove to Mexico in her new Town and Country convertible (bought with the money Barbara had given her when she married Marx) and got hitched.[379]

Sadly the fun and games ended all too soon. Within weeks of the marriage

Dardy following in Lili's footsteps, sandals and all

Jimmy was fired from his job. While Dardy continued working long hours at Carroll's he would take her new convertible and go out. Sometimes he came home, sometimes he did not. Eight months into the marriage Dardy discovered she was pregnant. Dardy continued working until she could no longer hide her growing belly.

MR. CARROLL HOPED DARDY'S HUSBAND WOULD TAKE CARE OF HER. Sadly he did not.

One night as Dardy returned home—earlier in the day she had warned Jimmy he needed to get a job as she was quitting hers—she found her husband and car gone. Forever.

The next day at the bank she was given more devastating news. Her account had been cleaned out.

In a panic, Dardy called her father. Soon she was hauling her suitcases to Ian's where he and his new wife Marge (Marguerite Green) welcomed her. Ian and Marge were living at Bedlam Manor where Marge graciously turned a bedroom into a nursery.

Dardy is on Earl Carroll's left, Barbara on his right

Dardy started divorce proceedings, alternatively devastated and angry.

Dardy gave birth to a beautiful boy she named Robert Scott, but was known as "Danny." He presumably never saw his father.

There was one more blow to Dardy. On June 17, 1948, her beloved boss Mr. Carroll and Beryl Wallace were killed in a plane crash on their way to a Philadelphia convention. The crew and passengers died from carbon dioxide before the plane plummeted to the ground. The bodies were so badly burned Beryl was only identified by the jewelry she wore. She was buried with Earl Carroll together at Forest Lawn, together eternally.

WHILE LILI STRUGGLED WITH HER OWN DISINTEGRATING MARRIAGE, Dardy waived alimony but was awarded $50 in child support for "month-old Robert" from "night club owner" Greenleaf.[380] She cited "cruelty" and the judge ended her nineteen-month marriage.[381] She hadn't expected her happily ever after to crumble so swiftly. But she was strong. Time to brush herself off and move forward.

Lili encouraged her sister to return to work. Alice could watch the baby, as she had offered.

"After Danny was born," Dardy said, "Grandma did come and take care of him. Alice would come and live at Lili's house when Lili was on the road . . . or between husbands. She took good care of Danny." Alice spent a great deal of her life raising other people's kids. To Lili Dardy would remain grateful. "She picked me up and got me turned around after my divorce. Got me back into show business. It was all Lili's idea."

Dardy went on the road with her guilt and doubt, attempting to regain a foothold in her business and to feel attractive after a pregnancy and a bad marriage.

Dardy brought little Danny to Canyon Drive and Lili would "coo over him," buying him expensive presents.[382] She purchased a gorgeous bassinet with monogrammed linens bordered in fine lace. Alice would make coffee downstairs while Lili shut herself in her bedroom playing with Danny. Something of a fair-weather aunt, Lili did love the baby, but Lili held no sentimental ties to her family. Especially children.

"She would have these little outfits made for him," Dardy said. "Little tailored monogrammed suits. For a two-year-old! I would ask her, 'Where is he supposed to wear this?' And she would say, 'To the opera of course!' She *loved* spoiling us."

But babies were never the end-all for Lili. She certainly didn't want one of her own. By this point in her life everything was about nurturing, building, and sustaining her career. She had her work and her romances and that was enough.

Lili wasn't resting on her laurels. She was inventing new scenarios, sewing costumes, and buying expensive gowns to add to her repertoire. She kept looking to history for infamous women to portray. She would borrow their stories and dance their dreams and dramas. Lili was traveling every few weeks, New York, Miami, Boston, New Orleans, Philadelphia, New Jersey, and on and on.

In Los Angeles when Paul would throw parties at her house for his friends, she would leave or lock herself upstairs. Their fights intensified. She was depressed. She wanted out of the marriage.

As was Lili's way, she wanted escape. She called Miles and begged to go back to Montreal.

"Trouble in paradise, sweetheart?" her agent joked.

"Just get me the hell out of Los Angeles," she told him. "Book me into Montreal. I miss it."[383] And Jimmy Orlando. Jimmy and his wanton ways seemed like a salve after Paul's bickering and put-downs. Every time she left Montreal, things remained in a state of uncertainty with Jimmy. She felt his lack of commitment, yet he wouldn't break with her, soothing her with his sweet talk and his lies, the "perpetual lover."[384] He was always happy to see her and they would start back

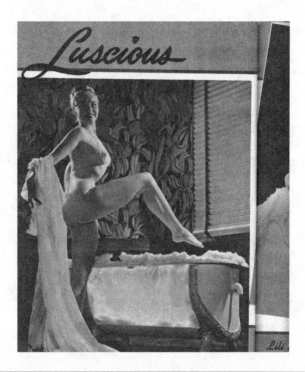

Luscious indeed

up where they had left off, forgetting the world around them. Forgetting other lovers or spouses. Their relationship never moved forward, only stayed swaying in place. Lili's heart broke every time she left, knowing her leaving didn't matter. There was always someone ready to take her place in bed. She would kiss him at the train station, hoping he'd come with her, or at least ask her to stay. But he never did. It would take her days to recover from their good-byes.

All Lili ever wanted from any of her relationships, husbands in particular, was love. She wanted to be adored. Her intentions were pure: love and affection. Words of encouragement and passion and support. She wasn't looking for a husband to support her or buy her things. But she didn't want constant berating and attacks.

With one easy phone call Miles booked her back into the loving embrace of Montreal and Jimmy Orlando.

RUNNING BACK INTO JIMMY'S ARMS WAS LIKE LEAPING FROM THE proverbial frying pan. In the three years she had known him, Jimmy hadn't changed, which, even Lili had to admit, was part of his charm. His infidelity

tormented her. His easygoing manner slayed her. He was romantic, manly, attentive to a fault—but only when she was within eyesight.

Arriving at the newly opened one-thousand-room Laurentien Hotel in April of
1948, "La Belle Lili" met Jimmy in her suite loaded with flowers from the Gayety,
Al Palmer, Al Capps, Eddie Quinn, and a host of admirers.

Her show that night—and in the weeks to follow—was standing room only.
Jimmy sent a car for her after her last show and they began their long and leisurely
crawl to their favorite blind pigs, listening to jazz, greeting old friends, sipping
champagne. It was good to be back. She had missed her pals. And they clearly had
missed her. She was waited on, stared at, whispered about, adored, and admired. She
was truly the "queen of Montreal night life."

After several weeks of bliss Lili was sent crashing back to reality. She heard a
young girl had tried to kill herself after a brief affair with Jimmy. When Lili confronted him about it Jimmy denied it. As he always did. The girl was a nutcase, and
besides it had nothing to do with Lili. He could barely remember the girl's name.
He tried to reason with her that besides being married she went out with other men.

She said she didn't sleep with them.

He told her it broke his heart every time she left Montreal.

And hers broke every time she returned, she said.

Then, unexpectedly, Lili got pregnant. Of course she wasn't going to keep it.
She had another abortion.

Throughout this time, the *married* Lili wasn't exactly faithful herself. Yet she
was utterly wasted by Jimmy bedding younger and prettier girls. It was his cavalier
attitude that bothered her. He was careless with her emotions. She took more pills.

Lili half-heartedly attempted suicide. She was found and saved and filled
with shame. It had been only a dramatic gesture, a wallowing in emotion that she
couldn't express any other way.

Lili would end up attempting suicide often, but never by any means that would
leave her maimed. She would never slash her wrists. She worked in a time when
many entertainers gobbled handfuls of pills theatrically claiming suicide. Lana
Turner would do it. Elizabeth Taylor. Judy Garland and Marilyn had too many
close calls to count. Those were the days of easy access to pills and studio-prescribed
addictions. There was no shame in pills to sleep, pills to wake. Pills to drown sorrow.
Many reached for an easy solution. Lili was just one more star seeking relief. Despite
her personal turmoil Lili rarely missed a show. Only a handful of times in decades
of engagements. Backstage Sadie comforted her employer, telling her to stop all this
"foolishness." *Mr. Jimmy wasn't worth it.* Her maid didn't trust him as far as she
could throw the good-looking bastard.

Lili finished her run at the Gayety. Exhausted from her nightly partying, her spats with Jimmy, she looked thin and fragile. The Gayety manager Conway begged her to take care of herself. "You are a star. We all depend on you." She did not want to disappoint anyone. "You have to take care of yourself." [385]

Lili was burning the candle at both ends. Responsibility and fun. Jimmy and Paul. Hiding and revealing. Stripping and dressing. The twin. Back and forth.

The reporters took note of her new blue hair color, which was really a light rinse. Some called it a "blue headdress." But it didn't matter. "Who looks at her hair, anyhow!"[386] Maybe it was to refocus Jimmy's gaze or an outrageous stunt to procure more publicity, but Lili (as she had with Paul) had washed her platinum tresses in a blue wash and columnist Al Palmer reported it to be "blue mink."[387]

Soon it was all the rage with Canadian "hairdressers reporting customers are seeking information regarding the process in an increasing number."[388] Palmer wrote she was "the tall doll with the blue-mink hair,"[389] as he announced Lili had signed for the title role of a film, *Wolf Woman*.[390]

IN JUNE SHE DEBUTED HER "SALOME" ACT. AL PALMER NOTED SHE GAVE "a fairly good idea of why she remains top box office attraction . . . year in and year out." The act was a "shock" to her audience and "brought the house down."[391] Still she could not tie Jimmy to her.

In July Jimmy greeted her at Windsor Station. The train station was crowded and Lili had a couple of attendants pulling her many trunks along the platform. One trunk carried "her entire collection of antique fans." In the "Salome" number she would wear a seersucker gown "dyed to match" her still "blue-mink" hair.[392]

Her suite was jammed with flowers. The phone rang. It was Eddie Quinn eager to tell her about Jimmy's new love trouble. Another girl. Another overdose when Jimmy refused to marry the girl after she became pregnant.

She confronted Jimmy.

Jimmy said the girl was sick. Lili crumbled in tears. He didn't understand how much she loved him. Or he just didn't care. She felt sick. So sick. She wanted to die.

Lili was back on the phone with Miles, this time begging him to get her out of Montreal. She finished the season before the Gayety closed for the summer "which earned for her the all-time top box office crown along Theatre Row" out of a lineup that included an accordion player, ventriloquist and dummy, juggler, and clown.[393]

"La Belle Lili" escaped to New Orleans. Normally she liked New Orleans only during Mardi Gras, though that meant ten shows a day, but Lili wanted to be done with Jimmy Orlando for good.

LILI ST. CYR

THE
WOLF WOMAN

BETWEEN ENGAGEMENTS, AN INCREASE IN HER SALARY, AND MORE demands from a wide variety of clubs and theatres vying for her body beautiful, Lili continued her on-again, off-again love affair with the bad boy of the ice throughout 1948. She made frequent trips to Montreal, always sucked into Jimmy's vows of "love."

Between turbulent, painful reunions with Jimmy Orlando and equally excruciating separations, Lili needed distraction.

Back in Los Angeles mentoring Dardy was just the thing to occupy Lili. She was going to get Teedles's mojo back. The two were at Lili's house, while two-month-old Danny slept in his beautiful Porthault linen–lined bassinet.

Lili promised to help her with some routines and to get Miles to book Dardy.

Dardy protested that she didn't even have the wardrobe. Lili reminded her that they both knew how to sew. Dardy drove Lili in the car Ian had bought for her as a replacement for the one her lousy husband had stolen to a nearby fabric store for new costumes.

Lili loved to buy beautiful fabric and lace and linen and satin ribbons. She paid for everything. When she died she still had a few plastic boxes filled with scraps of eyelet and ribbons and labels with her name embroidered on them, almost all that remained of her beautiful costumes and her expert handiwork.

Every day the sisters rehearsed at a dance studio on Vine Street that Lili rented, inventing routines for Dardy. Lili hired a piano player to tap out "Manhattan Serenade" while Danny slept in a basket on the floor oblivious to the music.

Lili was training Dardy with acts similar to her boudoir ones. Dardy would lounge on a chaise, dressing and undressing. Dardy worried it would be said she stole Lili's routines.

Lili in casual pants and top tied at her waist and wearing flat Capezzio ballet slippers shrugged her shoulders. She knew press was important, and maybe even better if the sisters were "feuding."

Dardy stayed up late sewing costumes, grateful for her sister's help. Though they often didn't see each other for long stretches that would grow longer in the coming years—life seemed to get in the way, and Lili was busy—Dardy knew Lili was always there for her. Dardy vowed to do the same. That promise, and remembering what her glamorous sister had done for her in her time of need, would sustain Dardy when she spent years running errands for her reclusive sister. It would—*almost*—help her erase the one man in Lili's life that she hated. In Lili's twilight years it would become harder, then impossible, then ultimately heartbreaking to be there for Lili. Going through a pile of evening dresses Dardy had collected over the past seven years, Lili made two piles. She knew a shop on Sunset that would buy them. Dardy ended up getting a few hundred dollars, enough cash for the road.

Miles Ingalls had booked Dardy for two weeks in Montreal, following Lili's two-week engagement. At her sister's suggestion Dardy changed her name to "Dardy Orlando."

The sisters planned to travel together in early September. "How are we going?" Dardy asked.[394]

"You can drive us," Lili said.

"What? Why not the train?"

"Because neither one of us has enough money."

It wasn't unusual for Lili to be short between engagements, which was one of the reasons she worked the better part of the year nonstop. Money kept Lili on the road. "I always need to pay for things," Lili explained.[395] The girls took Dardy's new car. Grandma Alice saw them off with a giant picnic basket filled with egg salad sandwiches. Danny lay in Alice's arms as Dardy waved good-bye.

Dardy loved speed, be it riding her horses or driving cars. She thrilled with her foot on the accelerator.[396] Lili, along with a fear of cramped spaces and heights, was terrified of speed and told Dardy not to go faster than forty miles per hour.

Dardy knew at that rate they would never get to Montreal. Lili sat, sunglasses on, a magazine in her lap, several road maps spread out. She gripped the car door handle. "Forty. And I'll be watching."

But knowing Lili, Dardy had Ian fix the speedometer so it wouldn't read above forty.

"Tweedle—it feels too fast," Lili would say, and Dardy would show her the dial. "I'm not going above forty. See for yourself."

In those days with no interstate highway the route was tricky. The sisters wound through long stretches of road with nothing to distract them, the sun pouring into their eyes until eventually a roadside café appeared.

After a quick bite they started out again with Dardy following Lili's directions as she perused the maps. After several more dull hours with Dardy tired and cranky behind the wheel, Lili exclaimed, "Oh, another café, let's eat. I'm hungry."

Dardy pulled the car over. "These places all look alike," she said. Inside they drank cups of hot coffee, ate steaks, and used the restroom.

"Does this place look familiar to you?" Dardy asked.

Lili looked around. "No."

The waitress came over and said, "Oh, I'm so glad you came back." She held a fur coat. "You left your coat."

The sisters were stunned. They had been driving in a circle. Dardy glared at Lili.

"You're fired from navigating," Dardy said, and grabbed the maps from Lili's hands.

A night in Illinois, the two stopped for a bite to eat as a layer of fog descended on the bus stop restaurant. They ate their hamburgers while the waitress told the sisters how the truck drivers had been complaining about the dangerous roads just north. By the time the girls left the fog was thick and stretched for miles. The two had no choice but to proceed.

"We can't be delayed," Lili cried. "I've never been late for an engagement."

"Well, how am I supposed to see the road?" Dardy worried. The sun had set and it was cold. She couldn't even see the car in the parking lot.

Later in life Dardy would say it must have been because they were both so young—and dumb—that she followed what Lili suggested. "I'll tell you what we'll do," Lili said.

With Dardy clutching the steering wheel she slowly pulled the car through the soup-like air. Lili, wearing her heaviest pantsuit, crouched on the fender of the car, her feet wedged for support on the driver's-side fender.

"I'll guide you by the white line in the road," Lili explained. "If you go over, I'll shout and bang the hood."

Dardy was petrified as Lili leaned out toward oncoming traffic shouting back directions at Dardy. *Keep straight. Veer right. Looks like a truck's in front of us, slow down.*

Dardy slowly continued through the night, thinking, *If Miles only knew what his valuable client was doing at this very moment, he would have a heart attack.* They drove until the fog lifted and a damp, frozen, and triumphant Lili slid back into the car and slept.

AT THE MONT-ROYAL THE SISTERS COULD BARELY NAVIGATE FOR ALL the flower arrangements from admirers piled over every surface of the suite.

Dardy suggested they see the city Lili had been bragging about.

"There's only a couple places we can go where I won't be recognized," Lili said. "I don't want anyone seeing us together. Yet." It was part of the surprise for her new number. It was imperative that no one knew Lili's look-alike sister was in town.

Dardy, used to Lili's idiosyncratic behavior, agreed to stay mostly out of sight for the next two weeks.

Dardy was astounded that her sister was mobbed even just waiting for a taxi outside the hotel. The strikingly tall creature in heels, wearing a full-length fur and diamonds, was too much for the average Canadian on the street. Everyone stared. Lili drew unseemly attention everywhere she went. Dardy had never seen anything like it. Never in New York or Los Angeles. Lili truly was the "Sweetheart of Montreal."

"Don't expect me to walk down the street here," Lili explained. "I can't." But she adored the attention. She played the star for all it was worth.

It was mid-September and Lili was booked at the Gayety for two weeks with the following two weeks headlined by Dardy (billed of course as "Lili St. Cyr's sister").

To Montreal Lili introduced "Suicide," a personal, stunning, revelatory dance that had the audience gasping.

"HARLEM NOCTURNE," A JAZZ STANDARD LILI ADORED, FLOATED OVER the expectant audience. The set was elaborate, a bed and dressing table.

Lili entered as though returning from a date wearing beautiful jewels and a gorgeous white dress. She was radiantly beautiful.

Moving languidly to the sultry music, Lili's entire body seemed encased in sorrow. She changed into a black transparent negligee. Desperation clung to her like perfume. At her dressing table she reached a despairing hand toward an ornate crystal bottle of pills and a waiting glass of champagne. Looking at a photograph of her love in a thick silver frame Lili pretended to swallow a handful of pills. With a last loving look at her "lover's" face she stepped behind a dressing screen on the set—where Dardy waited.

Dressed in an identical negligee Dardy stepped back onstage with her face away from the audience. Everyone assumed it was Lili—who had crawled backstage from underneath the curtain.

Like a sexy somnambulist, her body dripping with hopelessness, Dardy shed her black negligee. She was down to her G-string. Her long legs identical to Lili's. Overcome by the pills, she collapsed to the dark floor, where the shadows absorbed her prone body.

Meanwhile Lili, down to an identical G-string, had crawled back under the curtain behind Dardy, out of sight. Again the darkened stage helped hide her.

A scrim onstage rose, revealing a staircase and clouds floating in the sky (Conway had fought that expense). The lights changed and from behind Dardy's dead frame Lili's "ghost" or "spirit" rose, dreamily walking up the stairs toward heaven as ethereal music played from the orchestra.

It was a masterly piece of theatre and the audience gave her a rousing standing ovation as the curtain closed and Dardy vanished back to Lili's dressing room to hide.

No one had ever dared to bring such a realistic scenario like a suicide to a

"SUICIDE"

Disillusion, is the keynote of his fantasy of love and hatred in which death draws the final curtain.

striptease routine. Her buddy and sometime lover Al Palmer wrote of her "tricky finale" that she "slays the audience with a dramatic suicide bit," noting, "No one has ever died so beautifully on the Gayety's stage."[397]

It was revolutionary and personal. Surely at least some of her audience, especially her die-hard fans, had read about her overdoses. Historically Lili would never be given her due for bringing—even though romanticized—drama, artistic touches, and, more importantly and oft overlooked, *herself* to her work.

In a variation on the theme, Lili looks at a photo of a lover who has jilted her (onstage she was the one always rejected) and steps onto a window ledge to end it all. She thrilled as the audience screamed "no." Part of Lili's fascination and hold over the audience was the sense of expectancy she crafted into her scenes. Expectancy is anticipation, suspense, hope. Would she jump or would she find hope? The audience held its breath waiting for the answer. Would someone rescue her?

"I had to hide the entire two weeks I was in Montreal before I went on," Dardy complained. "Lili didn't want anyone to know how she did it. Oh, she was so proud of that act, and they went *crazy* for her." Lili had once again exceeded everyone's forecasts. All too soon the kind of "suicide" Lili would be known for would be one of rushing to the hospital, stomach-pumping reality. She would stop performing "Suicide" onstage, maybe because it was just too close to home.

CHAPTER NINE

1991

Aknock at the door. The seventy-four-year-old woman shuffled the few feet from the bathroom, her head bent like a wilted flower stem. She carefully kept her watery eyes on her scuffed and worn Capezzio slippers as she navigated—slowly so as not to fall—across the creaky wood floors. Ugly, old, spotted, worn through. She'd have to tell her sister she needed a new pair of slippers. Nothing like the mules she used to wear. The ones with fluff she had in every color. She could never stand, let alone walk, in those anymore. Osteoarthritis spreading throughout her joints. The pain in her back and feet and legs made walking difficult. She could no longer make it the mile to the post office for stamps. Her fans had to send her stamps if they wanted her to write.

One day soon she was going to lie in bed and be unable to get up. She would melt into that drab-looking bed. Gone was the smooth wooden showpiece. Her Montreal masterpiece. The gorgeous Italian antique she had stored and hauled and finally installed on Canyon Drive. *Boy, had that been a disaster.* That bed was constantly being confused with the one she had rented from a prop house that had been Gloria Swanson's from *Sunset Blvd.* All the half-truths, misdirections she had created about—everything—her life. Once. Upon. A. Time.

So many rumors. So many fabrications. She had herself to blame as much as the lazy reporters who had written whatever they were told, where she said anything that popped into her head. Anything but the truth.

Those two "biographies" she had "written" were mostly laughable and hadn't brought in the money she hoped. Sometimes she felt as if she were paying for her sins and this frustrated and angered her. She was so angry. Mad at her feeble body. Enraged at being trapped. Flight to another city had always been her MO. Now she was just old and broken down.

It was offensive, the weakening of muscles that had once been strong, a mind still sharp, but saddened. Everything beautiful gone . . .

Rage, rage against the dying of the light . . .

The knock again. "Come in," she called out. She switched off the bedside lamp, throwing the apartment into shadows. Reaching into her robe pocket, her "bank" these days, she retrieved a twenty. The door opened a crack and a young boy stepped tentatively inside. In his hand was the credit card he used to pop the rickety lock of her front door.

They recognized each other.

She handed him the cash. It was the same meal every night; same rice, same salmon, same twenty bucks, even though the dinner cost ten. He pocketed the credit card and left.

Every night that he worked he got the order and reluctantly peddled down Melrose Avenue, past the gates of Paramount, taking a left on Plymouth, finally stopping in front of the white apartment building. It was creepy the way the newspapers and magazines were taped to all the windows in place of curtains. The thick incense and cigarette smoke could be smelled from the walkway. The dust. The darkness and the old woman with the white cotton-candy hair sitting on her bed in the living room waiting for him like a spider. Her apartment smelled old and like cats; though the felines were long gone, the scent remained. Her soft voice, strangely so feminine, barely heard as she spoke in quiet tones. All alone. The tip was generous from someone who looked as if she didn't have much.

He left her with her memories as she scraped a plastic fork against the Styrofoam container. Not like the clink of silver on china at her beautiful dinner parties. Cocktails, everyone dressed. Seated among a gaggle of admirers, animated and in her element, entertaining her suitors. She had been so happy there, proud of her home that she had created, the epitome of everything she wanted out of life, elegant, refined, high-class, expensive.

Her house had been a showcase. The walls around her now were stained beige. Tom Douglas would be horrified. This wasn't the interiors he designed.

No more suitors. At least Lorenzo was still with her. *Like a weight around my neck.* Her only party guest. He'd brought the "party" to her years ago. Not his fault. He needed the relief for his crumbling body and she needed it—for everything. Now that she could no longer pack a trunk and rush to a city that would embrace her, throw cash at her, fill her with romance and adventure and headlines, she needed the adventure and calmness from the needle. It was like her pills, though faster and stronger.

She sat alone and picked at the rice and vegetables. She could cook a meal better than this. It had been a long time since she'd cooked. Oh, how her house had been so beautiful, with silver, and her linens laid out, all with her monograms: SLC. Everything would be lit by candlelight reflecting the crystal and antiques. The only house she had ever owned. Gone. Her dinner parties had glittered. With Tom and Clifton and Virginia. How much laughter there had been with the stars out overhead, the dark canyon cradling her house. After years on the road her house had been a haven. She had never been able to spend enough time there. The work. She had constantly worked. It had been both an addiction and a necessity. To pay the bills. Though she had the husbands and the rich boyfriends and the jewels and furs, her show was expensive, hauling the props (try shipping a silver heavy tub by rail from club to club) across the country, wearing the designer clothes, out constantly, the chauffeurs, the agents' fees. Then later when there was no more work and no income and an injured boyfriend to pay for, and medical bills and drugs . . . yes, drugs . . . the money had gone. The antiques sold, jewelry pawned, given away, maybe stolen, never to be seen again. Lost. And finally the sale of the house.

Twenty years ago and she still didn't have her house back. Back then, she had been in survival mode, taking care of Lorenzo and making the best of it.

Memory stung. She lit a cigarette, panicked she was almost out. She must call her sister. She had a list. She needed things. Things.

The worn men's pajama bottoms bunched around her knees. It wasn't even from her store, which was still in operation but she couldn't get there. She didn't put on makeup. Why bother? Who would she seduce?

She was left alone and . . . *it is a relief after so many years of "show business."*

Was Lorenzo home? Would he shuffle out of his room or would she creep back there and check on him? Poor pathetic Lorenzo. Once so handsome. Now nearly crippled. Maybe someone would bring her junk soon. Bring them junk and they could float together. That might be nice. There was little they did together besides share a needle.

CHAPTER TEN

Dardy Orlando's debut in Canada was a rousing success. Al Palmer praised her beauty, noting she was "one of four sisters" in the show business family. Lili might have confided in him, something she rarely did, but she was always comfortable with Palmer. He told readers that "sister Lili's tutelage has added to" Dardy's numbers.[398] He ran a gorgeous picture of Dardy. One wonders what Jimmy thought about seeing his name on the Gayety marquee.

Miles was impressed enough to book Dardy in Baltimore following Montreal. In the meantime, Lili carried on with Jimmy, and the sisters would go out after the show to the blind pigs. Dardy would come to cherish them as much as Lili did.

Lili was keeping company with several of the Mafioso that hung around the blind pigs. "Most of the gangsters were on the lam," Dardy said. She remained amazed at the fuss everyone in the clubs and restaurants made over her sister. She was spoiled and doted on. She went out every night. "What wasn't to like about the places? And the men." Dardy understood why Lili preferred Montreal to any other city.

Lili felt love from the audiences. She was making fistfuls of cash. Admirers and lovers sent furs and flowers and bought her expensive gifts. It would take her "hours to open them all."[399]

She would still meet someone for breakfast—or lunch, for a charge. Lili and her unconventional social mores were misunderstood. To Lili it was all publicity. Which meant money. And that's what it was all about. Whatever it took to keep them lining up outside. Whatever it took to keep Lili St. Cyr on top.

Her image also did much to keep Marie hidden. Lili wasn't going to appear vulnerable, except in her numbers; suicide victim, slave girl, or imprisoned queen. She had made Lili St. Cyr wildly desired and extravagant. She had added a dais underneath her bed onstage that "adds to her unattainability."[400] Lili's allure with the audience was that they knew they were never going to be with her.

Lili was living the image she had seen in dark theatres watching Greta Garbo and Jean Harlow. Now she was the one tossing furs and wisecracks. *She* was the one who had men trailing after her. *She* traveled, *she* was fussed over. *She* was a success. *She* had everything. And mostly she loved every minute of it. Who else would hold a champagne press conference for reporters at former wrestler Yvon Robert's Celebrity Lounge at the Mont-Royal Place?

Lili continued with new numbers set in her courtesan-like boudoir with the ever-present tub for the twice-daily shows at two thirty and seven thirty. The Gayety booked vaudeville acts (always an "anti-climax," as Al Palmer reported) with such talents as an accordion act, tap dancers Myers and Walker, acrobats, and Upside Down Emanuel, a girl singer.[401] On Saturdays there was an additional ten o'clock show. But it was the Sweetheart of Montreal people were flocking to see.

For her "Salome" number the audience howled. She mixed it up with the "Wolf Woman," "Love Bird," and "Leda and the Swan." She created a mermaid number with special lighting giving the illusion of being underwater while she "swam" across the stage. Audiences kept returning. *What will she think of next?*

BY THE FOLLOWING YEAR, 1949, PAUL WOULD SEE THE RELEASE OF three of his films: *Love Happy*; *House of Strangers*, a film noir starring Susan Hayward; and *Special Agent*, costarring future television Superman George Reeves. However, he wasn't busy enough to ignore whispers by "friends" eager to tell him about the drama being played out north of the border.

Lili's tumultuous relationship with Jimmy and their sightings around Montreal were chronicled in the papers, raising eyebrows. There were fights, reconciliations, denials of an engagement, of an affair even, denial of suicide attempts. It was only ever a matter of time before news reached Paul.

Paul confronted her in a fury.

There was screaming. Denials. Threats. She was besotted with Jimmy. He was in her hair and breath and skin.

Paul ranted and raved. He shook his finger in her face. Finally he slammed the hotel door behind him. It was August 4, 1949.

With him gone the silence exploded in her head. Her heart was in Montreal but her guilt was in New York. At the Gorham Hotel in Manhattan she threw herself on the bed and wept. She called Jimmy. The two fought.

Crying, she scribbled out a note on the hotel stationery:

PAUL, I'M SORRY I'VE BEEN SUCH AN UNSUCCESSFUL WIFE AND that everything I've tried to do has failed. Please give the money to Alice [she piled a stack of money on the desk] *and give my mink to Sadie. —Lili*

FEELING HOPELESS LILI REACHED FOR A BOTTLE OF PILLS AND SWAL-
lowed too many. She wished for sleep that "would last forever." She was exhausted
and felt as if the world had let her down.[402]

She closed her eyes and drifted.

Paul had, fortunately, returned to the hotel to continue the fight. Along with
the hotel's house detective they broke open room 6-F and found Lili lying nearly
unconscious with an empty bottle of sleeping pills. She was entirely nude. Paul
filled a tub with ice water. When she didn't revive he was forced to call an ambulance that rushed her to Roosevelt Hospital.[403] As furious as he was, Paul didn't
want to lose Lili.

Attempting to protect her privacy, Paul checked her in under her married
name of "Mrs. Marie Valentine." Paul would keep her true identity out of the
papers, initially, until he decided to exploit the fact and garner some press for
himself as hero and savior. In fact he would even turn over the $18 hospital bill
to the tabloids.

When Lili opened her eyes there was the humiliation of doctors and nurses and
tubes. She'd had her stomach pumped. She felt horrible, physically and mentally.

"You saved me." She looked into Paul's eyes, grateful. "So you must care
about me."[404]

Barely recovered she returned to Montreal and Jimmy.

Sadie was disgusted and told Lili Jimmy didn't deserve her. "He runs after a
hockey puck."

"Yes, she did attempt suicide," Dardy said matter-of-factly. "I don't think she
was trying to kill herself. She just wanted the attention. I don't know. When a love
affair went bad she would cry, 'Oh, I have nothing worth living for.'"

She would always say, "The absolutely irretrievable waste of my life . . . are the
times when I haven't been in love."[405]

Often it was Dardy who received the call. Lili had tried to kill herself. Again.
It would grow to such frequency that Dardy's daughter Ava would remember her
parents kept the doctors "on speed-dial."[406]

One time in the fifties, when Dardy was married and living in Las Vegas,
Lili called from Los Angeles. It was after midnight. She was in the hospital. Too
many pills.

Dardy flew there and went directly to the hospital. This was after other
attempts and Lili "wanted to get out before the papers picked it up." Dardy had her
released and took her back to Canyon Drive. "Lili went up to bed. I went downstairs
to sleep in the big bed Lili had in the living room."

She was awakened by a "clanking that disturbed me." Dardy thought, *What's
she up to now?*

The room was still pitch dark with the French shutters closed. Dardy assumed it was the middle of the night and she had been asleep only a short time.

"And I got up and here's Lili coming into the living room with this beautiful wicker tray with a lit candelabra on it. 'What the hell are you doing, Lil?'"

"I'm bringing you breakfast." She had squeezed fresh orange juice and made coffee.

"Lili, it's the middle of the night," Dardy protested.

"Oh, no. No, it isn't. It's eleven in the morning."

"Well, it's so dark in here."

"Well, who wants to have breakfast in the harsh daylight," Lili said, setting down the tray. She kept her shutters firmly closed. "Candelabras are much more flattering."

Lili, concerned with aging even at the height of her beauty, had begun to turn to tricks to flatter. (Soon reviewers would complain about the dim light she performed under.)

Dardy thought she kept the house in shadows all the time. "She'd do this with her lovers, no doubt," Dardy laughed.

Was she a good sister?

"Oh, the best. She was so good to all of us."

But there were times you didn't speak or see each other?

"Well, I couldn't. When *he* got her into drugs. I didn't want anything to do with him. I told her until she got rid of him I didn't want to be around. I couldn't *stand* him." Dardy shook her head, still worked up years after Lili's death. "I didn't know what to do. I didn't know how to help her. I couldn't." A long pause, then quietly: "I couldn't help her."

CHAPTER ELEVEN

One night at the Follies a man named Walter Kane asked to see Lili in her dressing room. Lili thought Kane seemed out of place in a burlesque theatre. Not the type seeking a quick thrill. He was instead all business.

"I work for Mr. Howard Hughes, Miss St. Cyr." Kane was in his fifties, dressed refined, spoke well. He asked her out for a drink and since Paul wasn't around she agreed. Kane's chauffer drove the two to West Hollywood and Kane's chic, bachelor's duplex.[407]

She admired the antiques that filled the rooms. Rooms that were small and painted dark colors, greens and grays and burgundy.

He called for a butler to mix martinis.

"We want to make a film *for* you." It wasn't the first time she had heard that nonsense, usually from someone who wanted to sleep with her. She enjoyed the gin martini and some appetizers that appeared hot and crispy on the butler's silver tray while Kane told her how much Hughes wanted to employee the lovely Lili.

He told her he thought she would be a movie star.[408]

They chatted for a brief time and then Kane called for his chauffer to take her home. She was astounded he hadn't attempted to kiss her. This behavior intrigued her. Most men alone with Lili St. Cyr made passes.

Unbeknownst to Lili, but not to others in the industry, Kane was known to procure and proposition women for the reclusive Hughes. Kane managed Hughes's myriad of starlets stashed around Hollywood. And though most certainly Hughes had arranged the meeting, nothing happened with the eccentric billionaire. Lili probably never even met him. She never mentioned him and she wasn't shy about naming lovers.

Kane himself wasn't known as a lothario, but he did develop a friendship with the leggy stripper. She would claim in her biography to have fallen in love with him, though he wasn't her type, neither rugged nor overly hunky or even particularly wealthy. He was sweet and she always appreciated a man with impeccable manners. Maybe because of the turmoil with Paul and Jimmy she needed attention from someone new, someone to take charge and take care of her. Maybe she was holding out hope Hughes would appear. As starlet Jeanne Carmen would describe it, when Kane came calling for her on Hughes's behalf, she was impressed by the charming, "dapper" man.[409] Like Lili she had endless meetings with Kane, waiting for Hughes to show up—who didn't in the six months the farce played out.

Paul would later claim that "Lili turned on her charm" for Kane because of his movie connections.[410] But Lili cared so little for being an actress. She would do it, but she hardly pursued it. The stage was her domain and Lili never had delusions about where her appeal lay.

A pattern developed where Kane's driver showed up at the Follies to chauffer Lili back to his apartment for drinks and a late dinner. Perhaps Kane was working off instructions and waiting for Hughes to make his move; most likely the apartment was owned by the millionaire and kept for trysts.

Lili grew dependent on this older man. He became the support she wasn't getting at home. Kane seemed to make no demands of her. She was impressed with the chauffer and butler. During the worst of the fighting with Paul, Kane persuaded her to move out.

He paid for a suite at the Roosevelt Hotel, which looked across at Grauman's Chinese Theatre. She was melancholy. Another breakup.

Days later Lili finished her run at the Follies and noticed the absence of Kane's chauffer. She called Kane. She missed him and their chats.

"I have to call you back," he said abruptly, and hung up. She had three days of no work before she would have to leave for New York. She waited. No call. It wasn't like him. Attentive, sweet Walter. She called again, no answer. She began to feel desperate. Had she done something wrong?

She turned frantic. Impulsively she swallowed a handful of pills. "I had nothing to live for," she explained later.[411] In her Canadian biography she wrote she took "thirty-six pills," which in Canadian slang meant one hundred. But whatever amount she took it was enough to do the job.

Her last thought before she fell unconscious was, *I won't have to pay my damn taxes.*

Two days later she woke, her body paralyzed. She managed to crawl to the phone with great effort, her head pounding, her limbs shaking. She had to call someone. Who, Walter? Paul? Her mouth, dry and heavy, couldn't form words. She felt darkness descend once again though she tried fighting it. Her eyes closed. She stretched a hand toward the phone before succumbing.

Someone at the hotel discovered her, half-naked, sprawled as if dead across the bed. Walter's chauffer showed up. Perhaps the hotel manager, who knew who was paying the bill, had alerted Kane. Lili's semiconscious body was dressed, coffee poured down her throat. She was made to walk the length of the room.

Someone was saying, "You're really a lucky young woman."

"I don't feel lucky," she either replied or thought she did. Husband trouble and income tax woes weighed heavily on her.

Why did Kane never show up? He was said to be genuinely caring and would have been empathetic toward Lili. He too had taken an overdose of sleeping pills before Christmas of 1947.

It would be Paul that drove Lili home.

She flew to New York for an engagement at the Samoa. "I never miss an opening," she told Paul when he protested.

"You must really have wanted to leave that Mr. Paul if you took a plane," Sadie commented. Lili looked and felt terrible.[412]

Sick and dizzy all week, Lili soldiered on. The Samoa was home. Work was safe. Once again Lili had survived but she was left disheartened and uninterested in the men flocking into the club trying to reach her.

Sadie tried to cajole her out of her bad mood. "It's not like you, Miss St. Cyr, to not be interested in men."

"Maybe I will be next week." Lili told Sadie to get her off her back.[413]

LILI CONTINUED TO BREAK BOX OFFICE RECORDS WITH HER "CHRYSIS" act (Chrysis was a courtesan in the French-language novel *Aphrodite*). Her latest character was a woman proud of her figure and how men fawned over her.[414] Her creations were infamous, immortal, and steeped in history and mythology.

In August Paul filed for divorce, "citing cruelty." Lili read about it in the papers. Paul, in his usual dramatic fashion, had told reporters "the only time I saw her much was when she was working in Los Angeles. She was cold and distant to my friends. I couldn't even turn on the radio because she hates music and comedy." He griped, "Everyone could see more of her than I could." Lili "would lock herself in her room and did not speak" to him or anyone else. Except for seeing movies starring friend Clifton Webb and listening to Jack Benny on the radio, she was "antisocial."[415]

Lili was despondent. Romance once again had slipped between her fingers. Why couldn't happiness find her?

Sadie urged her to forget Paul. Sadie had the right—usually funny—thing to say. She was nobody's fool and she always stuck up for Miss. St. Cyr.

Lili, never contentious, quickly worked out a settlement with Paul. He would be allowed to stay in her beloved house (that she didn't yet own) for two years.[416] She was permitted to keep "title to the couple's Hollywood home" provided "she will keep up the payments" (which it has to be assumed meant the rent).[417] As she was booked solid for the next year, that wouldn't be a problem.[418]

Lili (and Dardy) would always claim Lili was the first woman in California to pay alimony. "She didn't have bitter divorces."[419] Lili would set her exes up in business or pay for apartments. So friendly did the two become postmarriage that she continued to let Paul choreograph for her. They even posed for a photo shoot in Malibu. She liked Paul much better now that her responsibility to him was legally severed.

Catty columnist Dorothy Kilgallen claimed Lili's "divorce boosted her fame and popularity" and she benefited from the publicity surrounding such, commenting that her autographed pictures were flying out of the lobby at performances.[420]

In May of 1952 Paul would marry Flaveen Sultana Abdul Ali Khan, daughter of an Iranian businessman. They would start a mail-order lingerie business and Paul would rechristen her as "princess" Flavine Ali Khan, claiming she was the shah of Iran's niece. The lingerie business was a venture Paul had once encouraged Lili to start.

Paul would spend the rest of his life toiling in small parts in films into the eighties, telling whoever would listen that he was responsible for Lili's unprecedented success. Though by then, sadly, few remembered—or cared—about Lili St. Cyr.

CHAPTER TWELVE

For Lili life continued to be a series of alternating highs and lows. From Riley's in Saratoga Springs in August of 1949, where she was noted for "tasteful strips that induce a session of orb-popping," to the low of September when her divorce from Paul came through.[421]

The finality of the divorce sent Lili into a tailspin. In a fit of hopelessness, she was once again depressed. She swallowed a handful of pills. Unlike her character onstage she was rescued and returned to earth before she had a chance to ascend to heaven.

Lili was once again single. But not for long.

By October Lili was ready for a new man. "I like to spoil men. That's my hobby," she proudly stated.[422] She didn't have time to watch TV, no *Lone Ranger* or *Kukla, Fran and Ollies*. She probably didn't listen to Perry Como sing "A Dreamer's Holiday" or even Sinatra's "If I Ever Love Again." Sinatra was something of a regular at the Samoa, having haunted the street in the thirties listening to jazz and then the strip clubs in the forties and fifties.

She was thirty-two years old, besieged with suitors. *Lili, can you meet me for a drink? Lili, can I take you for a walk? Lili, can I do anything for you?* The chauffer-driven limos would line up outside the club waiting for her. Champagne corks would fly. There weren't enough hours in the night. The men would do anything for her, pay for hotel suites, buy her jewels. Lili tried to believe she was happy.

THE 1950S WOULD BE A TIME OF TREMENDOUS ACTIVITY FOR LILI. THE name Lili St. Cyr and her exploits would fill columns and pages inside numerous tabloids and newspapers. Her lustful form would grace countless men's magazines. She was celebrated, envied, lauded, gossiped over.

There was growing expectation about her shows. Could she keep topping herself? Audiences expected a lot from the "uninhibited and exotic Lili St. Cyr."[423] It was a lot to live up to when they were screaming, "Exotic, svelte charming Lili St. Cyr is the outstanding striptease of the nation."[424]

Lili's stomach was constantly upset. If she wanted, she could drink some of that newly invented Maalox, which helped the burning.

Added worry was when Sadie spoke of her children, back home in New York. Lili was afraid Sadie would abandon her permanently for them. Lili resented the pull children had (Barbara, Dardy, Sadie, husbands, later the mere mention of someone getting married would make Lili worry they'd have kids and she'd be left).

The average person's salary in 1950 rose to $3,210 per year. Significantly less than what Lili pulled, now upwards of $2,000 a week. And oftentimes in cold, hard, undeclared cash.

Lili rarely took a day off. If she had had time to see them, she would have loved that year's crop of films: *Samson and Delilah, Cinderella*, and *Father of the Bride*. All different forms of fantasy. Right up her alley. Diner's Club introduced the first credit card, nothing Lili bothered with, as she trusted neither banks nor borrowing. She preferred to stuff cash in her purse, her garter, and wherever else she could hide it. Fats Domino, Nat "King" Cole, and Patti Page dominated the charts. Eight million homes had television sets, which even after a brief rise in burlesque began the slow death march of many nightclubs as audiences opted for the ease of being entertained in the comfort of their own homes. Television, along with the loosening of standards, would eventually erode Lili's audience. For a while Lili remained safe, but the times were changing and she was not unaware of it. For now she continued selling out, still a one-of-a-kind legend that everyone wanted to see.

After her Montreal debut, with a two-week break before starting in Baltimore, Dardy returned to New York. She hooked up with Miles, who began escorting her around introducing her to important people, as he had done for Lili years earlier.

At a party at the Waldorf Astoria, Dardy, now platinum-haired (as she had to be for "Suicide"), sat off to the side, like Lili intimidated by social settings. She too felt less sophisticated and interesting than the other guests, which often made her come across as stuck-up. A man sat near her. He was wearing a tweed jacket and smoking a pipe, attractive, but not ravishingly so. She liked his eyes. Gentle, warm, and humorous.

"Hello," she said.

"Hello," he said. He was soft spoken. He lit her cigarette.

"I'm Dardy Orlando."

"Hmmm." He looked her over. "I'm Harold Minsky."[425]

The Minsky family was the biggest name in burlesque. A Minsky had introduced stripping to America in the twenties. Harold was a second-generation

burlesque producer. His father Abe and Abe's brothers started producing shows at the Winter Garden theatre in New York, first showing racy films and then bringing in vaudeville performers. Legend had it that Mae Dix in 1917 removed a sleeve cuff in a Minsky show and the crowds went wild. Stripping had sprung from the genie's bottle and burlesque exploded with peeling—and peelers—in demand.

Harold, Abe's adopted son, started his career as a teenager taking over the running of theatres in the summer while his parents vacationed in Europe. One summer he made over "a million dollars" when he didn't close the theatre, as was typical of the time because there was no air-conditioning. On his return Abe told young Harold, "It's all yours," and handed over the reins.[426]

When Dardy met Harold he was thirty-five and still living with his overprotective, overcontrolling mother.

Harold's most recent plan was to open the Colonial Inn in Florida. Originally built as a gambling casino, mobster Meyer Lansky had bought the club for $80,000 from Lou Walters in 1945.[427] With a handshake (and supposedly $200,000), Minsky took it over from Lansky when gambling was outlawed.[428]

When Dardy was ready to leave the party Harold offered to see her home. All the while she was thinking, *This is who I want to be with. Forever.*

Instead of dropping her at her hotel Harold took her to Toots Shor's for dinner where they stayed until 2 a.m.

Dardy finally fell into bed at her hotel, unable to sleep, entranced by this brown-eyed man.

The next morning Miles called and told her she had booked the Colonial Inn.

Harold sent Dardy dozens of roses and a telegram telling her to call him as soon as she arrived in Florida.

In Florida Dardy headed straight to the Colonial Inn where rehearsals were in full swing. It was November and the club was set to open December 24. The club sat one thousand and Harold planned to sell drinks cheaper than the competition.

Harold dropped what he was doing and came over to greet Dardy. "You'll have dinner with me? Tonight?"

THAT NIGHT THEY DROVE TO PALM BEACH. IT WAS A BALMY, STARRY night with a salty breeze blowing off the ocean. They were suddenly and unexpectedly in love and the only obstacle was his jealous mother who quite literally held the purse strings. Harold insisted they hide their relationship, telling Dardy his mother didn't approve of girls in "show business."

LEFT: *Dardy and Harold Minsky, partners on and off the stage*

Dardy could only wonder what that meant. His brothers and father had all been in "show business." She put off thinking about it. Months would pass blissfully as they began a grand romance.

"MINSKY'S FOLLIES" PROVED TO BE A HIT WITH THE "HOITY TOIGHTY" crowd that jammed the place. A "lavish affair," exclaimed the trades. Dardy, "a parade whose act is more display than strip," was working on a bill that included Lili's old friends Corinne and Tito.[429] The show featured a popular juggler who bounced balls on the floor while upside down, eighteen chorus girls, and Carrie Finnel, the heavyset grandmother of strippers, (probably in her late forties at the time) whose enormously popular act generally consisted of bouncing her enormous boobs in and out of her dress.

Very soon Dardy became an integral and invaluable part of Harold's life, both onstage and off. Eventually she would help him train and name strippers. Harold would conquer Las Vegas, Chicago, and every major city that had burlesque.

Answering an ad in the Chicago paper, Lili's old friend and choreographer Ivan Fehnova was hired by Dardy and Harold to choreograph at the Rialto Theatre. He would work there for years.

In the meantime Dardy was frustrated with how things weren't progressing—personally—with Harold. Or rather, with Harold's mother. Working a club in Wisconsin, Dardy got a call from Harold's friend, Charlie Hogan, vaudevillian agent and future agent of Bob Hope.

"Harold's in the hospital, doll," Charlie told her.

"What? And I'm stuck here in Wisconsin." She was frantic but managed to make it to Chicago.

Both the mother and sister were outside Harold's room. They refused to let Dardy see him.

"He's resting," the mother said.

"He's only seeing family," the sister said.

Upset, Dardy went back to her apartment and called Fehnova. He rushed over and the two drank copious amounts of vodka until they were both so drunk they ended in a heap of tears on the floor.

A couple of miserable days later Harold called, and Dardy told him it was over. "I'm leaving," she said.

"Why?" He sounded so pathetic her resolve almost ended.

"Because you will never stand up to your mother." She related her humiliation. "And I was so worried about you."

Harold didn't want to lose Dardy. He asked her to be his wife.

"What about your mother?" Dardy didn't believe Harold. They had been through forced separations due to his mother traveling with Harold.

"She'll have to relent," Harold assured her.

"I doubt that." What Dardy didn't know, and wouldn't discover for years, was that Harold made an agreement with his mother; to appease her he agreed to give his mother half of everything he earned.[430] The disapproval of Mama Minsky even made the papers, which reported, "Friends are trying to reconcile Harold Minsky and his mother."[431]

On a spring day in 1950, Harold and Dardy, with Fehnova in the backseat, drove to Elkhart, Indiana, to get married. Fehnova popped a bottle of champagne that was chilling in a bucket of ice as soon as Harold started driving. He and Dardy indulged, as did Harold. And then another bottle was popped.

During the five-minute ceremony, the very drunk Fehnova could barely stand, crying throughout. In his usual dramatic fashion he dabbed an oversized white silk handkerchief to his eyes.

A kiss on the lips between bride and groom and the small party piled back in the car to return to Chicago. Fehnova and Harold dropped Dardy at the apartment and continued on to the theatre. The show must go on.

"No honeymoon trip," Dardy would write in her unpublished biography.

Dardy headed to California to retrieve three-year-old Danny from Alice, who had been "raising him."[432] Lore in the family would have members believe Danny renamed himself (he was originally born Robert) after Harold adopted him. But an interview Alice gave when the toddler was still living with her clearly shows Danny was called by that name prior to Harold's adoption. It most likely was Alice who named him Danny after her father, Daniel.[433]

Neither Harold's mother nor sister had spoken to Dardy since the marriage.

When Ava, Dardy and Harold's daughter, was born in 1953, "the mother" (as Dardy referred to her) thawed "slightly," thrilled with having a granddaughter. Dardy invited her mother-in-law over for pie. Dardy served a beautiful apple pie she had made herself. Unbeknownst to Dardy—who was never very domestic—she had substituted salt for sugar. Harold's mother choked. "I never tried *that* again," Dardy said.

Life got very busy for Dardy, working for and with her new husband and now with two children to raise. She and Lili sometimes went months without speaking, let alone seeing each other, unless Lili was booked into a Minsky theatre. They kept in touch when they could, both experiencing ups and downs, rarely letting the other know the source. They had never been *that type of family*.

CHAPTER THIRTEEN

Lili returned once again to Montreal and another fight with Jimmy. Deeply wounded she confronted him about his latest affair. Now that she was free of Paul she wanted Jimmy to marry her.

Jimmy tried smooth-talking her. "I suffer when you are away." His dark eyes bore into hers. But she was really angry this time.

She swore at him. "I'm done, Jimmy. I'm really truly done."[434]

He too was growing weary of their fights.

Lili could never trust him. He was full of lies. He was never going to marry her.

Shortly after she broke it off with Jimmy, she started an affair with his younger brother Fortunado. "Frankie" was cute, rugged, a miniature Jimmy. Lili entertained Frankie at her suite at the La Salle. It wasn't solely to get back at Jimmy, though surely that played a part in her decision to bed him. He too had played hockey, for the Wimberley Lions. He was calm and reliable, things Jimmy was not. But there was no swirling passion either. She would never feel about him the way she did about Jimmy.

Frankie couldn't believe his good fortune to be dating the "Queen of Montreal." He believed Lili when she told him Jimmy was in the past. She kissed his doubts—and hers—away.

Frankie adored Lili and was attentive, faithful, and kind. He was a "relief" after Jimmy, who acted as if he didn't care.[435] Jimmy began dating a showgirl nicknamed "Bunny," whom he would marry. Lili avoided Jimmy when she could but in the tight-knit world of Montreal their paths often crossed. Several times the two couples were in the same club, mutual friends waiting for a fight to break out. One that never did.

Lili acted as if she'd never even been with Jimmy. Finally the pretense got to Jimmy and he confronted her at El Morocco. In a lather he stopped her on her way to the ladies' room.

"Why my younger brother?" Jimmy asked her.

"Because he's here," was her not-so-romantic reply. "I like him. He's nice."[436]

She was cold to Jimmy. She didn't owe him any explanations.

Jimmy left Montreal—for where, Lili didn't care—and the tension dissipated.

Lili's and Frankie's favorite restaurant was the Samovar, which looked like old Russia. Waiters bustled around in traditional Russian costume. The food was interesting and afterward Frankie would take her dancing at one of the clubs, like the roof of the Mont-Royal or Bellevue Casino. And then Algiers. Everyone dressed to the nines. The night and the partying never seemed to have an end. The same faces meeting and mingling night after laughter-filled night. Lili enjoyed the rush when she made her jaw-dropping entrances, hand on hip, surveying the place to see whom she knew, to make sure others had time to recognize her. Waiters bowed, customers turned and followed Lili's saunter as she made her way—slowly—across the crowded room. They whispered, they watched. She dressed for effect in gorgeous gowns, off the shoulder, white taffeta, diamonds on her neck and wrists. Black fur over her shoulder. A white mink stole.

OCCASIONALLY A MOMENT MIGHT BE RUINED BY SOME IDIOT WHO unknowingly asked, "Where's Jimmy?"[437] She ignored them and clung to Frankie, making it clear she was with him.

Saying good-bye to the deeply infatuated Frankie, Lili and Sadie packed their trunks for Florida. Lili was headed to the Colonial Inn.

Over the coming years Lili would work at many Harold Minsky–run theatres between standing contracts with other producers. She generally liked working for Harold, whom she admired greatly.

In Florida one day Lili looked up and a plane overhead was writing her name in smoke across the sky. Harold, an inventive showman, thought to take advantage of Lili's name in his club in a spectacular way. Harold would do anything to make Lili happy. She brought in more money than anyone. Harold treated her with great respect, catering to her every whim, including filling her beloved basket full of cash.

With crowds lining up to get a look at Miss St. Cyr, Harold would ask Lili to add another performance (in Chicago that sometimes meant six daily). Cheerfully she would take out a little basket woven with pink satin ribbon and ask, "How many shows do you want, Harold?" Lili didn't give anything away for free.

"What do you want? Name it. I *need* to add another show."

"I need a set of sterling silver flatware," and she proceeded to tell him exactly which set—Dardy had the same.[438] And Harold would send someone to buy Lili a set of the Reed and Barton Baroque pieces she wanted. Or she would ask for an elaborate silver tea set. Harold didn't mind. She was worth every ounce of metal.

The basket traveled with Lili, who told other producers to fill it as Minsky did.

All was well in Florida until Frankie showed up. Lili didn't appreciate the surprise. After a couple of days she begged him to go back to Montreal. He was cramping her style.

It was one thing to have him take her out in Montreal, quite another for him to trail after her on the road. It can be assumed without the eyes of Jimmy on her Frankie lost his appeal. A dejected Frankie left.

With the amount of shows and little sleep Lili could become irritable. She wasn't always having fun on the stage. It was a lot to prepare for. But she kept on. Always tired, always needing to sleep. Needing her pills.

She would start claiming she didn't like being on the stage anymore but the money was too great to stop. She even spoke of friction with her new brother-in-law. Lili was feeling the pressure.

OUT OF THE PAST, LILI'S FATHER, EDWARD VAN SCHAACK, WROTE HIS famous daughter, saying he wanted to meet.

Lili asked Alice's advice. Alice told her to ignore the letter. Lili did, with no regrets. He would never try contacting her again.

She was thirty-three, making her own way, and she didn't need him. Daddy Ben had been the only father she had ever known and Ian a warm substitute. There was no room for anyone else. Edward Van Schaack would die in 1962 in Spokane, Washington, without ever having met his adult daughter Marie.

CHAPTER FOURTEEN

By the summer of 1950 Lili was madly, deeply in love again.

Armando Orsini was five years her junior, born in New York, but Italian by nationality; he had lived in Rome until recently. His birth name was Cocchi, but "it sounded too much like 'cock,'" he explained. "I didn't like it."[439] So he (like so many in Lili's life) changed his name to Orsini—which was the name of a Roman noble family dating back to the eleventh century.[440]

Armando was 100 percent Lili's type. Dark, handsome, impeccably dressed, and sophisticated with beautiful manners. After the disasters that were Paul Valentine and Jimmy Orlando, Armando's worldly manners, kindness, and over-whelming sophistication fed Lili's heart and ego. She would write that he was the only one that made her forget Jimmy. He was powerful in bed. Passionate and tender, though oftentimes she woke bruised.[441] The only evident problem was Armando barely spoke English, which wasn't enough to stop them from embarking on a whirl-wind affair. His interests were in architecture. He had been trained as a civil engineer at the University of Rome and his father had been an engineer graduating at the University of Torino. He had come to America to build not only a career and a life but a new persona. The typical immigrant making good, shedding his name and past to become who he wanted, who he invented. They had a lot in common.

They met at a party in Greenwich Village. They began to meet after her show at the Samoa. He had been in America seven months.

Columnist Earl Wilson reported a different story. He wrote that even though Lili was making $1,000 a week she was still supplementing her income by charging men for dates. Armando overheard a suitor asking if he could telephone Lili. Everyone knew that Lili "charges $150 for her phone number."[442] When the suitor balked at the price she told him to send two roses with a $100 bill wrapped around each rose. The suitor left. Armando stepped in and told Lili he would pay, "but on the installment plan." Lili was charmed.[443]

"We didn't communicate," he recalled. "My accent. Love. Passion, but not communication."[444] He didn't know the language barrier had nothing to do with it.

There was something about the smooth, sincere Mediterranean that—for a time—soothed the restlessness in Lili. He didn't pick and berate and demand of her like Paul. Nor was he cavalier with her feelings like Jimmy. He wasn't clingy and insecure like Frankie. He wasn't like the dozens of others who tried to woo her, sans manners and elegance and charm. He was every inch the prince. She wanted to be with Armando. She wanted to smother him with attention and love. Just one caveat, she was booked for months in advance and the only way they could be together was if he followed her, putting any kind of career he wanted on hold.[445]

In the beginning she kept him away from the clubs where she stripped. "I never saw the show," he claimed.

Armando put his plans, his "construction company building a school in Queens," on hold and followed the enigmatic goddess. He would be her loyal, attentive lover. In return she promised him her work would be temporary. "I'll be quitting soon, Baby," she assured him.[446] And maybe, for a time, she actually meant it.

Five months after their affair began he was driving her to Los Angeles for an engagement at the Follies. Spending the night at motels across the country he was surprised to find she would huddle inside, refusing to go with him to sunbathe at the pool. He thought it was because she didn't want tan lines. With Lili he was never exactly sure. Their verbal communication was limited. But he knew he loved her. She was exciting in bed, and he was a fierce lover.

"*Leelee*, come with me to the pool," he begged.

"I can't give them for free what they have to pay to see in the theatre," she explained, lying in the hotel room, reading her endless supply of magazines. "You go sit by the pool, baby." She would become increasingly sensitive and reclusive about being seen offstage, fearing sightings of a nearly naked Lili would decrease her paying audience.

In Flagstaff, Arizona, Armando drove the convertible she had bought him into town.[447] The city alongside Route 66 was near enough to the Grand Canyon to be a popular tourist destination.

"Marry me, Lili." He pulled the car to the side of the road and took her in his arms.

They checked into a hotel and with the help of the manager found a justice of the peace.

Armando's knowledge of the English language was so appalling that Lili couldn't help but laugh during the brief ceremony. The justice of the peace thought the two were being disrespectful and gave them a lecture that if they weren't taking the ceremony seriously, he wouldn't marry them.

They assured him they were deadly serious, and "in love," Lili added, clasping Armando's hand.

After the ceremony Lili sent telegrams to Miles and Dardy.

With Paul thankfully out of her Canyon Drive house Lili was free to settle back into her beloved home.

However, habits were hard to break, and when Armando asked about her family—he would meet Dardy only once—she told him her parents were dead. Same with her grandparents. Was it just easier for Lili? Did she think Armando wouldn't be around long enough to discover the truth?

Armando would never hear of Jack and Betty, who were completely out of the picture by now, having been totally erased from her biography.

He would meet Barbara, who apparently wasn't completely out of Lili's life, though soon she would be "forbidden to talk to Lili."[448] Armando remembered a conversation Lili had with Louis Marx in her home. "I will give you $100,000 to open something . . . a lingerie shop . . . a hat store . . . something respectable," Louis Marx offered.

Armando thought Marx was a "son of a bitch." The type that made deals, *if I give you this, you must do this* type. But Lili was too independent for Marx and his offers.[449]

Lili stared at Marx and continued smoking. Why the hell was he offering to set her up in business? He was uptight and seemed to care so much about appearances and bettering one's self. Marx was controlling, admittedly star-struck—he could have been simultaneously attracted and repulsed by Lili and her profession. Lili had seen it in the faces of many men. They desired her yet wanted to tame her. Thought less of her. *Stripper.*

Just to look at her Marx knew she was doing well, diamonds around her throat, pearls on her wrists. There was a car out front, a house. She had beautiful things scattered around her house, crystal and silver sets and antiques.

The house was quiet. Barbara, Dardy, and some friends were on the patio. Did Lili remind him Barbara had been in the same line of work? Did that make Marx determined to buy Lili out of stripping?

She always had fantasies about designing clothes and lingerie but she was a *star* now. And she did not like being told what to do.

"Take your $100,000 and shove it," Armando remembered Lili saying. How she must have relished towering over the diminutive bully. She wasn't going to let Marx get to her. The sisters were close. Nothing could come between them.[450]

Not long into Barbara's—now Idella's—marriage, Lili found it increasingly difficult to reach her. Phone calls went unanswered for long stretches of time. "Lili loved Barbara," Armando said. "She was very hurt by Barbara."[451]

Despite her new marriage Lili immediately returned to work, eight sold-out weeks at the Follies. Then an offer came from a prominent nightclub that would change her life forever.

THE 1950S SAW A "SHUTTERING" OF MANY BURLESQUE THEATRES.[452] The old comedians were dying out. No one young was getting into the business. To compete with movies and television the few remaining theatres and nightclubs added more strippers.

The fifties was still a "romantic" time, but an earthy rawness and the loosening of sexual taboos were changing pop culture. Where did Lili fit in? For the time being she was staying firmly in fantasy with her dreamy stories and her tame sort of tease. She was experiencing an unprecedented amount of work and fame. It would be her most prolific decade—both personally and professionally. One can wonder, with the grueling pace she kept, how she managed to stay at the top, but indeed it was the relentless working, being seen, traveling from club to club, and no days off that kept her name glaring from the marquee and the newspapers.

On February 23, 1951, Lili debuted at the swank Los Angeles nightclub Ciro's, a hot Hollywood watering spot. It was a very big deal for Lili and she knew it. All of Hollywood would be there. Movie stars, producers, directors.

On the night of her debut she was scheduled to open with a show at 11 p.m., but didn't end up going on until close to 12:30. As she entered in a long gown and big hat, a hush fell over the crowd.

It was the usual boudoir setting with the centerpiece being an ornate transparent bathtub with colored lights beneath. The stage was "designed to resemble two connecting rooms, a posh bedroom and an oversized bath."[453]

Off came the $5,000 mink, then the opera-length gloves and gown. Stepping behind a shimmering screen her clothes were shed. She gingerly stepped into the tub. Sadie was there to wrap her in a huge towel. Lili danced lightly, then proceeded to dress.

The applause was refined, which reflected the caliber of the audience, not her performance. *Variety* noted Lili performed "no bumps" but she was derogatorily called "lower Main striptease."[454] It would have no bearing on the box office for the two weeks she was booked. Lili St. Cyr was a must-see event. One clever columnist noted the stars seeking the "new and exciting were hardly disappointed at the gal who might now be remembered as 'Lili St. Cyr-o.'"[455]

In March Lili returned to Ciro's, smashing all prior records for a standing-room crowd of 650. Hedda Hopper marveled that Lili's engagement was "bringing out many of our stars who seldom go to nightclubs."[456] An ordinance banning

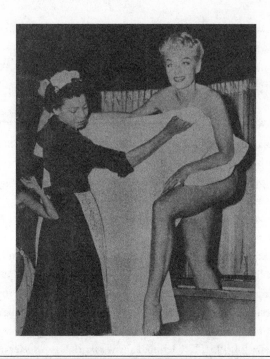

Lili and her beloved Sadie

strippers had been passed in Los Angeles, yet that hadn't stopped "Mayor Fletcher Bowron and Sheriff Eugene Biscailuz" and at least "100 city fathers" from attending Lili's show, enjoying Lili splashing in her tub.[457] It seemed the city's fathers were only too happy to allow Lili her act.

She returned again in April though the "city bigwigs" were cracking down on burlesque in clubs. STRIP-TEASE ENDS TONIGHT, the headline screamed. An ordinance was passed by the board of supervisors to "control obscene nightclub shows." Stripping along with female impersonators was now illegal "in county territory."[458]

ONE NIGHT WITH ARMANDO LILI VISITED STRIP CITY TO SEE GAY Dawn, a Doris Day look-alike who was being compared to Lili, but whose average beauty was no match or threat. Dawn performed a vigorous bathtub strip. She was a protégé of Lillian Hunt and Lillian wanted Lili to see her. Lili was nothing if not loyal.[459]

So popular was Lili's act that Ciro's began hawking her bubble bath in the lobby. "The perfumed water" was the "first time strip act plugged a scent." *Billboard* marveled as she was "smashing" records for the club.[460] She was on top of the world.

Unbeknownst to Lili there was hunting in the air.

DARDY AND HAROLD WERE IN TOWN, STAYING AT THE BEVERLY HILTON and attending an event when mid-cocktail Dardy started to feel "dreadfully ill" and doubled over. "I really feel bad," she managed to gasp to Harold. In minutes she was being rushed to nearby Cedars-Sinai hospital in excruciating pain.

"Call Lili," she instructed Harold as she was being examined. Dardy thought, *Lili will know the top doctor.* Alice had recently had her gallbladder removed and the procedure had gone well thanks to Lili, who handled everything, even choosing the doctor. Harold found Lili at Ciro's. Lili promised to come as soon as her last show ended.

About two in the morning, a gorgeously made-up Lili St. Cyr swept into the hospital looking for her little sister, a fur draped over her arm, a veiled hat on her coiffed head, diamond earrings dripping from her lobes.

Harold ushered her into Dardy's private room where Lili tossed her fur on a chair and took control. "Dardy, what is it?" Lili bent over her sister's bed. Harold was sweating, near tears, "a wreck." Dardy had been given four or five shots of morphine but nothing was helping.

"Gallstones," Dardy croaked. "They want to operate. I don't know any doctors here. I need your help." Dardy was scared.

"Let me speak with the doctor," Lili got up. "Where is he?"

In the hallway Lili conferred with the doctor. "It is very serious," he assured her. "We need to operate soon."

"Will she have a scar?" Lili asked.

"She will. I don't imagine it will be too bad—"

"But she will have a scar?"

"We need to operate, or she could die."

Lili turned and clicked her high heels back into her sister's room. "Dardy, can you hear me?" Her gloved hands rested on either side of Dardy's shoulders. Lili's face was grim.

"Yes, I can hear you." Dardy was pale and shaking. "Please, can I have some water? I'm so thirsty."

The nurse standing by shook her head no. Lili went to the sink and wet her linen hanky and patted Dardy's parched lips.

Lili inched her face closer. "Dardy, do you understand what I'm saying?"

Dardy's pain was ever increasing. "Oh, please let me die. I'm in such terrible pain." She had never felt such agony.

From his seat Harold moaned in sympathy, "useless," unable to deal with the situation.

"Dardy, listen." Lili sat on the edge of the bed, a waft of White Shoulders comforting Dardy. "Can you hear me?"

"Yes." Dardy was becoming impatient. *Why wouldn't they all just let her be?*

Lili's face was somber. "They have to operate or you might die. But if they do, you will have a *scar*." She paused dramatically. "Now the choice is yours."

Dardy explained decades later, "You have to understand. To Lili having a scar was the worse choice. Lili would rather die. It's why she never had any children."[461]

IN JUNE, LILI AND ARMANDO TRAVELED TO MONTREAL. SHE WAS excited to show her husband the city she loved and that worshiped her in return. He had no concept of her celebrity. Unlike Paul, who had wanted to change—even stop—her career, Armando seemed to accept what she did.

Burlesque and stripping wasn't a part of the Italian culture. Armando had never seen a show until he saw Lili on the Montreal stage. He thought his wife elegant and classy. "She didn't know how to do a classical strip tease act," Armando claimed.[462] Or Lili had him believing.

Even half a century later he thought she did not know how to do a typical bump and grind. She had dragged him off to clubs to see what other girls were doing. The language barrier was so thick between the two possibly he merely misunderstood and of course Lili wasn't filling him in on her past.

Strictly speaking, Lili wasn't lying. She did not do a "traditional" strip, coming on, bumping, grinding, flinging clothes off, and leaving (though in fairness not all the girls did that). Maybe she dragged Armando to the clubs to see what she wasn't going to do. Lili always strove to set herself apart, to be different.

In Montreal Armando attended all her shows, dining with her afterward. She naturally introduced him to her favorite blind pigs. Apparently they didn't run into Jimmy or Frankie, as she never mentioned it. She caught up with her old crowd, who were courteous to her new husband and wished her well.

Gayety manager Conway greeted his star exuberantly, happy to see her.

"Oh, you know, Mr. Conway, I only feel safe playing here," she told him.

"Why is that, Lil?"

"Because I trust the engineers here." Not all theatres took such care with the lighting and sets.[463] The Gayety never let her down.

Lili worked hard prepping, performing, and then partying afterward. She got as little sleep as ever but she was happy with Armando and being "La Belle Lili."

"Lili," Conway said. "You're a star. Everyone depends on you. Take care of yourself."[464] She was burning the candle at both ends and it was beginning to show.

Lili decided to perform as dual temptresses. Salome and Eve. The timing could

not have been worse as Quebec readied for its national holiday, Fête de la Saint-Jean-Baptiste. Given John the Baptist's head on a platter after her fiery dance as Salome, Al Palmer reported in 1948 it, "came as a shock to regular theatre-goers." Still he lauded Lili for being an "accomplished actress."[465]

BUT MONTREAL HAD BEGUN A "WAVE OF REFORM" AND THE CANADIAN politicians were in no mood for Lili's sense of humor.[466] As burlesque had been run out of New York by Fiorella La Guardia in 1939, so too were the politicians of Montreal trying to "clean up" the city's image.[467] Lili stood as one of the most prominent symbols of supposed sin pervading the city and corrupting the morals of its citizens.

Marie-Joseph D'Anjou, a Jesuit priest, hated all things Lili, meaning the vice and gambling and drinking dens in Montreal that she represented with her wanton displays of sex and flesh. He wrote a scathing article in the city's French-language paper Le Devoir, pushing the city's fathers to run Lili St. Cyr and her filth out of town.

Author William Weintraub described D'Anjou's hatred of Lili in his book City Unique. "Whenever she danced, he [D'Anjou] wrote, 'un relenet de frenesie sexuelle empeste le theatre'" ("the theatre is made to stink with the foul odour of sexual frenzy").

With the choice of Salome in 1951, was Lili baiting D'Anjou? She claimed she was not aware of the anti-Lili feelings building. Lili had never tried to be—nor wanted to be—"discreet or modest" in her act.[468]

With the Public Morality Committee on his side and with D'Anjou's unrelenting campaign, Lili was arrested in June of 1951, along with the manager of the Gayety, for "behavior that was 'immoral, obscene, or indecent.'"[469]

Lili was embarrassed and failed to mention to Armando that this was her second arrest. Released, she was allowed to continue with her show as long as she made changes.

The police flocked to the theatre to keep an eye on her, which increased her jitters. She took pills to calm down, pills to sleep, and drank a little more. Her stomach gave her increasing problems. She was anxious and lost weight. She appeared unmoored with all the vitriol the papers were spewing at her.

Lili told Dardy the Gayety was "being nasty to her."[470] She told them she wouldn't go on until they filled her basket with cash.

Armando and Lili met with a bilingual attorney at Café Martin. The café was situated in a nineteenth-century house on Mountain Street that served French food and was one of Lili's favorites.

Lili trusted the attorney because he reminded her of George Raft, one of Dardy's old gangster boyfriends. The attorney calmly and mysteriously assured the nervous couple it would be all right. "Have confidence in me," he said. "It's all been arranged."

"What you mean?" Armando asked but was ignored.[471]

On June 27 Lili arrived in court wearing a skirt suit and fur, her equally well-turned-out husband at her side. The proceeding was held entirely in French, of which she understood nothing.

While the authorities testified she was "evil," several police officers swore they had seen the act and saw nothing wrong with it.

Lili sat stone-faced. Armando, a stranger in a strange country, was nervous.

At the end of the day Judge Edward Archambault, unable to find any evidence against the stripper, had the charges dropped.

Lili complained to reporters about the "prejudice" leveled at her from those who hadn't actually seen her act. "I don't like vulgarity—I think it is ugly—and on the burlesque circuit they think I'm high hat."[472] Lili acted as if she wasn't fazed by the latest ruckus. Burlesque and her show was the only thing she knew how to do. Montreal had always been on her side.

But Lili was shaken to her core. It was one thing to be arrested in the country where you were at least a citizen and quite another to be a foreigner who did not understand the repercussions. And though the papers clamored to her defense, the city that had embraced her, made her a name, lost a bit of its luster. She would no longer feel safe there. She had survived an abusive boyfriend, an unfaithful lover, but always she had felt nurtured and loved by Montreal. Now she wasn't so sure.

It would turn out to be a trying summer all around. On July 5, a group of patrons at the Gayety stood packed together under a staircase watching the show. As Lili seduced onstage, a fire escape crashed down, killing two and badly injuring another.[473]

When Conway was informed of the mishap he made everyone promise not to tell Lili. Lili's seemingly cavalier attitude about an event she knew nothing about fueled her critics (religious and political) to confirm she was an evil, uncaring woman. She received anonymous threats, including one that warned acid would be thrown in her face. She no longer felt comfortable shopping on Saint Catherine Street. Conway made sure a car was available for her and Armando at all times.

One night Lili was hissed at by a group of women as she was leaving the theatre. "Bitch!"[474] The city that had embraced her, titled her "La Belle Lili," had become ugly. The Gayety closed two days later for the summer, ending Lili's four-week run.

Lili felt this role of an evil woman had been thrust on her and she didn't like it. She liked to be in charge of the "bad girl" image she projected. Things were out of her control. She decided to put distance between herself and Montreal, hoping the storm would pass.

She and Armando packed their bags and left.

She would not perform again in Montreal for another fourteen years.

CHAPTER FIFTEEN

Beldon Katleman was a charming, gruff, deeply tanned man in his late forties who fancied himself an expert ladies' man. He had inherited from his Uncle Jake the first resort hotel and casino to sprout improbably in the arid Nevada desert. Situated on Highway 91, the El Rancho, sprawled across fifty-seven (some accounts list it as being sixty-six) acres, consisting of a main building, pool, badminton courts, and a gas station. At the El Rancho guests drove up to their separate bungalows and parked just outside their door. The one-story bungalows were individually decorated and most had their own kitchen, lawn, and porch.

Built prior to the Last Frontier and Flamingo, the El Rancho did much to help boost the growth of Las Vegas, which was in the nascent stage of tourism, catering to fantasy and escape. It would suit Lili's sensibilities perfectly.

The El Rancho was marked by a tall windmill reaching up to the desert sky. STOP AT THE SIGN OF THE WINDMILL, it read in neon. Audiences packed the El Rancho to see the top entertainers of the day, including Sophie Tucker, Rudy Vallee, Betty Grable, Dorothy Dandridge, and the ever-present El Rancho Girls, an extended line of statuesque showgirls. It was the first self-contained resort, or destination spot, when Beldon took over running it. He made extensive renovations, expanding the club, the Opera House Theatre, and the casino.

With the help of Tom Douglas, a former child actor turned interior decorator (who would figure large in Lili's career and life), Beldon added a French provincial motif to the bungalows to include a dash of fancy, but most everything else was western-themed. It was an odd mishmash that worked. Lili would think it charming and rustic.

Douglas had been pulled out of retirement by Katleman to rejuvenate the place. With his extensive background in theatre and films, Douglas took over designing the sets and staging the shows, eventually producing many—including Lili's—successful and groundbreaking numbers.

Born in 1896 (he would claim 1901) in Louisville, Kentucky, Douglas was left largely to himself by his parents who thought he was peculiar because of his love of dance. At an early age Tom migrated to London and became a "gorgeous" child actor in films starring Tyrone Power Sr. and Lionel Barrymore.[475] He starred opposite Dorothy Gish in the 1922 film *The Country Flapper*. In unpublished biography Douglas described a meteoric rise in the theatrical circles of London, hob-knobbing as one of the "bright young people," one of the "elite,"[476] running with the Noël Coward/Cecil Beaton crowd of bon vivants, a homosexual group of gorgeously dressed young men.

Tom was a distant cousin to Tallulah Bankhead, with whom he most likely cultivated his love of outrageous behavior and desire to "shock the fuddy duddies." After five years of London triumph he returned to America and landed in New York. (In his biography Tom makes no mention of the rumor that he had to leave London after a dead body was found on his doorstep. Scotland Yard failed to believe his cries of innocence and allegedly revoked his permit, and he fled the UK.)

He soon befriended Garbo and Carole Lombard. A career change came when his neighbor Kay Francis asked him to decorate her house. Tom began working on homes for Myrna Loy, director Alfred Hitchcock, Cary Grant, and Billie Burke. Douglas claimed a high-class madam ran a whorehouse across the street from his home in Los Angeles and he gave Lionel Barrymore's wife, silent screen actress Irene Fenwick (who died of anorexia at age forty-nine), a pornographic painting that she hung in her powder room.

Billy Wilkerson asked Douglas to model Ciro's and Café Trocadero after London and Parisian clubs. He did in a lavish and most spectacular way with silk green walls and a red painted ceiling. At the opening of Ciro's he sat beside Marlene Dietrich.

Douglas was in demand and highly paid. He was a frequent club-goer and caught Paulette Goddard under the tables of Ciro's with Anatol Litvak, whose pants were crumpled around his ankles.

Tom spent vast amounts of time in Lili's company, involved in her photo shoots and decorating her beloved home to reflect his taste. They were so close the papers would periodically announce their imminent nuptials, which amused the homosexual Douglas and the usually married Lili. He gave her a diamond ring worth $12,000, which set tongues flapping.[477]

At El Rancho, Katleman and Douglas would have a tumultuous relationship, eventually falling out after years of arguments. A year after commencing work, Tom would write Katleman a glowing letter stating "nothing can ever really change my regard for your integrity." In his unpublished biography he wrote of a money dispute and was still owed money by his former friend when he left Las Vegas forever. Tom admitted both were "stubborn as hell" and could be "charming when he wished to be."[478]

Douglas did a magnificent job on El Rancho, greening up the grounds surrounding the all-white buildings with palm trees and shrubs and made sure the lawn was perfectly manicured no matter the scorching heat.[479] The lake-shaped pool was twice as big as any other.

Beldon was the first to introduce the soon-to-be de rigueur buffet. The Chuck Wagon Buffet offered continual late-night dining, of mostly cold cuts, to keep hungry gamblers going. Eventually renamed the Buckaroo Buffet, patrons could stuff themselves silly for $1. It was another innovation that took over Vegas.

A clever businessman, Beldon sought to provide everything a traveler might need, including clothing, gift shops, even a health club, so there was never any need to leave his resort.

The large, neon-lit windmill atop the main building could be seen for miles in the desolate desert night. The windmill reminded Lili of the Windmill in London and surely gave her a sense of continuity and comfort.

Beldon first caught Lili's act at the Follies in Los Angeles. He wooed her to his desert oasis with a generous salary. Starting in September of 1951 Lili would perform her bathtub act in the Opera House, a large ornate room with painted ceilings, chandeliers, and white tablecloths for diners. The schedule was not demanding; shows were at eight, midnight, and on Saturday at two fifteen. Entertainment was kept short to get the gamblers back to their tables. Beldon introduced her as the "Contessa," signing her for a six-week-a-year, multiyear guarantee. Eventually it would grow to a ten-week-a-year guarantee.

Entertainment was first-class in the growing city. Just weeks earlier Sinatra had made his debut at the Desert Inn. But Lili was the first stripper to work Vegas. She was there before the high-rises, the escalating salaries, and the topless dancers.

Vegas in those days had a population of twenty-five thousand.

As stripper Dixie Evans related, "They're catering to the gambling crowd . . . they would want some exciting type of acts," and classy ones.[480] There was no more elegant striptease than Lili. She would pave the way for the risqué acts that are the staple of Las Vegas today.

Beldon Katleman was a man who took up space. From the beginning of his association with Lili, though married to Mildred Halbreich, he would display a mad crush on his employee and she in return adored his wily ways, always charmed by a scoundrel, especially one that treated her well and paid her even better.

Beldon showered Lili with gifts. He was courteous, accommodating her every wish, stocking her bungalow with a stream of expensive items, always a way to Lili's heart. Her bungalow at the El Rancho was redecorated by Tom Douglas, whom she bonded with immediately. The two became fast friends and would remain so for years.

Tom Douglas with his hand on Dick Ogden's shoulder

Tom and Lili had much in common. His aesthetic tastes were ornate and sophisticated. Often referred to as "the millionaire interior decorator," Douglas, like Lili, was always in search of a new romance to spice up his life, though for years he traveled and roomed with Richard Ogden, a beautiful blond man years younger than himself.[481] It would be a painting of Ogden that hung on the wall during Lili's act. Douglas would categorize himself as "asexual."[482]

THE EVER-FAITHFUL SADIE ACCOMPANIED LILI AND ARMANDO TO LAS Vegas. Armando would remember it as his first encounter with American racism. The majority of hotels did not "permit Negro artists," let alone maids, to sleep on the premises.[483]

"I was shocked," he recalled. "She couldn't go in the clubs. She couldn't stay at the El Rancho. I had to drive her to a not very nice hotel for 'her people.' It was really very shocking for me. I had not seen that before."[484] Sadie stayed in an area of Las Vegas know as the "Westside," little more than "a slum."[485]

Lili made a spectacular debut at the Opera House on September 12, 1951.

Douglas had outdone himself redecorating the room. He had stretched a curtain the length of the long narrow stage and placed square tables jammed against the stage. The Ted Fio Rito orchestra sat off to the audience's right. Tom told Lili he had designed the set as if she were a jewel in a gorgeous jewelry box.

While she rehearsed during the day, Dick Ogden drove Armando around the desert. Armando couldn't tell if the ex-RJO Army Air Corps who had flown B-24s up and down the coast of California was Tom's boyfriend or not. He seemed interested in women and vice versa. In fact, Dick Ogden's nephew didn't know either, though at the beginning of the relationship Dick's family was concerned when he moved in with the older man. The two had met literally running into each other in Los Angeles. Dick was entranced with the glamorous Tom Douglas and his show business friends. The two remained together for years. Tom's scrapbooks show the two on many exotic travels around the world. When Tom died he left Dick many of his personal effects including the scrapbooks and his unpublished memoirs. [486]

Beldon gave VIPs the use of a yacht to tool around Lake Mead, which Dick utilized to keep Armando company while Lili and Tom rehearsed.

Lili opened with dance bandleader Richard Winslow and his wife, singer Alice Tyrrell. Neither of which are remembered today.

Like Montreal, Lili conquered the desert city in one triumphant night.

LILI'S ACT GAINED A LOT OF ATTENTION, AND NOT JUST FROM THOSE in the audience. Lili garnered another indecency charge from the Las Vegas police. The district attorney was on a crusade for the "battle of the red light district," though the El Rancho was by no means a part of it. District attorney Roger Foley said he was having dinner during a September show when Lili "dropped her towel" in front of the children and families attending the show. Foley stopped Lili's show and, to the dismay of all, carted her down to jail.[487]

Beldon paid the $1,000 bail.

Coming on the heels of the Montreal trial, it was too much for Lili. She skipped the hearing and returned to Los Angeles with her thoroughly mystified husband.[488] She downplayed any significance of the arrest. To Armando, a foreigner, police and jail meant trouble of a serious nature.

They threw themselves into work. Her work. Armando helped her build sets and picked out antiques to decorate them. They were working for her continued success. She never relaxed. She wanted to create an enduring place for herself in show business.

Armando was pained by her obvious "insecurity." She would complain about her lack of education and so many things she didn't know.[489] A voracious reader himself, he encouraged her to read.

The newlyweds traveled constantly. Armando kept asking Lili when she was going to stop. She assured him she would rather he worked and she stay at home playing the traditional role of a 1950s American wife. They couldn't travel from city to city like circus people forever, she laughingly reassured him. A life she was fine with, by the way, but failed to be honest about.

Armando had grown tired of packing, schlepping to a different city where he didn't know anyone, with little to do. Life on the road was aimless. He wanted to work and support his beautiful wife. She worked too hard, rarely slept, was constantly surrounded by people wanting to sit with her and drink till the sun came up. He wanted to protect her.

Armando truly loved Lili. He always would, but there was little about her that he actually knew. He would die never really knowing her, unable to reconcile "all the lies" she told him.

"She wasn't domestic at all," Armando said. "Sadie cooked or we went out. Lili [*Leelee*, he would say in his charmingly thick accent that remained even into his late eighties] never took a week off. . . . We practically lived in the clubs." Always before their lovemaking he asked her if he should use protection. "I can't get pregnant,"[490] she said. Whether true or not she never became pregnant in the time they were together.

"Quit, *Leelee*," Armando begged her.

"I will, *Caro*." She used his endearment for her. "Another couple of engagements and I will." And those engagements would pass and then she would have "just a few more." He would raise his eyebrows. "I can't turn work down," she whined. "They are paying me so much. And I've such debt, Armando. *So* much."

He wanted to sweep away this debt she talked incessantly of. "I am an engineer, *Leelee*, not a man who follows women. We go back to New York and I will work. I am builder of buildings."[491]

Did he want her to quit?

"Of course. Of course. I was no gigolo. I couldn't keep following her around to clubs."

Armando had a friend with money to invest and with some of Lili's money they could build "retirement villages" for people over sixty. It had never been done. His friend had an option on some land back east. Armando would design it. If Lili would quit the road, all three would go into business. They would make a fortune. Lili wouldn't have to work so hard.

Armando was a forward thinker and perhaps it was another thing that drew them together, both dreamers.

"Soon, *Caro*, soon," Lili would dismiss him. "Just let me finish this next

LEFT: *Lili on stage, "Scherazade"*

engagement, then we will talk. I want to quit. I do." She didn't really. She was in demand; she couldn't turn down the money, the headlines, her name on the marquee. She told Armando what she thought he wanted to hear. And maybe she did want to quit. She often fantasized about doing nothing. She hid her ambition and her love of her career. But she would sacrifice everything for it—relationships, family, even her health.

Lili continued to dash from engagement to engagement.

"You are my wife, *Leelee*," Armando said. He shook his head, sick with disappointment. Though he would never ask her not to work. If she would only have told him the truth, how much it meant to her, he might have been able to live with it. He felt toyed with, which wasn't something he could stomach for long.

Fed up, he told her he was leaving. "This isn't working, *Leelee*. I cannot wait for you any longer. You are never going to quit."

She started to tear up. She again promised him she would.

He was furious but would not entertain thoughts of sleeping on the couch, "an American idea." In the morning he would go.

Sometime in the middle of the night Armando woke to Lili's soft moaning.

"What is it?" He turned on the bedside light and shook her.

Her eyes were closed, her forehead clammy. He couldn't get her to respond or open her eyes. He tried shaking her.

"*Leelee!*" Alarmed, he rushed to her side of the bed. Several bottles of empty prescription pills—her "sleepers"—were scattered on the floor. A frantic Armando grabbed her by the arms and propped her up on several satin pillows. She kept sliding down. Her eyes remained slits. He didn't know what to do. "*Leelee.*" He cradled her head and kissed her falling curls. She smelled of alcohol and cigarettes and the faint jasmine of her perfume.

He dashed downstairs and made coffee, managing to get her to drink some. She was barely responsive.

Out of desperation he tore at her nightgown, kissed her breasts. "*Dai.*" Come on! He shook her. He realized he didn't know her. Not the woman onstage who enchanted her audience with her grace and elegant ballet, nor the woman offstage who could turn distant, and quiet, who never opened her heart to him. She walled herself off. They never spoke of significant things. And it was more than the language barrier.

He grasped at her nightgown. He did the only thing he knew how to do. He made love to her.

CHAPTER SIXTEEN

1992

The hand shook as she penned a note to a fan. Some young man who had never been to a club to see her perform. He hadn't even been born when she was dancing at Ciro's.

Her apartment was cold. Outside her window white frost coated the lawn. Inside her breath showed in the apartment. Her heater was crap. She kept the oven on low and the door open. An oven she never used for cooking.

She couldn't cook now. Not anymore. The pain that racked her back was intense. Her feet were stiff, the toe joints bent and gnarled. Once-beautiful feet.

She would need to ask one of her "touches" for some money.[492] She needed to eat. She had been sick and unable to send photos in the mail. Her little business was temporarily sidetracked. Al's Liquor store down the street wouldn't cash any more checks for her. It was impossible to walk the couple of blocks anyway. She was feeling desperate. And she was out of drugs.

The phone rang. She clutched at it. The time had been prearranged.

"Hello?" She answered as if it were a question.

"*Cara mia.*"

"I'm scared," she blurted.

"*Perche?*" He forgot his English. "Why? I'm here. Tell me what is wrong."

She poured forth a litany of troubles. The neighborhood was dangerous. She had no money. It was cold. She was sick. She was alone.

He promised to send more money. His monthly checks supplemented her Social Security—and Lorenzo's. Not that he knew anything about Lorenzo. She told him she was scared and alone living in a drug-crazed, dangerous neighborhood. He promised to send what he could, though it was not so good a time for him either.

As always they talked about the past. People they knew. His beloved brother Elio.[493]

"What else do you need, *Cara*?"

"Nothing, baby. Well, a little money if you could—"

She never asked about his wife. He never talked about her or the affairs he had. Did he remember the last time he had seen her in person? It had been New York. At his restaurant. Decorated as she suggested, in red. A seduction spot for the multitude of women he would seduce, trying to forget Lili.

She had stood there in full-length fur, blonde hair piled on top of her regal head. Gorgeous. Maybe fifty. Her body was still strong and slim. She was still working.

"Love you." She hung up and sighed. It depressed her to think of him. She had tried to get him back. Too late. She had messed up so much in her life. Him most of all.

What a mess. She looked down the length of her terry cloth robe to her slippers. Somewhere inside that old woman's body was her real self.

Where was the woman that had been adored by so many? Where was the young beautiful dancer with the gorgeous skin? Desired. Sensual. Erotic.

Sometimes she couldn't believe her life. Trapped in her apartment, the sun kept out by newspapers taped to the windows. The green courtyard beyond her windows was quiet. Lorenzo could barely negotiate the three steps into the apartment. He was entirely bent over now. He had to lean on a cane and look up at everybody. And he had been over six feet tall. Poor Lorenzo. She had been sucked into the responsibility of caring for him. She would never make him leave. She didn't want Armando to find out about him.

She took her responsibilities seriously. She had never been late for a show. She rarely even missed a show. She kept looking after men long after the feelings had fled. She had felt obligated to their feelings. It made her cold and seemingly uncaring. And she had been at times. *Forgive me, Armando.*

The apartment remained silent as if caught in time. Her beautiful antiques were long gone. She was stuck waiting for the end of her days, terrified she would be carted off to a home for old people, helpless, stared at by strangers. No privacy. There would be whispers, *That used to be—well, look at her now.*

There was no one to bother her here. Maybe that was the problem. After a lifetime of being stared at, she lay in bed, no one looking, no one seeing her. Occasionally someone knocked on the door asking for her. Strangers, fans. She never answered the door. They couldn't see her like this. They needed to keep their memories of her. She would keep hers.

Life beyond Plymouth Boulevard was passing her by. She was angry and bitter. She had no money. She clung to memories, furs thrown over her diamond brooch, rooms full of roses, glowing press reports.

Her days of trying to off herself were over. They hadn't meant anything. Now she clung to life; she didn't want to leave it. How ironic.

Who could she call? Dardy wasn't an option. Her whole family gone. She regretted that but it was too late.

Still Armando had called and made her laugh. He always could. A good man. What had been wrong with her to push him away? That was how she had been then. She thought only of her career and getting ahead, reaching for some unattainable okay from who knows whom to validate her existence. The romances and the men had fed her, but her work was all. Without it, what was she?

What had her life been about?

PART THREE

INTERLUDE BEFORE EVENING

"As my earnings went up,
my act got to be more refined"

—LILI ST. CYR

How Jerry Giesler

e Famous Hollywood
wyer Has Heard
ndals That Would
ock A Hardened
iminal. But Here's
Case Where He
eally Had 'Em
olling in the
ourtroom Aisles.

CHAPTER ONE

The year 1951 was filled with passionate, poignant art in movies and literature. *An American in Paris* and *A Streetcar Named Desire* were playing in theatres. The popular novel *From Here to Eternity* was both steamy and gritty. Couples were dancing to "Hello, Young Lovers" and "Kisses Sweeter Than Wine." Romance was slamming up against reality.

Smoke settled over the heads of the movie stars like halos worn in heaven, or at least MGM's depiction of the hereafter. Lana Turner canoodled with her latest love. Ronald Reagan was there. Actor Gilbert Roland drank a martini. Mickey Rooney was off to the side being his usual obnoxious self. Maroon tuxedo–clad waiters wove through the crowds of diamonds and décolleté with trays of Manhattans and martinis. The orchestra lowered their swing to background music, waiting for the star attraction, an act that had been much ballyhooed in the papers. A peeler with a cold, hard Nordic beauty that kept the stage-door Johnnies hanging around the bar every night.

A drunk Bogart was eyeing the curtained stage. He had seen the ads. Betty was at home with their baby Stephen. The *Key Largo* actor hadn't yet won an Oscar for his latest film, *The African Queen*. He downed another scotch, scowled, and smoked another cigarette.

In the background the blonde's husband waited patiently. He was Hollywood handsome and spoke somewhat better English now than when he had married her. The Italian with long tapered fingers lit a cigarette. The ladies eyed him hungrily: a head of thick black hair, chest hair to rake lacquered nails through in ecstasy, and a killer smile to match his brilliant blue eyes.

It was early October and the air was cool outside. Inside, the place was steaming and Armando kept an eye on the crowd. He would go backstage but Lili didn't like him there before a show. Even after a dozen years stripping she still got preshow butterflies. Bad. *Leelee* would end up with ulcers, he thought. Her problem was she cared more about her show than these bums ever would. They were arrogant movie types who didn't give a damn about her. They just wanted to see her tits.

"We went shopping for beautiful gowns," Armando recalled, a fondness and frustration still evident in his voice. "She had five gowns. Two were Balenciaga, which were quite expensive. I chose them."[494] She also wore Balmain and Dior. If she was going to be among the well-heeled movie stars, he was determined that she would outshine them.

Armando watched the crowds. The movie stars were drunk. The place was loud. Food was good. Phyllis, the beautiful cigarette girl who looked like a Debbie Reynolds knockoff, pranced by, smiling and holding out her formidable chest over packs of tobacco. To be nice he bought four packs. Phyllis smiled and continued on her rounds. In the old days, he would have fucked her. But not with Lili in the wings. She was all the woman he needed.

The nightclub stank, despite plumes of expensive perfume and the gardenias Phyllis sold. It wasn't a smell that ever left the building: old cigarettes and booze ground into the maroon carpets and gold drapes. It was even in the white starched tablecloths and leather banquettes, despite the bleach. It was the sweaty, salty smell of the rich and famous.

Lili had filled out nicely over the years. Still lean and thin like the ballet dancer she had always wanted to be, she had grown fuller in the bust and hips, and her legs were powerful and strong. She wasn't overripe like Elizabeth Taylor, more in keeping with Ava Gardner's trim physique. Lili looked strong and fit and healthy. She was tan, the influence of her sun-loving husband and a private courtyard at her house. Not a movie star in the place outshone her.

Laughter rose from the table where beautiful redheaded Arlene Dahl rested a diamond-encircled glove on the table. A handsome B actor kept his hand squarely on Dahl's back as if to say "she's mine" and tried to act as if he weren't trying to garner the attention of a columnist a couple of tables over.

Backstage, Lili changed out of her pale blue robe and made the final adjustments to her costume, a pair of flesh-colored net panties that clung low to her hips worn over her rhinestone G-string.

When Ciro's owner Herman Hover[495] had caught her performance at the Follies, he immediately forced his way backstage past Lillian Hunt and announced he wanted to book the bathing beauty for his nightclub. No exotic had ever played Ciro's—or any nightclub on the Sunset Strip. He wanted to create a sensation. Ciro's wasn't doing so well at the time due to stiff competition across the street from the Brazilian-themed Macambo. Macambo's décor was courtesy of Tony Duquette with white-and-black-striped wallpaper and cages filled with live parrots.

Ciro's booked big acts—all the clubs did—such as Xavier Cougat and Duke

Ellington and Herb Jeffries, French chanteuse Edith Piaf, Marlene Dietrich, and Mae West. When Dean Martin and Jerry Lewis performed at the club, they became stars. When they were booked elsewhere, commanding $100,000 a week, they would loyally return to Ciro's for their old rate of $7,000. Lili's newest pal and Vegas costar, comedian Joe E. Lewis, had reopened the club in 1942 when Hover took over ownership, hoping to put his brand of splash on the Los Angeles nightlife. [496]

The Sunset Strip was packed with clubs fighting for the movie stars. Hover believed Lili would bring in the audience. Though she never liked his "character" she signed a contract and would work for him for years.[497]

According to Louella Parsons, Hover agreed to "book her as an 'Ecdysiast.' Which, according to the dictionary, Parsons noted, was "an insect which sheds its outer shell." [498]

Tom Douglas convinced Hover to spend thousands to accommodate Lili's tub, advertised as having a royal pedigree, supposedly once belonging to the Empress Josephine (unlikely). Under Douglas's direction Hover got rid of some tables, built out the stage, and added curtains and lights. Lili appreciated the way both men understood what her act needed. He placed a picture of his roommate, Dick Ogden, on a low table center stage. Lili would cavort to his bedroom eyes.[499]

Ciro's was like "going to the moon" in terms of career advancements.[500] She knew the audience would be more critical of her. "She had never worked so hard." Her nerves were raw.[501]

Over the murmur of the crowd, Lili reached for the oversized bath sheet. She waited in the hallway to go on. Nervously, her hands flitted to the curtains and gripped them. Her success, marriages, and applause hadn't made her any more comfortable with herself. She was truly at ease only on the stage.

Ready to go on, her maid was overdressed in silk and taffeta.[502]

The lights dimmed out front. A hush descended over the crowd. It was time to go on.

THE DRUMS BEGAN TO ROLL. THE EMCEE ANNOUNCED, "THE BEST dressed, undressed lady in the theatre, ladies and gentlemen, Lili St Cyr . . ."

Trumpets added their call as a sax rang out and a clarinet chimed in. Lili breathed in the expectancy from the room, swathed in mink and jewels. She began her version of a "classical" striptease wearing G-string, panel, and pasties, doing a mild "imitation" of bumping and grinding. This lasted all of two to three minutes. Curtains parted revealing a bath. She sauntered over to it and undressed. The lights

---

RIGHT: *With Sadie. Note a picture of Armando sits on the vanity.*

dimmed. Lights underneath her tub illuminated her long legs—and more—as she sank down into the delicious bubbles.

Her bathing ritual was long and leisurely; she raised one leg, then the other. As she stood up, her maid blocked her, then wrapped Lili in an enormous towel. Lili leisurely began the process of dressing for her date. She tried on several long dresses. Hats on and off. She fussed in the mirror. The maid pointed to Dick's handsome face, then to a fancy French clock to indicate Lili must hurry. A boy entered carrying a box from a jeweler's. A string of exquisite pearls. The maid tested their authenticity by running her teeth across them. She nodded and tossed them to Lili. The doorbell rang. Sadie exited to answer the door, reentering with a top hat and gold walking stick from the gentleman caller. With only her panties on, Lili grabbed a long, thick sable coat and slipped it on. The crescendo of music followed Lili offstage.

Another successful night.[503]

LILI'S CHIC STYLE, ON DISPLAY THAT NIGHT, WOULD BE EMULATED BY the movie stars in the room. Bette Davis immediately went out and got a new "poodle haircut" after catching Lili sporting her new short hairdo.[504]

Lili's Ciro's success led to a contract in Palm Springs at the Chi Chi. The Chi Chi was a giant supper club, bigger than Ciro's, that lorded over Palm Canyon Drive in the heart of the desert, one hundred miles from Los Angeles. The price of a show was $5. It was decorated in the popular Polynesian motif that had sprung up in clubs after Trader Vic and the Luau, owned by Lana Turner's husband Stephen Crane in Beverly Hills. Mai tais and ham steaks with pineapples were all the rage.

Klieg lights pierced the black velvet night in front of the club. The Chi Chi's long square architecture was reminiscent of Ciro's. Inside, above the Starlite Room ceiling, lights twinkled above a circular stage.

The Chi Chi was another upscale club with movie stars and gangsters that the leggy dancer easily conquered. Audiences thronged to the desert feeling privileged to take in the ecdysiast everyone was talking about. She said she felt she was "always proving" herself.[505]

CHAPTER TWO

I t's impossible to guess how Lili's debut in February differed from her grand return in the fall, except that the stakes had risen for Ciro's to outdo the other nightclubs, and buzz about Lili's performance was spreading like wildfire. By October, those who had dismissed the novelty of her engagement were now demanding to see what all the talk was about.

It was a month before the Thanksgiving holiday and Ciro's continued to sell out to audiences eager to see "the stripper on the strip."[506] Hover was thrilled Lili was filling his coffers. Soon everyone was booking classy strips in their club. But he had the original. He made sure to treat her with the respect the incoming dollars deserved.

LILI PERFORMED TWO SHOWS NIGHTLY FOR THE MAGNIFICENT SUM OF (her reported) $1,250 a week.[507]

At her entrance the audience clapped enthusiastically, if not wildly. The show was "elegant" and "erotic" but not "dirty. Everyone came to see her."[508]

After the second show of the night, Lili, wearing a long silk robe, dabbed at the sweat on her face. There was a knock on the door of her dressing room that soon flew open and a female cop burst in, a male officer trailing behind her.

Sergeant Ann Hunter seized Lili's G-string.

Captain P. L. Sutton, a large good-looking male officer, told her she was under arrest for an indecent performance and lewdly exposing her person.

Lili stated that she had "worn a similar costume without interference from the law in less arty surrounds of burlesque."

"I can't be guided by what they do on Main Street," Sutton scowled, referring to the Follies.[509]

Armando rushed backstage. He was smoking angrily. He didn't understand these arrests and had hated the spectacle of her trial in Montreal. Escorted by the officers, the couple made their way upstairs to Hover's office.

Minutes earlier Florabel Muir, a fiftysomething columnist and former police reporter, had sat smoking a cigarette when an officer burst into Hover's office looking to arrest the owner.

"What do you silly bastards think you're doing?" Muir, unafraid to mince words, demanded. Muir was a hard-boiled journalist, a thin-lipped newspaper reporter working for the *Los Angeles Mirror*. In 1949 she had been injured along with Mickey Cohen when a bullet hit her in the rear.[510]

Outside Ciro's, crowds of newspaper men and photographers had "mysteriously" and "suddenly" appeared, tipped off—they lamely offered—not to witness Lili's arrest but because Mickey Rooney and his estranged wife Martha Vickers were seen together.

Hover, like the rest of the club owners on the Strip, enjoyed a "special relationship" with the LA Sheriff's Department.[511] Supposedly nothing went on in the clubs that the sheriff didn't know about. "Insider tips were as prevalent then as they are today. If there was an arrest going down, Hover would know." If someone was in the paper, it was because Hover wanted it in the paper. According to author (and Hover's niece) Sheila Weller, the club's publicist Jim Byron had tipped off the sheriff. [512]

The sheriff's office insisted they had received complaints about Lili's act. But the papers noted that the "press agents were coincidentally on hand" to capture her arrest. Lili claimed the ensuing "publicity is not a press stunt." She reasoned, "It would be the worst sort of propaganda for me."

To Lili, it felt like a setup. The police issued citations for Lili and Hover, who were ordered to appear at the Beverly Hills Police Station Monday morning or a warrant for their arrest would be issued.

AT HOME LILI AND ARMANDO HUDDLED WITH DRINKS. ARMANDO WAS completely out of his element. "I don't know what to do," he kept saying.

"I'm calling Tom," Lili said, reaching for the phone. All her earlier bravado had vanished. She was "terrified."[513] "He'll know what to do."

Lili tearfully explained the situation to close friend Tom Douglas.

"Hire Giesler," Tom suggested. "He's the right one, Lili. You can't mess around with this. Call him first thing in the morning."[514]

Of course Lili had heard of Jerry Giesler. Errol Flynn had been a guest at the Florentine when Giesler was defending him against rape charges involving Peggy Satterlee, who had even danced briefly with Lili at the Florentine.

Sometime later Armando and Lili crawled into bed exhausted. Lili couldn't sleep. She tried some sleeping pills. Nothing worked. In hindsight it seemed to her to be a cheap publicity stunt, something Hover was capable of. He was low-class. Lili thought him crude.

This was her fourth arrest. If she could stop the arrests, if she could prove what she did wasn't "indecent," maybe then they could never threaten her or stop her show again. Lili St. Cyr was headed once again to court.

THE HOMELY SHORT MAN IN A DOUBLE-BREASTED DARK SUIT TOLD her he smelled a setup. Like Lili he was impeccably dressed on the Saturday afternoon when they met.

Lili had relayed her story to the lawyer. He took notes. She hadn't expected a man as soft-spoken as herself. "Money is not an obstacle to avoid prison," he warned.[515] He would be expensive, but it was no guarantee of a favorable outcome.

Armando sat nervously at his wife's side. "But—" Giesler paused for dramatic effect. "I rarely lose."

Lili liked him. Walking into his building on Wilshire Boulevard in Beverly Hills she felt reassured. His name and reputation was substantial in the courts. She instantly felt comfortable with him but at first feared he wouldn't take her case.[516]

"Mr. Giesler," she addressed him. Theirs would be a "formal relationship."[517] He in turn called her Miss St. Cyr.

"Miss St. Cyr, in the past have you had any other incidences? Arrests? Your shows stopped?" His round, kindly face was like that of someone's grandfather.

Lili waivered for only a second. "No. Nothing." If she told him about her Follies arrest, he wouldn't take her on, she was sure. And he didn't need to know about the Canadian arrest. As for Las Vegas, she had blocked it from her mind.

He looked at her thoughtfully. "Okay."

First lie.

They had a long conversation wherein he instructed that she must "follow his orders."[518] Armando was always to be with her. She would appear less of a "dangerous woman, less of a threat." He wanted to show that she was a respectable, married woman.

Armando of course said he would do anything for *Leelee*.

"You must always stop by my office before going to court. I want to approve what you are wearing." He told her to dress as if going to church.

"Understood." She was already planning her wardrobe in her mind.

Her attorney waived his hands, small, elegant, a sapphire on his finger—a bit of flash, a gift from his second wife; he told her he'd have the jury made up of her *peers.* His mind was quick and brilliant and was the reason Charlie Chaplin and Flynn had retained him, and why someday Lana Turner would call him *before* she phoned the police to tell them she had a very dead body spilling blood all over her white bedroom carpet. Giesler was the best.

Lili was stumped. A jury of her peers? Giesler's original idea was to have a jury of strippers on the panel so the case would be laughed out of court. He knew that would be an impossibility, so he planned to lobby for a jury filled with artists who would appreciate the "artistic merits" of Lili's act.[519]

Sitting erect and perfect, Lili looked every inch the lady. The blonde hairs on her arm were delicate. The lobes of her ears translucent. Her elegance was intimidating to many, but not to the attorney. Nothing unnerved the confident and experienced lawyer. Most of Giesler's clients needed his help. The three strikes against them—famous and rich and good-looking—made for a jealous desire to rip them from their pedestals.

He told her they would meet in court Monday morning.

DESPITE THEIR AGE DIFFERENCES—LILI WAS THIRTY-TWO AND THE lawyer sixty-five—they had much in common. He had been born Harold Lee Giesler, but found Jerry suited him better. He was as smart and tenacious as he was homely. He would go to any length to win his clients' cases.

By the time he met Lili he had already successfully defended Charlie Chaplin against charges of violating the Mann Act, when the actor purportedly transported and paid for twenty-two-year-old actress Joan Berry to travel across state lines to have sex with him.

Earning upwards of $100,000 for his brilliant defense of the "Little Tramp," Giesler won the case. No elitist, Giesler never charged a caller for talking to him on the phone and had an open-door policy, available night and day. He was interested in defending the rights of clients whom he felt were persecuted.

In 1943 Giesler fought against Errol Flynn's already-tainted reputation after two nubile young women accused the actor of statutory rape. He won. The married Robert Mitchum hired Giesler after he was set up and arrested with a young starlet smoking marijuana in 1948. On Giesler's advice, Mitchum did sixty days of public service, and his career didn't suffer. And Mitchum's long-suffering wife Dorothy publicly forgave him his trespasses.

Giesler had been practicing law since 1910, first as a lowly clerk for famed defense attorney Earl Rogers, after whom Earl Stanley Gardner patterned the fictional Perry Mason. Giesler made his name when Rogers was defending Clarence Darrow, accused of bribing a jury. Henry, as Jerry was known then, was asked to research a point of law. When he turned in a hefty report of over thirty pages, his boss was impressed. With Darrow's acquittal came Giesler's promotion.

"Get me Giesler" would be a catchphrase after the 1958 acquittal of screen goddess Lana Turner's daughter Cheryl—some whispered it was Lana—who plunged a ten-inch knife into the hairy stomach of her mother's greaseball mobster lover Johnny Stompanato in Lana's Beverly Hills boudoir, after the fourteen-year-old overheard a particularly nasty argument.[520]

His was a lucrative, demanding practice and his wife, Ruth, tolerated his late-night preparations. Giesler had a reputation for meticulous preparatory work. He interviewed witnesses oftentimes before the police. He visited Ciro's, plotted where everyone had sat on the night in question, and used Ruth as a "guinea pig."[521]

Giesler planned to be ever present in the stripper's life. He would be seen hovering close by. With Giesler nothing was left to chance. It was the image he wanted to perpetuate, deference to her statuesque beauty.

She explained to Giesler that being nude, the stripping, had never bothered her. She never felt she was doing anything "bad." It was a dance. Art. "When I finished disrobing, I was no more nude than many girls you see on the beaches."[522]

The claim was a little bit of a stretch. Even with the first bikini being worn on the beaches in 1946, the brave souls who wore them were arrested; Lili was hardly more clothed than in a bikini. Her stage bras and panties were see-through—though, like almost all the burlesque girls at the time, they wore two sets of panties, a larger net panty over a rhinestone G-string, and always pasties. There was little "real" nudity.

Giesler was going to refer to Lili as an "artist" and begin to change the public's perception of her.

HOVER ASSURED LILI THE SHOW AT CIRO'S COULD CONTINUE. "WE'LL tone it down until the trial is over. But already we're getting calls from VIPs begging to get in," he gloated. "We are sold out." He planned to take ads out capitalizing on the arrest. He would challenge people to come see what the cops saw . . . what was so naughty that she had to be arrested . . . he knew how to sell this.

She agreed to meet police officers at Ciro's and show them modified costumes, but she stood them up. Perhaps that is why Hover backpeddled and announced he was cancelling her three-week engagement, at a now widely reported $5,000 dollars a week.[523] Hover claimed that "her act . . . was not the same one she did downtown."[524] Some papers were listing her pay as high as $8,000 a week, and it might have been by the end of her standing-room-only triumph.

Lili issued her own formal statement. "I sincerely hope the fact that I am not

Lili and her attorney on their way to court

appearing tonight will not be construed as an admission by me that I am guilty of having appeared in an unsavory performance. I am absolutely sincere when I say I was surprised and bitterly disappointed when this citation was served on me. I had been assured by the management that my act conformed to every regulation and was in no way offensive."

Rules regulating what a stripper did ranged from the required G-string and pasties, to bumping and grinding in an "upright position."[525]

Los Angeles had passed a set of ordinances including "A performer was not permitted to pass her hands over her body in such a manner that the hands touch the body at any point."[526]

Monday morning, at an hour when she was usually still asleep, Lili "breezed" into court in a gray suit and fur stole.[527] A silk scarf covered every inch of her chest and neck.

Giesler asked the court for a continuance. "I need more time, Your Honor, to study the accusations against my client."[528]

Hover was in court representing himself. Since canceling her act, a furious Lili would neither speak nor look at him.

Lili was "enchanted" by Giesler. Speaking calmly, he was the epitome of respectability. He reeked of confidence in himself and in her.

His request was granted.

Lili paid a $250 bail.

First round won.

HOVER WAS FEELING THE DAMAGE CAUSED BY CANCELING LILI'S SHOWS. Only seventy-five people showed up for the replacement act, the Nicholas Brothers. He asked the AGVA (American Guild of Variety Artists, the representation for live performers and acts) to review Lili's act.

Lili agreed to put on a special 2 p.m.—as opposed to her usual 2 a.m.—show for members of the vice squad, Sheriff Biscailuz, and others from the sheriff's office along with representatives and attorneys for AGVA with "more complete costumes" to obtain permission to continue with her performances. Afterward, AGVA representative Eddie Rio said, "I wouldn't be ashamed to take my own daughter." They demanded three changes concerning her movements in the tub, on the couch, and how low she unzipped her dress.

Officers told Lili she was free to dance, but warned if her act returned to its prior incarnation, she would once again be arrested. If her act was decent, she could "dance until kingdom come and it's all right with us."

That night, October 23, Lili was back onstage, albeit in a "modified version" despite the headlines screaming Ciro's very license was in jeopardy because of the ban on burlesque. Two-faced Hover told reporters, "I intend to fight this thing all the way."

Despite *Variety*'s reporting that someone complained that "his wife's new bathing suit was more revealing," Lili was packing in a "hefty attendance" to see the show "all of America is talking about."[529]

Lili, Tom Douglas, and Armando decided that all they could do to spice up the watered-down act was add a multitude of glamorous gowns by Marusia and Dior and Balenciaga. Lili would recall that she had fourteen changes and complained, "If I have to perform in more clothes, it'll ruin my whole career." [530]

Variety reported Lili lost "some of her appeal due to her endless array of gowns." The alterations to her act "dismay the ringsiders."[531]

Officers Hannon and Sutton, self-appointed "art-critics," attended the shows and refused to applaud, complaining that "it still looks like a strip act to me."

Unexpectedly, things took a serious turn. What Giesler (and no doubt Hover) had thought would be a simple misdemeanor charge with the consequence of a small fine had turned into a felony charge with a possible jail sentence. Because Ciro's sat between the municipality of Los Angeles and Beverly Hills, it fell under the jurisdiction of Los Angeles County, not the city.

On October 25, in a black floor-length mink and hat with short veil, white gloves, and pearls, Lili sat quietly in court next to her attorney while he entered a plea of not guilty and asked the judge for a jury to be made up of fellow "artists and business people who appreciate art."

Giesler asked, "If my client is found to be innocent, and I assure you she will, I respectfully submit all charges against Mr. Herman Hover be dropped." Hover had finally hired his own attorney.

When Lili and Giesler, who kept a respectful hand on her arm, exited court, reporters shouted questions. Giesler, no stranger to the power of publicity, warned Lili he was going to use the press to her advantage. The more she was seen in the papers looking as she did—cool, elegant, classy—public sympathy would be on their side. He would first win public opinion, then the jurors'.

Giesler addressed the reporters. "This wasn't an indecent act. This was an artistic show." He maneuvered Lili through the crowd. "Miss St. Cyr is a symbol of ambition, of American enterprise. That's what this case is about. And that's why I took it on. To defend the American way."

Giesler intended to keep Lili, as a "symbol of liberty," free.

The trial was set for December.

Lili was, maybe for the first time, self-consciousness on top of her normal anxiety back onstage at Ciro's. She worried about every swing of her hips, every mild undulation. She was a wreck. She protested, "What is there to tone down?" What remained lacked all manner of sex. The crowd who cut into their steak tartar and speared escargot didn't seem to notice she felt stiff.

Despite this, her arrest was paying off. Lili was breaking the records previously set by Martin and Lewis the year before. Everyone wanted to see and meet Lili St. Cyr. In the audience was Paul Valentine's former costar Robert Mitchum and finally the king himself, Clark Gable. "That was probably the most exciting night of the engagement," she proclaimed.[532]

Until she returned to court Lili remained tense. The police haunted the club while she was onstage. She was now taking off her dress behind a "small screen. A very small screen." She was allowed to wave one leg, not two from the tub.

"I'm so afraid someone is going to grab me off stage and say 'you're under arrest' again," she complained. She was unable to sleep. She didn't eat much.

Lili was turning into a celebrity, but one that was portrayed as the "bad woman."[533] She felt it was unfair. And it made her defiant.

Tom told her to enjoy it "and ask Hover for a raise." She did.[534]

CHAPTER THREE

Appears in Mink, gushed the headlines.[535]

It was December 4, 1951, Lili's and Armando's first anniversary. Lili woke and prepared for court.

Unbeknownst to her husband she was booked far into the future. Lucky, as she would have to pay for her defense and Giesler wasn't cheap.

Armando stood before her, not a dark hair out of place. His muscles were like steel underneath his custom-tailored silk shirt. His piercing blue eyes devoured her. Sometimes all the men had to offer was their looks, but with Armando it was different. He wanted a future *with* her.

BEFORE JURY SELECTION GIESLER PROMISED LILI HE WOULD GET twelve fair-minded jurors. He wanted as many women on the jury as possible, as he believed they would be more sympathetic toward her. Despite what Lili believed, women did like her. Armando would be a bonus; a handsome husband, solicitous and always at her side. She would be seen as a victim.

Giesler had poured over every article his team of secretaries, research assistants, and law clerks could find. He would be ready.

IT IS IMAGINABLE THAT THE MIDDLE-CLASS HOUSEWIVES AND OTHER potential jurors gasped as Lili "strolled" into court at 9:30 a.m. looking like the proverbial million bucks. Lili knew how to make an appearance and was dressed to impress.

She wore a dark blue knit suit, blouse, dark full-length "ranch" mink coat, a hat with a veil, and green gloves. And pearls.[536] Every inch the lady. It was a fine line between dazzling the court and intimidating them. Giesler would make sure she didn't cross it.

Armando and Lili admiring her new ring

Lili said, "I wanted to look as middle-class as possible." And though she was wearing a fur, most middle-class women at the time owned at least a stole. They could both relate and aspire to be like her.

"There's no need for the judge to know I'm wearing a Dior suit," Lili thought. *Or a Capucci fur, or watch by Cartier.*

Giesler addressed the courtroom, explaining he was looking for a jury that would "understand and appreciate the arts."

Judge Henry Draeger raised a skeptical eyebrow.

Lili sat in her place next to Giesler, knowing every pair of eyes in the courtroom was on her. She was being examined from hat-capped head to low-heeled pump.

In front of thirty prospective jurors Lili smiled and told them she was ready to "demonstrate the decency of my act any place, any time."[537]

Giesler offered Lili's act, tub and all, to be brought into the courtroom. He asked each prospective juror if they had any "prejudice against persons in the entertainment world."

Giesler used his famous bumbling routine to put the potential jurors at ease. He fumbled for words. "He was known to appear so ill-equipped that jurors would feel sorry for his clients before testimony even began. It was all an act."[538]

District Attorney Bernard Gross and Giesler whittled the potential jurors down to the required twelve. Ten women and two men. Carefully chosen, from Giesler's point of view, for those who might appreciate or at least understand Lili's "artistic performance." By insisting on a jury with an artistic bent, of which he knew not one of them was an artist, it did accomplish one thing. The jury looked at Lili not "merely as a stripper" but as someone doing a performance with "artistic meaning."[539]

Giesler explained that the first and only time he used a curse word his mother washed his mouth out with soap. He did not swear.

Lili thought about her own mother. Idella. Nothing but coldness there. Idella had inserted herself in to the press surrounding the trial, telling a reporter, "Nudity is essential to her act." Portrayed as a "matronly Hanford housewife," Idella said she was "sick and tired of hearing Lili accused of being naughty." Humorously she added, "At $5,000, I'd take fifteen baths of that kind a night. It's that decent." She claimed her dear daughter had "been artistic from the day she was born."[540] To another Idella commented that she'd caught Lili's show only "a couple of times" and lauded her daughter. "I think Lili carries a lot of dignity." Of course adding, "But I'm just a homebody."[541]

The questioning of the jury had been boring and tedious. Giesler offered to have the jury driven to Ciro's where Lili would "reprise her act."

Giesler's request seemed to wake the courtroom. It could be assured that a good portion, if not all, of the women on the jury had never been to a strip show. Or Ciro's, for that matter.

During a break, Giesler rushed out to do an interview with a reporter. Throughout the trial he would tirelessly plead Lili's case to the public.

Back in the courtroom Lili sat demurely while Giesler gave his opening remarks. He softly stated he would prove that what Lili had done on the night in question and what she continued to do on the stage was "art." Pure and simple.

For the first witness, DA Bernard Gross introduced Sheriff C. H. Conner, a tight-lipped, middle-aged deputy who lounged arrogantly in the stand as he described Lili's offenses.

"She took off her dress." He described seeing her buttocks and most of her breasts that were "barely covered" by the pasties and bra.

On cross-examination Giesler approached the testifying officer and politely asked him to explain what he was doing at a show that featured a well-known stripper. "Eating dinner," the officer replied, as if it was perfectly normal for a sergeant to dine at Ciro's on a cop's salary.

Giesler made a point of asking if Lili's performance at all "excited" him.

He denied that it did. He just continued eating his dinner.

What did he think of the act?

"Indecent," the dark-haired officer said.

Giesler never raised his voice. He was unfailingly polite, sometimes searching for his words. His approach in the courtroom came off as comical, which made Lili uneasy. At first.

Giesler's intention was to show the court the ridiculousness of the case. His client had not committed a "serious offense." He explained, "It is hard to believe a show is lewd when you are laughing about it."[542]

"Did you applaud the act?" Giesler asked.

"I did," the officer acknowledged.

Giesler winked and the jury laughed. Lili tilted back in her chair, a fur thrown over the back, and suppressed a smile.

Next up, Deputy Ann Hunter looked the polar opposite of a chicly outfitted Lili and answered questions from the DA.

Before Giesler could cross-examine, the judge adjourned for the day. That night Armando presented his wife with a beautiful flower-shaped ring with a pearl in the center for their first anniversary.

THE NEXT DAY LILI SHOWED UP AT GIESLER'S WEARING ONE OF HER favorite pantsuits.

"No," he shook his head, "that won't do at all." Armando raced Lili back home to change. She returned instead in another tailored skirt suit.

Eighteen men and three women half-filled the small courtroom on December 5, the second day of testimony. Outside the courtroom interest was great. *Variety* would devote more columns than any other story all week in reporting the antics in Judge Draeger's courtroom.

In the same issue of *Variety* was a small announcement that Lili's old bosses, the Duncan Sisters, were being honored as guests at a Paramount Studios luncheon. The studio was preparing to make a "bio pic" of the sisters. It would never come to fruition.[543]

Ann Hunter resumed the stand. Giesler asked her to repeat testimony regarding Lili's performance. She testified Lili had performed "more or less the motion of the bumps."

Giesler pounced softly. "Was it a full bump, or just half a bump?"

Hunter paused.

"Maybe it was just a quarter," Giesler prompted, "or one-eighth, or one-sixteenth? Or maybe a thirty-second?"

After more discussion she decided it was a "baby bump." She knew because she'd seen one in Ensenada. In a café.

"Oh, those," Giesler smiled. "Those bumps they do at Ensenada, those are bumpity bumps." The jury tittered.

On stage at Ciro's

Why was she at Ciro's?

She went with Officer Hannon and Captain Pete Sutton.

"Did anyone sit with them at the club?"

"Jim Byron from Ciro's." The deputy "pouted" that neither men bothered to introduce her to the club's publicist. It was as if she were invisible, or the three men had no manners. She was not included in the conversation. She said not a word, just watched the show.

Who paid her cover charge of $1.50?

Hover paid everyone's cover charge and drinks.

Did she notice the celebrities in the room?

No. She didn't stare or look for any. She watched the stage. She added she "only took one sip from her drink." It had been her first time at Ciro's.

The other officers in their complaint had stated that Lili's maid had stood between Lili and the audience. Hunter said Lili emerged from the tub without anything on while the maid was standing "on far side" of the tub, leaving Lili's nudity exposed for all.

"But Captain Walker had testified that the maid held a towel in front of Lili and the audience?"

Hunter remained firm that "there wasn't much you couldn't see."

"As Lili got down to bare essentials was it a little too bare for public taste?" Giesler asked.

The deputy admitted Lili never took off her bra and panties. But she could see the "outline" of Lili's "private parts" even though Hunter sat thirty-five feet away. Lili gritted her teeth. No one liked having their "private parts" discussed.

Giesler approached. Did the deputy actually see the "outline" or was she "influenced by knowledge they were there?"

Hunter repeated that "there wasn't much you couldn't see."

Giesler turned to the jury. He presented his claim that the officers went to the nightclub with the intention of arresting his client. Someone had decided, before she poked one painted toenail into her bathtub, that her performance was going to be indecent.

Giesler got Hunter to admit she had been taken that night on "special assignment" and that the table had been reserved ahead of time. She admitted she was from the transportation department. A little out of her league policing vice on Sunset Boulevard.

Next the prosecution called Captain Walker "Tex" Hannon of the antivice squad division of the Hollywood Sherriff's Department.

Though Lili's act had lasted less than fifteen minutes, the long-winded captain took a bloated twenty-five minutes to describe how Lili "bumped" and grinded."[544] Something Lili had a reputation for *not* doing.

The officer stubbornly described Lili's performance as being an "indecent exposure" of herself. Miss St. Cyr had "caressed her body while looking at a man's picture and slid her hands over her thighs. Then she gave a couple of Mae West wiggles. She unzipped her dress to below her buttocks. Her rear was exposed. You could see through her black panties." The captain continued. "She held her dress in front of her and walked sideways, leaving her rear exposed. She stripped to a flesh-colored net bra and panties." Hannon pointed to the offending articles (exhibits A and B) on Judge Draeger's desk. "She lay in front of the picture and kicked her legs. The bra and panties did not adhere too closely to her body."

As she "wiggled," the result, he said, was that "a line of men came closer from the bar."

The captain saw the "outline of her privates" but "no pubic hair . . . she was shaven." Lili's face remained stoic.

Hannon related that while Lili bathed she "gave a couple of little bumps to the timing of the drums" as she dried herself off.

When it was his turn with the witness, Giesler asked the captain to define a bump.

"A movement wherein the muscles of the buttocks contract and [the] lower part of the spine bends forward sudden-like—throwing the front portion of the body forward."

Giesler asked if he had said to Miss St. Cyr that he saw nothing wrong with her show but was there because he had received telephone complaints. Hannon denied this.

Next up, arresting officer Captain Sutton said Lili "peeled down to a couple ounces of transparent chiffon" and as such "she worked her knee back and forth in the air."[545]

Next was a long discussion regarding French bathing suits and whether they were proper or not and whether what Lili wore was similar.

The questioning proceeded on its ridiculous track. Sutton stated that he didn't know what a bikini was. A "French bathing suit" was a bra and panties.

Giesler's let the court know he found it hard to believe such an experienced cop would be shocked by Lili's act. He led Sutton through attendance at the club, the location of the bar, the stage and other logistics.

Then he inquired about reporter Florabel Muir. "You did talk to Miss Muir about arresting Miss St. Cyr?" Sutton concurred. "What did Miss Muir say?"

"She called me a silly bastard," the good-looking officer said.

"Was she mad at you?"

"Oh no. That's the way she always talks to me." The courtroom teetered.

Giesler asked what Lili wore when she stepped out of the tub.

The officer said she wrapped herself in a towel.

"About how big?" the lawyer asked.

"About twenty, twenty-four inches."

Giesler had the officer repeat his answer.

During the lunch break Giesler asked if someone could go to Ciro's to retrieve Lili's towel. Either Armando or someone drove the ten minutes to Lili's dressing room and retrieved the towel she had used the night of her arrest and every night since.

After the break Giesler again questioned the officer as to the size of Lili's towel.

"Twenty, twenty-four inches," he insisted.

With a grand flourish Giesler stood up, holding the folded white Maison de Blanc bath sheet Tom Douglas had purchased for her show. Giesler opened it up and draped it over his shoulder.

"Does this look like the towel Miss St. Cyr used?"

After some squabbling of whether it was or wasn't the towel in question, Giesler made a big show of unfolding the towel to its grand size of six by eight feet.

"Tell me again it was about twenty-four inches?" The courtroom laughed.

Giesler laid the towel on the floor. He had made his point loud and clear.

Lili was relieved to see a friendly face. Giesler's first witness was Tom Douglas.

The decorator was now in his fifties and had lost his golden-boy looks. He was overweight with thinning dark hair. He gave his address as 8426 DeLongpre in West Hollywood. He clarified that a "bikini" and a "French bathing suit" were one and the same.

He explained he wrote and staged Lili's current show. He "suggested" orchestral arrangements for her to use. Why suggested? Douglas paused. One didn't tell Lili what to do. It was better to suggest. The jury perked up when he promised the offending tub was a genuine antique once owned by Empress Josephine.[546] He proudly testified they had spent $6,000 to $7,000 on the act and other "embellishments" (so far), including editing the program.

Giesler let that sink in. Six thousand. And he hadn't even gotten to the cost of her gowns. Pretty rich stuff for a stripper.

Giesler was thorough in his presentation as he set the scene, knowing most had probably never set foot inside the nightclub. He brought into the courtroom a large blackboard. Carefully sketching where the cops had sat, where the orchestra was, even where Lili dropped each item of clothing. The diagram showed the location of where the best seats in the house were.

DARDY CALLED THAT NIGHT TO CHECK IN. SHE WAS IN LAS VEGAS WITH the kids while her husband was supervising a room full of chorus girls at the Desert Inn.

She read that a bus took the jurors to Ciro's for a special show.

Lili explained Giesler had offered but the DA wasn't going for it. They talked about some gowns Lili had sent her. Lili regularly sent discarded costumes, as the sisters were the same size.

Dardy said Marx—or more likely Barbara—had sent a box of toys to Danny from the Marx Toy Company.

Dardy told her Danny would love to see his "*Tante*." Lili had insisted she be called *Tante* Lili. The French term sounded so much better.

Lili thanked Dardy for her "sleepers" and asked her to get more. Dardy had a pharmacist in Vegas where she got them cheap. For Christmas she would send Lili beautiful cut crystal bowls filled with her pills.

Lili took "massive" amounts. "Lili just loved pills!"[547]

CHAPTER FOUR

"Lured by the thought she'd do her act," the courtroom drew a "near capacity crowd" on December 6. *Variety* reported the jury "alternately tittered and slept through Hover's and columnist Florabel Muir's" testimony.[548]

Giesler wanted Lili to present "Interlude" to the jury, but he no longer wanted her to perform it in court. The DA opposed the jury traveling to Ciro's. The judge hadn't yet made up his mind.

Lili wore a beautiful brooch and a light coat and slicked back her hair.

Hover was called to the stand.

He testified that *he* had started in show business as a chorus boy, then went on to say his star attraction worked long and hard for her $1,250 a week.

They discussed "spins." The DA had claimed Lili's "spinning on the floor" was a "lewd dance." Giesler had told the jury it was an "artistic, interpretive dance."

The DA and Hover got into a nitpicking discussion of the definition of bumps. Frustrated, Hover jumped up and said, "You're deliberately trying to confuse me."

Hover testified he always watched the shows and he had sat with his fiancée on the terrace above. Yes, he was aware the sherriff's office was in attendance.

The DA wanted to know if Hover interrupted his watching the show to talk to his fiancée.

"We don't talk when the show's on," Hover answered.

"You were looking hard?"

"Well," Hover smiled. "When my girlfriend's there I can only look so hard." More laughter in the court.

"You were watching the show separately?"

"Separately but together."

"Well, would you say your minds were running along the same channels?"

"Gosh, I hope so." Hover added for emphasis, "Lili is not like the ordinary person. She is graceful."

Hover acknowledged Lili paid her maid, who "never got undressed." More giggles in the court. And Lili paid for her music arrangements and set. She owned the set, props, walls, and doors. He testified that she twirled on her toes while reclining on the lounge.

The DA instructed the clerk "to put down T for toes" on the diagram to the amusement of everyone in the room. There was something farcical about the whole questioning, just as Giesler had anticipated.

Once again Giesler asked Hover what he considered to be a bump.

"You want an illustration or a description?" Hover said.

Giesler said he'd accept both.

"A bump," Hover said, "well, a bump is a pelvic propulsion. That's it." Then the portly Hover "rose like a bashful kewpie doll," put his hands behind his head, and did a bump, not terribly well.[549] The courtroom burst into giggles that "grew into a roar."[550] Hover demonstrated a grind, which he said was a "circular movement of hips without moving any other part of the body." More laughs.

The judge interrupted. "I would say that a bump is a forward pelvic motion." The attorneys stared at Judge Draeger. "I'm only judging on what took place here," Draeger explained.

Giesler smiled. "I'll stipulate, Your Honor, that you are not an expert."

"A grind is a circular movement of the hips where the feet don't move and the body shouldn't," Hover continued.

Asked if he had seen Lili do either in his club, he vehemently denied it.

As to the purpose of rhinestones on the panties he said, "It reflects the light. When the stage is properly lighted, the light bounces off and it's impossible to see what's behind the rhinestones."

The next witness was long-time columnist Florabel Muir, who had been scooping stories for nearly thirty years.

She said she thought the whole arrest was a publicity stunt manufactured by the club. No, she never saw Lili's "private parts." No, she never saw "the nipples of her breasts, or pigmentation." She said the act never ceded the boundary of good taste, nor did Lili expose herself. "My husband didn't see anything like that either. Otherwise I wouldn't have let him stay," she cracked.

The DA repeatedly interrupted Muir with "Madame—"

Muir flushed. Leaning forward she gave the DA a dirty look. "Don't call me Madame." Composing herself she added, "Call me Florabel."

Again the courtroom burst into laughter.

"No further questions." The DA backed down.[551]

"LANGUID LILI" TOOK THE STAND FOR MOST OF THE DAY ON DECEMBER 7. She was "conservatively garbed" in a blue tailored suit with a brooch, her hair once again carefully swept back.[552]

Giesler rose. He asked her to describe her act and her life as an artist. She looked through photographs taken of her onstage. The jury watched her every feline move.

Lili stated, "As the curtain opens, my maid stands there. I enter, fully dressed, carrying hat boxes. I look at some cards on the tray.

"My maid says my sweetheart has not called. I am disappointed. I walk to his picture, on the wall, kiss my fingertips, touch them to his lips.

"I try on a hat or two. Then I undress. The maid is preparing my bubble bath. As I undress, I am finally left wearing a black lace brassier, a garter belt, and stockings. But always my maid is between me and the audience."

Giesler asked if she had "any intent to expose your person lewdly at Ciro's in your performance?"

"No."

The jury listened, enthralled by the soft-spoken stripper. Armando clasped his hands nervously.

Lili testified she paid for her maid and her agent. "Money keeps dribbling out." She was composed and ladylike on the stand. Serene. "I get $1,250 a week, but with those expenses and everything I'm lucky—after taxes—to keep $1,000 of it." She paid $500 for arrangements, $1,200 for costumes, and $50 for "little things."

She denied taking it all off. There certainly were "no bumps, grinds, or wiggles." What she did was a "pantomime of Russian ballet."

Fully clothed, Lili slowly and calmly went through the motions of her act; stepping in and out of an imaginary tub, twirling, pirouetting across the courtroom, with nary a bump or a grind.

"I'll be the maid," Giesler said, pretending to unzip her dress. "They'll be the audience." He pointed to the jury.

With a flourish Giesler produced the already-established sixty-two-inch-wide towel. As the "maid," Giesler stood in front of the jury/audience to shield Lili. Sixty-two inches covered her up almost entirely as she wrapped it around her torso.

The jury burst into laughter and Lili breathed a tiny bit easier.

GIESLER GENTLY LED HER TO A CHAIR SO SHE COULD SIMULATE DRY-ing one long leg after the other. Even with her heels on, her toes were pointed like a ballerina.

"Is this exactly the way you do it?" he asked.

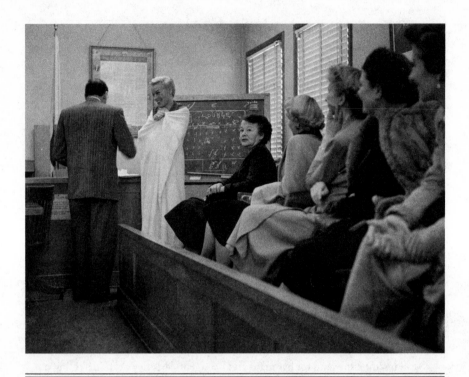

Lili wrapped in her towel for the jury

"Well, I usually have my shoes off." More laughter.

Slowly, methodically, Giesler took the white towel that was hanging on a rail and stretched it on the floor to its full six-by-eight size. He looked at it. The jury looked at it. He didn't say anything. Next he bent over, picked it up, and folded it in half. Then in half again. Then in half again before handing it over to be entered as an exhibit. He had made his point.

The DA approached.

Did she know the law was in the audience?

"Yes, a waiter told me before the show."

The DA asked if she then altered her performance.

"I did not change the performance because they were there." In addition to "scanty under things," she was covered by a "semi-transparent black negligee." And her maid protected her "modesty." The courtroom strained to hear the beauty with the high cheekbones and green eyes. Occasionally she leaned a white-gloved hand on her chin or held her forehead. She looked tired.

DA Gross asked if she made "bedroom gestures in one scene where she pantomimes an interest on the picture of a young man." One assumes that meant masturbating.

"No. I did not," she said calmly, smiled, and looked at the jury.

Gross asked if Lili had knelt during her act, suggesting a crude on-your-knees-type show. No, Lili denied.

Had she caressed herself?

No. Not at any time.

The DA was incredulous. "Do you take off your dress to try on a hat?"

"Of course." What a ridiculous question.

The DA cross-examined. "Where were A and B?"

Exactly where they should be.

Did she twirl around in a sheer negligee before or after getting into tub?

"Yes, but I always had People's A and B on," pouted Lili. She explained, "But always my maid is between me and the audience."

Testimony ended with a clash between Giesler and Gross. The prosecutor tried to spring a surprise witness on the court. A Reverend Bertil von Norman, who, along with another reverend, had been at the club the night Lili was arrested.

Von Norman, the pastor of the West Hollywood Presbyterian Church, was a Clark Kent dead ringer.

Giesler argued the pastor's testimony would add nothing to the record and the judge agreed. "If this testimony is admitted, I might call in Mickey Rooney and a lot of others who saw the show," Giesler articulated, "and let them tell what they think of Lili's act!"

The pastor was not invited to the stand, though it would have been interesting to hear why the two men of God had been in Ciro's in the first place.

THAT WEEKEND LILI CONTINUED TO PERFORM TO PACKED HOUSES. Everyone clamored to meet her afterward. Mostly she and Armando snuck out. She didn't want to chat with strangers. When she finally managed to get to sleep she slept until late afternoon. The strain was taking its toll.

Lili's case "grinds to close," *Variety* joked.[553] On Monday, December 10, Lili arrived in court in a white turtleneck sweater, a long tan coat thrown over her shoulders.

In closing arguments the DA addressed the jury, saying that despite the fact the defense had tried to "turn this into a burlesque," the issues were clear. "We can't look into the defendant's mind, we can only look at her body. We can only judge by what she did do." He looked sternly at the women and men deciding the case. "The issue is simple . . . who are you going to believe? . . . The deputies have nothing to gain. They get no bonuses for arrests. A rose by any other name would smell as sweet . . . so all this conversation about the expense of the act doesn't affect what was done that night."

Giesler let the air settle in the room. He rose. He calmly turned to the jury.

"Free this fine young woman. To send her on her way to bigger and better things."
In doing so the jury "would be upholding the finest traditions of Americanism."

Regarding his client being a "burlesque," he defended, "I've tried this case with
every ounce of respect for His Honor, the jury, and the integrity of the court." He appealed
to their sense of injustice and explained there were no set laws regarding "decency."

"Just think, one individual can tell an entire community what is right and
what is wrong." Giesler wanted them to really look at Lili. The lovely young woman
sitting beside her adoring husband. She looked like a lady. And as much as he had
gotten to know her she was a *fine* lady.

He reiterated that Lili knew the sheriffs were attending her performance on
that night and doubted she would "flaunt indecency in the face of officers."

"She's only trying to lift herself up. This is the American way and she has every
right to do it." He paused. "If I thought she intended to put on a lewd performance
I wouldn't touch this case. I don't need the money. I came into this because of my
faith in the great American law of justice."

During rebuttal Gross conceded Giesler was "a gentleman, scholar, and a fine
man.'" However "I think the issue is who are you going to believe, the officers who
saw Lili or the defense?"

The judge dismissed the "ten tired women and two mild, outnumbered men"
for the night.[554] They would all meet the next morning back in the courtroom for
instructions.

The next morning Judge Henry H. Draeger warned the jury, "Even if she did
indecently display herself, you must find her not guilty if it was done without specific intent to do so."

The jury filed out to weigh the evidence. *The Los Angeles Times* carried a picture of Armando planting a supportive kiss on the smiling Lili's cheek. He told her,
"Everything's going to be all right." She almost believed it.

LILI HAD A NATURAL "HAUTEUR AND DIGNIFIED ALOOFNESS" ABOUT
her, though it did not alienate her from the jury. Her beauty and obvious class
played in her favor.

After seventy-eight nail-biting minutes the jury was ready with their verdict.

While she wrung a lace hanky in her hands, the jury pronounced Lili innocent. Lili felt an explosion go off in her head.

"Oh boy. Oh boy!" exclaimed Giesler.[555]

"I'm relieved," Lili gushed.

The jury immediately surrounded her, reaching for her hands, wishing her
"good luck" and "congratulations."

Triumphant in court, Lili with her attorney

The jury told reporters they had balloted three times; the first time had been eight to four and the second ten to two, before ending in a unanimous decision.

Lili declared, "It's a wonderful and a real victory for the profession."

She threw her arms around Giesler and smiled for the cameras holding exhibits A and B, her rhinestone-encrusted panties and bra. The attorney himself looked satisfied, after "having that case laughed into acquittal."[556] He said he felt as if he'd just won the World Series.

Armando drifted toward the background, smiling, perhaps thinking he would finally be getting his wife to himself. But the fame Lili attained was about to send her career soaring into the stratosphere and he would never get his *Leelee* back.

On the way to the car Lili asked Giesler how much she owed him.

"How much do you have in your purse?"

She reached in and grabbed all her cash. Over $2,000 in bills. "Here."

"Fine." He reached for it. "We're settled."

Giesler's fame was forever cemented by Lili's touch of glamour. Lili's and Giesler's shared triumph in court legitimized Lili and sprinkled the attorney with more stardust than most of his movie-star clients. He was still a few years away from another blonde damsel in distress, Marilyn Monroe, who attended many of Lili's performances, claiming to pattern herself after the lean stripper. Marilyn would turn to the saggy-chinned attorney in tears during her very public divorce from Joe DiMaggio. He would stand patiently beside the pale-faced blonde who dressed in a conservative turtleneck as Lili had.

Giesler was the ultimate small-town boy with the midwestern work ethic determined to make good in the world. His career would go on for almost a half century.

The drama in the courtroom lasted six days and cost the county $1,200, less than a week's salary for Lili.

Variety declared Lili a "Symbol of Free Enterprise." Ironically, in a much smaller column in the same paper, Lili's old Florentine Garden codancer Yvonne DeCarlo was set to star in the film *Hurricane*. Lili received far more ink fighting for the "American way."

"Just because a girl's a stripper, you know," Lili described herself a week after the trial, "does not mean she hasn't got homespun values."

Lili's favorite subject to dish about remained men. To reporter Virginia MacPherson, Lili "shifted her mink coat" and launched into how she admired "stable, lovable men." She liked "permanent men. Men you can trust to stick with you." Lili's men stuck. It was Lili that usually didn't adhere to a relationship.[557]

Ciro's was "celebrating" Lili's triumphant verdict and promised patrons her performance had "reverted to her original act."[558]

Lili asked for more money and a week later Hover again "hacked" Lili, firing her because of her outrageous and exorbitant salary demands.[559]

Lili didn't care. There was a long list of places willing to fork over piles of cash to see the infamous Lili St. Cyr. She had been promised a twelve-week engagement at the Beachcomber in Miami Beach starting December 20, but first she had a return engagement at the Chi Chi in Palm Springs.

Suddenly clubs that had been inaccessible to her were begging her to perform. Lili's fame had been assured with her "million dollars' worth of free publicity."

"She liked the attention," Armando said. "She was a beautiful, beautiful girl. I was a handsome man . . . at the time." He chuckled. "Ciro's wasn't doing so good before Lili. In her three months at Ciro's she was sold out. It changed everything for her. And killed us . . ." He paused. "She was so famous after that." [560]

A-list producer Walter Wanger phoned. Wanger was the executive behind such films as *Queen Christina* (starring Lili's idol Garbo) and director John Ford's *Stagecoach*, Hitchcock's *Foreign Correspondent*, and *Joan of Arc*. Wanger wanted Lili for a proposed film, *Scherazade*, the music based on *A Thousand and One Nights*. Wanger drove out to the desert to talk with her after her show. The two got on brilliantly and ended up chatting all night, which is how long it took him to convince her to do the part. Wanger immediately drove back to Los Angeles and Lili went to bed in the early-morning hours thrilled. *Scherazade* was right up her alley. Just the kind of high-brow thing she wanted to take on. She knew her acting range was limited, but with Wanger she could make the leap to respectable films and out of burlesque.[561]

Fate, however, had other plans. Wanger chose the next day, December 13, at dusk to shoot his wife Joan Bennett's supposed lover, talent agent Jennings Lang, in a parking lot in Los Angeles. Lang was shot in the groin and would recover.[562] *Scherazade* was off. Wanger received a four-month jail sentence for "temporary insanity." His lawyer was Jerry Giesler.[563] Not to be entirely thwarted, Lili would create her own version of *Scherazade* for the stage.

CHAPTER FIVE

In January of 1952 Lili stood on the Follies stage. There were the usual touch-stones grounding her: tub, bed, filmy dressing gowns tossed over a chase, vanity, Armando's framed photograph.

"Lili, you ready?" Lillian Hunt's voice boomed from an empty row in the theatre.

This was no live show. Lili was about to film *Love Moods,* a seventeen-minute re-creation of her "infamous" (as it was forever after billed) Ciro's routine. She reclined on a blue chaise lounge and wore an evening gown, which she traded for a sheer robe. Down to her "scanty panties" she bathed in a "white and gold" tub, as Sadie hovered in attendance.[564] At the end of the act, dressed in jewels and a long fur coat, she wrapped a fur stole atop her shoulders. It was classic Lili.

Lili explained, "I sort of directed it myself." As only she would know how to do. She even "told the camera where to be placed."[565]

"The police said she was naughty that she showed too much Lili," claimed the trailer. However, *Variety* complained all Lili showed was "a fast look at her shapely thighs."[566]

Though it hadn't been fun at the time, the Ciro's arrest would turn out to be the best thing that could have happened to Lili. She was climbing the heights of a career no one could have imagined from a stripteaser, paid $5,000 for a day's work on *Love Moods.* The producers Willis Kent and Dan Sonney had approached her with the idea. "So everyone can see what they missed at Ciro's. It'll be a hit!"

IT WASN'T SUCH HARD WORK AND NO WAY WAS SHE TURNING DOWN that amount of money.

Though quicker than shooting a feature-length film, the process was still tedious, Lili standing under the hot lights waiting for cameras to be reloaded or

Lili's "Love Moods"

lights adjusted. There was constant powdering; her makeup seemed to drip off her face. She did like the exposure the short film promised to bring. Those too shy or hypocritical to come to the clubs could see her in all her glory. She would be immortalized on celluloid. It kept anxiety at bay. *I matter. I was here.*

Tom Douglas supervised her look and the props. Tom had become her rock, and though he tended to drink more she trusted him utterly. Armando, becoming more estranged following the trial, was nowhere except for in the picture frame she held in her hands.

Capitalizing on the trial, the producers edited and distributed the film within seven weeks of Lili's acquittal. The one-sheet posters proclaimed, "As Presented On the Sunset Strip in Hollywood."

When it debuted in February, critics complained all she did was "dress and undress"[567] yet in three days the film grossed $4,000 in Hollywood at the Paris Theatre, with tickets as low as 85 cents and as high as $1.[568]

Lili continued to elevate herself from her profession, taking exception at being called a stripper. She much preferred "to be known as the ballet pantomimist."[569]

As proof that Lili wasn't the only one singled out for persecution—and prosecution—the following year her pal headliner Betty Rowland would be sentenced to jail for four months for her "lewd" performance at the Follies (now called the New Follies).[570] It was a harsh sentence. Betty was thirty-six and was released after three degrading weeks that she never forgot.[571]

Lili was scheduled to appear on *The Spade Cooley Show,* a televised coast-to-coast variety show shot at the Santa Monica Pier Ballroom. Prior guests had included Frankie Lane and Dinah Shore. A fee of $500 was agreed on. However, at the last minute the show's sponsors, Chevy Dealerships, developed cold feet about having an infamous peeler on a family show and nixed her appearance. She was angry but still received her pay.[572]

Hover wasn't really done with Lili and she triumphantly sailed back onstage at Ciro's, no doubt at an inflated rate. She was loyal and also kept returning to the New Follies. Both places remained sold out.

One afternoon at the Main Street theatre she was performing as Cleopatra when she spotted a man in the balcony masturbating. It was a common enough occurrence in the theatres. "There was a certain seediness," explained stripper Dixie Evans. "One expected that sort of thing."[573] And toward the late forties into the fifties the New Follies had begun to slide toward a more base, more carnal show, as burlesque itself had.

Lili was strangely flattered and repulsed by the man masturbating. As Sherry Britton acknowledged, "I knew I was a part of that."[574] Like Lili she felt conflicting emotions about being able to affect such a response from her audience. Power and shame.

Lili felt empowered. Her beauty was her currency. They could all jerk off as she danced. Since the first kiss with boyfriend Jimmy Nichols, when she had felt his erection, she marveled at the response she could generate. In clubs like the Samoa where the men were only feet from her crotch, she could see the desire and the glimmer in their eyes and in their pants. She was neither afraid of the response nor repulsed by it.

Her shudder onstage reverberated up to the man in the balcony. He climaxed at the culmination of her dance. She looked up with satisfaction in her eyes. The man fled.

She designed her shows so there would be something for everyone. The women gasped over her clothing, jewels, and furs, and the men quite simply drooled over her divine figure.

Scripts for movies began to pile up outside the Canyon Drive house. Her phone rang with offers of work and requests for interviews.

Agent Henry Wilson, known for "inventing" Rock Hudson, Lana Turner, Troy Donahue, John Derek, and a bevy of other beautiful young (often homosexual) actors, called Lili. Wilson had caught the act at Ciro's and quickly signed her for representation in the movies.[575]

The forty-year-old agent looked like "Vincente Minnelli," slightly pudgy with a dark receding hairline. A dapper dresser, he wore three-piece suits and had a dry sense of humor that Lili appreciated.[576]

"He could build careers," said former client actor Tab Hunter. Wilson loved to escort "gals around. There was a touch of sleaze," Hunter admitted. But he was a "big agent. More like a manger."

The sophisticated Wilson was not only "powerful" but a "gay svengali."[577]

Wilson messengered scripts to Lili daily. Many roles were written specifically for her (though most came to naught). It was an exciting, high-pressure time. She had worked long and hard to see her career paying off. She later admitted it was head-turning. She paid less attention to Armando, who was adrift. He seemed a hindrance to her scaling the heights she wanted. She became arrogant with him and others. She didn't want to listen to anyone. It was her career and she wasn't going to stop. She didn't owe anyone any explanation for anything. The resentment and worry she had endured at trial came out as self-importance. And though she knew she wasn't being fair—mostly to Armando—she couldn't stop herself.

If someone asked her out, she went, as she considered it part of her job. Armando was sure she remained faithful to him, and it is doubtful he gave her a long leash, but if not physically adulterous, she could cheat mentally. She was retreating from him.

Tension was high in the house as Armando tried to hold his place in Lili's life. She largely ignored him, his friends, and his opinions. She cared only for Tom and Virginia and friends that fawned over her.

In June columnist Earl Wilson cornered Lili for an interview. "Are you tired of taking your clothes off?"

Her answer was revealing. "My *husband* doesn't like it." But Lili wasn't about to give up a rumored $5,000 a week. She was beginning to insinuate in interviews that she was on the verge of quitting, either to appease Armando or to fuel the theatre-packing that there wasn't going to be Lili St. Cyr and her see-through bathtub around much longer. At this point she was *two decades* from quitting. She told Wilson, "He's going to be very happy if I got into something else."[578]

Wilson was sitting in her suite at the Astor Hotel in New York (Miles Ingalls used the Astor as his business address). It was three in the afternoon. She had recently arisen and he noted she still looked sleepy, wearing a coat and blue pantsuit. She was still favoring pants, even though it was the hotel's policy to forbid women to wear them. He accused her of arranging her arrests for publicity.

"It's a heck of a nuisance . . . and it costs a lot of money." She said she wished not "to thrive on scandal but on art."[579]

She defended her act: "There are a thousand girls you can see without clothes on, and just doing that doesn't get them any place." She admitted she thought of herself as an artist. She wasn't for nudity, reminding Wilson, "I couldn't make any money if everybody was walking around nude!" [580]

Did she mind all the fuss made about stripping? She deflected. "I'm glad they do—they're keeping me in mink coats."

CHAPTER SIX

As a last-ditch effort to save his marriage Armando convinced Lili to take a belated honeymoon to Italy. Maybe because she was still tense and exhausted after the trial, she agreed. She rationalized if she gave him this time, she could return to her wall-to-wall bookings.

Armando asked her if she had ever been to Europe. She lied and said no. It was habit to lie. Armando wanted to show her his city, Roma.

In June Armando flew ahead to arrange for their accommodations. She would follow after the conclusion of her engagements. She flew to New York alone. Once in New York she boarded Alitalia for Rome.[581]

In her Canadian biography, Lili claimed that at the Rome airport they were plagued by paparazzi. She was surprised by her fame in Europe. Most likely she wasn't famous there. This author could find no evidence to support Lili's claim. Armando wasn't famous and the whole paparazzi-celebrity stalking didn't begin until Fellini's 1960 film *La Dolce Vita*. The word "paparazzi" wasn't even used yet. It simply wasn't in the zeitgeist in 1952 and Lili was not internationally known. She and Armando were no Liz and Dick, whose shenanigans were still another ten years down the road.

Exhausted after the long flight, Lili climbed into the tiny sports car Armando rented. Her head was exploding. Armando zipped the little car through the streets, excitedly pointing out ancient ruins to her. She nodded, not caring about the Roman Forum or the Capitoline Hill as the sun reflecting off the stone blinded her. She longed to lay her head down on a soft pillow and close her eyes.

"There is where the Coliseum—" Armando babbled as he drove past the half-crumbling monument dating from 80 AD.

"Armando," she pleaded, "can we see this another time? Must it be today?"

"*Bambina*," he grabbed her hand, his blue eyes shining with love for his city and his woman. "It must be today. We must see it today."

She nodded, her eyes glazing over. "It's beautiful. Beautiful." She could swear they had circled one particular grand building several times and was about to say something when he pulled the car in front of a pair of impressive gates.

A man came out, spoke briefly in rapid Italian, and pushed open the gates. Armando gunned the car up the circular driveway to an open courtyard.

She slipped out of the car as a steward popped open the car's trunk and starting removing her luggage.

"Armando, what is he doing?" Lili screeched. "Stop, please. Armando."

Armando gripped her by the waist and starting laughing. "It is all right, *Bambina*. Relax."

"Why are you laughing? I have my jewels in there—"

"*Cara*, this is where we are going to live. We need to have your luggage, your things here."

Lili stopped. They were going to live here? It was the most gorgeous place she had ever seen.

Armando led her to a suite of rooms richly decorated with ancient paintings and ornate gilding. Tall ceilings were painted with fading frescos. There was a set of marble fireplaces as tall as her.

"This is my family's home," Armando explained proudly, waving an arm about. "Do you like?"

She threw herself into his arms and kissed him deeply.

In Lili's biography she describes the fabulous building as being the Palazzo Orsini. She doesn't identify it as being the Palazzo Cocchi, which was Armando's true surname. Armando by no means came from royalty (perhaps it was fantasy of her ghostwriter). There is an Orsini Palazzo in Rome, but it would have been odd for it to have been Armando's unless it belonged to distant relatives. Lili never "outed" Armando as Cocchi, a name he didn't use. Armando told this author he rented an apartment in the old part of Rome before they traveled to Sicily, Tuscany, Calabria, and the Dolomites.[582]

No matter which palazzo they stayed in, their months together in Europe were some of their best times together. They were the closest they had ever been, or would ever be. Years later Lili would say the three months was the happiest time of her life. And one of the only times in her career that she didn't work. She would consider it the most "normal" time of her life with no strict schedule to adhere to. The memories would stay with her forever, though the honeymoon would usher in the end of her marriage.[583]

Lili recalled days spent exploring the fine old Palazzo that was in the process of renovations. There was a grand staircase that led to nowhere. There were old Roman mosaic tiles on the floor that shone like real gold. One room had only a bed in it—where she would take quiet naps sheltered in the cool darkness of the grand room. Another room was turned into her closet, grand and luxurious. Armando was in his element, showing his wife *his* life, giving her the luxury—even if only short-lived—that she strove to have.

She would spend days exploring up and down staircases. Armando led her to a suite of rooms above them to meet his mother, a gentle sweet woman who doted on her son. Signora Cocchi had experienced terrible things during World War II, which had left its mark on her.[584] According to Lili, Armando's father had been killed in front of his wife and Armando had been hauled off by the Germans.

Armando explained to Lili that he had escaped one night when the prison where he was kept was bombed. Free, he traveled on foot only at night so as not to get caught. He walked through destroyed villages avoiding the prowling German army. He saw countless dead bodies making his way back to Rome and his mother, just in time to witness Rome's liberation.

Armando's mother spoke not a word of English. Despite this, both she and Lili enjoyed each other's company.

In the midst of their bliss, one day Lili doubled over in pain. She had to have emergency surgery to take care of a painful cyst, the reason Armando believed she never became pregnant.

The doctors discovered too late that Lili was allergic to penicillin. She fell unconscious. Terrified, Armando remained at her side. When they returned to the Palazzo, Armando had the mirrors either covered or removed after she saw her swollen reflection and became desolate. *Oh, my face, Armando!* How would she ever work again? Luckily the swelling subsided and her beauty remained unscathed.

As the summer wore on, the steamy heat of the Roman streets began to oppress the couple. They decided to escape to the north. Traveling to Venice they checked into the magnificent Danielle on the Grand Canal. They spent happy days strolling hand in hand around the squares drinking strong espresso and eating sweets at Caffè Florian. She felt like a tourist. They never argued. They were in love again without the pressures of her work.

They next escaped to the beautiful island of Capri, which in August was at the height of the season. Lili thought it was glamorous and fun and they sipped lemoncello in La Piazetta, the crowded little square in the heart of the town with dozens of dark-skinned Italians gossiping and flirting and laughing.

TOP: *Lili and Armando in Capri*
BOTTOM: *Very much in love with her "Prince" in Capri*

A PICTURE OF THE TWO OF THEM ON THE TERRACE OF THE HOTEL Caesar Augustus high above the water shows them smiling. They are a stunning pair, Lili wearing a striped pants outfit, her jewelry casual, her hair cut short. Armando by her side. They both glowed with a Mediterranean tan.

AS THE DAYS WORE ON LILI BEGAN TO GROW ANXIOUS. THEN BORED. She complained about things, the lack of clean bathrooms, the food. *It was too hot.*

Armando became impatient. They left the island.

In Switzerland he dragged her up cool green mountains. She was restless. No longer content to roam aimlessly. She missed the stage. She was wasting time. What was going on back in the clubs? Was someone taking her place?

She received a telegram from Miles Ingalls. She had been listed as one of the ten most beautiful women in the world, along with Ava Gardner and Bridgett Bardot. Las Vegas named her the "cherished child."

She wanted to go home. Time was passing her by, time she couldn't get back. Her career was based on beauty and a strong young body. She scrutinized herself in the mirror. Everything she had worked hard to achieve was slipping away. Armando became the enemy.

"What is wrong, *bambina*?" Armando would ask.

She didn't know how to tell him all the things spinning in her head. She pushed him away.

"Let's go back to New York," she suggested. She didn't want to lose him, but she didn't want to lose her life either. She missed being someone. She agonized over Armando and the hurt she saw in his face.

"Please take me home," she begged him.

Armando, still so in love with Lili, reluctantly agreed. They returned to Rome, packed, and kissed his mother good-bye. On August 29 Armando and Lili boarded a DC-6, Linee Aeree Italiane. The name of the aircraft was "I—Love Italian." Flight 437 made fuel stops in Paris and Shannon, Ireland, before landing in New York on the thirtieth.

In New York Armando looked at property and toyed with the idea of opening a restaurant or a coffee bar like the ones in Italy. There was nothing like it in New York.

Lili encouraged him, thinking it a splendid way for him to drop his retirement villages plan. She suggested décor ideas and would be very proud of the interior of his future establishment, Orsini's.

CLUBS WERE BETTING ON LILI BRINGING IN BIG BOX OFFICE REVENUES and the New Follies had offered her a whopping $10,000 a week—outrageous for a burlesque theatre—outbidding several clubs.[585] "The largest sum ever paid by a theatre for a burlesque queen."[586]

The noise of applause was welcome after months of silence. She was back in her element. She felt strong and powerful. She became secretive around Armando, refusing to tell him where she went. While he believed her heavy work schedule shackled her, she felt shackled by him.

At the New Follies Lillian Hunt's husband, straight man Leon DeVoe, announced Lili to the expectant audience: "Ladies and gentlemen, we present for your enjoyment and entertainment the incomparable Lili St. Cyr."

From the orchestra pit the music began. A spotlight flickered across the dark stage searching for Lili. DeVoe moved center stage. "Ladies and gentlemen, I'm sorry to inform you Miss St. Cyr does not appear to be in the building."

From the back of the audience Lili burst in, dressed in a day suit loaded with shopping bags. "Wait, Miss. St. Cyr is here. Please come down." Lili walked down the aisle in all her magnificent beauty. A small step appeared at the foot of the stage and she slowly walked onto the stage. She leaned into DeVoe's ear and whispered. "It will be a few minutes, folks, she'll be right back," continued DeVoe. Lili again whispered in his ear. "Well, since she is going to be taking it off, why doesn't she just begin as she is?"

From there Lili proceeded to strip. "She never flashes a lot of her body," Hunt's granddaughter Pearl recalled.

The tub appeared and Lili slipped into a negligee. Sadie handed her a phone. On went an evening gown and she exited. All to "Rhapsody in Blue." Pearl claimed it was the only thing she used at the Follies at the time. She had her own orchestration of it, perfectly worked out, using only the parts that went with her choreography. Pearl remembered the sweet smell from Lili's bubble machine backstage. Her specially made tub had a cutout window so the audience could gaze at her.

The "movie stars came." Burt Lancaster, Mickey Rooney ("Well, he came all the time"). Though Pearl had met two of Lili's husbands—Valentine, who "followed her around," and Orsini—Pearl said there were "always rumors of lots of boyfriends."

ONE AFTERNOON AT THE THEATRE, LILI SENT WORD FOR PEARL. THERE was a bar next door that had "great hamburgers." "Lili wants to talk to you," Hunt told eleven- or twelve-year-old Pearl.

Lili, still in the habit of coloring her hair pink, blue, or lavender, was wearing a "very subtle" shade of pink.

Lili would use many different style tubs to bathe in

Lili asked the young girl if she wanted a cheeseburger? *Oh yes!*

"Pearl," Lili said, "I just want to tell you when I was a little girl I looked exactly like you do now."

Pearl, struck by the incredible beauty of Lili, was thrilled. Would she grow up to look like Lili?

With her beautiful hands Lili delicately maneuvered a messy hamburger. "She had a special cloth, like a hanky" that she retrieved from her purse to wipe her mouth. She was incredibly glamorous and exotic, dabbing a finger at her lip. But apparently not chatty. Besides remarking on her looks, it was the only conversation the two had the entire meal. "She didn't have a personality," Pearl said.

Lili presented her with a little box. "Open that when you get in your dressing room." It would turn out to be a scarf with French poodles on it. Something Lili had picked up in Europe. "She was incredibly sweet," Pearl said.

Lili, always savvy about publicity, was most likely the one who cooked up a feud in the papers between Dardy and herself. Lili, the paper said, (coincidentally along with Paul Valentine's ex-girlfriend Sally Rand) wanted to portray Lady Godiva in a pageant in England. Lili said she would wear a long blonde wig, claiming she was most qualified because she was shy like Godiva. Dardy bragged she was more qualified because "I am a lady. I believe nudity should be reserved for the theatre." Dardy "accused" Lili of "cheapening their profession."[587]

Other papers played up the fact Dardy had "stolen" Lili's boudoir scenario. Most likely Lili helped her younger sister create her own version of the act.[588] Even Al Palmer noted that she worked under "sister Lili's tutelage."[589]

DARDY WASN'T THE ONLY ONE IMITATING LILI'S SIGNATURE ACTS. There were several look-alike bathing acts wetting audiences in New York. It irked Lili, but she knew she was the original everyone wanted to see. She said burlesque was "one of the most unethical forms of show business."[590]

On December 28, 1952, after a night working the New Follies, Lili returned home around 2 a.m. to an unpleasant surprise: She had been robbed of a $10,000 black-diamond mink, a Christmas gift from Armando. The coat had been magnificent—lined with white brocade, it had a large collar that she could use either as a hood or cape.

They called the police. The next day Lili refused to answer the flurry of phone calls from reporters, leaving Armando the task of fielding calls while she slept. It infuriated him. Reporters kept calling him her "unemployed civil engineer" of a husband. He didn't like how she was treating him like an employee. *Do this, do that, answer the phone, tell them this . . .*[591]

Henry Wilson continued fielding calls for his client to appear mostly in B movies. The trades kept announcing Lili's impending appearance in one film after another, yet Lili remained on the stage.

There was tension in the Canyon Drive home. Armando was frustrated with little to do and Lili was angry that his future seemed dependent on her.

Tom Douglas picked Lili up and took her to her hairdresser in Hollywood. "She was a terrible driver." Dardy claimed Lili rarely drove anymore.

The phone rang. His English was not good enough for the telephone, but Lili was gone.

It was Henry Wilson.

"She have to call you back," Armando told him.

After some small talk Henry boasted his client was "booked solid for the next year." He had clubs begging for her.

The agent's words echoed in Armando's ears. *She's booked for the next year.* It also promised to be a good year of work for Lili's sister, advertised as such.

Armando was incredulous.

He sat in the quiet of *Leelee's* house, surrounded by *her* things, and knew he

Dardy in "her" boudoir scene

couldn't stay. He realized "this woman will never quit." She was never going to stop working. Oh, maybe in five or ten years when she got too old to take her clothes off. But not now, not in time for him, in time for *them*. He had wanted to believe her. But he couldn't live his life like this. She wanted this life. She couldn't stop collecting the dough. And "she's not gonna trust this Italian guy."

He was tired of her promising, "One more year, Armando, then I'll quit." Or, "But they are offering me $10,000 for the week. Let's wait another month before I quit." Every time she booked another three-week engagement she told him they should wait. "I'm a precise guy," Armando explained. "Lili, now is the time to build and invest." His partner had been waiting two years for them.

"I was kept. It was a beautiful life. She was very proper. She was never unfaithful. But I couldn't live that way anymore."

Though she had grown cavalier in her treatment of Armando, mostly because she saw him as a threat to her continued success, in the last months they were together she was afraid without him. She had wanted it to work, but ultimately chose flight. She had come too far in her career and didn't want to jeopardize it. Once again she let the man in the relationship be the one who ended it.

Armando packed his things and left in the car she had given him. "She didn't believe it." But Armando had his formidable pride. "I'm not a gigolo. I had a project. I left."[592]

Decades later Armando said, "She would always ask, 'Can I take this job?' I would say, "Of course.' Then another job would come up. 'But Armando, they are giving me this much money.' 'Take it,' I would say. I never tried to stop it. But I couldn't go on." He sighed. An old man still frustrated at what could have been.

Armando did eventually open a coffee shop, Café Orsini, in 1953, and it was a huge success. In the fifties there were no elegant coffee shops like the ones in Europe. It was a small place on West Fifty-Sixth Street. At first there were fifteen marble tables and in back six tables for diners, mostly for his friends, Oleg Casini, Ali Khan, Porfirio Rubirosa, and a host of wealthy bachelor playboy friends who all belonged to the same tennis club and trawled among the same New York socialites for mistresses and occasionally wives. Café Orsini was elegant, with candlelight and red velvet walls—all Lili's suggestions. There were chandeliers and brass and waiters in formal attire. Clients would include Jackie Onassis and Gloria Vanderbilt among the moneyed ladies who lunched.

Eventually Armando added more tables, and society came for the excellent Italian food and the handsome owner who always paused to kiss a lady's hand. He filled the place with antiques and was a success, as Lili had predicted he would be. Eventually it grew into a large restaurant, and along with his brother Elio, Armando bought the building. Upstairs was a small apartment where Armando bedded many women in his long and prolific life as a Manhattan playboy.

After Lili, Armando spent decades tearing through scores of beautiful women, married and not. When she was working in New York Lili would sometimes meet him for lunch. She even would see his mother when she came from Rome. But their romance was over. Not the love, but the *in love*.

She would write, "I didn't realize how much I really cared until I looked back."[593] He was the one she would regret losing. "This was the best one."

He kept going and so did she. Then one day she started writing him letters of regret, realizing the "sunburst" he had been in her life when she had been so "lonely and unhappy."[594] But it was too late. And she was still working, still starring as the notorious Lili St. Cyr. Their time had passed. He too for a time used drugs when the discos took over New York. Sex and drugs. He was mad with it. Poppers. They had almost killed him. He was once pulled screaming from an airplane, calling for his mother like a baby. His mind snapped.

Armando's second wife, Georgianna, a poet, asked him not to write or to call Lili. If they were to have a go of it, he had to let Lili go. And he did. Sort of. Out of respect for his wife he made Elio the middleman. Lili would call Elio when she needed something and Elio would call Armando and he would send cash, gifts, and messages. Armando would be there for Lili to the very end.

PART FOUR

BIRD IN A GOLDEN SWING

*"The more I stay with X the more
responsible I feel towards him.
My freedom is cut off."*

—LILI ST. CYR

Lili St. Cyr

Her royal wedding night in Monaco number gives Las Vegas a sequel to Grace Kelly marriage.

CHAPTER ONE

Armando was still legally married to Lili but he was in New York and she was working the Rialto in Chicago for brother-in-law Harold Minksy, whom she adored and respected.

Dardy was running Harold's shows. "We used to get these little girls and turn them into the most wonderful strippers."[595] The name Minsky on a marquee meant gorgeous costumes, a full line of elaborately dressed chorus girls, and strippers that were the cream of the burlesque circuit. Dardy was proud to sign the name Minsky.

Lili thought the world of Harold. "They both loved each other," Dardy said. "Harold loved to spend money as much as Lili did. One Christmas when Ava was about three, Harold and a few of his hangers-on—he always had an entourage—went to get a Christmas tree. Now, Harold was Jewish, so he had never had one before. They went to a lot and came back with the most gorgeous tree. He said, 'I asked the owner which is the most expensive tree on the lot.'" Dardy laughed. "That was just like Lili."

Every morning Harold got up early and went to get fresh bagels for Dardy and the kids. However, first he would stop by Lili's hotel and bring her whatever she asked for, usually a croissant or petit fours. "She wasn't a bagel girl," Dardy explained.

In his New Jersey theatre Lili asked Harold to put a bed in her dressing room, after he had the dingy room painted and wall-papered. She had decided to sleep nights in her dressing room to save time traveling back to her hotel in Manhattan. Harold naturally obliged. "If Lili . . . comes to us with some unusual, difficult technical ideas in order to make for a better act, we supply what's needed."[596]

Dardy explained, "When you're doing six shows a day and you have an hour between shows and your show is two hours long . . ." There was no time to go anywhere else. Instead of driving to the Astor, Lili preferred her dressing room.

Working together again in Chicago it was like old times for Dardy and Lili.

Mutual admiration society: Lili and her brother-in-law, Harold Minsky

And there was Fehnova, who was choreographing Harold's shows. He and Lili would barricade themselves in her dressing room and drink champagne, howling with laughter.[597]

PHIL SILVERS WAS A FORMER MINSKY COMEDIAN AND FRIEND OF Harold's. Silvers was at the height of popularity with his hit television series *The Phil Silvers Show* playing Sergeant Ernest Bilko. Harold told him to come to Chicago to see Lili perform. The comedian admitted he desperately wanted to meet her.

Silvers arrived at the theatre and Dardy knocked on Lili's dressing room. "Hey, Lil, it's me. Open up, someone wants to meet you." When the door opened Lili was sitting in a sheer black robe with pasties and G-string, all her gorgeousness on display. Silvers was beside himself. Lili was polite and after a few minutes of conversation she asked, "And what do you do, Mr. Silvers?" The actor's inflated ego was deflated. "I got a good laugh out of that for decades," Dardy beamed.

"Lili would never go out with crowds but she'd go with me and Harold," Dardy said. Minsky's Rialto Theatre on State and Van Buren was near a little place called the Silver Bar. "Lili and I would go in for drinks after her show. I would introduce her to all the gangsters that hung out there. I mean big, *big* gangsters. The Fischetti brothers. They were just wonderful guys!" Dardy laughed. "And then I would tell Lili, 'He's on the FBI's 10 Most Wanted List.' She loved it. She said to the bartender, 'What a wonderful clientele you have here.' I mean she always wanted to go there after that."[598]

Dardy persuaded Lili to join her and Harold at a nightclub in the tony Gold Coast neighborhood. The Chez Paree was a top nightclub with talent such as Sophie Tucker, Jimmy Durante, Danny Thomas, Lili's Vegas pal Joe. E. Lewis, and Frank Sinatra. Inside the Chez Paree was a private members-only club called the Gold Key Room. Members were given a gold key for a fee of $100 with their name engraved on it. The key inserted into a padded door at the end of the large dining room that allowed entrance to a smaller, more informal club.

Harold and Dardy were members. Local newscaster Mike Wallace and his Italian-born wife Buff Cobb stopped by their table while Lili was there. Wallace and Cobb begged Lili to come on their radio show that was broadcast live from the Chez Paree. Reluctantly Lili agreed. It was a disaster.

"She froze," Dardy said. "The first question they asked her. She absolutely froze and didn't say a word the entire time."

Another night Lili, Dardy, and Harold joined a late-night dinner group of friends discussing the upcoming July 1952 Democratic National Convention. Lili arrived fresh off the stage from her midnight show.

The talk among the group was all about the candidates. Dardy was vocally an Adlai Stevenson supporter. She was pregnant at the time and not drinking. Lili sipped a gin martini and remained quiet.

Someone argued how indecisive Stevenson was. "A snob, an intellectual," they snorted.

Dardy argued back that some "intellect" was needed in the party.

After a half hour of debate Lili got up without saying a word. Halfway across the room Dardy caught up with her.

"Where are you going?"

"To bed. I'm bored with all this political talk." She yawned.

"Aren't you interested in who becomes president? Everyone else is. We're just excited and the convention will be here. Harold promised to take me."

Lili rolled her eyes.

Dardy put her hands on her hips and narrowed her eyes. "You don't even know who is running for president."

"Yes, I do," she paused. "Eisenhower!"

Dardy was amazed. Lili never read a newspaper or listened to the radio. "How did you know that?"

"*You* told me," Lili smiled, turned, and left.[599]

THE REST OF 1952 WAS A BUSY YEAR. AT THIRTY-FIVE SHE DIDN'T HAVE time to think, just dance and rake in the money.

By October Lili was back in Las Vegas pleading guilty to her September misdemeanor charge. She paid a $250 fine (or rather she had Beldon pay it) for the arrest prior to Ciro's so she could return to the El Rancho, now more infamous than before.

Her show was described as a "fashion show" wherein she changed in and out of numerous designer gowns.[600] She had gone "chichi."[601] Little cards were stacked on the cocktail tables informing the audience that her gowns were by Simonetti Visconti, an Italian designer whose clothes Armando had introduced her to. Visconti was a fellow Roman jailed by Mussolini and would in the future live at a leper colony. Visconti had Lili's kind of aristocratic glamour. Lili's hats were made by Jose Fernandez of Madrid and her jewels set by Boucheron.

Lili counted the music and sailed onto the stage to the first wave of "ahs." Her gown swirled around her. She moved like a queen. It was all second nature by now.

She moved about the set, which was dominated by an ornate vanity, bathtub, and chaise. A photograph of Armando hung above her vanity. She supposed when they divorced she'd have to take it down. She knelt in front of the mirror. Kicking her legs up for Sadie to take off one thigh-high black stocking after the other.

Reviewers weren't all complimentary with Lili's familiar pantomime. "Gone are the days, alas, when the St. Cyr strip was bouncy and gay."[602] Some complained the act had become "set." It was. But that was because it worked and it is what audiences expected to see.

The critics sensed a certain ennui pervaded Lili. A hardness was freezing her. She was still taking her pills. The dressing rooms were still mostly crummy; rats and cockroaches and the smell of old cheese. She had become polished, but she was no longer fresh; she was preserved and crystallized.

She continued to keep her large salary—usually paid in cash—out of banks and on her person. She had a pocket sewn into her garter belt where she would stuff $100 bills at the end of the night.

"I always knew when she had a lot of money," Dardy said. "I mean she'd have thousands of dollars on her. But she loved to spend money. That was part of the fun of having it."

Lili ended the very eventful year with a tribute at the New Follies in Los Angeles by the new owners. A dinner at the Sportsmen's Club was thrown after the last show on December 29 with comedians and fellow strippers. It would be one of the only tributes for her in her long career.

AS LILI RUNG IN 1953 SHE TRIED NOT TO THINK ABOUT ARMANDO.

Maybe she would have Tom arrange a dinner party at her house. She would put on her glittering hostess face, not at all upset over her latest wreck of a marriage. She would show them she was the happy, hard-hearted love-'em-and-leave-'em Lili. No one would know how despondent she really was.

The reporters asked where Armando was. "Are you divorcing, Lili?" they wanted to know. "Who's the new romance?"

"No one. And of course we're not divorcing," she lied.

Lili went on a nonstop jag of work, dates, and pills. She announced she would be doing a musical of *Carmen* (nothing would come of it). She submerged herself in Vegas working, sleeping, seeing Dardy and the kids when she could. Her stomach gave her trouble. Her appendix acted up. She ignored everything.

She had no harsh words for Armando—ever. She regretted his leaving but wasn't ready for the applause to end.

Besides minor health issues these were the golden years for Lili, who was making anywhere between three and $5,000 a week. Huge sums for the 1950s when the average income was $4,000, and the cost of the average home was $17,000. Gas was 22 cents, a stamp 3 cents. And this was her "official" income. She always went home with much more from tips if she sat with a customer or if the theatre added another show.

It was rumored that her bubble bath routine at Ciro's pulled in between nine and $10,000 a week. Audiences—and club owners—demanded Lili keep the tub in the act.

None of the imitation bubble bath routines that kept popping up—sometimes on the same street—made a dint in her appeal. Lili was the original and Lili was a smash success.

She traveled with truckloads of antique furniture, spending enormous sums of money to haul her props from town to town. Her gowns and furs and jewels cost thousands, all supervised under the careful eye of Tom Douglas.

She headlined at the Beachcomber in Miami with a "conventional type burlesque show," including a line of chorus girls, comics, and dance teams. She premiered a new stage designed by the ever-faithful Tom.

Las Vegas was inviting and invigorating for Lili, though *Variety* noted that the "reception is mild."[603] Lili didn't care. She felt at home with the cactus and the cold nights. She adored the beauty of the sunsets and the solitude of the land.

Dardy and Harold had a daughter, Ava, born in 1953. Lili didn't understand why Dardy wanted children. "Don't you know what's going to happen to your breasts?" she asked.[604]

When she was old enough to know her aunt, Ava thought Lili considered her—and all children—a "nuisance." Lili couldn't be "bothered."[605]

Alice visited Dardy and the kids frequently in Las Vegas. Idella rarely visited because "no one wanted to spend time with her." When Ava was about five or six her grandmother came to visit. Ava remembered everyone was inside the Minsky home when there was a knock on the door. Idella answered, spoke briefly with someone, then turning to her granddaughter said, "He hit your dog with his car and it's dead!"

When the little girl started to cry, understandably, Idella told her to go to her room and refused to speak to Ava for the remainder of her visit. "She was lacking in any maternal qualities."

VERY OFTEN IN THE CLUBS LILI WOULD DRINK A BIT HERE AND A BIT there (less over time as she no longer wanted to mingle or make champagne sales) as she circulated, which ended up being more than she wanted to consume. The next morning she would be left wrecked.

Instead of champagne sales she would prefer to curl up with a man and make love inside her house or hotel room and forget she was an "exotic dancer." She didn't have friends to confide in or hang with. She never went anywhere she could meet someone who wasn't another stripper. She would rather go back to her room and have Sadie grab her food or, if a man was interested, eat in the club.

Lili loved her lifestyle and the things it brought; however, she wasn't attached to money for money's sake. Perhaps if she had been, she might have watched her money better or invested. She hired an accountant but couldn't be bothered to monitor him. Taxes didn't always get paid.

To the outside eye Lili wasn't an obviously driven person. But from the time she stepped on the stage of the Florentine Gardens she never stopped working, plotting, planning, preparing. She was smart enough to know how to capitalize on her notoriety and was never above a good publicity stunt. Fame and fortune seemed to rain easily down on her. She liked being successful. But she would always feel it was a hollow fame. *It* didn't satisfy her.

Maybe it was at Armando's urging, but finally Lili turned to books with a vengeance. "Oh, she read everything. She would read about pearls," Dardy explained. "Then she would know everything there was to know about pearls. She just loved to read books. I mean she read *everything*. Except the papers. That didn't interest her." Laugh. "She wanted to educate herself about everything."

Lili filmed *Striporama*, a burlesque review with Bettie Page, Georgia Sothern, and Rosita Royce, who stripped by having bird food sewn into her clothes so her live doves would peck until her clothes dropped. Into its seventeen-week run at New York's Rialto Theatre, *Variety* noted there was "no closing date" in site. For what it was it did well, making over $108,000.[606]

Lili accepted every offer of work. As much as she was working, somehow it wasn't enough.

CHAPTER TWO

Somewhere after her split from Armando and before her next marriage (between 1952 and 1954) Lili would meet the least known and most mysterious of her lovers. She would say he "stole into her life."[607] He would be a memory hard to track down. But he would give her her greatest gift. Her house.

Lili was in her dressing room getting ready for her show at Club Samoa.

The club had a couple "royal boxes" for high-paying guests, where they could sit somewhat privately, paying of course for the privilege.[608]

Being such a tiny place, Lili was able to see most of the patrons, not that she acknowledged them, but she was aware of who was in the club. This night she noticed an elegant man sitting alone drinking in one of the boxes. He was the type of gentleman she didn't usually see at the club. Conservative.

After her show, the owner Nick knocked on her door.

"Come in," she purred.

"There is someone who wants to see you," Nick announced.

"Let me guess. The elegant, nicely dressed man in the box?"

Sadie puttered about Lili, getting her clothes ready.

"Actually, no," Nick said.

Sadie stopped. Lili frowned.

"The table near the front. The two gentlemen from Florida."

LILI SHRUGGED, TOOK HER TIME, AND EVENTUALLY JOINED THE TWO Florida businessmen. She was disappointed. Who was that mystery man? She was sure he would have asked to meet her.

The next night the same gentleman was back in his box drinking and watching the show.

During intermission Lili sat at Nick's table and the two ate steak sandwiches, which was about the only thing on the menu. Presently a waiter sent over a bottle of champagne. "From the gentleman in the box."

"Is there a note? Does he want to meet me?" Lili asked.

"No note, Miss St. Cyr," the waiter said, and left. The place was crowded as usual.

The next day in her dressing room four dozen red roses appeared without a note.

"This is getting strange," Sadie said. "Does Mystery Man want to meet you or not?"

"I don't know," Lili said, intrigued. She liked a good game of cat and mouse as well as the next.

After her last show, near 2 a.m., Lili decided to take things into her own hands.

She breezed over to the gentleman's table and paused, hand on hip. "Good evening. You're back."

"Good evening," he stood. He was at least thirty years older than her with gray hair and piercing blue eyes. While not handsome, he certainly was not unattractive and had a sophistication about him that appealed to her.

He introduced himself as Charles B. (Barney) Murphy and he had a slight stutter. She was surprised he was eating soup, which was not on the limited menu. But Murphy had persuaded the owner to make beef bourguignon. He was on a strict diet due to an ulcer.

They had a pleasant conversation about the show, New York, his business. He told her he was in real estate. Among his vast holdings was Sunkist and he owned the Murphy Ranch in Southern California. He purchased Paradise Valley and founded Ox Yoke Ranch, a fifty-thousand-acre cattle ranch in Montana. Slowly the club emptied out. He offered to escort her home. His driver drove her to the Astor Hotel.

Over the next few weeks they fell into a pattern. She would arrive at her dressing room to bigger and more elaborate flower arrangements. The flowers were exotic and arranged in expensive vases.

Murphy would watch the show. At the end a fresh bottle of champagne and two glasses would be waiting. She let him know that when she sat with a client of the club's she would be given a tip. He took to handing over an envelope with five crisp $100 bills in it. She adored her new relationship.

They would eat, chat a little, then she was driven home. Sometimes he rode along in the backseat, sometimes not.

Charles Murphy was an enigma. Wealthy, she could tell. Charming, yes. Obviously he was interested in her, yet he didn't make a move. He wore a wedding ring but didn't speak about his wife. She didn't ask.

She wasn't falling in love—she fell only for hunky Adonis types—but she did feel affection for him. He never attempted to touch her and was unfailingly polite.

Lili at the Samoa

She enjoyed the Dom Pérignon he ordered, the tip, and his attention.

One night Lili sat down next to Murphy and told him she would be leaving at the end of the week for an engagement at the Follies.

At week's end they said their polite, awkward good-byes. Lili caught a train to Los Angeles and began working at the Follies.

After her show she would go out for drinks with various men courting her. She caught up with Virginia and Tom and their crowd. But soon that engagement ended and she was back in New York at the Samoa for another ten-week run.

Her first night back she sat with Murphy as he somberly poured her a glass of champagne. She could tell he was in a dark mood.

"I am sailing to Europe," he admitted. "I have to forget about you."

Lili wouldn't be heartbroken. She assumed that was the end of it. She had made some extra cash, had some fun, received the attention she needed.

Weeks later Murphy reappeared at his usual table. Lili admitted she was glad to see him.

He explained that the plan hadn't worked. He couldn't forget her and had asked his wife for a divorce. He looked distressed. She felt sorry for him.

To her amazement the next night Murphy showed up with his wife. Nick came backstage to warn Lili.

Nick offered to share the table with the threesome along with a friend of his.

The table was tense and awkward. Murphy's wife didn't say a word, nor did Lili. Soon Lili had had enough. She got up to go.

Mrs. Murphy finally spoke. "You are not to see my husband any longer."

Lili thought, *That really is his decision, not mine. I don't have control over your husband. Obviously, neither do you.*

THE SUMMER WAS A HOT ONE IN NEW YORK FOR LILI AS SHE WAS CON-ducting a heated affair with actor Yul Brynner. *The King and I* actor's dressing room was "nearly across the alley" from the Samoa. Years later Lili would say it was the greatest summer because of the Russian-born actor who sent "tons of flowers to the Samoa" to fill her dressing room.[609]

Quite possibly she acquired a taste for waiting limousines from Brynner, who claimed to hire limousines even when he was broke. It is exactly the kind of extrava-gant behavior Lili admired (and soon imitated).[610]

Making thousands every week, her fees kept climbing along with the demand for her.

Lili returned to Las Vegas and Murphy showed up to hunker down for a six-week divorce. He appeared at the El Rancho during her shows. He swore he didn't want her for a mistress. He wanted to make her his wife. Lili continued affairs with others. She was fighting to "feel frivolous" and "youthful," as she once had.[611] She felt no obligation to Murphy. She was not going to take responsibility for his divorce. She flaunted other men in front of him. Murphy was respectful and kind but lacked sweeping lustful gestures, the very thing Lili thrived on. He patiently suffered her casting him aside for younger, more handsome men. He bided his time.

Lili might have pushed him away entirely if he hadn't delivered the coup de grace. The timing was right and he gave her most of the money to purchase her beloved Canyon Drive home, even paying for the renovations she had been plan-ning. No questions asked. Anything she wanted. He told her to send the bills to him. She didn't have the kind of cash Murphy offered. She had been in love with her house for years. It would be the only home she ever owned.

Murphy had the deed put in her name. Perhaps he was the one who persuaded the owners to sell. In any event, in July of 1953 Lili obtained title on 2639 Canyon Drive. (As the house was purchased prior to her divorce from Armando, he gra-ciously signed a quit claim deed giving up any claim to Lili's retreat.[612])

Lili was now the proud owner of a home. Though she was making between

$1,500 and $2,500 a week, and performing nearly every week out of the year, Lili would always be short of funds. For $30,000 with a loan of $15,788, she owned her first and only home, included in that price was the empty corner lot next door.[613] She signed the grant dead erroneously, either through her own fault or the notary public's sloppiness, as Lilli St. Cyr.

In an all-out assault Murphy showered Lili with jewelry, a pearl necklace and bracelet, and he even sent her a new car that she expressed an interest in, though by now she had stopped driving altogether. Lili was cautious, not wanting to feel as if she "owed" him. He assured her she was free to make her own decisions and come and go as she liked. "I'm living in the moment," she would tell Tom, as they both commiserated about their romances.[614] Tom, as usual, was going through a painful breakup with some young thing. A *too-young* thing. He was still living with Dick Ogden.

Lili wished Tom would find happiness. "But maybe neither one of us is lucky in love," she sighed.[615]

She wanted her desires fulfilled no matter how selfish. She believed she needed to get as much as she could get out of her relationships. The beautiful presents and envelopes of money proved she was worth something.

Murphy had to travel up north to Arroyo Grande, a city in San Luis Obispo County, to check on some forestry he owned. Knowing Alice lived there and hoping to seduce Lili's grandmother to "his side" in his quest to marry Lili, he stopped by Alice's for a visit.[616]

Alice was living in one of the foreclosed homes Idella's husband had obtained for a song.

Murphy and Alice had a lovely visit and Alice served fresh pie she had made. Over coffee she wrapped a large shawl around her shoulders and shivered.

"It's always so cold up here," she complained mildly. "I need a fireplace."

After another cup of coffee and some talk about Lili, Murphy left.

The next morning workers showed up to begin constructing a fireplace. "Courtesy of Mr. Murphy," the foreman explained.

To top the whole gift off, Murphy sent a truck that deposited a whole cord of wood.[617]

"Isn't that wonderful?" Alice telephoned Lili. "And you know he also delivered beautiful cashmere blankets. I am going to have to be careful what I say to him in the future."

Lili knew what Alice meant. Whenever she mentioned something she admired, Murphy would get it for her. "But why did you ask for a fireplace?" Lili scolded. "A *mink* coat would have kept you much warmer."[618]

CHAPTER THREE

In 1953 Lili received an offer from Howard Hughes to be in a movie. The movie was *Son of Sinbad* and she would play Nerissa, one of the girls in a harem who dances. Of course Lili would bathe in the film. It didn't seem to be much of a part, and of course she'd never be a Garbo. In the meantime she had other engagements.

In Las Vegas Lili reached for a tall glass of tea. She was tired. Four shows a day on the weekends. Beldon was throwing thousands at her. She'd been up early posing for a men's magazine. She had to keep up the publicity that kept her in front of the public's eyes.

Notes for *Son of Sinbad* sat on her dresser. She imagined herself costumed like Garbo in *Mata Hari* with pastel-colored veils. She had the obligation at the El Rancho to complete, then it would be back to Hollywood. Was Walter Kane still working for him? She had to wonder.

Lili defended her place in Hollywood to Hedda Hopper. "If Gypsy can do it, so can I," Lili told the gossip columnist, more confident than she felt.

"How do you feel, Lili," Hedda asked, "about the Hays Office condemning the hiring of *you* as a *stripteaser*?"

Lili lay back on her chaise. She had a half hour till the first show. She liked the El Rancho. It was glamorous and familiar. Visiting celebs sat front row at her shows. Actor Ronald Reagan came along with Garland and Bogart, with wife, Lauren, this time. Lili was feeling confident. "Obviously Mr. Hughes made the perfect choice."

With her contract signed Lili was besieged by reporters. Philip Scheuer wrote that Lili greeted him in a "black broadcloth Balenciaga suit, a matching hat with pink rose in front, and earrings. A mink coat was draped beside her." She pretended to be angered at the comparison to Rita Hayworth's dance in the film *Salome*. "I was doing this long before." When asked what she thought about while performing she claimed, "Victor Mature," whom she hadn't yet embarked on an affair with, but

would in a few short years.[619] She said, "Every time I passed him on the lot it was better than getting my salary."[620]

Son of Sinbad was filmed at RKO in 1953. Hughes planned it to be a big 3-D event. Being driven through the big gates off Melrose, Lili held her breath. She felt ten times as nervous as she did before her shows. She knew she would have to hold her own among professional actors. She didn't want to look the fool. This wasn't *her* stage.

And though her part was little more than bathing and a dance of the seven veils, she did have lines. *Son of Sinbad* turned out to be a silly film about a pirate (Sinbad) in pursuit of gunpowder, or "Greek fire." The press felt it was Hughes's solution to a bevy of starlet's contracts he held. The reclusive playboy was known to promise jobs to numerous women and perhaps this was payback time.

The film was shot in Technicolor and Lili looked stunning. The film gave Lili a chance to show her graceful dancing and unique beauty to a broader audience, a "legitimate" audience. It was a big distinction.

Lili hated the process of making movies. She felt unmoored at the lack of "control" she had on a movie set. She didn't like to be told to "go here" and "go there." Lili said she felt "tied down" on a movie set. She was used to doing "as I please" on the stage even if it meant failure, something she hadn't experienced in quite some time. She was also expert at making up her face and complained about others doing her hair and makeup. "I was used to doing my own hair and costumes," she said. For her the movies "took away my independence" and amusingly "made me feel like a Barbie doll."[621]

"I don't like the hours. Up at six and work for twelve hours. It's hard work."[622] In films she wasn't able to be Lili, saying, "There is not enough room for self-expression."[623]

Soon her nerves turned to sheer boredom. She waited doing nothing while men fiddled with lights. There were endless "technical difficulties." Director Ted Tetzlaff, an Academy Award–nominated cinematographer known for such classics as *Notorious* and *My Man Godfrey*, stopped her often. She overheard him complain about the quality of her voice. And in the end she was entirely dubbed. Others on the set complained that Lili was "difficult" and "snooty," not realizing it was terror and shyness manifest as coldness. She appeared haughty. She was intimidated on the set.

She was delighted to see her former lover Walter Kane. She hadn't seen him since her suicide attempt when Paul rescued her. He turned out to be a prince, driving her home in his limousine every night, where they laughed and played cards. This didn't help the jealousy and gossip directed at Lili from the cast.

Sinbad actor Dale Robertson didn't like Lili, especially when he found that his monthly contract with RKO was a fraction of what her daily rate was. Whether out of thwarted desire or envy Robertson teased Lili incessantly, laughing at his own stupid jokes. Fellow costar Vincent Price tried to keep the peace as best he could. "Small egos" were everywhere and Lili complained of petty conflicts.[624]

To pass the censors Robertson was required to keep one foot on the floor while he lay atop Lili, both fully clothed.

Though the film was packed with dozens of beautiful women, Lili easily stood out. She looked her regal best, with a white beaded bra and layers of chiffon. In one scene she wore a gorgeous dress with two peacock heads arising out of her breasts.

Often before important engagements she would go on a juice fast for a few days and rent a dance studio on Vine to practice ballet till the sweat dripped down her back and her muscles ached. She hated exercising but was disciplined nonetheless.

Lili heard the girls sniping that she was vain. *What did they think?* She made a living off her beauty and her body. It was all she had. Her beauty. Her body. When it vanished, her way of making a living, her place in the world would be gone. She was clinging on as tight as she could and she didn't give a damn what the little starlets thought. Let them go on the stage and draw the crowds she did and have men throw jewels at them. If caring about her appearance and taking care of herself made her vain, then so be it.

It says much about Lili's remarkable health, good genes, and reasonably healthy lifestyle that she did as well and looked so fantastic during the filming. She was performing nightly at the Follies, arriving early at RKO each morning on very little sleep. Despite this, she was never tardy.

Not seeing her discipline, others considered her self-destructive. Lili was striking while the iron was hot, in whatever direction work came, fearful the money would stop and the gigs would end. She appears very thin in the film. The stress and lack of sleep soon caught up with her. On May 25 Lili was taken to Good Samaritan Hospital after suffering from an appendicitis attack on the set. She was pushing herself like never before.

BECAUSE OF *SINBAD*'S HIGH PROFILE, LILI DID NUMEROUS FLUFF PIECES for several magazines. Gossip columnist Sidney Skolsky visited the set and wrote about her costume, or what little costume it was.

Lili reclined in a "simple gray linen sheath" and described her "beauty routine" to Lydia Lane. She varied her oft-repeated story of seeing the Ballets Russes when she was young. This time she claimed to be six and Alice had taken her. Her family didn't like her in burlesque (failing to mention her two sisters who were in it), but she hadn't quit because she was "independent." As a firm believer "in creams" she rubbed lanolin over her face and body every night and her flat abdomen was due to "dancing and exercise."

Lili told Lane she took care of herself, getting plenty of sleep, and that, believe it or not, she dressed for women. Not men.[625] Which is what most women do, only Lili was honest enough to admit it. She knew she could make little effort and impress a man, but for her sharpest critics, women, she strove for perfection.

Lili loved indulging in her beauty routines, soaking her nails in bowls of oil; applying egg white masks to her face, waving it dry with her collection of delicate lace fans. She used Ponds to remove her makeup. She preferred neutral nail colors like Elizabeth Arden's Sky-Blue Pink.[626] She loved nothing better than to spend an afternoon pampering herself. When she shampooed her oft-bleached hair she used an oil-based shampoo and soaked her hair with oil the night before to keep it from drying out.

Her RKO-written biography states in part that "her ambition is to make a million dollars . . . she loathes sports and parlor games." Her "recreation" is reading. She didn't let on that she was on the outs with Armando, her "restaurateur" of a husband. And her favorite food was "chocolate soufflé with whipped cream." Surely a fantasy she didn't often indulge in.

She explained her pantomimes and what went into them. "I usually do a little number about a girl who gets up in the morning and dresses for her date. Naturally, she takes a bath, she'd have to take a bath." She explained it was women who came to see what she was wearing. "Marusia did my clothes at Ciro's—as many as four-teen different changes," which explained why she was "always broke." She was at the time earning s$7,500 a week.

Marusia Toumanoff Sassi was a Russian costume designer who worked on the *Loretta Young Show* (1953–54) and *Rosemary Clooney Show* (1956). Her designs were exclusive and chic. And nothing was too good for Lili.[627]

Lili was doing everything she could to remain a unique attraction. She com-plained everyone was copying her act. She said she would not give up performing live.

Son of Sinbad would be condemned by the Catholic Legion of Decency, partially due to the casting of Lili. Yet the film held its own, typical for the type of fluff that it was. *Variety* called it "no better and no worse" than others. Frank Morriss in his "Here There and Hollywood" column noted, "It would be a little difficult to tell you just what *Son of Sinbad* is about." He mentions Lili but doesn't point her out. "*Son of Sinbad* is strictly a grade B movie."

Lili was amused by the controversy she caused. She didn't like censorship of any kind.

In July Armando's divorce came through. She admitted her fourth divorce to reporters. "I guess we just drifted apart."[628] When pushed, her old charm came back. "Yes. I am single. And looking for trouble."[629] She laughed, tossed her hair. The myth firmly in place. She was moving on.

SINBAD WAS NEITHER A HAPPY EXPERIENCE NOR A PARTICULARLY rewarding one. It would be another two years before the film hit theatres and Lili would be humiliated when she heard her voice dubbed. Dardy assured her no one would know. Despite Hughes's hopes the film was never released in 3-D.

"I hate making films," she declared, all thoughts of being the next Greta Garbo over. "The stage is so much easier."

Maybe critics were right, she thought, and she had no talent for anything else. One headline exclaimed, "'I can't sing or dance,' admits stripper Lili St Cyr. But her shapely figure is talent enough!"[630]

Finishing out 1953, Lili shot *Bedroom Fantasies* and *Cinderella Love Lessons*, two quickie shorts, variations of her stage acts, and *The 3-D Follies* (which was never shown in 3-D). Early exploitation producer Sol Lesser, who signed Jackie Coogan to a contract in the early 1920s, dreamed up *The 3-D Follies*. It was to be five separate shorts, but probably due to financial difficulties the project was canceled after Lili filmed her one piece, *Carmenesque*, dancing to the beat of Bizet.

Lesser had hoped to release the proposed ninety-minute film as the first 3-D color musical. However, *Variety* reported production halted after he could not sign Milton Berle as the emcee.[631] Later, Lili's short was released in 2-D and then a version was bizarrely intercut with a parrot and played for comedy. It wouldn't be until the 2006 World 3-D Film Expo II in Hollywood that *Carmenesque* would be screened as it was originally shot. *Carmenesque* had a first-rate cinematographer, Karl Struss, who in 1927 had won the first Academy Award for cinematography for *Sunrise*.

Cinderella Love Lessons begins with Lili as the titled character, her hair in a white washerwoman's cap, wearing long white bloomers and high heels (naturally), scrubbing the floor. With the wave of an offscreen fairy godmother's wand she is transformed. Her cap becomes a tiara, her bloomers stockings. In her princess ball gown she rushes to the palace where she meets and falls in love with Prince Charming. They dance. As the clock strikes midnight her ball gown disappears in stages; panties, top, until she sits cowering on the floor covering herself up modestly, the next cut and she's back in bloomers and cap.

The piece was ironic and filled with humor as Lili's pantomimes tended to be. And a very clever way to disrobe.

Lili filmed a small, uncredited part in a B gangster picture, *The Miami Story,* again essentially playing herself. By October she was complaining she hadn't yet been paid, which did nothing to further endear her to movie making.

It was another boom year for Lili St. Cyr. Though by now the veneer she had been creating, the hardness was beginning to constrict. Still it failed to hide the deep sadness of an "unhappy woman whose life is far more serious than her bumps and grinds."[632]

CHAPTER FOUR

W hat kept Lili happy was renovating her home. She spared no expense. She would spend a great sum of money decorating with the help of Tom Douglas. A dream had come true. Her beautiful Tudor-like home was legally hers. With big windows that faced the mountain across the street she turned it into an elegant, refined sanctuary. Lili sat with Murphy and showed him Tom's vision for the five-room house and all the work proposed, including an enclosed patio (what she would call a covered lanai), a twenty-two-by-twelve-foot outdoor wooden deck, bar, new floors, and new walls. She wanted to add four fireplaces, move an existing wall, and add windows and doors.

Tom did a marvelous job and would be worth every overpriced penny. There was flocked red wallpaper at $13.50 a roll for the downstairs bathroom. Ten rolls were posted from New York at nearly $10 a roll for her office, and that at 1953 prices. There were yards of "carnation pink" fabric for the six dining room chairs. The home was trimmed throughout in gold, except for the bathroom, which was done in silver. She bought her first television set for $425.

Lili went ahead with the work, making "capricious demands" for the renovations and sending the bills to Murphy's attorney's office.[633]

Between July 1953 and August 1, 1954, she paid $17,000 to Tom Douglas. There was plastering and painting and wallpaper to be hung, marble work, restoring furniture. Everything had a perfumed femininity to it. She had a beautiful carousal horse—or horses—installed downstairs at the bar instead of stools.[634] She had bleached the antique furniture that she had been buying for years. There were hard French lavender chaises (she would pose on many for photos), a big silver tea set, and a curio cabinet she was especially proud of. The remodel and decorating came at exorbitant prices, happily paid for by Murphy. Lili loved to decorate and would say "your home should always be a work in progress."[635] She

A very gilded Lili in her treasured home

would tinker with the decorating and redecorating for over a decade. The empty lot she had purchased adjacent to her home remained vacant and she apparently had no plans for it.

MURPHY PROPOSED AN AROUND-THE-WORLD TRIP ON A LUXURIOUS ocean liner, knowing how much she enjoyed traveling in such style. He clearly wanted her off the stage. He most likely did not plan on his future wife remaining a stripper.

Lili hesitated. It wasn't a good time to vacation. She was in demand. *A vacation?* She didn't even know what to think about that.

"It will give us a chance to see if this will work."[636] He meant them, as a couple. A *married* couple. She found his ideas old-fashioned.

She knew *they* would never work. There was no future for *them*. She grew anxious and panicky and as usual she began to behave badly as she did when feeling cornered. She wanted him to leave her. She didn't want to hurt him. She didn't want her bills to stop being paid for. But she didn't want to marry him either.

How could he expect her to walk away from everything that made her Lili? To be the new Mrs. Charles Murphy. She didn't see that life for herself. She didn't want that life. "Lili St. Cyr would cease to exist."[637] She couldn't let that happen.

"Okay," she stalled. While he made plans she escaped into work.

After his meticulous planning Lili was desperate and depressed as she often became when a romance wasn't going as she wished. She felt torn between him and all she still wanted from the life she had created. She called him. "I can't go."

He didn't say anything for several seconds. Then, "Why?" His voice sounded tight and angry.

"I just *can't.*" *Why did they always want an explanation?* She knew she had burned her bridges as she stared at the dining room table made possible by his generosity. She could not throw away her career.

She felt miserable and sent her Filipino houseboy away for the rest of the day. With heaviness in her heart she crawled into bed with a lit cigarette and cried. She was distraught. Why couldn't she give it all up and have Murphy take care of her? It would make him happy. But could she walk away from what she had created? If she stepped one foot on that cruise ship, she would be committing herself to him and she didn't want that. It would be a death sentence for Lili St. Cyr. But most importantly, she didn't love him. At all.

Charles Murphy, like the quiet gentleman he was, withdrew from Lili's life.

A few years later, after Dardy and Harold divorced, Murphy appeared in Las Vegas and in *her* life. They began to date.

One dull afternoon Murphy showed up at Dardy's house.

"Get in," he instructed her, and she climbed into his Cadillac. He drove her to the parking lot behind the Sahara Inn, parked, and popped the trunk of his car.

There was no one else around in the wide parking lot surrounded by miles of sand. Murphy pulled out two perfect expensive Hammacher Schlemmer fishing rods and proceeded to spend the next few hours teaching her how to fly fish.

He asked her to marry him. She too said no.

"I was a dancer. I guess I had good timing [about her fly-fishing abilities] because I rather impressed him," Dardy said. "I could never have married him. He was crazy about Lili. But I did like him. A really charming man."[638]

CHAPTER FIVE

Lili took an engagement at the El Rey theatre in Oakland for the standard two weeks. The fifteen-hundred-seat theatre was open from noon to midnight, showing B movies between three live shows each and every day. Along with her bubble bath routine she portrayed "Carmen," a Spanish dancer who was "a little devilish."[639]

The *Oakland Tribune* appreciated that Lili was "different than run of the mill strip-tease." With her act "she is the lady at all times." Praised for her uniqueness, the reporter acknowledged she was the only exotic who "comes equipped with her own scenery and props."[640]

Between acts she entertained a circle of reporters sipping coffee and feeding her sweet tooth by munching on a donut. She was personable with reporters, clearly in her element.

Her traveling did not slow. After a stint in Birmingham at Cane Break Supper Club she was back in Las Vegas in 1954 with Joe E. Lewis, a "popular pairing," the papers noted. She would be held over. Douglas bragged that Lili was worth every cent of the $10,000 a week she was making at the El Rancho. Her salary vacillated between high and extra high, depending on the venue. She was not turning down any work. And though the El Rancho paid a generous salary—enormous for a stripper—top-tiered stars like Marlene Dietrich, playing down the street, were pulling in $30,000 a week.

On weekends couples from California and nearby poured into the growing desert town. Rooms were booked, slots were ringing, and Lili's show was packed. The men dressed in black tie and the women in diamonds and furs. Las Vegas thrilled Lili. She felt cocooned in a small exclusive world. She didn't want—or need—to venture far. The camaraderie was better than a cold movie set where you were asked to be intimate with someone you had never met prior, disliked, and, worse, would never see again.

Her act ran approximately twenty minutes. Sometimes as short as ten. Billed as "the most fabulous girl in the world," Lili surprised her audience one night, perching on a throne eating grapes to "Strangers in Paradise."[641] There was no end to her inventiveness.

Her thousands were going straight to her accountant to pay outstanding debts and taxes. Dardy couldn't believe the money Lili pulled in flew out just as fast. It was never enough for her lifestyle. As she would say, "If I want something, I want it and nothing will stand in my way. I earned it, I'll spend it."[642]

Lili sat in her bungalow painting her nails. "Hey, doll," a voice called out. It was Joe E. Lewis. Lili disdained most baggy pants. "I didn't associate with them," she would say.[643] But Joe E. was a gentleman. They occasionally shared a preshow drink. "Need some company?" Joe E. asked. He held a racing form in one hand, scotch in the other. His brow was in its ever-present furrow.

She hadn't talked to Alice in a while. She made no effort to see Idella at all. She hadn't heard from Barbara in ages. Divorced and without Murphy she had been complaining she was lonely in Vegas.

He suggested Dean Martin, who had been at her show.

Lili eyed the scars across Joe E.'s cheek and another at his throat. It was a terrible story.

One night in Chicago, 1927. Joe E. had been singing at a club owned by a Capone lieutenant. Lewis was popular, packing them in, and the club wanted him to return. But when he was offered a fatter contract at a rival club, Joe E. took it. Some of Capone's compatriots were none too happy and had Joe E. pistol-whipped, slashing his throat and cutting out a part of his tongue. He was left for dead. Capone was furious when he found out, claiming he knew nothing about the assault. He wrote Joe E. a fat check for $10,000 to help him recover.

Joe E. let Lili know his buddy Sinatra was coming up for the weekend.

Lili shrugged. The singer wasn't for her, though she spent a fair amount of time with him. She never liked a man who had women throwing themselves at him. She remembered him from the Samoa when he used to come in with Ava Gardner. He had been so obviously in love with the dark-haired beauty. Frank was too skinny and short for Lili. Not her type at all.

Joe E. would throw chips at Lili whether he had a good night at the table or not.

The next night after the show Lili met up with Joe E. and Sinatra for dinner and a show at a nearby casino.

Someone introduced Frank, who got up, mic in hand. "There are a lot of celebs in the audience tonight," he looked around, waiving a lit cigarette.

Lili sipped her martini and lowered her eyes. Vegas was always full of celebrities

Onstage

who wanted to meet other famous people. It was the oddest thing, she thought. Even famous people felt it was okay to intrude, slapping backs and kissing cheeks. It was too familiar for her.

"And over in the corner we have . . ." Sinatra mentioned someone in the room.

Lili waited her turn. Everyone in Las Vegas knew Lili St. Cyr.

Sinatra continued. "And of course my friend Joe E. Lewis, you gotta catch his show at the El Rancho."

Frank sat. No mention of Lili, who wasn't exactly a wallflower with her platinum hair and dripping diamonds. Later when Sinatra swaggered to the restroom, Lili mentioned the slight to Joe.

The next day the largest bouquet of yellow roses appeared in her bungalow with a note from Sinatra, apologizing.

LILI WAS APPROACHED BY NEW YORK–BASED PHOTOGRAPHER AND SELF-styled "Pin-Up King" Irving Klaw to perform two of her routines for his movie cameras and a "quick" photo shoot afterward.

Klaw, who sold his bondage and erotic photos through the mail, shared the business with his sister Paula. They had been selling "damsel in distress" photos since the early 1940s. Lili made it clear she was not doing any of "those" photos. If some little tramp like Bettie Page wanted to pose with handcuffs and whips, she could keep the corner on *that* market. "Fucking slut," she would say when asked about Bettie.[644] Though sharing title in the film, they worked separately.

Klaw assured Lili her performance and photos would strictly be about "her act."

The money was excellent, and, as usual, no matter how much she was pulling in, "I always seem to be a year behind in my bills," she lamented.[645] She never seemed to be able to stop working; not that she wanted to, but it was a good excuse to stay in it.

The limousine turned the corner at Third Avenue onto Fourteenth Street, cutting through a steamy summer morning. Humidity poured off the asphalt. In the backseat Lili stared at the various shops selling pianos and watches, a haberdashery, and two Hungarian restaurants. The car slowed in front of the Jefferson, a former vaudeville theatre, now barely hanging on to its dignity like an old dowager. Squashed next to the theatre at 212 East Fourteenth Street was Movie Star News studio. It was 1954.

As her uniformed driver opened the door Lili studied the painted window, which screamed, IRVING KLAW MOVIE STAR PHOTOS. The store was small and crammed with glossies of faces famous and nearly so.

Lili started up a narrow staircase to the third floor. The walls pressing in on her were an ugly green, dust gathered in the corners. She was used to dismal theatres; in fact she liked them. Dark. Dives. Reminded her of Jimmy. And romance. And the forbidden.

In the loft upstairs men in suits were scurrying about, pulling cables and setting lights that heated the room. Girls were putting on makeup, practicing their routines.

Irving, a forty-four-year-old Brooklynite, unattractive and short, sailed around directing traffic in the studio. He wore a wrinkled white shirt and saggy brown pants. His sister Paula, a frizzy-haired brunette with dimples, put out platters of food and supervised the models.

Bettie Page worked through a rehearsal dressed in a red harem outfit, a sparkly crown on her head. What she lacked in grace she made up for in enthusiasm.

The previous year Lili had performed in Klaw's *StripoRama*, as had Bettie. Lili was still furious that Klaw had featured Page in "her" bathtub act. The film had pulled in an impressive $80,000 in theatres and done much to bring Page greater fame and accolades. Lili's number "Cinderella's Love Lessons" had been used by Klaw as its own short feature, which he assured her was a compliment.

Lili didn't trust him. She was concerned with the quality of his work and how she would come across, appearances being of the utmost importance.

He assured her he was going big-time with a professional crew and this would be shot in marvelous Technicolor. Klaw's stock in trade for his shorts were shot in black and white on an eight-millimeter camera.

Klaw planned to shoot four scenes with Lili. Covered in diamonds and a thick ankle-length fur coat, Lili walked down the hall to the set.

It was hot and airless. Irving rocked from foot to foot next to the camera. Paula fussed around the sparse set, arranging Lili's requested props.

Lili would work barely half a day and there would not be many takes, but she was prepared. She didn't need endless takes; she had been performing similar routines for nearly fifteen years.

"Action," Klaw called, and Lili entered the set, a dressing room with vanity and chair, a coat rack and a paisley-covered couch. A dressing screen stood in one corner. She began to undress, tossing on a black sheer robe over her black thigh-high fishnets. Her hair was curled and to her shoulders. Reaching down she plucked her heels from her feet, shook out a gown to try on. Lying back on the couch she stretched her legs into the air, all the while aware to give the camera her best angles.

"Cut." Lili took the opportunity to powder her nose, reapply lipstick, and change outfits. In the next setup Lili sat at a dressing table wearing a green sheath dress that matched the color of her eyes. With the camera rolling she pinned up her hair, admiring herself in the mirror. In her own world, yet aware of the sounds around her.

After a short break and a cup of lukewarm coffee, Lili relaxed in her room. She kept mostly to herself. As in the theatres she had a way of surrounding herself with an invisible wall that did not permit trespass. Lili had never been one of the girls, gossiping and sharing makeup. And she never would be.

She changed into what would be her pièce de résistance. Back on set, which was now a stage, she was adorned with an ornate diamond necklace and earrings (but no one need know), bra, and panels made of sheer red chiffon to match her cherry-red lips.

Paula started the music from a record player. Playfully, Lili tossed the panels of her skirt as she caressed her body, doing little in the way of actual dancing. She teased in front of a gold curtain, hastily and unevenly hung, that no one had bothered to smooth. The wrinkles didn't matter because Lili drew all eyes to her. The film would make her immortal, she hoped.

Stagehands began to break down the set and prepare for the next setup with Spanish dancers Peppe and Roccio. Lili was free to change.

Klaw led Lili back to her dressing room setup to take photos, which he would

later sell downstairs. Lili knew she wouldn't share in these profits, but she considered posing part of her job. All part of the ongoing and relentless publicity necessary to keep girls like Bettie billed only as co-features.

It didn't mean she liked Klaw's "flat lighting" and endless poses.[646]

"He made an endless amount of money on me off those terrible photos." She would hate the photos and would refer to Klaw as "the pig."[647]

THE END RESULT WAS THE DISAPPOINTING *VARIETEASE*, A LACKLUSTER revue of strippers and burly acts. Previewed in August 1954 the film was lambasted as being "strictly for skid row joints." Lili was singled out as being the exception to the "substandard" fair.[648]

In the summer an article entitled "My 10 Favorite Men" appeared in *Top Secret* magazine, supposedly penned by Lili. (It was more likely dictated by her. "She couldn't write," Armando claimed.[649]) Declaring that it "takes ten men to make one good man," she lists the qualities she appreciated, starting with "sex appeal" on down.[650]

Victor Mature won the top spot for looks. She called him "Mr. Sex Appeal in person." And she would know. Though Mature was married (from 1948 to 1955) Lili had an affair with the hunky actor. She swooned over his rugged masculinity.

Number two was another lover, Yul Brynner, whom she praised because he was sophisticated and suave, making note of his intelligence. She admitted to being "spellbound" by his "reminisces."[651]

Number three, Artie Shaw, was another lover. She privately recalled how every time they were together he tried analyzing her, insisting she used men as "pawns" and had so many marriages because she had never known her own father. The hypocritical and oft-married (seven times) Shaw was a proponent of Freud and a misogynist. He told Lili *she* hated all men. She cried foul and told him that was the furthest thing from the truth. And she had the husbands to prove it.

Number four was actor Clifton Webb, her gay friend whom she praised for his wit.

Number five was Armando, whom she appreciated now that they were divorced. He was continental and gallant.

Paul Valentine made number six, listed for the help he had given her for her bathtub act.

Harold Minsky was number seven because he was practical and she admired his business acumen.

Number eight was Tom Douglas because he was the most generous person she knew, a lavish gift giver like herself.

Number nine was Monte Hale, for reasons not wholly clear. He was an out-doorsy type, something she truly hated.

Number ten was hunky actor Fernando Lamas.

INCLUDING COWBOY ACTOR MONTE HALE IN HER LIST WAS ODD GIVEN an incident that occurred one night in Las Vegas.

The papers were speculating that Hale would be Lili's next husband as "he's nutz about her."[652] Dardy and Harold had settled into a beautiful round house centered on a courtyard with a pool in the center. Glass sliding doors opened onto it. A tall wall surrounded the house. One night Dardy answered a frantic knocking on her door. "Dardy, open up. Open up, please. Quick." It was Lili, nearly hysterical. Her hand cradled a fresh bruise on her cheek.

Lili was shaking. "He's trying to kill me." She slammed the door. "Dardy, lock the door. Lock it quick."

Dardy got Lili to calm down just enough to explain that Monte Hale had flown into a rage. "He *really* hit her," Dardy emphasized. The Oklahoman Hale was a former vaudevillian performer and now B actor who had been in dozens of westerns. He would be remembered for his role as Rock Hudson's attorney in the 1956 blockbuster *Giant* starring Elizabeth Taylor.

Hale had a ranch in Las Vegas and was constantly showing up at Lili's bungalow at the El Rancho, despite her involvement with other men.

Dardy ushered Lili safely inside. But she wouldn't sit. She was trembling and pacing.

Not a minute later there was a terrible pounding on the walls outside and the doorbell repeatedly rang. Lili started to scream.

"He's going to come over the wall," she shouted. "Call the police."

Dardy did. Officers showed up within minutes.

"They had their bull horns, shouting, 'we got him,'" Dardy laughingly recalled.

The officers quickly had the actor in handcuffs. Tentatively, Dardy opened the door with Lili crouching behind her peeking out at all the commotion.

"There must have been six cop cars," Dardy said, "with two cops in each car."

They walked outside. Lili was terrified of more bad publicity. "And she didn't want to be linked with that cowboy!"

Lili ran back inside and grabbed her purse. She then proceeded to waltz among the officers trying to pass out $100 bills to keep the "unpleasantness" out of the papers. "Just like she was serving hors d'oeuvres, saying, 'I just want you to get him and keep him away from here.'"

LILI'S SUPREMACY WAS NEARING ITS ZENITH. WANTING TO CAPITALIZE on her popularity, in February of 1954 she opened a small club called the Boudoir in a "tonier" section of New York in the Park Avenue restaurant at 46 East Fifty-Second Street. *Variety* noted that it was like "going from Woolworths to Bergdorf Goodman."[653] What they didn't understand was Lili was never a snob. She didn't care if the joint was high- or low-class. She just wanted as many people to see her as possible.

She had calling cards made: "Mlle. Lili St. Cyr invites you to her BOUDOIR just off Park Avenue."

Owner Johnny Ruggierio refurbished the upstairs to suit her tastes. There was an elevated stage for her tub, now "an essential part" of her act. She sold $75 bottles of champagne and performed with the loyal and devoted Sadie. A harp player accompanied her, and jazz musician Gene Bianco (who used his harp like a jazz instrument) was featured.

It was elegant and unique. There was a living room–like set surrounded by mirrors reflecting a multitude of bejeweled Lilis. Her number lasted all of fourteen minutes from the moment she entered swathed in mink and a "swish of silk."[654] Lili lit a couple of candelabras (the papers compared her to Liberace). The show, the space, and the stripper dazzled the audience. Some complained it was too short a show for the $3.50 minimum. No matter how brief her appearance, the place was packed.

Even ex-suitor Peter R. Gimbel of the department store Gimbel's came—with his wife. He shocked the table by pulling out a photo of Lili from his wallet. Lili didn't imagine that was a very smart thing to do as his wife grimaced. Lili smiled politely and excused herself, satisfied she was still number one with Peter. But he no longer interested her. Lili was mesmerized by a new hunk who was demanding all her attention.

It seemed Lili was destined to meet her husbands (and lovers) where she worked. Of course, her life revolved around the clubs, theatres, restaurants, and bars near those establishments. There were little other places—or times—for Lili to meet men. Besides Virginia and Tom, she didn't have real friends. Life revolved around work.

One night after a show, she was introduced to a tall, dark-haired man. And though she warned Dardy never to go out with "an actor, bartender, or musician," she found herself drawn to the handsome actor currently on Broadway in a small part in *The Caine Mutiny Court-Martial*. The prestigious production starred Henry Fonda and was directed by Charles Laughton. T. H. Jordan was merely a "member of the court," though he talked as though he was an important "lynch pin" to the whole play itself. Lili couldn't have cared. He was incredibly handsome and she was ripe for a new romance.

Jordan's persistence and insistence on meeting Lili paid off. He told Sadie he would wait "all night for her."[655]

"What does he look like?" Lili asked when Sadie came backstage to tell her a certain young man wanted to meet her.

"Well, he's very . . . clean cut." Sadie laughed.

"Clean cut? What does that mean?" Lili was slowly changing into an evening gown.

"Well," Sadie said, "I'd call him 'Mr. Spic and Span.'"

"Would I *want* to meet him?" Lili persisted.

"Yes. Most definitely. He would be someone pleasing to you. I think he spends a lot of time on his looks."[656]

Not elegant like Armando, the bit actor was rugged and "uncouth."[657] Part he-man, part con man, a bit of a scoundrel, and an adept bullshit artist, he was humorous and made Lili laugh. Not many could.

"I like his scurrilous ways," she would tell Dardy. Dardy would roll her eyes and think, *There she goes again, another disastrous relationship, for all of two minutes.*

Mr. Spic and Span had been born Ted Friedman in Ohio. He had one older brother, Ben. At fifteen, the financially strapped family moved to Los Angeles, settling into a small apartment in Beverly Hills.

Ted Jordan would recall feeling "like a duck out of water" with the more affluent kids who attended Beverly Hills High. It grated him that they were "poor little hicks." In a school filled with the sons and daughters of famous actors, Ted aspired to be one himself. He got work as a lifeguard and masseuse, no doubt bitter he had to work while his schoolmates enjoyed generous allowances. His sense of inferiority would stay with him his entire life and influence many of his choices.

Ted's father was not happy that his son wished to attend acting classes, but Ted rebelled and moved out. He was, he admitted, a "know-it-all."[658]

Ted was the nephew of musician, singer, and popular bandleader Ted Lewis, known as "Mr. Entertainer." Ted worshiped his uncle and his career. His most memorable song performed was "Me and My Shadow."

HE CLAIMED THAT PRIOR TO MEETING LILI HE HAD SPENT THE PREVIous year performing in nearly a dozen films, in small uncredited parts.

Unlike her new suitor, Lili's name and photos were constantly splashed across the tabloids and trades. She was making gobs of money. With Lili the struggling actor saw a chance for the recognition he sought. He grabbed at it.

With her new endeavor at the Boudoir, Lili had the potential to make great sums, as she was on the "percentage deal." [659] However, the deal would be short-lived.

Dardy and Lili with Eddie Lewis, presumably Ted Lewis's brother

Lili performed at the Boudoir several times between February and July but, as she later claimed, the Park Avenue's owners—mob run—who had their own club downstairs were stealing her clients by telling them as they entered that the Boudoir was full, so they might as well stay downstairs at their club. Lili, never a fighter, closed up shop and never attempted to run any sort of establishment again.

Ted tried to buoy her up. He told her he had practically stalked her when she was performing in LA sometime back, claiming to have seen her at the Follies and with his girlfriend Marilyn.

Did she recognize the name Marilyn Monroe? *Gentleman Prefer Blondes* and *How to Marry a Millionaire* were huge hits the year before in 1953. Of course she knew who Monroe was. But she would hardly care.

Many claimed they had seen Lili at this theatre or that. It was amazing how many people professed to be in the audience the night she had been arrested at Ciro's. It seemed so long ago now. She had performed literally hundreds of dates since her arrest, traveling back and forth across the country via plane, train, and car. She had every tabloid in America spilling gallons of ink about her adventures, real and imagined, yet she still relied on the flattery of men. And Ted flattered her, not that she believed half of what he said.

She knew most of what he said was pure exaggeration. Or lies merely to impress.

Jordan bragged that he had convinced Marilyn to study Lili, her moves, her look—everything. He claimed Monroe owed much of her success to him.

Of all his preposterous inventions, Jordan claimed to have become not only a lover of Marilyn Monroe for twenty-odd years, but also a lifelong friend, remaining intimate through her marriages, even speaking to her on the night of her death. He would brag that it was Marilyn who dragged him to first see Lili St. Cyr in Los Angeles. Now three years later he was in New York with the object of Marilyn's obsession.

Ted Jordan was seven years younger than Lili when they met (Lili lied and told reporters she was thirty-three). She was not overtaken with feelings for him. But he was a man and he did pursue her relentlessly, early on asking her to marry him.

It had been a long time without someone steady in her arm. She let "the Actor," as she called him, buy her drinks and take her home.[660] Their attraction was animal and physical.

Tom Douglas had a spectacular idea for a new show at the El Rancho. By April he announced to the trades that a "cage act" was coming.[661]

He told Lili what he had in mind. He would have a track run around the ceiling of the Opera House where she would perch like an exotic bird in a gilded cage. From above the heads of her audience she would peel off her panties and bra as the cage moved around the room.

Lili thought he was crazy. She reminded him she did not like heights. She refused to consider it.

Tom knew his friend. He started plying her with gifts. First with jewels, of which he sent the bill to Beldon, then he offered to redecorate her cottage, painting it gray and green. Then it was a luscious silver-colored fox fur she had admired at Neiman Marcus. Finally Lili agreed.

The debut of Lili's "Gilded Cage" act was far from smooth. Tom had orchestrated a row of chorus girls to come out on the stage and sing. From the back of the room, in the dark, Lili would climb up a ladder into the cage. During the first show, she panicked and refused to get in. The audience grew restless as they waited with the lights out. Finally, Lili managed to get into the damn thing, terrified and shaking and started her trajectory around the club. The audience looked up mesmerized.

After gliding around the club, tossing her clothing as she went, just barely out of reach of the upstretched hands, Lili jumped down into the arms of two muscled boys onstage. As she turned, the still-moving cage smacked her in the back of the head, knocking her out and stopping the show.

Tom worked out the kinks (and Lili's nerves) and every night, seven nights a week, twice a night, the golden bird of striptease in her gilded cage would shed her clothes from her perch above as "the diners shriek their pleasure."[662]

Lili's cage act

IT WAS CLEVER AND HEADLINE GRABBING. LILI (AND TOM DOUGLAS) kept packing the room. She received so many inquiries from women in the audience asking where to get the beaded bras, panties, and garters she dropped—along with a note saying, "With Love from Lili"—that Lili decided to start manufacturing lingerie. And thus the birth of "Lili St. Cyr Unmentionables, Inc."

In December she was at the Knickerbocker Hotel in Los Angeles to complete the deal selling lingerie through a mail-order catalogue. Lili was going into business. Would she finally quit stripping, as she kept threatening?[663]

Tom Douglas purportedly helped financed Lili's new venture, which makes sense. Lili rarely had those kinds of sums on hand. She would model for her own ads and comic book artist Bill Ward drew her exaggerated figure, almost Wolf–Gal like. This would be the first incarnation of what would become "The Undie World of Lili St. Cyr" store, which she began in earnest in the 1960s though she would not trademark the name "Undie-World" until 1970.[664]

THE CROWDS LOVED THE BIRD IN THE GILDED CAGE. LILI, PREENED panties in hand, exalted above the crowd, looking at men's thinning hair and the women's little hats. The cage displayed her beautifully as she tossed her panties into the crowd, hoping it would land on some celebrity's plate. Once again she was "setting new attendance records."[665]

Plop went a garter. Then the rhinestone bra. There were the expected gasps from the thrilled audience.

Columnist Harry Ingraham rhapsodized about Lili:

Many great things my walls have graced,
Because I possess such "crazy" taste—
But nothing could bring heaven quite so near
As the Bra that was tossed to me by Lili St. Cyr.[666]

On the stage she was once again asked to tone down her "bed reclining contortions" after someone complained. Once again Lili was a target for moral outrage.

If some thought she was trying too hard, she was. She had to remain a step ahead of other acts. She began to push her sexuality. However, days later she relented and "deleted her objectionable bed-reclining contortions."[667]

The Helldorado was an annual western festival celebrated in Las Vegas with a parade that had been enlivening the town since 1934. It raised money for local charities with costly and elaborate floats sponsored by the hotels and casinos.

In May of 1954 Lili was asked to participate in the Tom Douglas–designed El Rancho float, bathing for the duration of the parade, cheering crowds on either side of the street. Tom suggested some hunky Adonis types (he had his eye out for those) to pour water over her as she cruised down the street. Lili thought it was fun publicity. She found a lifeguard from the Sahara. Gordon Werschkul stood six-three and weighed 215 pounds with a fifty-inch chest and thirty-inch waist. He was a prime specimen.[668]

Lili immediately hired him. In her usual manner she renamed him Gordon Scott. Scott would go on to replace Les Barker in the *Tarzan* film series. He and Lili were friendly in Las Vegas but after Hollywood took him away Lili ran into him at a party where he had hooked up with actress Vera Miles (later they would marry) and Scott ignored her. Lili believed he didn't want to be reminded—or remind others—that he had once been hanging out at Las Vegas pools looking for a break.

By July Lili was performing to full houses in Oakland, with lines starting at 1 p.m. for her sold-out show that brought in a record $42,000. Her salary was reported to be $4,500.[669]

Variety reported that Tom Douglas, "irked by a succession of beefs," no doubt with Beldon, was calling Lili's "Bird in a Cage" act his "swan song."[670] He was finally quitting Beldon.[671]

RIGHT: *In her dressing room*

CHAPTER SIX

I t was a relationship fraught with problems from the start. Two gorgeous yet deeply insecure creatures. Both selfish and egotistical, demanding, lazy, and ambitious. Stubborn to their deaths. Inventors of their past and their present, petrified of the future.

Very quickly the egotistical Jordan resented the way Lili sucked up the spotlight wherever they went, and he was consigned to the shadows behind her. He felt like a nobody, a feeling he had been fighting his entire life. Maybe he felt what his friends claimed, that he was "merely a convenience to Lili."[672]

She never trusted him. She wasn't stupid. She had the suspicion he was a star fucker. He would never be interested in her if she wasn't at the top of her game. She felt Ted was using her as an anchor to something. To what she didn't know, or care.

Dardy couldn't understand why Lili fell in love with him. "A little schemer. Plays every angle." He was like a "bull in a china shop." He was big and awkward. But he "intrigued her."[673] Jordan became possessive and sullen and depressed, accusing her of caring more about her career than him (true). He didn't know about the men she slept with on the side. There were always ways to evade his constant vigilance. She could have an affair in her dressing room or hotel.

The name St. Cyr was everywhere. In a 1955 episode of the popular *The Honeymooners* starring former burlesque comedian Jackie Gleason, Lili's much-celebrated name was highlighted in "A Woman's Work Is Never Done." When the Kramdens hire a maid, buddy Norton quizzes Gleason's character, Ralph:

Norton: Is she anything like that maid we saw in that burlesque show?
Ralph: What maid?

RIGHT: *A Ciro's cover, May 1955*

MAGAZINE

Lili
St. Cyr

Norton: You know that one that helped Lily [*sic*] St. Cyr into the bathtub full of wine. Is she like that?

Ralph: No, she's not like that maid. She looks more like the one that installed
the bathtub.

And earlier on the *Alice Faye & Phil Harris Radio Show* there was this para-
phrased exchange in which Alice takes her husband, Phil, to task for being a slob:

Alice: Honestly, Phil—the way you leave your clothes lying around the house
after you take them off is ridiculous. Why, it's like living with Lili St. Cyr.

[Phil gives no response. Long pause.]

Alice: Phil? Phil? Why don't you answer me?

Phil: I'm just thinking about what it would be like living with Lili St. Cyr!

TED SANK INTO DEPRESSION WHEN LILI REFUSED TO MARRY HIM. SHE
in turn became anxious. He reminded her of herself. She sympathized with his lack
of confidence and his longing to be somebody. The swaggering and boasting was a
flimsy cover.

In April she was back at Ciro's with a new scenario, "a cheap hotel in the trop-
ics." Gone was her tub; instead she bathed "in a bowl." *Variety* complained that her
act had "worn a bit thin."[674]

Men were constantly dancing attendance around Lili. Sinatra pal Sammy
Davis Jr. asked her out. She declined because she considered him "too forward."
That and the fact he stood five five made him most definitely not her type.[675]

Lili was conflicted. She wanted the all-consuming passion but didn't feel it
with Ted.

In August she relented and announced she would wed Ted after her run at the
El Rancho.[676]

In September she applied for a wedding license, claiming she would retire and
run a lingerie shop in Beverly Hills. Those taking odds would have known better.

There was another "surprise" announcement that they would definitely wed
after her 2 a.m. show.[677] Beldon and his wife Mildred gave Lili diamond and pearl
earrings and brooch worth $11,000.

The pronouncement was premature. Lili faced reporters once again and said
the wedding was delayed. "Friends said it was permanent."[678] By October 8, Earl
Wilson was reporting in his column that the nuptials were off, but Ted would still

RIGHT: *Another wedding day*

be using St. Cyr as his professional name. Lili claimed "the marriage is postponed indefinitely because of a career difference."[679] He had none and she wouldn't let go of hers. She had now publically delayed at least three times. Jordan had to be feeling the sting of humiliation.

In Las Vegas she was seen with Jordan *and* Vic Mature, who was having "marital "woes."[680] He would continue to carry on with Lili throughout the fall.

Jordan was persistent and on October 28, 1955, Lili applied for a wedding license while she was working in San Francisco. But come December it was still a promise that she was going to wed "soon."[681]

After months of dithering, Lili finally caved. Lili and Ted Jordan were married on February 21, 1955, after midnight at the El Rancho between shows for a guest list of reporters. To boost the publicity, Lili had a photographer "constant at her side" during the reception in the lounge after the private ceremony held in Beldon's cottage.[682] Neither of their families attended. For the first time she had made and wore a white wedding dress with yards of chiffon. Beldon with his perpetual orangey tan stood in as best man. It was as Vegas as could be. Shiny, flashy, temporary.

While flashbulbs popped Ted leaned into his famous bride as if soaking up her fame. The atomic bomb had recently been tested in the desert and the chefs at the El Rancho whipped up an atomic cloud–shaped cake with the sign Happy Wedding Day Lili St. Cyr. There was no mention of her groom.[683]

SOME CYNICS CLAIMED THE ATTENTION-SEEKING COUPLE PICKED that day because it was when the "national media would be in town for the nuclear explosions."[684]

Not in love, she found herself again "responsible" for someone's well-being both physically and spiritually. She wanted to please him. She wanted to make him happy. She wanted to be "good," knowing how hard that was for her when her head was so easily turned by another gorgeous hunk.[685] How hard it was when she wasn't in heart-stopping love. She liked that the newspapers spotted them dining at Louigi's three or four times a week in the coming months. The littlest mention made the papers, of this she was grateful.

She felt that old push-pull of love and togetherness. Wanting to give her all, wanting to be overwhelmed by her relationships, she hated how it changed her. "When you marry someone, or even when you establish an intimate liaison—you're responsible before all else to that person. I detest the situation because it's a vicious circle. The more I stay with X, the more responsible I feel towards him. My freedom is cut off. I'm not able to be myself any longer." She wanted her relationships without strings. She wanted bondage to a man yet autonomy. It was a conflict that destroyed all her relationships.

CHAPTER SEVEN

I t was 1955 and burlesque was changing.

Lili, the "Stripper with Imagination," was dissatisfied. Reporters continued to complain about a noticeable weariness during her act. After one performance it was noted she "appeared less bored" than she had in previous months.[686] Lili was finding it hard to hide the monotony after decades of stripping.

The papers stirred trouble, citing that Lili's only real rival was Tempest Storm. Nearly a decade younger than Lili, Tempest had a completely different sensibility to her work and look. She was brash like the times and Lili didn't like it one bit.

Born Annie Banks, Tempest was raised in crushing poverty working in the cotton fields. There was a horrific gang rape involving five boys when she was a teen. Marrying her way to Los Angeles she found a mentor in Follies Theatre manager Lillian Hunt, who had Tempest lose weight and straighten and dye her frizzy black hair, turning her into a headline-making sensation.

Tempest was a new breed of burlesque dancer: bigger, bolder, brazen, flashy, and clearly enjoying herself. With less restrictions on costumes she got away with more. She was not a great dancer, flinging herself forward and back, but she had charisma. And huge breasts. Obscene, exaggerated, cartoonish. And audiences embraced her. She would boast of affairs with both JFK and Elvis Presley, among dozens of others.

Lili despised her. The newspapers played up a rivalry between the two very different burlesque queens, one that had started a couple of years earlier.

The Follies was packed. The stage needed a good sanding, everything smelled decades old. Backstage Lili waited for the co-feature—the buxom, vulgar-looking redhead with hips out to here and an excess of rhinestones—to finish. Everything about her was too much. Even her name was a joke, Tempest Storm. She couldn't keep time with the drummer. The stripper was running to and fro to a vulgar beat; she was animal and the crowd was roused. Lili could make out men on their feet.

Lili thought she was terrible, her appeal reaching only to "plumber" types.[687]

At the end of Tempest's act the theatre erupted.

Lili sailed onstage. The finale. The star position.

Lili felt a jab in her toe. She was dancing barefoot, as she preferred. At first she thought it was a splinter from the decrepit old stage. Kicking her leg over her head on the bed, as if it was part of her act, she plucked a straight pin out of her toe.

Furious, Lili stormed off when her act ended.

"Goddamn it!" Her voice cut through the backstage noise. Lili confronted Tempest, who was still half undressed, her white naked flesh an obscenity.

Lili accused her of purposely leaving her straight pins onstage.

Tempest denied using straight pins. Furious, she gathered her things to leave. "I don't have to take this crap, Lillian." Tempest was crying. "It wasn't my straight pin."[688]

To appease both girls, Lillian booked Tempest into the El Rey in Oakland. She—and her type—might be out of sight. But it was too late.

A storm called Tempest had arrived.

THE INTRODUCTION IN 1955 OF MILTOWN, VARIOUSLY CALLED "MOTHer's little helper" and "anxiety aspirin," was the answer to 1950s angst, the welcome precursor to Valium.[689] It was so popular a tranquilizer that Milton Berle, a rabid devotee, called himself "Uncle Miltown" on live television. Berle's wife claimed "most of the comedians in television are taking it right now." The pill was so widely regarded it flew off shelves and was publicly praised by many celebrities including Jerry Lewis at the 1956 Academy Awards.[690]

By 1957 there were thirty-six million prescriptions filled in the United States.[691]

Lili "loved it." She was grateful for anything that would subdue her anxiety. Dardy knew a wholesaler in Las Vegas who supplied the little white round pills for her. Lili was hardly alone in her addiction. "Everyone was taking them at the time," Dardy explained.[692]

And Lili had a lot to be concerned about.

Burlesque theatres were desperately struggling to keep an audience as pornography became readily available. Burlesque entertainment was becoming passé. Lillian Hunt hung on despite the owners cutting the musicians and chorus girls. When the theatre across the street started showing adult films, Hunt prophesized, "That's gonna hurt."[693]

The business was changing. Theatres were rapidly closing. Hunt managed to stay afloat because in addition to managing the Follies she was co-owner of a talent agency, Winsor Hunt, booking strippers jobs wherever available. It was through

Tempest Storm a threat to Lili

these commissions that Hunt made the majority of her money, especially in the coming years when burlesque struggled to compete against television and movies and nudie magazines. Lili was lucky to have her contract in Vegas where burlesque-type acts were thriving.

One night at the El Rancho she premiered a new number: "Sadie Thompson," the original prostitute of the South Seas who tempts poor Reverend Davidson.

Tom Douglas—back in the picture—built a little hut onstage with palm leaves. After the first dance Lili undressed behind a see-through wall of palm fronds, a burning candle lighting up her lithe silhouette. She was supposed to blow the candle out but didn't, and she failed to notice when she danced to the front of the stage that the candle fell and started a fire.

Because of the lights in her eyes Lili couldn't see the audience beyond the first row of tables. But she did see actress and singer Mitzi Gaynor, a regular performer in Vegas, sitting at a stage-side table becoming "agitated."[694] Lili had no idea a small fire smoldered behind her. The audience took it for granted that the flames were another part of Lili's sophisticated act.

It wasn't until she turned, parasol in hand, that Lili saw flames leaping from the hut. She started to panic, dancing toward the side of the stage to signal a stage-hand. She was not about to stop her performance, especially as this was an opening night. More importantly, she did not want the audience to panic.

In the audience Ted Jordan leapt from his seat and started smacking at the flames until the stagehands came around. All the while Lili continued to dance, hoping to avoid a disaster. Finally, the curtains were drawn and fire extinguishers broken out. Jordan's burns would be treated at the hospital.

Variety would report that her new "sensuous interpretation" was "her usual attempt to frame a story within the realm of the strip." She would toss her "laced scanties" (panties) out into the audience from behind an umbrella, instant advertising for her lingerie business.[695]

Reviews remained favorable. As bolero played she took a "whimsical bath" and "gyrates" on her bed.[696]

Back at Ciro's with her new act, the compliment was backhanded; "at her trade she's a virtuoso" even if the "novelty seems to have worn a bit thin."[697]

With Lili's help Ted signed with her film agent Henry Wilson. Her own film career was nonexistent, but Lili was making upward of $10,000 a week "for about thirty-six minutes a night of work."[698] For those thirty-six minutes a night, her world revolved around her shows. Lili was serious about her career, no matter she kept claiming she would rather be doing something else.

She noticed others' work ethic was changing. Stagehands weren't as meticulous as they had been. Everything was becoming "good enough."[699] She didn't want good enough. One of her recent falling-outs with Dardy had been after a screw-up at the Rialto. For the opening her lights were changed at the wrong time because of a lack of rehearsing and Lili was furious. Back in her hotel room she told Sadie to pack their bags. She called Dardy and told her to tell Harold the rest of her engagement was off. And she was gone.

Harold would say his star was a "perfectionist." "She requires expert lighting and expert production work." Lili was "critical of her work, far more than any other star we've played." Still, Harold had let her down. He considered her "serious" and "highly aesthetic."[700]

The sisters didn't speak for months. It wasn't the first or last time the sisters fell out. Sometimes they just were busy with their own lives; other times it was the clash of two stubborn wills. Interestingly, Lili complained to a reporter that she hadn't seen Barbara in months.

Back in Las Vegas a restless and insecure Jordan saw potential lovers everywhere his wife disrobed. She tried helping his career, hoping it would give him something to do. "Come sing in my show," she offered. He pouted and refused, then said okay.

They announced they would be starring together in *Kiss Me Goodbye*, a staged

Playing Mr. St. Cyr, an increasingly rare moment of tranquility
between Lili and Ted Jordan at home

comedy at the El Rancho with Beldon producing. It never happened. Lili wasn't
going to memorize lines for Ted.

She caught him in bed with a showgirl from *her* show. Furious, she slapped
his face and fled to a gig at the El Rey in Oakland, living barricaded in her dressing room.

Ted showed up. Begged. She took him back.

In LA he was no better. He wanted to be a movie star but nothing was going
his way.[701] She invited influential friends to the house for parties. Still no work. He
resented singing to the side of her show, practically offstage while chorus girls "went
through their routines." He was reduced to planning and working the lights on her
shows. He hated feeling like a "kept man." He deeply resented the way "she always
has to be walking a few steps in front of me."[702]

Like the husbands before, the never-ending living out of a suitcase took a toll
on Jordan. The gypsy life was fine for her.

Ted compulsively poured over the trades, noticing the slow successes his contemporaries were having, some from *The Caine Mutiny*, who had "stuck to it." He

felt he'd made a wrong choice with Lili. His career was going nowhere while he had been playing Mr. St. Cyr.[703]

LILI FLOATED AROUND THE HOUSE, LIGHTING HER ORNATE SILVER candelabras she had placed around the dining room. The fireplace was lit. Every inch of the small house was, as Tom would say, "gilded within an inch of itself."[704] Fancy French furniture, ornate wallpaper in the design of trees. She had the table set with Reed and Barton silver. There were bowls of cut crystal filled with flowers, cigarettes in glass boxes.

Sadie laid out monogrammed napkins with fancy script spelling "SLC" on the cream-colored linen.

Lili floated into the kitchen to check on her meal. Soon her guests arrived, the actors Clifton Webb and Lloyd Nolan, who had performed in *The Caine Mutiny* with Ted. Virginia showed up swathed in a fur capelet, chic as always, giant drop earrings dangling from her ears.[705]

LILI'S DINNER PARTIES WERE FILLED WITH HER SMALL CIRCLE OF mostly gay friends who were both flamboyant and connected in Hollywood. Oftentimes there would be Gaylord Hauser, Swanson and Garbo's health guru, sometimes Jerry Giesler, also the actor Joel Grey, whom she worked with in Las Vegas. She was comfortable with *her* people in *her* place. She enjoyed her dinners with her friends, comfortable with those that adored, protected, and supported her.

"She was a fantastic cook. She could make anything," Dardy claimed. "They had beautiful parties. First Tom would throw a dinner at his house, then Lili. They were very social even though Lili was shy." She didn't like to be around strangers. "When she wasn't on the road she was doing this." Her crowds were great wits and "the dinner parties carried on through several marriages," Dardy claimed. Days before a party, Lili and Sadie would polish and wipe the crystals in her chandelier. "She would spend all day cooking," Dardy said. "Grandma had taught her how to cook. She made the best cream puffs." The laughter around Lili's table flowed until the wee hours of the morning.

Ted tried to fit in with his wife's friends but mostly struck out. He was merely husband number five. Things had soured in the marriage and everyone knew it. They ignored him and he pouted.

She suggested he make the rounds, or whatever it was that out-of-work actors did. She was tired of his lounging around the house.

Lili near the fireplace, Virginia to the left

She again locked herself in the bedroom, furious to be trapped in another suffocating marriage. Ted moved into the guest room. Their lovemaking ceased. They each had meaningless affairs. She had no passion for him. When she had a rare day off she laid around in bed, "having breakfast served to her" by Sadie. He complained to others she only watched TV all day.[706]

Another source of contention was the way she spent money. *Her* money. "If I want to throw it away, that's what I'll do." She kept a suite at the Astor in New York, a limousine service on standby twenty-four hours a day. He thought it a colossal waste of money. Ted complained but realized "I can't change her. This is the way she likes to live." He deeply resented the way she acted like "a goddamn queen."[707]

Though she was "gorgeous," for Ted "it wasn't enough."[708]

Lili contemplated her upcoming obligations; another run at Ciro's, a five-year contract had been her wedding gift from Beldon. Undoubtedly, it was just publicity, as Beldon would have renewed her contract anyway.

Harold Minsky approached her to return to Newark; he promised no misplaced lights this time. She had an engagement at the Old Howard in Boston. She wasn't *in* the game, she *was* the game.

With the Sunset Blvd. *bed*

THE PAPERS WERE FILLED WITH THE NUPTIALS OF GRACE KELLY TO Prince Rainer of Monaco. Lili was entranced by the movie star's romance. It would remind her of Aunt Rosemary. As a tribute Lili premiered her "Royal Wedding Night" at the El Rancho in April of 1956. Though *Variety* sniped the act was "brief" and her "interior set is much the same," it was still beautiful, Lili entering in a white corset.[709] She debuted her spectacular new prop, a very royal bed.

Center stage sat a boat-shaped, hand-carved ornate wooden bed. Tom had found it in a movie prop house in Los Angeles. It turned out to be the very same bed Norma Desmond writhed on in *Sunset Blvd.*[710]

Longtime critic for the *Los Angeles Times* Kevin Thomas explained the bed made famous by Gloria Swanson in the 1950 movie had graced several films prior. It first showed up in the Lon Chaney 1925 film *Phantom of the Opera*. It was also in Howard Hawks's *The Twentieth Century* starring Carole Lombard before being immortalized in *Sunset Blvd.*

Long before its illustrious movie career the bed was rumored to have been in the possession of the king of Portugal's mistress.

At one point the bed was even on display at the department store May Company at Eighth and Broadway in Los Angeles displaying Italian linens. "I think

"Wedding in Monaco"

Lili rented it from a prop house," Kevin Thomas guessed. "I know she took it on the road. It was sturdy, but delicate. I mean there was a carved waterfall on the back. It was absolutely gorgeous. Originally green, I think she painted it chalky grey."[711]

With the help of photographer Bruno Bernard and Tom, the trio concocted a fantastical story for the papers; on a trip to Europe Lili found the bed as "she rummages through antique shops," the bed had formerly been the love nest of "Madama [*sic*] Pompadour."[712] It was unique, as only Lili's props were.

Bernard, the Berlin-born photographer, though only five years older than Lili, had lived a life far more worldly. As a child his parents put him in an orphanage because of their terrible poverty. As a Jew he fled Nazi Germany in 1937.

Delving into his childhood passion of photography he collaborated with pinup artist Alberto Vargas in 1940. It wasn't long until he was the go-to photographer for starlets and burlesque girls.

Lili enlisted Bruno for countless shoots. He shot photos for *Man*, the Adult Picture Magazine, and wrote a six-page spread extolling her virtues and why she was "the most daring thing" the audience had ever seen.

BY 1956 HER ACT HAD GROWN MORE INTRICATE. SHE ADDED A FAUX fireplace, soft blue lights, and the revolving stage.

In May Ted was performing in a revival of a Herman Wouk piece at Equity

Library Theatre in Lennox Hill entitled *The Traitor*. Though *Variety* called the production "inept," Ted received decent notices as a "personable" lieutenant.[713]

In August the papers reported the pair were separated though Jordan continued to appear often enough in her act. They seemed to reconcile whenever "Lili called him back" or when Ted crawled back "to think things over."[714] The couple continued to fight, reconcile, then live apart.

Periodically Lili announced she planned on winging it to Europe for a vacation. But it never happened.

HAROLD AND DARDY HAD BEEN LIVING IN NEW JERSEY WHERE FOR A time they enjoyed "a normalcy which Harold and I had never known."[715] Dardy was trying to control her husband's drinking, take care of the children, and help with the shows at the Adams. But by 1956 Harold and Dardy landed permanently in Las Vegas, living at the Dunes. Ava Minsky remembers looking down from her room on the back of the forty-foot Sultan's turban that stood at the front of the casino. The following year Harold would introduce customers to "Minsky Goes to Paris" and it would be a game changer. The January 10, 1957, debut was the first topless review and shocked many, but not enough to close the show. It was a smash success.[716] And it changed the Las Vegas landscape.

Dardy had all but retired from the stage, preferring to help Harold produce. She had her own one-woman show displaying her paintings. At Dardy's urging, Lili started painting, sitting in her dressing room or home, concentrating over a canvas. She loved to paint but it was hard to find time to pursue it. "The only one I remember," Dardy said, "is this really beautiful one with flowers that had eyes and she painted long eyelashes on them."

Dardy hosted a local television show, interviewing celebrities. She begged Lili to appear.

"Don't you remember *The Buffy and Wallace Show?*" Lili recalled sitting speechless in front of the radio microphone at a loss as to how to put a sentence together.

"You just didn't know what to talk about. Come on and we'll talk about—" Dardy thought fast. "Packing! You are always traveling. You know how to pack. It'll be great fun."

Lili did the show and talked nonstop. Dardy said, "You just had to get her to talk about what she knew."[717]

LILI FILMED *BUXOM BEAUTEASE* FOR IRVING KLAW. THE 1956 FILM included Tempest Storm and the West Virginia–born Blaze Starr with the size

38-DD chest who was conducting a messy public affair with Louisiana governor Earl Long. At least there was no Bettie Page for Klaw to fawn over.

Lili stood in a steaming-hot theatre in New York waiting for the lights and Klaw to be ready. Her skin was tanned. She had been laying out in the nude in the privacy of her courtyard.

THE TIMES THEY WERE A-CHANGING. THE COUNTY'S MORALS HAD loosened but so had Lili's. She went further than she might have just a few years earlier.

Variety claimed she was "bare-bosomed" at the El Rancho for her "Carmen" number.[718]

But Lili had to keep up with the Tempests and the Blazes. She was paid and paid well and lauded for her performance even if it was nothing more than wiggling and kicking her legs in the air. *Buxom Beautease* didn't showcase half her talent but did show her beauty to perfection as she again bathed in a translucent tub.[719]

Because of her association with Klaw and his with Page, in later years Lili would be asked endless questions about what Bettie was like.

"Whore," she would snarl. "She made everything cheap. I didn't even know her. Passed her backstage once. What she did was pornography. I did art."[720]

By July of 1957 she announced that she and Ted were divorcing. Their relationship would remain very much on and off again.

"Why do you stay with these men, Lili?" Dardy asked.[721]

Lili shrugged. It was all too much effort to extract herself from a relationship that wasn't working. She had heard Ted's brother telling someone there wasn't a man, waiter, or bartender she wouldn't sleep with. It helped cement her notorious reputation. She didn't care.

IN HER CHALET-STYLED BUNGALOW AT THE EL RANCHO ONE AFTERnoon, bored, as she so often was, Lili spied a tall handsome man outside her windows.

Later that night she spotted him gambling at the tables.

"Who is he?" She pointed him out to Beldon.

It was Zsa Zsa Gabor's latest heartbreak, Derek Goodman.

Lili wanted details.

Beldon told her what he knew. Goodman was a millionaire. A polo player from South America. Family in gold mines. He was in Vegas "recovering."

"Recovering from what?" Lili asked.[722]

Zsa Zsa had tossed him over for Rubirosa.

Lili had met Porfirio Rubirosa of the rumored eleven-inch-penis fame. He was

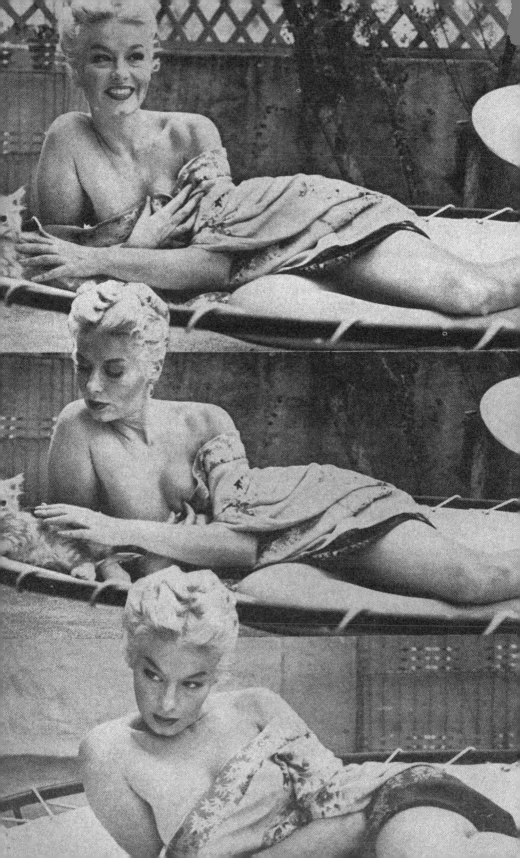

a crony of Armando. She never liked the Dominican and thought him a "hood."[723] Yes, he was charming but not at all attractive. And he was short. Lili liked her men tall and handsome.

She made Beldon introduce her to the thinly mustached Goodman, who stood six-four and had brilliant blue eyes. The married-though-estranged Derek soon began having dinner with Lili—and even Lili *and* Ted. Lili liked flirting with him. She wanted Ted out of her life. For Derek's part, the playboy returned some interest but was still pining for the tempestuous Zsa Zsa, who was off in another city with her lover, Rubirosa.

Perhaps she was bored, or perhaps she had decided to help Derek—as she often helped others' romances—in any case, Lili hatched a plan to make Zsa Zsa jealous. She called Bruno, who had opened a photographic studio at the Riviera and traveled between Las Vegas and Hollywood.

She told him to come and to bring his camera.

The next night, August 23, during dinner (as Bruno and a few reporters just *happened* to be in the Chuck Wagon buffet of the El Rancho), Derek and Lili huddled together eating. Ted arrived and sat with them. Soon thereafter, Ted theatrically and *loudly* jumped to his feet and shouted, "Hey, nobody talks about my wife like that."[724] Even the line sounded like that of a badly written script.

Goodman—playing in the same bad B movie—twirled his mustache and shouted back, "Perhaps you're right . . . but if she were *my* wife, I wouldn't let her out of my sight for thirty minutes, as you did."[725]

"Why you—" Ted balled up his fist.

Derek stood up quickly. Soup was knocked over. Lili jumped up and screamed, attracting everyone's eyes. Blows were exchanged. Derek fell to the floor at Ted's feet. Lili tried to separate the two men. All eyes were on the trio. The pair of flailing men crashed into the Chuck Wagon, upsetting bowls of salad.

Photographers snapped a series of pictures that was seen—or so it was hoped—around the world, or at least wherever Zsa Zsa might be.

The papers ran headlines: "Zsa Zsa's Friend Put Out of Fight?" and, "Salad Battle Ends."[726] Ted had a cut lip; Derek sported a black eye.

Zsa Zsa didn't seem to care. She never contacted Derek.[727]

"I was forever known for that damn stunt," Lili complained in old age, though it still amused her. "Whenever they write about me they mention that night, me spilling my soup, Ted hitting Derek."[728]

Conveniently, Ted and Lili were leaving the next day for New York and a scheduled vacation. Beldon had given Lili $5,000 in cash as a gift.

LEFT: *Lili sunbathing in the privacy of her yard*

THE BRAW
OVER
LILI ST. CY

1

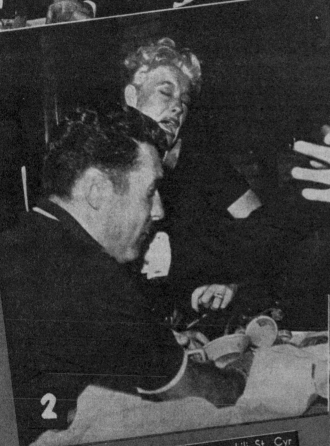

2

3

All was serene at Rancho Vegas when stripper Lili St. Cyr sat down with Derek Goodman, ex-beau of Zsa Zsa Gabor. He was a South African millionaire and Lili was intrigued.

The thirty minute tete a tete proceeded delightfully until Ted Jordan, Lili's husband, came by and heard something that made him decide to wipe the floor with Lili's millionaire.

Security officers finally managed to halt the brawl. Ex-champ Jackie Field helped Goodman to his feet. Lili hovered in the background. SUPPRESSED got only exclusive story and pictures.

In New York the two caught a cruise on the Cunard line for South Hampton. The line, though luxurious, wasn't what Lili remembered from her days sailing. The charm of the old ships had been replaced with steel and modern conveniences. They lacked the "mystery and elegance" of prior years.[729] To make things worse, she and Ted weren't speaking. Both sought attention elsewhere. He spent time with some "younger members of the crew," a vicious swipe that would have hurt.[730] Lili claimed she found respite in the arms of a "French steward."[731]

In London Lili worked up enough nerve to tell Ted it was over.

Her way to break the news was as they were cuddling in the hotel room. Ted was stunned. He suspected Derek, that the staged fight had never been about making Zsa Zsa jealous. What confirmed Ted's suspicions was the fact Derek *happened* to be in London at the same time. Ted tracked the millionaire down at the Brown Hotel and confronted him, punching him in the face. This time without the benefit of photographers.

No grand romance blossomed between Lili and Derek. She was unhappy and restless, increasingly relying on her sleeping pills. She felt as if she was hanging on. To what she didn't know. Desperation descended on her.

Ted returned to their hotel crying, distraught. She asked him to leave. He refused. She gave him money to go. He went to Paris.[732]

BACK IN LAS VEGAS, ALONE, LILI CONTINUED HER LONG TRADITION OF joining Joe E. for a $2 rare steak, peas, and drinks. The comedian was in the midst of writing his memoirs, seemingly unworried the mob might want to finish him off after they read it.

Both performers forgot about their troubles as they went onstage. Joe looked dapper in his tux as he warmed up the audience. He held the microphone in his hand, kidded the audience, and snapped his fingers at them. Then the hottest thing in Vegas sailed onstage.

The stage was dark except for a spotlight on Lili in a long stiff white coat, tiara, hair pinned up. She took her time. She never rushed the stripping. Eventually down to a white merry widow, tame by any standards. She loosened her shiny hair. She ran a hand over her cheek (a move Marilyn Monroe copied). Nothing was wildly provocative.

Lili was forty and had to feel it. Still spectacular looking, if not a little more worn, a little harder in the morning light. She was still having fun, but her underlying sadness, which had always threatened to overcome her, was visible more often.

LEFT: *Lili, Goodman, and Jordan in Las Vegas*

For Lillian Hunt, Lili danced in another short film, *Kiss Me Baby*, with stripper Taffy O'Neil, billed as "stripper by night, mother by day," who rose early to take her son stricken with polio for treatment in Santa Monica.[733] Also in the cast were Joy Ryder, Pat Flannery, and Lady Midnight, whose father was comedian Monkey Kirkland.

Astoundingly, Lili agreed to do Mike Wallace's television talk show. Possibly hoping to redeem herself after her previous encounter with the reporter, to show a different Lili, a lighter side. Besides which she wasn't one to turn down publicity with the likes of Tempest and Blaze burning up the tabloids behind her.

She had no idea what she was letting herself in for.

It was October 1957 and she had been working at the Crescendo, a preeminent jazz club (Count Basie was a regular) at 8572 Sunset Boulevard in West Hollywood, missing one night claiming to have overslept after staying up all night with Dardy.[734] She performed for twelve minutes.

For a $2 cover charge audiences saw Lili "shake, rattle, and roll." But the "sparse turnout" was underwhelmed by her tame sort of entertainment. Dressed as a geisha she undulated at the "shrine of a sacred goat." Special effects were a "flash of red powder." *Variety* noted she was "skilled" at performing her "dubious act" but the band "used up more energy than the headliner." It was noted "what has been for years a striptease is still that and no more."[735] With reviews like that she undoubtedly felt the need for some national publicity.

Wallace sent a couple of his producers to Lili's house days before for a pre-interview (according to Dardy). Wallace himself attended the Crescendo the night before the interview.

On camera Lili wore a demure scoop-neck dress with three-quarter sleeves, her hair short and curly, a three-strand pearl necklace around her neck, pearl earrings screwed into her ears.

Lili was optimistic about the interview. It would prove to be far more torturous than she could have imagined.

From the first moment it was obvious the thirty-nine-year-old Wallace didn't approve of Lili St. Cyr as a woman, as a performer, as anything. After a few cursory questions, in a superior snarky tone he pulled out his verbal knives.

His opening marks were prophetic of what was to come. "Tonight we go after the story of a beautiful blonde who has made a fortune by taking off her clothes in public."[736] He indeed did go after her. Wallace looked uptight and buttoned down and ready to eviscerate her.

Before introducing her he teased the audience, repeating a Lili quote, "'If I were a man I'd never bother to get married.'" He continued, "She makes more than $100,000 a year . . ."

Lili's appendix had been bothering her. (The following month she would be in the hospital to finally have it removed.) She was suffering dreadfully and it showed in her strained appearance. She appeared stiff, lacking wit or spontaneity of any kind, clearly not having a good time.

The first thing Wallace wanted to know was her "personal opinion of the men" at her shows.

"I'm flattered by their attention." She didn't judge them.

She looked hard under the harsh lights. Bags under her eyes, the skin on her cheeks showed slight scars. But even with the flat lighting her bone structure couldn't be denied. There was a reason she had been a headliner for over a decade.

Lili smoked throughout. She was thoughtful and honest. She defended her audience; they weren't only lonely men, as Wallace implied. He couldn't understand why someone would go to a strip show.

He had a palpable disdain for her and her profession. He tried to reduce her to a thing, a stripper, something abnormal.

When she told him she was a fan of striptease, he seemed surprised. Yes, she liked a beautiful woman dancing.

She thought actors were "panty waists," too feminine for her. She didn't like men on the stage. One can only wonder what Ted was thinking as he watched.

Wallace continued. "What do you think about . . . when you go through the gyrations . . . what do you *actually* think about?"

"I think about what I'm going to do next." She explained she had no feeling toward the audience. She thought only of her performance.

Wallace brought up her "three or four" arrests.

"Naturally I don't agree I arose any lust. . . . I don't believe I do anything that I believe is wrong."

"Ninety-eight percent of your audience goes . . . for the implications in the act . . . isn't that so?"

"I can't answer for the audience."

In her pre-interview she had said that most people were hypocrites and needed to loosen up. People pretended to be shocked by something they were actually attracted to. On camera she defended her opinion. "It's a joke to think I could demoralize anyone with this little act." Others might act as if they were shocked by strip teasing, but her audience was filled with men and women.

Why then did the law go after her?

"For commercial reasons," she said. "I'm an easy victim to pick on." Wallace made much of that, as if she deserved to be arrested for tantalizing men.

Lili thought the law should go after things that were more important than her.

She got a genuine chuckle out of Wallace, though too late for her to relax, when he asked her if she had ever done anything she was ashamed of.

"Yes." Effective pause. "But he was so handsome, I couldn't help myself." The joke fell flat. She delivered the line joylessly. She was underwater, struggling. Lili was never a verbal fighter, debater, defender. Her MO was to retreat into her interior world.

"What are you trying to do for an audience?" he asked.

All her answers were thought out in the moment. "Amuse them . . . for a few minutes." It was enough for her. Until he made her feel it wasn't.

"Do you consider yourself an artist?"

"No." In courtrooms she had told judges her dancing was "art" only to be sniggered at. She was tired of defending herself. She didn't explain further.

"Do you wish you did more than you do in show business? Are you proud of what you do?" Double punch.

"No."

"No?"

"No . . . I'd rather be doing something else."

"Like for instance?"

She wanted to be in legitimate business.

He scoffed when she told him she suffered from nerves. He didn't realize she was terrified nightly, not because she was taking off her clothes, that never bothered her, but because she was performing in front of others and knew they were judging her. She didn't want to let anyone down. "I'm always so stage frightened. I don't like having people look at me." Lili looked down at the desk.

Wallace was amused. Naturally, he didn't believe her. "You let people look at all of you."

"It's just as difficult to walk into a cocktail party . . . when people are looking at me it makes me nervous. On stage I'm a little more terrified." Even though she loved the attention, she always felt she had to live up to something. She had spent her entire career frightened.

She grew stiffer and more uncomfortable under Wallace's lashing. He put her down at every opportunity. She didn't let the cigarette out of her hand. She tried to answer his questions candidly.

Lili looked grim, mentally and physically unwell. Occasionally she would squint her eyes, suck hard on the cigarette while she thought how best to answer his questions.

Why do you do this? Why not another profession? Wallace's disgust for what she did, who she was, was humiliating.

"I must make money," she explained. "I've had to work my whole life." Nobody gave her a break. She hadn't married a wealthy man. She had made something of herself. "I'm not trained for anything else."

Wallace thought because she was married she shouldn't have to work— hardly a foreign concept from a 1950s male—but then he didn't know Ted Jordan.

"Well, I haven't always been married," she defended.

Wallace would never understand that dancing fulfilled her on so many levels. It was "easier" than being a waitress. Most people would rather she did that, a menial job, than reach the heights by stripping.

Stripping—and she thought of it as dancing, performing—gave her everything. It was who she was.

He suggested she might want to go to a psychoanalyst. She demurred; after all, she would be getting out of the business.

Wallace told his audience he had seen the show at the Crescendo and it was "affective." Between puffs of smoke he admitted it was a "beautiful kind of act."

He kept wondering if she were his wife, how would he feel about her taking off her clothes in front of strangers who were "vaguely intoxicated"?

"How does your husband feel about . . . disrobing?"

"My husband's very anxious to go into business and to have me stop it." She didn't mention she was anxious to get rid of said husband.

Well, why didn't she just stop and get out of that filthy business, Wallace implied.

"I'm always one year behind in my debts . . . now I'm caught up and I'll be stopping."

"What kind of business . . ." would she get into?

"I'll be the housewife and forget the bright lights. Gladly." She did occasionally have that fantasy. But it wasn't what she wanted. It was what others wanted to hear.

"It's a false business," she said. That was true. She was the one who felt false. After all, Lili St. Cyr was invention.

She knew she "wasn't really contributing anything . . . to anything." This was perhaps her saddest moment among many depressing moments in the long painful interview. Doctors and nurses and builders contributed more to society than her. She wanted to leave a lasting mark on the world. She didn't know how to do anything that would matter after she was gone.

"I'd be much more proud of myself," she said, if she could do something constructive.

"You don't like yourself very much." It wasn't even a question.

"No." Wallace was surprised at her sincere reply. Was she going to raise a family when she quit her job? After all, that's what "normal women" did.

But Lili had never felt any "obligation to contribute any more babies." It wasn't that she didn't like them, but her body was everything. A child didn't fit into her life.

How would she go on the road and have adventures if she had a child?

"Do you think you'd be a good mother?"

"Yes."

"But you don't want one?"

"Quite often women who have no other interest certainly need children." What did Wallace expect? That she would hang up her G-string for an apron and a bunch of children?

What would her interest outside of the business be, then, once she quit?

"I don't know."

Though on her fifth marriage, she said she didn't feel the need to legalize a union with a man. If she were a man, she would never get married. She didn't tell Wallace, but she could pick up and discard men like they did. Since it was "illegal" to just live with someone, she married them.

"What do you think of our alimony laws?"

She thought them unfair.

She was progressive in her views but not a feminist. Far from it.

"You said, 'I believe in flying saucers . . . that there is life on Venus.'" She had even gone further to say that the men on Venus would have "less lust and less greed."

To Wallace's audience Lili must have sounded like a kook when she admitted she believed aliens were "obviously more advanced people than we are." There had been many sightings of UFOs and she had read stacks of books on the subject. She didn't apologize for her beliefs. "So they must be more advanced in their emotions."

She went on to explain, "I believe they exist and . . . their manner of flying indicates they are many, many years ahead of us."

He asked about her religious belief (for obviously she must not have any). She explained she had her own religion. Which was doing the right thing, never hurting anyone, and helping anyone if she can. Echoes of Alice.

Politics didn't interest her, she said.

"Out of your field?"

"I'm not interested in it."

"Why not?"

Long pause. "I can't tell you why . . . perhaps I've always been so busy with my own little world that I haven't had time . . ." She laughed, trailed off. She never tried to be smarter or more sophisticated than she was. She could have. She could have lied and said anything. Instead she presented a guileless Lili.

"What is your most consuming interest . . . yourself? . . . What excites you?"

Wallace just didn't understand.

"I'm always so busy working. . . . I have no one helping me. And I must answer all the letters, and make all the arrangements, and do so many things all day long. . . . I never seem to have time for a hobby. I like to read."

What kind of things did she read?

"Everything."

Was she afraid to grow old and ugly?

"Yes." *Terrified.*

He asked if she had "anything" in her "spiritual bank" to rely on when she lost her beauty. A cruel question for a woman who lived off her looks.

"I don't know." It was a devastating moment and one that seemed to hit her hard.

"Lili, you don't respect marriage . . . you have no particular interest in children, politics. . . . What kind of a world do you think this would be if everyone were like you?" He must have loathed her.[737]

"Well, since I don't hurt anyone . . . then no one would ever hurt anyone else."

Because of the callous questioning many refused to "talk to Mike." After the "lethal barrage" aimed at Lili, Hollywood had "no interest," explained one anonymous "star." "He'll dig . . . junk outa the dead past that I'd just as soon not uncover. . . . The basic commodity of his show is shock."

Wallace was satisfied with the interview. "I was more interested in getting the real story—in showing the real Lili St. Cyr. Her insecurities. Her dislike of things she does. And that's the story I got."[738]

Others thought he left her "dangling before the nation with her life as naked as an open wound."

LILI HAD BEEN STRUGGLING WITH HER APPENDIX FOR A VERY LONG time. At her request doctors repeatedly froze it. As early as 1956 Dorothy Kilgallen was reporting Lili was "flirting with disaster" by having her appendix frozen five times, and her doctors were "frantic with worry."[739]

Dardy acknowledged Lili was "vain."[740] Though in terrible pain, Lili would not let them operate.

"I will not have a scar, Dardy."

"Lili, you can barely stand up."

"I don't care."

Dardy had enlisted Harold to convince Lili to have it removed. "We'll get you a plastic surgeon."

"I can't go on the stage with a big hack mark, Dard."

"Oh, Lili!" Dardy couldn't see dying over an appendix just not to have a scar. Good God, how would she ever grow old, Dardy wondered. Dardy could never imagine how bad it would get.

Finally, in November of 1957, after the third or fourth time, Lili was taken to the hospital and the doctors called Dardy. "Or maybe Sadie called me. I don't remember, it was so long ago. Now remember we're talking sixty years ago!" Dardy said, stunned by the sheer amount of years that had passed.

"Lili was in the Los Angeles Angel's Hospital, off the freeway near downtown," Dardy recalled. As she was walking through the hospital entrance Dardy, beautifully made up, was met by a "stunningly" good-looking doctor. "God, he was *good* looking," she remembered. "And I wasn't so bad looking myself." In distress Dardy caught the doctor's attention.

"Can I help you?" he asked.

"My sister is in here somewhere."

"Who is your sister?"

As luck would have it, *he* was Lili's doctor. He walked Dardy to Lili's room. *Oh, Lili will like him*, Dardy thought. It was just like Lili to have a movie-star-handsome doctor attend to her. *She'll work this*, Dardy thought. *Probably walk away without being given a bill.*

Lili's appendix was dangerously close to bursting, the doctor explained. "We need to operate," he told Dardy outside Lili's room.

"Oh, Tweed," Lili cried in relief. "You came. You did."

"Of course I came."

"Oh, Tweed, don't make me do this," Lili moaned. Sweat stood out on her brow and upper lip.

Dardy sat on the edge of the bed while the disapproving nurse stood in the background. "We go into surgery in fifteen minutes."

"Thank you," Dardy said in that cold tone that dismissed people. The nurse said she would wait outside.

"Lili, they have to operate or you're going to die," Dardy implored her.

"No. I can't have a scar." Lili stubbornly shook her head though she was in great pain. Perhaps thoughts of Betty maimed by a scar running down her face haunted her.

"The doctor has already talked to a plastic surgeon," Dardy pleaded. "You won't have but a little teeny tiny—"

"No," Lili raised her voice. She was pale and sweating. She looked thin and tired. Working too much. "I won't have them carve me up! No. I won't. I won't do it," Lili said. "Don't have them maim me."[741]

Exasperated, Dardy took the doctor outside and asked if he had any pills he could give Lili. "To calm her down. Give her anything. She likes pills."

The doctor promised to give Lili something.

A short time later Dardy ventured back into the room to see how Lili was doing.

Lili was calmer. "Really out of it," Dardy explained. "The pills were working just fine. I asked her, 'Have you thought about it? Are you going to go along with this or are you going to die?'"

"Oh, no, it's fine. Go ahead. Whatever they want to do. Anything is okay by me." And Lili did end up with a small white line, never noticeable.

CHAPTER EIGHT

Everyone at the party was dredging up that old murder.

"She had pretty hair. I remember that," John Gilmore, at the time a seventeen-year-old aspiring actor, recalled. He was the type Tom liked.

The group was at Tom Douglas's house. Lili was made up simply, just lipstick and her hair down. Her agent Henry Wilson was there. Ted was trying to monopolize the conversation. He bored everyone, ceaselessly turning every conversation to Marilyn Monroe. "She called me," he said.

Gilmore and Ted both claimed to be all-important in Marilyn's life. "No one believed Ted."[742] Lili seemed to Gilmore to be "withholding in a resentful way." She and Ted were on the outs. Lili told Gilmore the *only* time she ever even spoke with Marilyn was in some nightclub Lili had been working. Gilmore said Ted was known as a "crackpot" around town.

At the party Lili stayed quiet, seated on a chaise wearing dark slacks and a long-sleeved, high-necked black sweater, which surprised Gilmore. She was barefoot with her legs tucked under her. Simple, he thought. And elegant.

Gilmore thought Lili refined, not at all voluptuous for a stripteaser. "I kissed her hand," Gilmore said. "And she said, 'What a gentleman.'" She liked his manners. She was shy and pleasant and concerned about others. She asked him interesting questions about himself.

"Tom," Gilmore said, "went to all of George Cukor's parties." Director Cukor held notorious invitation-only Sunday afternoon soirees filled with good-looking gay men in show business who lounged around his pool.

Tom, now past sixty, was attempting to romance the quasi-juvenile John Gilmore. Heavyset and balding, he no longer resembled the "bright young thing" he had once boasted of being. He was drinking too much. For some reason the topic of conversation this night was on the nearly four-year-old murder of Elizabeth Short, whom the press had dubbed the Black Dahlia. In the 1990s Gilmore would write a book about the sensational murder.

After Lili and Ted departed, in the Cadillac she had bought him, someone mentioned a recent suicide attempt by Lili, which brought tears to Tom's eyes. "She's such a dear." He refused to speculate on her motives. He didn't gossip about Lili.[743]

LIKE GYPSY ROSE LEE WHO OFF-LOADED SOME OF HER STRIPPING responsibilities as she aged to a bevy of younger things sharing the stage with her, Lili planned a "stable of strippers," but so far had only one stripper, Sharon Knight, a Lili look-alike.[744]

Possibly pushed into the idea by Ted, who was always scheming up things for Lili, the project never got off the ground. Lili was notorious for her lack of follow-through.

Ted was destined to live his life in the shadow of others, first his famous uncle's, then his infamous wife's. He was desperate to be noticed, desperate to take credit for both Marilyn's and Lili's careers.

Lili tended to stay in the sanctuary of her home. "She was a hausfrau," Dardy claimed. Ted was taking up the air around her. She longed to be on the road. She thought often of Jimmy and Armando and the terrible mistakes she had made. She was unhappy and it showed in her face.

Dorothy Kilgallen reported the St. Cyr–Jordan marriage had "reached the end of a rocky matrimonial road" due to some "other woman," and Earl Wilson reported the two living separated in Las Vegas.[745]

ONE NIGHT IN 1958 AT THE EL RANCHO, LILI WAS SURPRISED BY A PAR-ticularly distinguished guest. Former First Lady Eleanor Roosevelt dropped in to catch Lili's gilded cage act, which by now had been perfected.

After the show "the Form Divine" changed into a beautiful satin gown and long gloves and went out to meet the guest, who was enchanted by Lili's performance. They posed for pictures together, wearing pearl necklaces, hair up. Both Beldon and Joe E. honed in on the photo.

THE FORMER FIRST LADY WAS HAVING THE TIME OF IT IN LAS VEGAS. "I must tell everyone. This Las Vegas is certainly something. I've lost nearly $3.00 gambling!" she exclaimed. The former First Lady was in Vegas on behalf of the United Nations Association.

Lili had some very distinguished guests in Las Vegas

Lili rarely missed a show; it happened so infrequently that when she did, it made the papers. Comedian Martha Raye took her spot, burlesquing a hilarious take on Lili's bath act, with her clothes on.[746]

Lili appeared in another movie, *Josette from New Orleans* starring John Loder. She played another stripper among a group of racketeers. Her pace never slowed.

Bullfighting was a popular pastime, with Americans flocking across the Mexican border to enjoy tequila and watch the handsome bullfighters strut in the ring wearing their "suit of lights" in Tijuana. Lili sewed a black velvet bolero jacket with fringe (sixty years later it still looks new) and created a matador act. In the number Lili seduces a painting of a toreador. Though she had been portraying Carmen since at least 1953 she renamed the number "Carmen Fantasy." She ended the dance by spinning around the stage throwing her "scanty panties" to the audience. Ted, and at least once Joe E., came onstage as the matador who appears to step from the painting on the wall. It was a sultry, sexy number and Lili looked her finest.

LILI WOULD FILM "DANCE OF CARMEN," A FOUR-MINUTE SHORT, PROBably for Irving Klaw. She enters wearing a frilly Spanish-style dress, a mantilla

Point *cover*

with a feather fan blocking her face. She dances toward a poster of a sexy matador, keeping her back to the audience. When she turns she dazzles with a smile and discards the mantilla. Her hair is elaborately curled; diamonds dangle from her earlobes. She does her signature twirling, leading by turning her head over her shoulder. Eventually she reclines on a chaise down to black lace panties and bra. Shimming to the poster she grabs a cape and twirls it; she is in a flesh-colored G-string and pasties, but modestly keeps her arm covering her breasts. She looks model-thin, fragile even.

EVEN WITH LAS VEGAS GROWING RACIER, LILI'S DATED ACT CONTINued to pack them in. The town had grown steadily. Lili felt the town was losing its western charm. The hotels were trying to outdo themselves in size, amenities, and décor. Everything was to lure folks to drop wads of cash at the gambling tables. Everything was open twenty-four hours—beauty parlors, grocery stores. It was too much. Las Vegas was losing its luster for her. It had always been a transitory place, but now even more so. It was gaining a reputation as a town where bad behavior was tolerated, not quite yet the "What happens in Vegas stays in

Vegas" but barreling toward it. The desert night was brighter, the days louder. A different kind of people were filling the town.

It was as Roosevelt observed: "A strange place and a strange life."[747]

Lili also noticed a change in celebrity. Fans would engage in unbecoming behavior. Rex Bell, former actor and husband to Clara Bow, now lieutenant governor, had people literally running after him.

Lili noted that visitors were either going someplace or coming from somewhere. No one was there to stay. It was easy to have affairs. It felt shallow and unreal with no meaning.

Too many wanted to intrude on Lili; it "exhausted" her.[748] She saw faces she hadn't seen in years and would never see again. Vegas was a melting pot of desperate people acting rashly with nonstop partying. She hid in her bungalow more than ever, sewing her signature label on her scanty panties.

She did make one concession to the changing times and posed topless for a magazine. It wasn't her first time, though she pretended it was. She had posed topless for photographer John Reed when she was just starting out. Still it was a departure for Lili at this point in her career. She was doing everything to hang on to her crown.

AT FORTY LILI LOOKED AS IF SHE HAD AN "INDESTRUCTIBLE BEAUTY." "Time seems to flow around" her as "millions of men" feasted their eyes upon her increasingly popular figure.[749]

The "implication of Lili's name" was cause to "fill rooms every night."[750]

At a dinner party in Las Vegas she found herself seated next to Frederic March. *The Best Years of Our Lives* actor soon had a hand exploring up and down Lili's thigh. She removed it discreetly, so as not to disturb his wife sitting directly across the table. Lili knew of March's reputation and wasn't thrilled. When the hand wandered back, she turned her back on the actor and devoted her attention to the playwright William Saroyan seated on her left.

Lili had a long list of contracts ahead of her: the Black Orchid in Chicago, the Hotsy Totsy in New Orleans, the Sho Bar in New Orleans, Casino Royal in Washington, DC, the Adams in Newark, and the Chi Chi where she performed in a giant champagne glass—an act Tom Douglas had designed for her in Las Vegas.[751]

Sadie had quit probably around 1958. Dardy thought she quit after she was busted in a club, accused of stealing a patron's purse, though Lili bailed her out. In any event, Sadie—like Lili's husbands—had tired of life on the road.

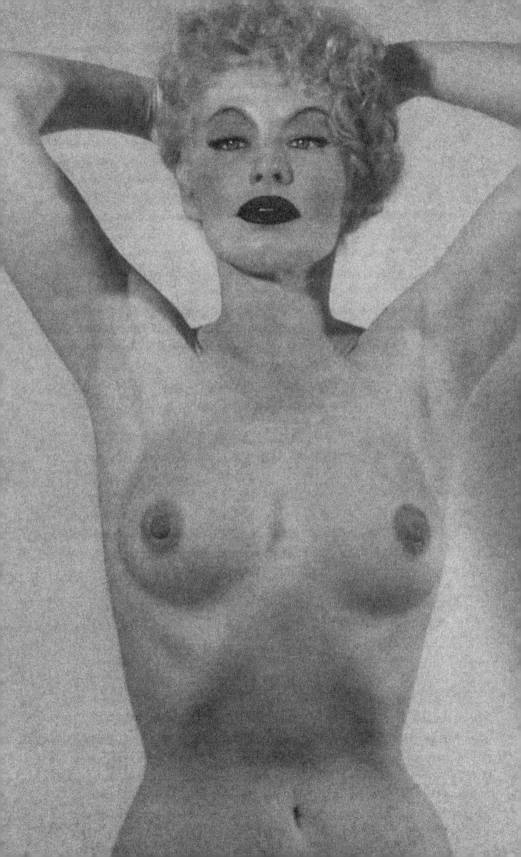

After years together the two presumably never saw each other again. Lili replaced her with another maid, Dell Gordan. [752]

Sleep was more elusive. She was grateful for Dardy's annual Christmas gift of sleeping pills in a cut crystal bowl. More pills to calm her. More pills to wake up. More pills to sleep. Until, accidentally, she took too many. It was one of the rare occasions when it was not a suicide attempt, though it would be reported as one. Ironically, it would be lover and costar Vic Damone who "filled in for her by singing a few extra songs" at the El Rancho to cover for a missing Lili while she recovered.[753]

It was another lurid headline. Why was this beautiful blonde willing to end her life? "She takes a lot of knocks," it was observed. "Under the glitter and glamour . . . is a frustrated and unhappy woman whose life is far more serious than her bumps and grinds would indicate," *Hush-Hush* magazine speculated. They blamed the "green-eyed monster" for why she couldn't stay married.[754] That every husband she had dealt with intense jealousy as Lili peeled for a paying audience.

Or were Lili's overdoses a cry for attention?

"Fake suicides with sleeping pills are an occasional problem here," noted policeman-turned-author Clinton H. Anderson in *Beverly Hills Is My Beat* of the epidemic of attempted suicides among the entertainers in his city at the time. Limelight-seeking folks trying to "get attention . . . or win back the affection of a straying sweetheart." He surmised that after a single trip to the hospital and the stomaching pumping it would end all other attempts. Nothing seemed to deter Lili.

Niece Ava Minsky remembered Lili's suicide attempts happened with "such regularity" that Harold "was always trying to cajole doctors into either giving her medication or extract a promise to not discuss her 'hospitalizations.'" Perhaps there were many more attempts that had been kept out of the paper. There were at least two doctors kept on "speed dial," Ava recalled.[755]

LILI WAS PERFORMING HER "NIGHT IN TANGIERS," ANOTHER EXOTIC number with a different title, but essentially the same act. As she left the stage her costar Vic Damone threw her an "admiring glance."[756]

Brooklyn-born Damone, born Vito Rocco Farinola, was a handsome, smooth-singing crooner. Married though separated from actress Pier Angeli, Damone occasionally shared Lili's billing and bed.

The *Hollywood Reporter* reported the couple, seen often in each other's company, wanted to be left alone.

With Lili's regular contract at the El Rancho (and other places), Dardy, ensconced at the Dunes, begged Lili to save some of her enormous salary.

Lili's lingere catalog

"Even if it's only a hundred a week, Lili," Dardy advised. "It will make me feel so much better. Put *something* in the bank."

Lili didn't seem to understand—or care; the lack of cash kept her working relentlessly across the country.

Billed as the "most expensive staged act," Lili was responsible for paying and getting her props from gig to gig.[757] Any additional income was certainly welcome and necessary.

Her ads were running in papers selling her "Scanty Panties" along with bras and corsets and slippers and other seductive items.

The slim catalogue of her "Intimate Secrets" was a black-and-white, fourteen-page pamphlet advertising a "breath-taking" line of lingerie. With dainty, jeweled panties to make every woman feel "like a princess!"

The catalogue showcased fishnet stockings, nylon mesh hose, patent leather heels in an array of colors including "flamingo red." She sold silver, gold, and pink star-shaped pasties. There were harem pants, skirts, flowing nylon negligees with lace cuffs. There were leotards with cinch belts. And she sold photographs of herself. A ten-by-fourteen went for $2.

With names like "No Mystery," "Coy Miss," and "My Secret," everything was sent in a black gift box resembling a diary with Lili's signature in pink on the cover. There were four-inch Lucite glass mules with marabou fluff. There were panties with rhinestones. The bras were named "Sweater Girl" and "Six-Way Sorcerer." Many were "fully padded wire broadcloth . . . for every occasion." There was a "Top Secret" padded push-up. Everything was fancy and feminine and very Lili.

Capitalizing on her performance in *Sinbad* she sold flat leather "Harem Slippers" bedecked with jewels in red, turquoise, pink, white, or black.

Included in the catalogue was the chance to own *Bath of Salome,* an eight-millimeter film starring Lili, either in black and white for $4 or for $10 in color. A sixteen-millimeter color copy was $30.

She promised to "let me thrill you—as I've thrilled millions!"

Check, cash, or money order was to be sent to a post office box at 806 South Robertson Boulevard in Los Angeles.

It should have been a success but it's no longer possible to determine the amount of her financial achievement with this venture. Most likely it was negligible, certainly not what she made performing.

It was, however, one more distraction from an unsatisfactory husband.

RIGHT: *Lili at home*

CHAPTER NINE

Hollywood and its horny producers kept trying to do something with Lili. In February of 1958 director Raoul Walsh offered her a part in Norman Mailer's *The Naked and the Dead*.

Lili was forty-one and disenchanted when her agent told her the news. Another stripper role. She might have felt inadequate as an actress and disheartened by the roles offered but she wasn't going to turn down the opportunity.

Sipping a beer from a champagne glass at the bar of her home she told a reporter she was dissatisfied with her costume. Playing a stripper, she was to strip down to a "bathing suit"–type garment. Five scenes had been written for her, her dances purloined from her stage acts.[758]

She dreaded filming. For her, acting was "too much mental effort."[759]

Lili found Walsh delightfully eccentric. The director walked around the set in riding pants and boots wearing a monocle. He had perfect gentlemanly manners. On the first day of shooting he knocked on Lili's dressing room and respectfully escorted her to the set as if she were the biggest star in the world, or in his film, even though she wasn't.

The film starred Clift Robertson, Raymond Massey, and L. Q. Jones as the hillbilly whom Lili's character adored.

Barbara Nichols, another stripper, was the female lead. Lili and Barbara were friendly, having played together at various nightclubs, maybe as far back as the Latin Quarter in the 1940s. Often the pair would sit off-camera and gossip. The waiting on set for everyone else to do their jobs was agony for Lili. But she seemed to enjoy the former "Miss Dill Pickle" who was a brassy blonde, gum-chewing Brooklynese babe.[760]

At night Lili returned to the Follies to perform. She knew she was wearing herself down, but it was never a question of stopping. Or even slowing down. Every time she turned around there was someone younger and bigger breasted dancing behind her.

Raoul Walsh later explained in an interview why Lili was cast in the film: "I went to Warner Brothers [*sic*]," Raoul Walsh said. "Jack Warner asked me if we were going to put any 'tits' in the movie. And that's the term he used. Literally. He said, 'Raoul, will you put some tits in it?' And that's what he did. He got Lillie [*sic*] St. Cyr to do a strip tease that had nothing to do with the book. The budget should have been a couple of million, instead of the $900,000 they spent. They cut every corner possible."[761]

It would be Raoul's last picture for Warner Bros.

Though Lili filmed a handful of strip numbers, only one survived the cutting room floor. She has a few lines in a dressing room at the beginning of the movie prior to her strip, but nothing memorable. She admitted enjoying filming her scene in front of actors cast as soldiers because it reminded her of dancing during the war years when soldiers had been grateful and appreciative.

Lili danced and imagined herself back at the Florentine, twenty-three and happy with the world ahead of her.

The film grossed a surprising $11 million. Lili was featured prominently in all the advertising, on posters and billboards, though her role was miniscule. She was touted as being the highest-paid peeler.

Critics were pleased. Lili, who managed to "excel in next to nothing"—a possible double entendre meaning quite literally her next-to-nothing costume—"is a knockout."[762]

Claiming to have gained ten pounds for the role, Lili "engaged a dietician to help her take off the poundage without changing her curves."[763]

Back in Las Vegas, Beldon knocked on her door while she drank a glass of champagne and prepared for her second show of the night.

"Lili," he shouted as he came in, surveying the room loaded with roses. "Lili." He sat on her delicate green chaise. "I'm hearing rumors."

Lili smiled and continued drinking.

"Are you really going out with Vic Damone?" Beldon rubbed a hand across his lined forehead. "Or is it Victor Mature?"

Lili said nothing.

"Come on, Lili, give me a break. Who is it? Is it both?" The owner with the perpetual tan and his hair slicked back hadn't changed in all the years she had known him. He was fascinated by her love life. He would have done anything to sleep with her.

Lili remained silent.

"Listen, I'll give you $5,000 if you leave the shades of your room up when Vic—or Victor—next comes over. Let me watch you, Lili."[764]

Lili was noncommittal, smiling. Of course she would keep her blinds closed. And yes, she was having an affair with both.[765]

"Beldon had a big crush on Lili," Dardy explained. "He offered her a lot of money to go to bed with him. He was twisted. He was married to Millie, and her father was someone big in the garment district or something. She was from New York, smart, attractive. She and Lili became great friends. And Beldon, see, Beldon was 'cock of the walk' in Vegas. There weren't so many casinos back then. Beldon was 'the thing.' Well, Beldon got into a fight with Millie and that led to a divorce. She went to a lawyer and froze his assets. Vegas didn't put money in banks. It was a *cash* business." Dardy nodded for emphasis. "Everyone skimmed off the top back then and had safety deposit boxes. Every hotel had huge ones. Millie tied him up for a settlement; she knew where the cash was and she knew how much of it she wanted. Lili loved that story. She was glad Millie got the best of him. But she did like Beldon. She knew he was a crook. Lili loved men like Beldon. Scoundrels. He was amusing to her. She never slept with him."[766]

The year 1958 saw another film for Lili. Actually, she had agreed the year before to be in the movie, then forgot all about it. She was in New York at the Samoa when the producers reminded her about her one-day commitment. Frantic, she hopped a flight to LA, worked all day, and then caught a red-eye (that day or next) back to New York to finish up at the Samoa.

The film was *I, Mobster*, a crime drama that would become a cult classic in France if not quite that in America. Again she was required only to be Lili St. Cyr—even using her name on the marquee—and re-create her act. She didn't have any lines in the film.

After having been on set since ten in the morning, it was close to midnight before they began to rehearse her scene. She "appeared with well-worn bathrobe over her blue jeans."[767]

Roger Corman, the smiling, wide-faced director—he couldn't have been older than thirty-two—approached her with his hands outstretched.

He wanted her to get rid of the towel in the last shot. *How would that get past the censors?* It wouldn't. But in Europe they weren't so prudish. And there would be a lot of publicity.

It was surprising to Lili—and later to others—that she hadn't protested. She didn't care. She was bored filming. Bored with her dancing. She needed something to shake up her existence. She couldn't shake the feeling that her act—as it was— was becoming irrelevant.

Lili retired to her dressing room while Corman ordered everyone extraneous off the set. She reappeared in a pretty robe this time.

The tub was filled with bubbles. She did what she always did, what she had been doing for years: reclined on the chaise, took off her robe. Her breasts were covered with skin-colored gauze and skin-colored panties and she knew how to maneuver her arms to cover. She climbed in the tub and began to soap herself.

The camera starts with a close-up of her satin-heeled shoe before traveling up to her face. She is wearing an unflattering wig. Still beautiful, she doesn't radiate the fresh, excited, and exciting performer she had once been. Her face is devoid of expression, an unflattering mask, as if to say, *I've done this too many times to get excited.* Not until her final close-up where she drops the towel does her personality and beauty shine through and we are reminded why Lili is a star.

I, Mobster turned out to be "well made and ably acted" in the tradition of *Scarface*, a realistic and sometime brutal formula.

Variety called it a "well-turned-out melodrama."[768]About Lili they said she "goes through her strip bathtub routine with the usual mopey facial expression that is supposed to be super sexy."

Reporter Vernon Scott interviewed Lili at the time. "I've never disrobed entirely before an audience. . . . I don't know what they'll do with the shots except to show them to their friends." Scott noted that the crew had fun with "retake after retake" and "on one occasion the camera accidentally ran out of film." [769]In all there would be three versions shot, with and without nudity.

But the sixties was a time of change in cinema. Films were becoming more graphic in theme, nudity, and violence. European standards were influencing Hollywood, and with "films from France, nudity has become increasingly popular with movie-makers."[770]

Decades later Corman, through his secretary, would dismiss Lili's participation in the film, saying she had worked merely "an hour," contradicting the accounts of reporters who had been on the set for nearly twelve hours.[771]

Hardly credible, as Lili related, "I don't think anybody realizes how long it takes me to get ready . . . my hair-do is a two-hour job."[772]

Though paid $1,000, Lili's contributions to the film were minimized. Perhaps the film had been a disappointment to Corman, who rejected the film itself in his book *How I Made a Hundred Movies in Hollywood and Never Lost a Dime.* He relegates only one paragraph to the production, dismissing it as "conventional."[773]

Lili complained that once she paid for her flights to and from New York, she lost money on the deal.

"Censorship is holding back progress," Lili pouted. "I should get out. All the girls do these days is come on naked." She moaned. "Burlesque is dying." Stripteasing was "washed up," which must have sent her panicking.[774] What would Lili St. Cyr do?

In August a church group objected to her appearance at a club in Bakersfield, California. "No one church has the right to appoint itself as a censor," another church group defended.[775] Lili was allowed to go on. It was a battle Lili was growing tired of, especially as she had a fight of another kind right at home.

More recently Lili had claimed she and Ted had bought a "movieland man-sion."[776] She was once again threatening to quit the striptease circuit and was working at the El Rancho only for her contracted ten weeks out of the year. Both disinformation.

According to Dardy, Lili convinced her to tell Ted she was divorcing him. And though Dardy had to wonder why Lili wasn't mature enough to break the news her-self, she went ahead and did it. "Lili could always get people to do what she wanted."

The tipping point, according to Dardy, had occurred at a dinner party in Lili's garden. The candelabras were lit and Ted took his two big paws and swatted a moth dead as it flitted around the flame. "And that was it for Lili. It was over."

AT THE EL RANCHO SOMETIME AFTER MIDNIGHT ON NOVEMBER 1, actor/stuntman and sometime "boyfriend" Fred Carson arrived after Lili's midnight show for dinner. Carson found Lili on the floor in a pale blue nightgown and pink robe "unconscious." Carson hustled her into a cab and took her to Southern Nevada Memorial hospital, where she was released the next morning. Reporters had a field day, noting, "The dancer is separated from husband Ted Jordan."[777]

Weeks later she asked for a "sealed court order" when filing for a divorce.[778] Her Reno attorney claimed the case could not be heard because Lili "doesn't know the whereabouts of her husband Edgar H. Friedman."[779]

In December Lili's lover Vic Damone and Pier Angeli were making their own headlines from a Santa Monica courtroom, divorcing after four years of marriage.

Reports circulated that Ted was dating Baroness Mildred de Palambara. However, by the end of the year he reported that he "will wed singer Marianna La Faugh" as soon as Lili shed him.[780] Walter Winchell reported Lili and Ted were "experimenting" and possibly would remain together. Reporters soon were spread-ing rumors that Lili had a new man and he would become husband number six.

Offstage Lili was leading a quieter life. While her social life calmed down—by choice—she wasn't hiding from the world. She had her beloved dinner parties with Clifton Webb, Joel Grey, and Tom—dear Tom, her beloved friend—and occasion-ally Virginia.

LILI POSED AT HER HOME FOR A SERIES OF ELEGANT PHOTOS THAT SHE claimed was shot by Russ Meyers, sexploitation producer/director of *Faster Pussycat! Kill! Kill!* (1965) fame. Lili is elegant and very much clothed.

RIGHT: *Lili was proud of her elegant home*

Even though she was forty-two, she was still very much in demand. Where her contemporaries were retiring or winding down, content with babies and husbands, Lili remained on the road still able to "hold an audience spell-bound with scant material."[781] Her body was still magnificent despite growing aches and pains.

The playing field was changing for Lili. Ciro's went bankrupt in 1958. "They should have made me a permanent fixture," she joked. Many of her favorite haunts were gone. Her beloved Gayety had closed in 1953. She bemoaned the fact audiences didn't dress as nicely as they once had.

Hush-Hush printed her photo with the headline "What Drove Lili St. Cyr to Attempt Suicide?" They detailed several overdoses from the insecure and unhappy stripper, dredging up one that involved Paul back in 1949, as told by an "insider." Obviously, Paul. She "managed to retain her reputation—but only at considerable cost to her self-respect."

"She has talent, money, millions of admirers, and her cheesecake pictures sell like hot cakes. She even has brains and a high I.Q. under that coiffure blonde hair."[782] But she also had a "desperate despondency" that wouldn't stay hidden.[783]

The tabloids could be vicious and were becoming bolder. *Confidential* got ahold of her mug shot from her 1947 arrest and splashed in across their pages.

Reviews remained positive but there was too much dwelling on suicide attempts, on too many husbands. *Hush-Hush* alleged that she was under the care of a psychiatrist, an idea Dardy pooh-poohed. "Lili didn't *talk* about her feelings." None of the sisters did.

The tabloid asserted that she was tormented by the breakup of all her marriages. *Too many husbands . . .*

And she was about to take another. Her last.

BY THE TIME THE MUSICAL *GYPSY* OPENED ON BROADWAY IN 1959, thrusting G-strings and gimmicks back into the limelight, Lili was seeing Joe Zomar exclusively. They had met at a bar in Hollywood. Joe Zomar, who would be misnamed as Zomar, Zoomar, Zonar, and Gomar, was tall, not necessarily handsome, but rugged. He caught her eye. Joe was thirty-nine; she was forty-two (though she told reporters she was thirty-seven).[784] He was neither sophisticated nor elegant. He was working-class and manly, a nice change after the fussy high-maintenance Jordan. And he had a job.

Joe came from a family of special effects masters; both his father and brother worked on movies. Joe was a special effects engineer in such films as Annette Funicello's *Beach Bikini* in 1964 (credited as Joe Zonar.) His last films would be director Robert Zemeckis's *Used Cars* and Steven Spielberg's *1941*.

Dardy called him "unpolished." Neither refined like Armando, who made "best dressed" lists, nor lithe-bodied like Paul. Zomar would never hold her heart like Jimmy Orlando, nor offer her a chance of escape like Cordy.[785] Still he had his charm and Lili liked to have a masculine man about.

He was about to start work on *Have Gun Will Travel* for MGM, shooting in Sun Valley. At his invitation Lili followed him to the location. By the time they returned to Los Angeles they were a couple.

Lili gave a disingenuous interview declaring that she was definitely planning on marrying Zomar as soon as her divorce from Jordan was final, which was going much too slow for her. It was deceptive in the fact that she wasn't sure she wanted another marriage and she refused to settle in Reno for the required six-week divorce, which she easily could have done

Twice divorced, Joe was insisting on marriage. She fixated on the fact that he had a job and wouldn't rely on her income. She told a reporter she was going to "learn how to cook," even though she already was quite skilled in the kitchen.

By July the papers noticed Ted—who would waltz in and out of her act for at least the next year—sniffing around trying to get Lili back; more likely he was trying to keep himself employed.

By the eighteeth of July, Marie Van Schaack Friedman was in Reno to start divorce proceedings against Edgar H. Friedman (sometimes alternatively spelled Freidman).

On July 22, 1959, Lili waltzed into court and obtained her freedom. By the end of the month Ted would be dating future *Gilligan's Island* star Tina Louise.

After a four-week August engagement at Mapes in Reno, Lili and Joe were married on September 21, 1959, in Tijuana.[786]

IN OCTOBER LILI WAS PERFORMING AT THE 365 CLUB IN SAN FRANCISCO and applied for a marriage license. Wanting to make sure it was legal she and Joe Zomar were married once again—for safety—on October 30.

For one of the ceremonies Lili wore a beautiful white bride's gown and she looks lovely if not absolutely overdressed, be it a Tijuana courtroom or a San Francisco one.

She presented Joe with a gold watch and promised him a car.

In the beginning Lili clung to Joe, doting on him and her new role as Mrs. Joe Zomar.

Joe was eager to introduce Lili to his young kids, Joe Jr. and Gail, his from two prior marriages. Lili, never comfortable or interested in children, resourcefully explained she didn't want to meet them, as it would remind her he'd slept with other

The second time Lili dressed as a traditional bride for her last – and sixth – marriage.

women. It temporarily appeased him. Instead he would bring his son over to Lili's house—now theirs—when she was out of town.

Like most of her marriages the two hadn't known each other long enough to really understand whom the other was.

Joe would later brag that she had made a pass at him. Lili the famous stripper had wanted to get married. He didn't know much about her past or her family. He didn't ask. He was willing to share her home with her many feline companions.

For several years Lili had been collecting stray cats. Living at the end of a street that petered out before it became rural, it was perfectly situated for people to drive up and dump strays, which Lili would take in and feed. At one time she had a dozen cats. The empty lot she owned on the corner had only a big oak tree, a short fence, and not much else. Lili built a little structure for the cats, all of them except her beloved Teeny (or Tiny), who lived in her house and whom she doted on like a baby, fixing up a bassinet with Pratesi linens and feeding the cat off fine china.

Lili went through a terrible spell when the cats caught some terminal disease. Their massive demise sent Lili into bed despondent for weeks, grateful her beloved Teeny had been spared.

IN THE BEGINNING JOE TOOK A LEAVE FROM WORK AND JOINED LILI ON the road to Reno, Chicago, San Francisco, Hollywood. Now that stagehands rarely did much for her, it was Joe's job to help maneuver the massive tubs and props. He even set the stage. Lili hired his sister Helen who was a seamstress to tend to her wardrobe, but the clubs "didn't want him around" backstage.[787]

Lili finished out the year with an engagement in Denver, three times a night in and out of the tub. She caught a cold and returned to Hollywood to recoup.[788]

Joe quickly tired "of that life" and returned to the studios.[789]

While Joe tinkered in the garage Lili cooked and fussed around the house. She loved nothing more than carrying trays of food and drinks out to him. She rose early and made chicken-salad sandwiches, carefully cutting the crusts off the bread for his lunch to take to the studio. She whipped up delicate pastries, including cream puffs.

Joe hadn't asked Lili to stop stripping, but she decided she wanted a break. She told the papers she wanted to develop her domestic skills. She bragged about staying at home taking care of Joe when he got home late from the studio.

Lili still kept a chauffeured limousine on twenty-four-hour call, something Joe hated. It idled at the curb, mostly unused. A waste of money. Joe was astounded to discover Lili didn't care about money, spending or saving it. She was used to her extravagant lifestyle but she was also in considerable debt.

In 1960 Lili St. Cyr was forty-three, by no means old. But her world was changing. The El Rancho had burned to the ground. One rumor circulated that Beldon had started it. When the fire department called, Beldon was said to have replied "but that was supposed to happen Friday."[790]

"You know," Dardy said, "there was a gas station next to the El Rancho. After the fire everyone was saying, 'There's Beldon pouring gas on the El Rancho.' He had insurance that paid him for the loss of the business. He didn't rebuild anything. They had to pay him every year."[791] Dardy relished the gossip. "And you know Beldon had a thing for twelve-, fourteen-year-old girls. Nearly went to jail. One mother—he had to pay her off."

Dardy clarified that Beldon was no better and no worse than any of the others. "Doc Bailey owned the Frontier," she said, "he was a cowboy, but he had a penchant for young girls too. He died in bed with one. The big joke everyone was repeating, 'He was coming as he went.'"[792]

CHAPTER TEN

Domestic bliss was fleeting at 2639 Canyon Drive. Joe turned out to be jealous and what Lili had thought was a hobby turned out to be a serious gambling problem. He bet on the horses and blew through his money. The relationship soured though they would remain married if not necessarily together for the next five years.

Zomar's young son, Joe Jr., about nine at the time, would recall meeting Lili only once during those five years. He said Lili hid upstairs when the kids were over. For meals their father would drive down to Sunset Boulevard and sit with them at the counter at Schwab's ordering burgers and shakes while Lili stayed in her tub reading Proust.

Joe Jr. would sleep with his dad in Lili's "giant bed" when she was on the road.

Joe Jr. liked exploring Lili's "secret" room while she was out of the house. "You could get in through the master bedroom closet. There was a door that looked like the wall of the closet and it led to a small room with a window that looked outside. I never really knew what it was for but now I assume maybe it was a 'safe room.'" Most likely it was Lili's "cold storage fur closet," explained her second cousin Kris Plasch, who recalled trying on Lili's furs when she stayed at Lili's house with her great grandmother Alice, who was watching the house while Lili was on the road.[793]

Lili had redecorated and the walls were red and black. There were white carpets throughout. She had up-to-date appliances in the kitchen. A television hung over the bar, so she could watch the popular *Flintstones* show, which had premiered in September. Lili thought it was amusing and the cavewomen glamorous. Her favorite films—who knows when she had a chance to see them—were the Miss Marple series of films starring Margaret Rutherford.[794]

The courtyard had "uncomfortable wrought iron furniture" that was not child friendly. Joe Jr. remembers seeing her at his grandfather's funeral, but Lili didn't speak to him. "She was always gone."[795]

Lili was still keeping engagements at the Moulin Rouge, (where she was called "lynx-like," doing her act in front of a faux fireplace[796]), Mapes, the Dune, and other familiar haunts that kept her out of the house as much as possible.

Though she couldn't be bothered entertaining children she wasn't unfriendly and she did make sure a box of Marx Toys was given to Joe Jr.[797] Maybe Barbara and Lili spoke and Barbara sent the gift.

Lili became stifled by Joe, who was "possessive and dominant."[798] He was drinking a lot, perhaps he always had; it would be an issue in his next marriage too. Joe was belligerent and reprimanded her when he got home. He hated finding her in bed, as she often was when she wasn't working, her head buried in a book. He had no idea of the miles she had logged. She deserved to rest.

He was soon working less and it fell once again to Lili to be the breadwinner. To keep the peace she lavished him with expensive gifts.

On weekends he wanted to go to parties. She preferred to stay in. When she had guests over he would start a fight and storm out of the house.

The unhappily married couple fell into a pattern. They would argue. He left. She left. The arguments would grow ugly. He pushed her hard against a heavy table. She screamed and called for an ambulance and was out of work because of an injured back.

The papers had a field day spotting Lili, Joe, and Ted Jordan in Las Vegas ushering out the decade around Christmastime.

The violence grew and Lili obtained a restraining order against her husband. In August of 1961 they split. A sad Zomar was found sitting alone at the Bantam Cock's bar in Los Angeles. Across the bar sat Ted Jordan.[799]

The separation didn't last. Lili and Joe got back together again.

The Intimate World of Lili St. Cyr opened at 8104 Santa Monica Boulevard. The tiny store sold Lili's lingerie creations from her catalogue. Everything was labeled with Lili's signature in thread.

A SAD FIRST FOR LILI—AFTER YEARS OF AVOIDING IT—WAS PERFORMING as a talking woman for comedian Ken Murray, a vaudevillian ham she was costarring with. As burlesque was dying, it became up to whoever was left (mostly the strippers) to act in skits with the comedians. Historically it wasn't something headliners did, or wanted to do. But with the chorus girls gone, Lili had to shoulder more of the burden onstage.

Lili and Murray performed a "blackout" skit that Murray had been recycling for the past twenty years. They performed at eight thirty, eleven thirty, and one thirty at the Sky Room at the Mapes Hotel in Reno.[800]

There were too many changes for Lili in both her personal and professional life. She was fighting to remain relevant as the whole business was falling apart.

She continued to inspire other artists. Seeing her act performed in a giant champagne glass, sculptor Tony Berlant would create a giant sculpture entitled *Lily After Dark* in 1990.

LIKE MOST OF THE WORLD LILI PROBABLY HEARD ABOUT MARILYN Monroe's death on the radio. She was in her house on Canyon Drive. The announcement caught the world off guard. Lili remembered when the timid and nonfamous young starlet with the round, rather fat bottom had sat at the various theatres and clubs catching her act. Marilyn had made columnist Walter Winchell take her to see Lili perform. According to Ted Jordan he escorted Marilyn to Lili's shows prior to their marriage. Many remarked Marilyn's voice changed, growing softer and whispery like Lili's.

Ted claimed to have talked to Marilyn on her last night on earth. Lili knew better. *He'll probably say the same thing when I die.* She would have been amused to know he did.[801]

In 1989 Ted would write a highly imaginative biography entitled *Norma Jean: My Secret Life with Marilyn Monroe.* He claims in his book Lili mentored Marilyn. At a Ciro's show Lili supposedly drew on a napkin how she should do her brows. Of course Jordan reported this was in 1949, though Lili wouldn't appear at Ciro's until 1951. He would throw his own uncle under the rug, claiming Uncle Ted Lewis was Marilyn's "supply" to drugs.[802] He claimed her pill taking bothered him and he constantly warned her against it, yet he never mentions Lili's own addiction to pills. The fame-seeking Ted portrayed Marilyn as a crude-mouthed nymphomaniac and had them carrying on a ménage à trois when Marilyn and Lili weren't conducting their own torrid affair.

FORMER BURLESQUE QUEEN ANN CORIO HAD BEEN A STAR STRIPPER and rival to Gypsy Rose Lee throughout the thirties and forties. Corio was such a popular headliner at Boston's Old Howard theatre that it was said "you couldn't graduate from Harvard until you've seen Ann Corio."[803] In the 1960s Corio, with her decades-younger husband Mike Iannucci, conceived of *This Was Burlesque,* a show honoring the glory days of burlesque. Corio brought the show to Broadway and toured with it for nearly thirty years, stripping well into her eighties. Former

RIGHT: *Lili posing for an artist in New York*

stars of burlesque such as Sally Rand and comedians like Dexter Maitland guest starred for short runs. Ann asked Lili to be one of the star strippers but Lili declined. She wasn't interested in a nostalgia show when she was still performing in what real burlesque remained.

Lili missed the old clubs and theatres. She appeared regularly in Vegas at the Silver Slipper, for Harold. But Las Vegas was different. Burlesque was all but dead, pushed out by pornography and risqué films. Lili began performing at county fairs, but for the first time in years—decades—she went weeks without work.

In June and July of 1963 a committee was formed to investigate how to protect postal patrons from obscene mail and communist propaganda. Lili's name was thrown into the mix.

The committee had decided to investigate certain magazines for "not only what they were offering, but where the offers were coming from." Looking at the ads "at random" they decided to investigate an address at 5880 Hollywood Boulevard that several mail-order companies used. Lili's "Intimate Lingerie" was one of them, and though she had nothing to do with other businesses deemed questionable by the committee such as "Vibra Finger" and "Men Only!" the committee lumped them all together as porno and set out to keep it from coming into households.

It was one man's "contention that if one ordered acne cream . . . one would be solicited for other degenerative things which will gradually lead you into the degeneration that they are selling."[804]

The hearings held before Congress came to naught. Perhaps Lili didn't even know about the investigation. She had plenty to occupy herself. Her home life was anything but tranquil.

Joe's drinking grew even heavier. He "became abusive and would cause unnecessary arguments and accuse me of things that weren't true."[805]

One night in August Lili and Joe returned after working a club to find her house had once again been vandalized. Her bedroom was ransacked. Gone was a fur coat, jacket, two stoles, two custom-made wigs, one blonde and one brunette, twelve pieces of jewelry, and an antique solid-gold dressing table set, with brush, mirror, and comb, all to the tune of approximately $10,000.

"I don't understand how they got it," she cried in alarm to the detectives standing among the mess of her things in her ornately wallpapered room with the mirrored closet doors.

The detectives surmised that the thieves had dislodged a glass louver from the window in the kitchen, at the breakfast nook window. She told reporters the robbery wouldn't stop her opening in Las Vegas at the Silver Slipper where she was engaged for a ten-week run in a few day's time. "At least the burglars didn't get my bathtub," she joked.

Lili divorcing for the last time

"SHE LOVED THE HEADLINES," DARDY CLAIMED ABOUT LILI'S splashed-about love life. "It didn't matter what it was. She was happy with people fussing over her."

One improbable headline had Lili retired and working in her lingerie store when a "rich Texan" bought up her stock of bras ($10,000) to get her back to work. It was a creative way to announce her return to the Silver Slipper and Latin Quarter.[806]

Fed up, she paid for a gorgeous apartment on the corner of Crescent Heights and Fountain in West Hollywood and Joe was out of her life. He moved in with a friend and she brought over furniture from her house for him. She vowed this was her last husband. Six was more than any woman should be burdened with. She would never again wed.

IN JULY OF 1964 LILI WAS OFFICIALLY DIVORCED FROM ZOMAR.

At the proceedings Lili looked chic, even modern in a half-capped sleeve-sheathed dress. She told Judge Martin Katz that Zomar "drank to excess . . . every evening before dinner and 'by 8 or 9 p.m. he would pass out on the sofa.'"[807] "He'd

Lili and Joe in happier times

call me nasty names and accuse me of things that weren't true."[808] She admitted to being in the hospital after one particularly rough argument.

One reporter asked, "I suppose you'll say you're through with marriage?"

"Yes."

"But you don't really mean it?"

"No . . . I hope not."[809] And after some reflection. "But I would have to be sure of the man."[810]

At forty-six she might be disenchanted with marriage but not with romance.

Lili once again waived alimony. Once again she would remain friendly with an ex.

LILI WAS STILL LIVING BEYOND HER MEANS. SHE TOOK OUT A $10,000 loan against her house in 1963. (She would repay it in 1972.) Joe helped by "cashing in his Motion Picture Fund to pay her debts off. It was a large amount of money." But still "he would do anything for her."[811]

Lili was spotted out with Ted Jordan, causing rumors of reconciliation, which were completely unfounded. In August Jordan, was in Vegas billing himself as "Ted Lewis, Jr." much to the "annoyance" of his uncle who was working down the strip. Jordan was sharing billing with comedian Hank Henry and Lili at the Castaways Hotel.[812]

Lili struggled to her feet after her divorce. She complained she had wasted five years of her life. Her business had changed entirely. She couldn't stand the current "whatever" attitude.

There was no help from the stagehands or managers. She found she had to do everything. The shows, always stressful, were even more so as she worried whether her props would make it onstage. Her ulcers flared up. Other strippers were decades younger. Lili held her head high but had to feel ancient in comparison.

Most clubs by the sixties had cut back on live musicians to save money, preferring taped music. It sickened Lili, who was used to dancing to an orchestra. At most there might be a couple of musicians. The Follies had closed; Lillian Hunt, dead from breast cancer.

It was difficult to transport a bathtub around. She began to pare down her act. She could always bring "Salome" out. Packing seven veils was easy.

Lili trudged forward.

CHAPTER ELEVEN

That same year, 1963, Dardy divorced Harold Minsky after thirteen years (other papers would claim they were married for sixteen years).[813] Like Zomar, Harold's drinking had become impossible. "I never saw him without a glass of scotch," complained Dardy. "He carried a briefcase full" of miniature bottles of booze.[814]

Harold wasn't functioning well, according to Dardy, who managed more of the operation of the shows. Many, though, would remember how involved he remained, even financing some of the strippers' education if they wanted it. Dardy tried talking to him about his drinking. She had the family doctor talk to him. Desperate, she had someone from Alcoholics Anonymous talk to him. Finally, she threatened to leave him. He quit for a year.

At sixteen, son Danny was working at the Frontier as a busboy.

Dardy, "thinking about divorcing" Harold and visiting Danny, noticed an empty store inside the Frontier. She opened a fur shop and it did surprisingly well.

When she and Harold divorced, Dardy ended up with custody of the children, alimony, and half the house, not knowing there were "over $300,000 in back tax liens against the property."[815]

Coming out of court Dardy declared, "Thank God, thank Judge Zenoff, and thank my lawyer."[816]

Harold would find himself back in court for not paying support after Dardy was "forced to sell household items to support the family." Harold claimed he was not only "unemployed" but also "living on money borrowed from friends and owed the government $100,000 in back taxes."[817]

It was a stressful time for Dardy. Her children were arguing, and since she was mostly at the fur store she was unable to "referee." And on top of that, "Harold kept calling and threatened suicide." Ava was at an especially rebellious age. "Every time I would ask her to do something she would call Harold and he would come and pick her up."

Lili in front of her house, changing with the times

She sent Ava to stay with her father, believing that if Ava was with Harold he wouldn't "dare attempt suicide." Days later Ava still wasn't speaking with her mother. "To this day I do not know if I made a mistake." Her relationship with Ava "has never been good since."[818]

Dardy would have strained relationships with both her children, echoes of Idella's legacy with her progeny.

Dardy moved to Los Angeles and got an apartment. She needed money and got a job working for the Automobile Club. It was a tough adjustment for the former Mrs. Minsky, but always pragmatic, she made it work.

Lili too changed as best she could with the times. Her makeup and dress reflected the sixties. She stripped from miniskirts and piled false hairpieces atop her head, lining her eyes with thick black liner.

LILI HERSELF HAD CHANGED. THOUGH STILL A STRIKING WOMAN, HER radiant youth was gone and with it any sense of security. Her jawline wasn't as tight. The erosion of her beauty left her bereft. *What was she going to do?*

Surely one of the last times Lili was professionally photographed

Lili was grateful for any work. She had bills and more tax mess. She *had* to work. She tried holding on to it as long as she could, but she knew the curtain would soon fall on that part of her life, the only part that had ever had meaning.

In the mid sixties Lili shot two shorts for director Robert Altman. The Scopitone was a coin-operated jukebox-type machine that played sixteen-millimeter films to songs, a precursor to MTV's music videos.

Altman, not yet the successful director he would become with *Mash, Nashville,* and *The Long Goodbye,* worked mostly in television and was "struggling."[819]

Lili met with the young director in his Westwood office. Altman had been married to a former Earl Carroll showgirl, who had been working at the time Lili was at the Florentine. That put Lili at ease. Altman outlined what he envisioned. Shooting would involve a gazebo that he had brought from Europe. She thought he must be romantic.

With a modest budget of $3,300 apiece, the first Scopitone was shot in the garden of William Goetz, Louis B. Mayer's son-in-law, at his mansion in Bel Air. The lush setting included a fancy chaise, a jewelry box overflowing with pearls, and a dressing screen.

The short had neither dialogue nor script. The music, "Speak Low" by a British band, would be added later. Altman talked Lili through the scenario, letting her improvise her dance. She said she felt "as if I was running and walking through a dream."[820]

On camera Lili arrived via Rolls-Royce wearing a cape before disrobing and frolicking in her boudoir in the garden. Closer to fifty than forty, Lili still had the firm body of a dancer, though her movements are stiffer. Lili's favorite novel was *Chéri* by Colette and later she said this was her little tribute to it.[821] *Chéri* is about Lea, an aging "richly kept courtesan." Lea has a magnificent "massive and indestructible" bed.[822]

IN THE SECOND SCOPITONE TITLED *EBB TIDE*, LILI LOOKS—THOUGH beautiful—like a different person in wig and bangs. It starts with the Malibu waves lapping toward the camera, as an Arabian knight is seen galloping on horseback across the sand while Lili voraciously eats grapes, resplendent in harem silks under a canopied tent.

The films would be neither high points nor low points in her career. They were simply more work.

CHAPTER TWELVE

Lili had had a falling-out with her beloved friend Tom Douglas. He was working at the Fiesta at the Tropicana in 1970. When he left Las Vegas for good he would claim Beldon still owed him money. Douglas moved to Mexico around 1973 or '74 and Lili lost touch. Tom would eventually die at age eighty-one in Cuernavaca.

Loss seemed to swirl around Lili. Virginia had died years before. Lili's small circle of friends was shrinking. Vegas became merely an obligation for her; the city had lost its charm. The small buildings were replaced by tall cement and glass buildings. The clientele was cheap. She called Vegas "the circus" and hid in her dressing room. For Lili there was too much partying and "sleeping around."[823]

Las Vegas was in the midst of a "hyperactive growth that would continue until today."[824] Lili no longer liked it there; it had lost its "fascination."[825]

On the road Lili stuck to her old routines like "Cinderella," "Carmen," and her bathtub scenarios. She would give her audience fantasy and escape. It was all she knew.

There were only twelve burlesque theatres left. She was running out of places to work.

Most of the old comedians had died off. Burlesque had become essentially a strip show. Some places showed hard-core porn behind the strippers as they danced to go-go music. It was not the world Lili knew.

SHE PLUGGED AWAY, WORKING TWO WEEKS AT THE MOULIN ROUGE IN Hollywood. The show "Naughty-Naughty" was sold out thanks to loyal fans. Lili didn't know how unusual it was to continue to sell out an act she'd been doing for fifteen years. The one-thousand-seat supper theatre was just down the street from her house, off Vine in the heart of Hollywood where she had played since she had begun stripping. The theatre was worn down. It had been at its height in the thirties when Earl Carroll had run it. Evidence of a different world than what she was dancing in.

Lili had a three-year contract at the Silver Slipper and another at the Latin Quarter in New York and at Bimbo's in San Francisco. For those she still managed to drag her tub, set up the stage boudoir, and use subtle lighting to hide her age. Some complained the light was too dim. Her body was still solid, but thicker.

In 1964 Lili appeared at city hall in Los Angeles. She and her neighbors had signed a petition to have the city put in sidewalks across the street from their houses. Lili complained she was receiving too much foot traffic in front of her home.

In 1965 Lili filmed *Runaway Girl*, her last movie role. In *Runaway Girl* Lili appears as a stripper who runs away from her life on the stage to pick grapes at a vineyard. An implausible story. There were no major stars. The film was directed and produced by Hamil Petroff, a sometime actor of little note. Grosses were a "sad $800 on opening," *Variety* reported.[826]

OLD FLAME JIMMY ORLANDO SHOT BACK INTO LILI'S LIFE, OFFERING her work at his club Champs Show Bar (sometimes Sho Bar). In 1965 "La Belle Lili" returned to her magnificent Montreal. It had been almost fifteen years since she had shimmied and shook in the city she so loved. Her fans welcomed her enthusiastically.

"She had them lined up. It was unbelievable. She was a legend . . . still beautiful woman though she was nearly fifty! And they couldn't get enough of her."[827]

Variety noted that "La Belle Lilli" worked "as close to the rules as possible" adding "an impish humor that gives the whole atmosphere a party touch."[828]

Montreal was furiously preparing for the 1967 Exposition. It would be considered the most successful world's fair of the twentieth century. There was a concerted effort to "clean up" the image of the city before millions of eyes were turned on Montreal.

Briefly Ted Jordan dragged along with his ex, still singing as Ted Lewis Jr. *Variety* deemed him "okay" but was working "behind another shadow," that of his ex-wife.[829]

Jimmy gave his former love a three-year contract. Where others were forced to hang up their G-strings, Lili was still signing multiyear contracts. There was one person not so thrilled by the return of Montreal's Sweetheart—Jimmy's wife "Bunny," whom he had married back in the fifties.

And though she would deny in her autobiography the two resumed their affair, there was nothing stopping Lili, who would always hold a torch for Jimmy.[830] And Jimmy was never one to be faithful.

Champ's on Crescent Street was a burlesque joint known for the "quality of the entertainers."[831] There was a big room that seated 250 with a long, mirror-backed bar. Rumors abounded that the pretty waitresses and strippers were hookers and could be put on one's tab along with a meal or a drink. Jimmy had been booking strip acts including Wanda, Irma the Body, and Blaze Starr.

According to her book, *The Weasel*, author Adriana Humphrey claimed Vic Cotroni (brother-in-law to Lili's old beau, Maurice) had an office upstairs and owned the club.

Jimmy jammed the place with tables as close together so as many eyes as possible could feast upon his glorious Lili St. Cyr.

Those lucky enough to have seen her back in the day were showing up with new admirers who wanted to see what all the fuss was about. Once again Lili shattered records. Young and old crowded in to see her. Her reviews were her best in years.

It was good to be back. Lili sat in Café Martin and had drinks and sandwiches with old friends. Al Palmer was somber; his only child, a daughter, had died of leukemia. She could see the pain in his face. Years of living lined his forehead. Nevertheless he gave Lili ink in his column "Uptown" for *the Montreal Gazette*.[832]

Lili adored her French city. And it loved her again. It was good to be back in Jimmy's arms.

She would never stop loving the former jock, still impeccably dressed, still a gentleman. His hair was threaded with gray; he gnawed on a diamond-studded toothpick. And though their past romance had been torrid they settled into a more even-keeled relationship. She no longer sent him extravagant gifts. Neither had ever been faithful to the other. And though there had been jealous fights and more passionate making up in the past, they were older, not necessarily wiser, but their passions didn't get out of hand so easily. So many lovers had passed between them. Jimmy was on a different marriage. She had gone through six. It no longer pained her that Jimmy hadn't made her his wife.

Lili was busy with the show and going out with friends afterward, exploring what familiar places remained. Much had changed. Familiar buildings had been demolished, including Frankie Orlando's favorite, the Samovar, now an empty lot.

Montreal was nearly a stranger to Lili. It had experienced a building boom. "I hardly recognize the old haunts."[833]

She felt nostalgic. How many more years could she pull off a big salary and a handsome man on her arm?

She hung out with Eddie Quinn and Al Palmer and they reminisced. They

RIGHT: *Lili "supposedly" living alone*

would go to Frankie Orlando's club after her show and talk. She felt as if her career was coming to an end. She tried to squeeze as much pleasure out of Montreal as time allowed. But everything had changed. She felt desperate to hold on to the life she knew.

BACK IN LOS ANGELES THE *HERALD EXAMINER*'S BILL KENNEDY DEVOTED his entire "Mr. L.A." column to a visit with legendary Lili. She had invited the reporter over for an informal dinner and chat.

In full domestic mode she prepared Kennedy a dinner of baked ham, wearing a lovely Givenchy dress. Kennedy was tickled that she had a rickshaw, a prop from one of her numbers, in her "enclosed patio."

She was living "alone" at the time, except for ten cats. She was back at the Follies doing her perennial bathtub routine using a tub made of wood with marble paper around the sides. She could only "bathe" for three minutes, as the water had to be drained before it seeped onto the stage.

She expertly mixed Kennedy a cocktail. She let him know how much care and expense went into her show. She wore $5,000 worth of jewelry, over $2,000 was invested in props, her designer gowns cost upwards of $1,000 each, and negligees were $300 apiece. Her bath towels were $35 apiece, "and I wear out $50 worth of hosiery and brassieres and garter belts every week."[834] But one thing hadn't changed: It was expensive being Lili.

CHAPTER THIRTEEN

Lili needed money. It always came to that. Decades of hard work to support her extravagant lifestyle, the ability to lavish cars and watches on men, presents to her family, plus the crystals and antiques she collected, the expense of hauling her furniture and props and paying for musicians; then there were her clothes and jewels. Lili always needed money. And Lili could feel her "career coming to end."[835]

As far back as 1957 she was claiming a desire to write her autobiography, but she had neither the time nor the discipline to sit down and do it. Leo Guild was, arguably, an author, a former Hollywood publicist turned ghostwriter in the mass-market paperback field. He wrote numerous "fairy tales" including biographies such as *The Loves of Liberace* and one about Fatty Arbuckle. Both books were fast-paced and obsessed with sex. He would ghostwrite Lili's autobiography, embarrassingly titled *And Men My Fuel*.

Guild was obsessed with the sex lives of the famous. In 1967 he would write the Hedy Lamarr biography *Ecstasy and Me*, whose opening lines pronounced, "I am a woman, above everything, let me start by saying that in my life, as in the lives of most women, sex has been an important factor."[836] The book, like most he put his name to, was rife with inaccuracies, fiction passing as fact, and outright lies.

Described as "the greatest hack ever"[837] Guild saw women as predatory and portrayed them as mercenary. From Lamarr's bio: "Every girl would like to marry a rich husband. I did twice. But what divides girls into two groups is this question— do you first think of money and then love, or vice versa?"[838]

Guild's promise to the stars was simple: "Fill fifty one-hour audio tapes talking with me, and I'll write your memoir." When he wrote actress Jayne Mansfield's bio he was seen trailing after her as she ran errands.[839]

Guild met with Lili for a series of sessions where she talked and he wrote and fabricated and expanded on her tales (which already often skirted around and over the truth), turning her life into a sensationalized serial. It would be a thin book, short on details, long on lurid claims.

He believed the public wanted sensationalism. And Lili possibly still wanted to hang on to her "bad girl" heartbreaker image.

Hedy Lamarr would sue Guild, claiming many scenes were salacious and pure invention. Like Lili, Lamarr was beautiful, ahead of her time in her views on marriage and men. She too had six husbands. Guild obsessed on both women's prolific sex lives and their seemingly cavalier treatment of men. He portrayed them as vulgar, hard, and slutty. Clearly neither book was written in either woman's voice. Guild was a hack looking for an easy paycheck.

Leo wasn't interested in writing about Lili's career, dismissing it over and over again with such banalities as "I pride myself about doing an imaginative strip tease." He wanted to write about men and sex, not "artistry."

The extent of his in-depth observation (as Lili) was, "When I want a man I get him!" And, "I look back on my life and think it was wasted."[840] It was a repeat of her Wallace interview, almost ten years later. She would tell anyone, no, she didn't like herself very much. No, she wasn't an artist.

And Men My Fuel, like her later French Canadian biography, *Ma Vie Stripteaseuse,* would be lacking specifics, such as dates and ages. Numerous names were changed. She (or Guild) disguised Walter Kane as "Joseph." Some family, friends, and lovers were omitted altogether.

The book also dramatized her many suicide attempts and supposed abortions. Guild writes that she had eleven abortions, then contradicts himself and writes seven.[841] Lili was portrayed as a love-hungry nymphomaniac who lived for adventures in her boudoir. Lili did live for adventure, and for love, but she or Leo marginalized how important her work was, the glory she felt, the reward, how it sustained her, how she spent hours—not lying around her bedroom, as implied—but working on her act.

In the book Idella had three girls and a boy. Either Leo didn't listen or didn't care, and one sister was erased.

It was a hastily published book. It was written to titillate. It exploited and expanded on her many headlines in the tabloids. Half-truths. Out-and-out lies.

Guild later added a chapter claiming it had been "too strong" for the original printing. In it he claims Lili bragged about having seven abortions, forgetting he had originally written she had eleven. He observed Lili was "still searching hungrily for love." Never mind that at the time she was still married to Zomar. Guild wrote Lili admitted to him that "there was a long period when one man wasn't enough for her,"[842] and after Lili has had a few drinks, "There's no telling what might happen." Of course Lili never confided in anyone, certainly not a stranger, her sexual feelings and desires.

Guild insinuates Lili told him things when she wasn't sober. And perhaps he plied her with drinks and then twisted her stories. But Lili was never a drunk. She would enjoy champagne and gin and vodka, but she was too disciplined to be a lush.

The final chapter revealing his opinion on Lili is nauseating and leads one to discount much of what comes before. The one true moment that was pure Lili came when she asked Guild to switch from black to brown shoes when he showed up at her house.

The older Lili would beg fans not to read it. "I did it for the money." Rightly, she claimed it was a "lot of exaggeration and outright lies compiled to satisfy her contractual demands."[843] The book was sold through the back of men's magazines and was supposed to be serialized in *Midnight* magazine, "the World's Greatest Tabloid," but this author found no evidence of that.[844] It could not have made a dint in her debt. Neither did it do anything for her waning career.

IN 1966 LILI'S AGENT DAVE COHEN, A RENOWNED AGENT IN BURLESQUE circles, sent her a telegram confirming an August engagement for six days, eight shows weekly (nothing like the two to four shows per day of her height, or indeed burlesque's height) for $3,000. A decent enough sum but not what she used to make. She would be the feature attraction and Cohen assured her she was following in classy footsteps, as Maurice Chevalier was "there this week."[845]

She was still returning regularly for sometimes month-long appearances at the Latin Quarter, still slipping into her tub, though *Variety* called her "handicapped" due to her age and the "youngsters who show as much as she." Most of her competition was now topless.[846]

Lili played the Shady Grove Music Fair in Gaithersburg, Maryland, a big arena-type theatre under a tent. Theatre in the round unnerved Lili, who much preferred a proscenium stage. She didn't like exposure on all sides.

At St. John Terrell's Music Circus, Lili starred in "Burlesque at its Best" on a bill that included comedians Joey Faye and Dick Postan for an August–September run. The advertisement showed a picture of Lili wearing a "skimpy cowboy vest" that was really a gun holster. She was forty-nine and the photo was at least fifteen years old.

Once again Lili inadvertently stirred up controversy. Though the *New York Times* ran the ad, four days later they refused to rerun it after receiving "about a half dozen phonecalls [*sic*] protesting" that Lili was too risqué and the *Times* demanded Lili's bosom be "decorously encased in a bra."[847] The producers cried censorship.

Lili appeared twice in the show, in the traditional headliner spot, before intermission and before the finale. It was summer theatre, again in the round, but with only one show a night, she couldn't complain.

WITH LESS GIGS TO FILL HER DAYS LILI BEGAN SPENDING TIME AT HER lingerie store. She had been selling her lingerie "in fine men's shops" and magazines and "The Undie World of Lili St. Cyr" would remain a catalogue business but also became a store, first at 1620 Vine and then 8104 Santa Monica Boulevard.

Dardy thought the origins of the store began when "some people" who owned a lingerie shop in Hollywood asked Lili to use her name, in return for a fee. Lili was paid a small amount and often spent days in the tiny shop helping young women, telling them how important "foundation" was under clothes. The store was later sold to owners of a shop on Santa Monica Boulevard.

Lili probably had some monetary interest beyond a nominal fee if she was spending time in the actual store. However, many would recall Lili there when they shopped, sitting toward the back of the tiny shop, carefully made up and with her hair done. After decades of work Lili needed to fill her days and she was generally interested in clothes and lingerie and such. She also needed the income. She would take another loan out against her house, this time for $4,000, repaid in 1967.[848]

In the 1980s television's Elvira, Cassandra Peterson, discovered a favorite item at the store. "I bought the bra I used in all of my Elvira dresses at the Lili St. Cyr store in West Hollywood when I first started Elvira in 1981. They were made by a company called 'Fanny' and when they later went out of business I bought their entire stock of those particular bras!"[849]

Eventually Lili's involvement became nil, and she received a small sum for the use of her name. The shop sold and closed in the 1990s.

RIGHT: *The photo that stirred up the controversy*

Down to Bare Fashion Facts

LILI ST. CYR
Stripped for action

New York

Lili St. Cyr and Blaze Starr are two names that will probably never appear on the best-dressed list.

But it won't be because the two strippers aren't choosy about the clothes they put on.

"I'm mad about fashion — in fact I wanted to be a designer," Miss St. Cyr said the other day while covered from neck to knee in a $2500 mink coat.

"Balenciaga and Courreges are my heroes," she added, "but Norman Norell is my favorite. He must have tailors who really know what they're doing. I get five or six years' wear from his things."

The blue-eyed blonde had less kind words for some of today's pop fashion trends.

"I wouldn't be caught dead wearing net hose, sequinned dresses or false eyelashes," she said. "Women who wear them in public remind me of strippers."

Miss Starr, on the other hand, makes most of her own clothes, including many of the costumes in her $20,000 stage wardrobe, which includes three mink coats.

She recently spent four months sewing and gluing hundreds of beads on a black lame gown that she made for $150. She believes it would have cost $500 in a store.

But the attire is strictly Poor Boy sweaters and stretch blue jeans when she's in Baltimore in her new $100,000 ranch-style home.

It is called "Belle's Little Acre." (Her real name is Bella Fleming.) She designed it herself, right down to the purple sunken bathtub and the modern Oriental furniture.

"I love miniskirts, too, but I can't wear them because I'm as wide as I am high," she said dejectedly. She is 5 feet 6 inches tall and measures (according to posters outside the theater) 48-24-36.

Both women said they earned $100,000 in "good years,'" a big chunk of which goes for clothes, wigs and cosmetics. But neither spends a cent on keeping her figure strip-shape.

Miss St. Cyr was born Marie Van Schaak in Pasadena and was a waitress in a Chinese restaurant there before becoming a stripper in 1942.

Now 49 years old — the same age, she said, as her sewing machine — she lives in an English country house in Hollywood with her seventh husband.

"California is really nowhere as far as fashion is concerned," she said.

So whenever she has a New York engagement — usually at the Latin Quarter — she stocks up on clothes.

Miss Starr, who is 30 ("say 29 — it's good for business"), was born on a farm near Logan, W. Va., the eighth child in a family of 11. Her father was a railroad worker.

One thing Miss Starr never takes off is a 5-carat diamond ring she said was a gift of the late Governor Earl Long of Louisiana.

They were engaged to be married, she said, but the governor died in September, 1960 — two months before his divorce from his first wife was to become final.

Her favorite offstage outfit is a $150 beige wool suit that she trimmed with opossum fur.

"Down home we throw those things away," she said with a medium-heavy drawl.

New York Times

CHAPTER FOURTEEN

Dardy and Lili drifted in and out of each other's lives, like storm-tossed waves, both in transition with their careers and personal lives. Both had new men, both younger.

There would be several times where they didn't speak or see each other for months—maybe years. Stripper Dixie Evans, a.k.a. the "Marilyn Monroe of Burlesque" because of her striking resemblance to Monroe, recalled playing at the Adam's Theatre in Newark for Harold.

Harold enlisted Dixie, a co-feature on the bill, to help patch things up between the sisters. "Harold told them, 'Girls, enough of this. Kiss and make up.' And they did."[850] All retired to a nearby bar after the show where Dixie spoofed Marilyn Monroe. Soon Lili was up imitating Monroe's distinctive walk, her bottom shaking back and forth. Everyone howled with laughter.

THE YEAR 1967 WOULD PROVE TO BE A DIFFICULT ONE FOR LILI, WITH the passing of her beloved Alice on January 2 in San Luis Obispo. Alice was ninety-one. She had been in a convalescent hospital after vomiting so severe that it led to aspiration pneumonitis (inflammation of the lungs), which in turn led to acute pulmonary edema and death.

Memories of Alice would haunt Lili's Canyon Drive home, of her sewing, laughing, glasses on nose. She was a combination of mother, grandmother, friend, flamboyant in her way, "full of life" and warmth and love.[851] Alice had thought the world of Lili, spoiled her, and loved her, and Lili had basked in that affection.

From Alice, Lili and her sisters learned their love of telling (and embellishing) a good yarn. Facts weren't important; neither was the truth. Alice was the "instigator" in shaping Lili and her sisters (and Idella) as flamboyant, colorful; storytellers who spun the tales they wanted to believe.[852] Which would make for much confusion. Each branch of Lili's family insisted the story they were told, such as the fiction that Lili was named Willis at birth (I believe Alice said this because she was sticking up for Lili after she changed her name—facts and documents clearly do not support it) was gospel.

That rock, the first woman to shape and influence Lili, was gone.

Lili hired a limousine to take her to Arroyo Grande Cemetery. She rolled down the window and listened but wouldn't attend the funeral. Dardy told cousin Ellie Hiatt that Lili had shingles on her face and wouldn't be seen. Another possibility could have been Lili was high on drugs. No matter, Lili was devastated by the loss. She was burying the only person who really knew her and knew her past.

IT MUST HAVE FELT LIKE CIRO'S ALL OVER AGAIN. EXCEPT THIS WAS Montreal and sixteen years after she had been acquitted. And of course Giesler was dead, having passed in 1962.[853]

It was February and Lili had just finished the 2 a.m. show. She was in her dressing room at Champ's. Jimmy was somewhere near the bar. There was a knock on her door.

She was under arrest.

No matter how the winds of change were blowing, no matter what the girls showed these days, someone was always after her. Because the Canadian politicians wanted to look tough and appear to sweep the dirt and vice from their city for the World's Fair, Lili and her G-string were once again being hung out to dry. The papers bragged that Lili's arrest was a "test case" as to what could and could not be performed in nightclubs during the World's Fair.[854]

A furious Jimmy barged in profusely apologetic. "I've already called my attorney and some *friends*," he growled. She knew he meant his "connected" friends.

She changed her clothes, not sure how many more times she had the fight in her.

Jimmy paid the $100 bail. It was possibly the final straw to his troubled marriage. Jimmy and his wife were fighting harder than ever.

Lili continued performing at Champ's while the case awaited its turn. When her gig was over she left Montreal and Jimmy.

At Windsor Station she was cold even though wrapped in fur. Piles of leather luggage surrounded her. She left with regrets. Bye, Jimmy and Al and Eddie. Bye bye, Montreal. Bye to an era. Bye to Lili St. Cyr.

IN MARCH, AFTER FAILING TO SHOW UP AT TRIAL—DUE TO A MISUN-derstanding, her attorney claimed—the judge issued a bench warrant for her

arrest. But Lili was already back in New York performing at the Latin Quarter. She would never return. She would never see Jimmy or her Canadian friends again.

AT FIFTY LILI REMAINED ACTIVE THROUGHOUT 1967. SHE RETURNED to the Latin Quarter in New York and during the summer months she performed weekly in various East Coast country music fairs. She was on the road for eighteen weeks with Dagmar in "Bravo, Burlesque." Billed as a "musical satire on the wonderful days of burlesque," Lili was given top billing. The "American Venus" (as she was lauded) would be performing her "Dance of the Seven Veils" and "Love Bird."

The show toured from the Camden County Fairgrounds in New Jersey, eventually coming to Melodyland in Anaheim, a theatre that later would become an Evangelical Christian church. It was a mediocre show with a "blah chorus line" and "lousy staging," considered a "seedy show."[855] Lili performed "Salome" and proved to her audience she was still in "fantastic shape," keeping audiences "on the edge of their seats."[856]

Mentally, it was a struggle for Lili. It wasn't what she wanted. She wanted Ciro's and the Gayety and the tuxedo crowd, which no longer existed. The comedian on the bill was terrible. Ironically, the crowd ate it up. They loved the tassel-twirler, the top banana Moe Raft. The show lacked any sort of artistry or elegance, once Lili's trademark. She was still in the business, but it wasn't the same.

RIGHT: *An older Lili on the stage*
ABOVE: *An older, still glamorous Lili*

PART FIVE

BON NUIT

"Now I have to stand in line like everyone else"

—LILI ST. CYR

To Don Barreca
From your old friend, with love
Lili St. Cyr

CHAPTER ONE

"Getting old was rough for Lili," Dardy said. Armando would echo the sentiments and many would speculate why the long-limbed stunner shut her door on friends, turned her back on the public, and disappeared from sight.

"Her looks were everything," her former husband lamented.

"I'm terrified of old age," Lili had said years earlier, "and the thought of losing my beauty."[857]

As a young girl Lili could never imagine being old. She didn't want wrinkly skin and saggy breasts. She wouldn't be the first—or last—entertainer accused of being narcissistic. In an industry based on charm, allure, and beauty, Lili's reputation as stunning was paramount to her identity. She floundered as her looks faded and she was no longer "La Belle Lili" who could "just come out and take a bow and still bring the house down."[858]

Katherine Hepburn once admitted she never wanted children because if the child got sick she would be forced to choose between it and making her curtain at the theatre. A career in front of the public is demanding and all-absorbing. It must be. Performers utilize their instruments—their entire bodies—and must maintain their assets as best they can. For a stripper, body and face were everything.

Lili was beauty. For decades critics and fans had lauded her good looks. It was her uniquely regal beauty that drew the crowds.

Growing up she wanted to escape the reality of poverty, the feeling of being ordinary. She wanted glamour and mystery, fantasy and adventure. She created that life onstage and off. It led to riches and fame and romance. It drew to her husbands and lovers. Without it, what would her future hold?

For Lili there was once last romance in store for her.

LIKE THE MEN IN HER ARMS BEFORE HIM, DONALD MARKICK WAS DEV-astatingly handsome. When they met in 1964 he was thirty, seventeen years Lili's junior. She didn't care. His youth and charm enraptured her. She was like the character in her favorite novel *Chérie* "A woman . . . the 'vampire,' who needs must feed off youthful flesh."[859]

Lili and Donald would play roles, swathe themselves in a make-believe world that would swallow them completely.

Born in Pennsylvania to a Yugoslavian-born father and a mother from Pennsylvania, Donald Andrew Markick was born February 11, 1934.[860] He was the lone male among three sisters. Charming, tall, and dark-haired he fit Lili's image of an ideal mate. And, as she told a reporter, she "prefers the company of young men to those of her age."[861]

It would be claimed that Donald Markick served in the Korean War as a para-trooper, and that his tour "proved to be tumultuous and risky."

Markick told others—so there is no reason to believe he didn't tell Lili the same—he "suffered from jungle rot." During the war he was "captured and held prisoner."[862] Perhaps it was his excuse to justify the hard drugs he took. Maybe he wanted to be a hero in the eyes of others and making up a past filled with danger and glory was the only way he would ever be that. Many would believe the lies of this gentle sweet man.

Sadly, his military records tell a very different story. Donald Andrew Markick did serve in the US Army from July 8, 1953, to July 13, 1955, *after* the fighting was over. He joined the Tenth Specialist Service Company.

In speaking with an expert at "The Korean War Project" this author was told "the Specialists were strictly an entertainment service." This was verified by the National Archives and Records Administration. "The unit's duties involved troop entertainment."[863]

As a private, Donald would have been no more than a "lifter and a toter, or a clerk." Whether he went to Korea or not, his hazardous duties would have been to "set up football fields or uniforms or equipment for movies to entertain the troops."[864] There were volleyball and softball games, along with horseshoes, theatrical shows, and miniature golf to attend to. Though he was discharged with a National Defense Service Medal, it was awarded to anyone who had served honorably. According to the command report, the platoon was operating "the library, recreation hall, entertainment, and motion picture projectors."

Lili wouldn't have known his elaborate tales were lies and she probably wouldn't have cared. She always loved a hopeless rascal. Donald was an unambitious loser building himself up in the eyes of others. He would never put to use his considerable charm for anything other than getting by with the least amount of effort.

Donald would claim he had been infatuated with Lili for years after having seen her picture in a girlie magazine. He collected some photos, found out where she was performing, and stalked the club. He would have stood out, as he was tall with a large build, with his thick "shaggy" dark hair and thick eyebrows over "interesting eyes."[865] He had a beautiful smile. People noted he had a wry sense of humor.

"They both adamantly believed that they were 'soul mates' and had been together before in another life."[866]

"I gave my accountant every single one of his gray hairs," Lili would boast. "'Fall in love with a rich man,' he'd say. I couldn't help myself. Looks and romance is what I wanted." For the first several years of their relationship she was still working regularly. She had enough money for the both of them.

He claimed he always wanted to be a magician. He admired Houdini.

As she had with so many, Lili set about reinventing him. First he needed a "more theatrical" name. She chose Lorenzo because it sounded "exotic." An avid reader, his favorite writer was Arthur Conan Doyle. His favorite character Sherlock Holmes. So Lili chose the name "Lorenzo Holmes."[867] His family was not thrilled with the moniker or his relationship with an older woman. They refused to call him Lorenzo.

Lorenzo soon packed his things and moved into her house. She was in love again. So was he. Not that it prevented her from seeing Jimmy when she was in Montreal. Faithfulness had never been her forte.[868]

Two months after her divorce from Joe was final, reporters were noting that her "fiancé" was following her to Las Vegas and Canada. But Lili told reporters that "her engagement to actor Lorenzo Holmes has been broken."[869]

The serial bride would never marry Lorenzo/Donald Markick, possibly because he remained married to Jeanie Linck, whom he had wed in 1958 in Reno, Nevada.[870] Or, if he was divorced, he had no further need to try marriage again.

ONCE AGAIN LILI HAD FALLEN FOR AN UNDERDOG. MAYBE SHE FELT sorry for this drifter, cutting him slack regarding his drug use because it soothed his pain, mental or physical. Lili knew about pain.

Somewhere along the way Lorenzo had developed injuries to either his legs or hips and, it being the "Age of Aquarius," he'd picked up a bad "habit" that Lili's friends didn't approve of. He smoked pot, but it wasn't nearly enough to dull the pain.

Once he moved in he seemed content to live off her; his only income besides what he received from the VA came from a more disreputable source.

"He was a glorified drug dealer," niece Ava Minsky Foxman recalled. "A whack job in a long line of whack jobs. I didn't pay any attention to him. He enabled her."

Most likely Lili didn't smoke pot with him. When marijuana was offered to her she would demur, "That's not of *my* people."[871] She wasn't being racist. The people she knew who smoked weed were the black musicians in the jazz clubs Orson Welles had taken her to years before. It wasn't what *her* gin martini crowd indulged in. For all her progressive beliefs in UFOs and talk of antimarriage, Lili could be quite conventional, one of the many contradictions of a Gemini. Pot was not for her. That wouldn't be the high she would share with her young lover.

To others Lorenzo came across as lost. Essentially lacking ambitious or talent he held the occasional odd job. He didn't like to be tied down. It was one of several things he had in common with Lili. They were both free spirits and saw in each other a refuge from a judgmental world. He didn't want to get married or have her quit stripping. He made no demands.

Together they would slip into their own cloistered world of play-acting, having dinners alone dressed in costume under a silk tent, à la the Arabian nights.

For a time Lorenzo trailed along with Lili to some of her engagements. Earl Wilson reported in August of 1965 that Lili had "announced she'd wed young Lorenzo Holmes." Amusingly other papers reported that she would wed "writer Lorenzo Holmes" and "actor Lorenzo Holmes."[872] Reporters waited for the announcement of marriage number seven.

Not all was love and light. Lili and her much younger boyfriend were caught "looking daggers at each other" out one night.[873]

According to Dardy Lili had finally saved a substantial nest egg, even putting money in the bank. Her assets included her house and the lot next door. There were her jewels and antiques. There should have been enough to live off comfortably. She was tired. Tired of travel, the way audiences had changed. There was loneliness and no one at the end of the road if she didn't make a final stab with this relationship. She could have been comfortable.

Lorenzo didn't mind her habit of living with the shutters and curtains closed, keeping out the harsh daylight, living by candlelight. He was usually high and perhaps loved the soft mellow moods, the womb she enveloped them in. He performed magic tricks he had learned. For once someone entertained her. Did he help her recapture her youth?

They began to slip into their own world, slowly leaving others behind. She would drift from her reality into his. She stopped working, didn't visit friends, no longer returned phone calls. She began to shed Lili St. Cyr. He would be with her for nearly thirty years.

CHAPTER TWO

There was one person Lili was eager to have Lorenzo meet. One she should have known better than to introduce him to. Lili invited Dardy over.

"I didn't like his smoking pot. Oh, I've tried it," Dardy said. "The 'magician,' or whatever he claimed to be, I don't think he did a lick of work ever. She supported him. He was too sick to work, he claimed. Bull!"

Did he do a lot of drugs?

Dardy waved her hand. "I wasn't around him much after that. Didn't like him. User. Of Lili and drugs. He's the one that got her doing terrible, terrible drugs." She shook her head. "I could never forgive him that." Lili's little sister thought the new man was "a scumball who was destroying" her.[874]

As Lili aged, her body began to betray her. She would remain strong and muscular from decades of dance, in marvelous shape well into her sixties. Even toward the end of her life her arms retained definition. But gradually there were aches and pains. Her feet, her back, joints. She developed osteoarthritis, a degenerative joint disease. There was tenderness, stiffness, aches, inflammation. Her toes especially, but also her hands, grew knobby and rigid. It was a throbbing dull ache throughout. She wasn't used to not feeling well.

Then there was the kind of pain that had afflicted Lili her entire life. Her insecurities and anxieties. Her fear of aging and losing her great beauty. It had to be agony for her to look in the mirror and see lines, sagging, a once-stunning woman becoming old. Worry and wariness was etched into her face.

Her *type* of career was essentially at an end. There was no need for her "tame" entertainment.[875] The crowds, the applause, and the fussing were leaving.

In 1970 Lili was engaged at the Aladdin working for ex-brother-in-law Harold in his "Minsky's Burlesque Review." Ironically, she replaced Tempest Storm, who *Variety* noted was very different than Miss St. Cyr's act, which still maintained "a premise, as always" as she performed her decades-old "Salome."[876]

Again a bed was the centerpiece in her boudoir set among mirrors. Her "auto-erotic" performance on the bed grew from slow undulations to "frantic writhing." She tossed off a pair of red panties to a member of the audience. A reviewer complained she looked washed out under her blue lighting. She performed for ten minutes, twice nightly, to "moderate" applause.[877] She was still packing in audiences, mostly out of nostalgia. She stayed March and April and returned in July, once again replacing Tempest.

While Elvis Presley was starring in a televised show at the Las Vegas Convention Center and earning a reported $1 million, Lili was fifty-three years old, decades older than most of the other exotics. She had been stripping for thirty years, several lifetimes longer than the average exotic. But then Lili had never been average. Vegas and Harold's shows had changed to keep up with the times. By 1966 the showgirls were nude. Harold wanted to keep a mystery about them, but no one was interested in that.

The Strip was crowded with acts like Tiny Tim and Don Ho, Dean Martin, Johnny Carson, and Alan King. In March the culinary worker strike caused a shutdown on the Strip, briefly canceling Lili's show.[878]

In September she was back bathing for "Minsky's Burlesque '70." While Joe E. Lewis was honored at a testimonial dinner at the Riviera with Sinatra in attendance, reporters sniped Lili "doesn't sing, dance, talk, play an instrument" but remained "a star."[879]

Her act had changed very little over the decades. Lili St. Cyr was a legend. Audiences wanted to see the original bathing beauty, even if she was the age of most grandmothers. St. Cyr gave more than they asked for. She gave a lifetime of care and detail. But now it was time for her to retreat. She was done with headlines and publicity and scandal. She didn't have the energy to pursue it any more. She was tired of traveling and packing. The production of shows weren't to her standards.

It was time to step off the stage and let Lili go. She would revert to Willis Van Schaack and, like a favored dress, "Lili St. Cyr" was carefully packed away along with the G-strings and the pasties and the clippings.

She assumed with what she had saved and what she continued to receive from the Undie World that she would be okay. Maybe she thought she would finally start to design clothes. Her next act was anyone's guess.

In retirement Lili spent hours doting on her numerous stray cats and Lorenzo. Without work she had the time and focus to spoil someone without resenting what it took away from her nightly performances. She bought Lorenzo a beautiful new Corvette and when that got old she bought him another.

She spent her time doodling lingerie designs.

NAVY BATIST DRESS
WHITE EMBROIDERY APRON
NAVY VELVET RIBBON TRIM & HAIR RIBBON

WHITE BATIST
WITH
BIAS RUFFLES

Some of Lili's hand-drawn designs

SHE TOLD LORENZO HER MOTHER WAS LONG DEAD. SO WHEN IDELLA Beck died on December 31, 1973, it barely registered. Not only was Lili numbing herself with drugs, but also Idella had never been much of an attachment for Lili.

According to Dardy, toward the end Idella "was pretty good into the gin" and suffered a heart attack, dying at home, probably alone, as 1972 was being ushered out. She was seventy-seven years old.[880] She would be cremated. The next of kin notified was Mrs. Idella Marx of New York.[881]

The death of the secretive, "crabby" Idella brought Barbara out west for four days.[882] Dardy and Barbara saw each other for the first time in twenty years. Lili was nowhere to be found. Brother Jack had become a paint contractor in Ventura and somewhere along the way, according to Dardy, suffered a bad fall. Jack had been "not too friendly" with what remained of the family.[883]

The long-forgotten Bettalee too might have passed by now. According to niece Ava Minsky, she thought her Aunt Betty had died in the 1970s. Her story too had a sad ending.

Betty was homeless and living on Spring Street in downtown Los Angeles, probably in some abandoned building. Idella had been sending her money care of the Utility Department. Apparently Betty stuffed it in newspapers because when she died the money was found.[884]

It was a lot of loss for Lili. It isn't known how much she even knew since she wasn't close with extended family. She probably was not in touch with either her Uncle Jack or Aunt Betty. Soon Lili would lose herself in serious drugs and wouldn't care about anything.

Lili began to live a life without travel and work, or accolades, but fraught with day-long worry. Gone was an adoring public. Gone was the applause. There were no more headlines. With all the time—time she had no idea how to fill beyond puttering and looking after Lorenzo and the cats—her thoughts and her fears settled on aging. Along with the increasing pain and stiffness in her back and joints, a mental anguish took over. Lorenzo knew how to help his beloved.

Lili had always liked her Miltowns and her sleeping pills. She liked to soothe the wolf yapping in her head. She would have been easy to convince. Maybe Lorenzo wanted her to slip into imagination with him. He could promise castles in the air. A place where they could go together. One wonders if Lili went easily. Did she hesitate? Know fear? Trust implicitly?

Heroin—at least the first time—is said to bring intense pleasure and relief from pain of any kind. And then every injection after becomes the chasing to recapture that first blissful euphoria. A dark road trying to catch the elusive pot of gold somewhere over the rainbow. Heroin can and does bring respite from depression and angst. Familiar symptoms Lili suffered from, not to mention the very real aches in her body.

No doubt Lorenzo suggested she try it. *Lili, it will help your back. Don't feel nervous. Relax. Let me help you. Here's a vein. Your arms are strong. I love you.* Lorenzo the Magnificent didn't need to do his magic tricks—she would soon levitate. The feeling was incredible. Happiness. As powerful as she had been onstage.

For Lili it was always about escape and relief. If she couldn't transform herself through her work and her romances, she could now through a needle.

For those individuals like Lili who rarely experienced ecstasy in life, heroin was beatific. It would release her emotional inhibitions and uptightness, which she surely had. It would enslave her like no other lover.

And Lili, "languid Lili," already known for her *je ne sais quoi,* became listless, her limbs thick and foggy. She could float, leaving her fears. She could breathe with heroin in her veins. She could drift and not care. *The future?* She would be fine. The couple could sail for hours.

But it is a drug that ultimately deadens: the soul, the spirit, hope, the future. Everything erased for an elusive grasping for the first-time flush of supremacy as the heroin courses through. Then the deadening as it kills what is left. It slays the "aches and discomforts of life." Warmth suffuses the user. Womblike. Protective. It "deprives the soul."[885]

Without it the body bucks. The insides churn in agony. There is nausea,

Lili on her corner lot with her cat Tiger

drowsiness, panic worse than any opening night, body chills, handshakes, stomach cramps, a stabbing pain.

There could be spells of crying and insomnia—sleep had never come easily for Lili. All too soon without her new "lover" the restlessness would return twofold and with Lorenzo's help she would reach for relief.

Applause and headlines were addictive to one Lili; this other Lili replaced them with heroin. It would substitute for the fawning and the attention and the love. It would have to sustain her until her dying day.

CHAPTER THREE

Toward the end of her life Lili told someone she had been taking morphine for forty years, which would have made her addiction start sometime in the 1950s. Morphine was widely available since the 1920s. Maybe she was first introduced to it to suppress the pain from her appendix attacks.

Many stars of Lili's day and prior had been addicted to morphine; actors Errol Flynn, Lionel Barrymore, Theda Bara, Barbara La Marr, Peter Lorre, and Wallace Reid. (La Marr, Lorre, and Reid became addicted after being prescribed morphine to manage pain.) Morphine certainly was not unheard of in Hollywood. However, what is interesting is when Lili begged someone in her final months to get her morphine she said, "Don't you know anyone in the army?"[886] The only one she knew that had been in the military was Lorenzo.

Maybe Lorenzo only wanted to help his love, whom he knew *suffered* from insomnia, ulcers, stiff feet, and an increasingly arthritic spine that left her frozen, not to mention her great fear and anxiety. She was in constant pain and spent much of her last years uncomfortable. Arthritis caused a gradual squeezing of the last of her freedom, depriving her of flight, something she had always been able to do. Lili St. Cyr could always get up and dance away, could always pack a bag and hop on a train and escape. And when she could no longer, she was trapped.

No one ever mentioned seeing Lili high or shooting up. Her performances were never affected by drink or drugs. No one saw marked arms.

Lili's new lifestyle consisted of sequestering herself inside her home while Lorenzo and his friends took over. "There were *always* people coming by her house. Going into the garage seeing *him*. He was selling drugs out of her house!" Lorenzo would be in the garage tinkering with his new Corvette. "Friends" would drive over for minutes, then drive away. "All the time. Every time I was there," Dardy said. "He was selling dope!"

The more they dove into drugs and the procuring it and taking it and stumbling through their fantasy life, the more Lili and Lorenzo hid.

Soon it was years since Lili had any real income. Where was her huge nest egg she had retired with? Dardy noticed furniture missing from the house. Antiques Lili had carefully acquired over the years where no longer there.

"Are you *selling* things, Lil?" Dardy asked.

Lili was evasive and said she was "simplifying." But Dardy knew.

Was all her money gone? Shot up her arm? And his?

Lili had become one of the "women past their prime, who abandon first their stays, then their hair-dye, and who finally no longer bother about the quality of their underclothes."[887] Lili had let herself go.

Unbeknownst to Lili, her niece Ava (probably around the time she stormed out of Dardy's house after living with her mother since the two fought too much) moved into a house near Lili on Carolus Drive. Nineteen-year-old Ava had no idea her aunt was so close, not having seen her for about a decade. One day Ava answered a knock on the door. There was a "weird fat old woman" in a "black shroud," wearing a long black skirt with a basket selling things. Ava felt sorry for her. Then Lili's funny squeaky voice gave her away. It was her *Tante* Lili, dressed "like a Muslim" and weighing two hundred pounds.

"Lili?" Ava asked, astounded her once-gorgeous aunt was completely unrecognizable.

Lili squinted. "Is that Dardy's daughter?" From there the two would enjoy a short-lived reunion. About Lorenzo, Ava paid "no attention to *him*." She was astounded to see he was driving a military tank, which of course Lili must have bought him.

Whenever Ava saw Lorenzo, he was "stoned most of the time." He "took the role of Lili's 'gate keeper' very seriously. Some might call it protective. I saw it as him keeping her isolated. According to those in the know, he procured drugs for her and was a well-known customer of the drug dealers that populated Bronson Canyon Park (also known as Needle Park) in the 'day.'" Ava also thought Lorenzo "paranoid."[888]

Ava spoke occasionally to her *tante* on the phone "until Lili didn't have a phone anymore."[889]

Ava slipped a note under Lili's door to let her know she was moving back east. Lili didn't respond. She had receded further into addiction and isolation.

Finally, Dardy had had enough. She stood in Lili's house. "I can't stand him." Lorenzo was upstairs. Probably stoned. Dardy despised him. She hated seeing Lili's once-beautiful arms marked with needle punctures.

Lili didn't say anything.

"You're selling your things for him, aren't you?" Dardy screeched. "Why?"

"He has blood clots, Teedle," Lili murmured. Her sister just didn't understand. Lorenzo was helpless. His poor legs filled with clots. Who would take care of him if she didn't? It didn't matter to her what it cost. She would sell anything.

Dardy didn't know Lili would wander to the end of her street where kids hung out to score drugs, desperate to get high.

Lili had to realize there would not be another romance, no other man she could ensnare, fall in love with, care for. She was no longer the queen of the stage. She was no longer beautiful.

"First he got a blood clot in one lung," Dardy said. "Lili got him the finest doctors. He was in the hospital for weeks. She saved his life, but it cost her $250,000. Then he got blood clots in his legs. He was supposed to keep them elevated. She waited on him hand and foot—brought him meals on trays. He was bed-bound for months. She wore herself out! Then he developed another clot in his lungs. Same thing. Surgery. She had to start selling things to pay for everything."

Desperate for money Lili sold her corner lot in 1969 for $10,500. She signed a grant deed to C.B.G. Murphy Trust, losing the first of her last two major assets. In her Canadian biography she implied an ominous meeting occurred in which two men came to her and *made* her sign some papers. It is more likely that the soft-hearted Murphy helped Lili when she was low on funds and seriously into a drug addiction by buying her property. Lili would have done it unselfishly. Like Alice she would give anything to help someone. The corner lot had served her well. She had never intended to build on it. She simply did not want someone else that close to her. Privacy was paramount for Lili.[890]

CHAPTER FOUR

Growing up in New Zealand in the 1950s, Richard Timothy Smith's "adolescence was swamped with joys that most of the fifties decent society decried as mindless, comics, rock-n-roll, B-movies."[891] He became fascinated with comic books and pulp fiction. In his town of Tauranga was a shop filled with kitsch and magazines. Lili St. Cyr. adorned many of those magazines.

Smith became fascinated with her. She "was one of the most beautiful women in the world and, by default, a transsexual's dream girl." Smith noted that burlesque "was aimed at the eternal adolescent in males." Lili clearly was the leading element of that "particular zeitgeist."

In 1973 Smith, now known by his stage name of Richard O'Brien, wrote what would become the cult hit *The Rocky Horror Picture Show*, both the musical and, in 1975, as a cowriter, the screenplay.

The character Janet, played by Susan Sarandon in the film, sings "Don't Dream It—Be It." It was inspired by one of O'Brien's pulp magazines asking the question, whatever happened to *King Kong* actress Fay Wray? The last line of the song is "It's beyond me, help me, Mommy—God bless Lily [sic] St. Cyr." And though it was just twenty-five years from her heyday in the fifties, most of *RHPS*'s audience had no clue who Lili St. Cyr was. The "inclusion of Lily [sic] was driven by the recognition of my own imagined self." [892]

O'Brien believes the LA stage version bought some of their costumes from Lili's lingerie store in 1974.

LILI WROTE DARDY THAT SHE WAS AT HER "WITS END." IT WAS JANUARY. She sent Dardy a package of bills, hoping like Scarlet O'Hara that "something would happen that I could pay them myself." Her luck had turned so much that

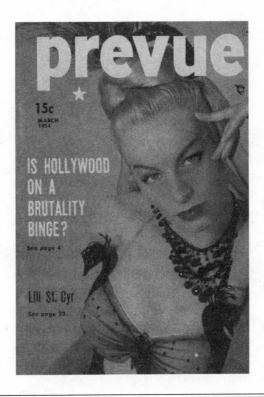

Lili's face and figure adorned many magazine covers in her day

"even my pen went dry." She owed money everywhere, including a pawnshop. "I am frightened," she admitted. She promised Teedle she would "try to make it up to you somehow."[893]

The rumor still swirls today, written as fact, that Lili was broke and literally put out on the street. That she lost her beloved house because she couldn't pay the taxes.

THE TRUTH IS THAT IN MARCH OF 1977 SHE SOLD HER CANYON DRIVE home for $72,500. By then it was her only means of providing much-needed income for both Lorenzo and herself. Lili could no longer afford to keep her lovingly decorated, meticulously arranged, cherished refuge.

After paying whatever outstanding debts she had, she squirreled away $40,000 into a Bank of America savings account. Maybe she sold her home to settle debts. But when she and Lorenzo departed Canyon Drive forever she had enough money to live on, at least for a while. She had sold almost all of her antiques at yard sales. She pawned and sold her jewels and her furs. Gone were

Lili's house as it appeared in 2015.

the elaborate beds, the carousel horse(s), the pagoda, the antique ivory fans she had collected. Gone was so much.

BETWEEN MARCH AND SEPTEMBER OF 1977 SHE WENT THROUGH THE entire $40,000—$1,000 here, $2,000 there. In six months it was gone.

Lili continued to make sporadic appearances at her Undie World shop, but around this time the boutique sold to new owners and though her involvement was only minimal she would stop going in.[894]

Lili's world was shrinking.

Unsure where to go, Lili and Lorenzo moved into a tiny dark apartment squashed alongside a row of equally grim apartments at 630 Plymouth Drive in Hollywood.

The front window looked directly on the plant-lined walkway and another apartment just feet across a narrow walkway. It afforded Lili no privacy. Neighbors were on all sides.

Though discombobulated after just having sold her house and all her lovely antiques, and surely disoriented from drugs, she was aware of the stream of Lorenzo's "friends" in and out of the apartment that would set the neighborhood talking with rumors of buying and selling drugs.

Lili entertaining in her beloved home

Lili had the forethought to put her name on a waiting list for a larger apartment a few buildings down on the same side of the street.

Finally she and Lorenzo moved into a large Spanish complex at 624 North Plymouth. Number 7 was (and still is) a bright, bottom-floor one-bedroom unit with tall French windows and a tiny kitchen with a back door. The ceilings were high. There was a front room that looked out on green lawn and trees. Tucked back off the main street it was quiet, a block from the famous Paramount Studio gates. It was a comfortable, airy apartment and she would enjoy working in the garden.

LORENZO TOOK THE SOLE BEDROOM TOWARD THE BACK OF THE APARTment. Lili moved a small bed into the living room and slept there. Lorenzo was in constant pain. His hips were disintegrating, according to an upstairs neighbor. Neither slept well. They needed separate rooms. Long past her two-year expiration date for passion, their relationship had lost fervor. Their intimacy had to have long since moved from sex to syringes. It was a matter of getting drugs and doing drugs to keep their fantasy world alive.

They argued frequently. The upstairs neighbor heard his voice raised, but never Lili's. "Lili's husband"—which is how Lili introduced Lorenzo—could be heard hollering at her.[895] Lili's soft murmurs went unwitnessed outside her walls.

"She wasn't friendly," the woman who lived with her parents above Lili's apartment said. "She would grunt for a response. I remember once when she was speaking with my mother on the street and a man came over and she told my mother to go. My mother was quite insulted. She [Lili] didn't like women." If he was a drug connection, she might also have feared being overheard.

How was Lorenzo?

"Oh, he was charming," the woman perked up. "He was real tall. But he walked holding a cane, completely bent over. He had this strange way of looking up at you. We became friends. He talked to me. Lili never would. She'd be polite on the stairs in passing, but Lorenzo was friendly. I'd see him every morning walking to the meth clinic in Hollywood. He was on outpatient. Or home services, something. So he could bring some back for her. We all knew they were on drugs. Some of the people that would come by!" Apparently Lorenzo liked to gossip with the neighbor. "Lorenzo told me she wasn't 'practical.' She wasn't good at business. She had lost the house on Canyon, *their* house, because she didn't pay the taxes."

When told that wasn't exactly true, she said, "He told me they were put out on the street with the furniture. Sold it [the furniture] right off the street. Are you sure?"

The neighbor claimed Lorenzo kept three guns in the house and they had some in-home help to take care of him. Lili would have been physically incapable of caring for six-four Lorenzo. For good or for bad, Lili had found the one man who was never going to leave her. He was physically incapable of abandoning her. And she was too deep in—to him, to drugs, and to the need to get them from his sources. She could not tear herself away.

In 1982 Lili again had conversations taped for a French Canadian biography largely written by Mathew Tombers. Canadian author William Weintraub claimed that Tombers wrote the book "aimed at the Quebec market . . . written in French, a language Lili didn't speak."[896]

This time the men and the sex talk was toned down. *Ma Vie de Stripteaseuse* was much less torrid than *And Men My Fuel*. Lili was happy to talk about her act. Again Lili is vague—if not downright lacking—about dates and times. She continued with her usual half-truths, keeping her private life hidden, though she seemed to make an effort to strip away part of the myth.[897]

She hoped to make great sums of money from the book; she needed it. The book would not be published in English and Lili would be disappointed once again.

CHAPTER FIVE

I t was around 1972.

Dardy was living alone in Los Angeles, still working for the Auto Club in a job she found surprisingly satisfactory. She was currently going through a nontalking period with Lili, who had sold her house and was living in the apartment near Paramount, when her sister Barbara called.

It had been a rough spell for Barbara. She was particularly close to her stepdaughter Patricia, who was married to an MIT researcher by the name of Daniel Ellsberg. In 1971 Ellsberg leaked documents that would become known as the Pentagon Papers to the *New York Times*. The documents revealed the US government was aware early on that there was no possibility of winning the Vietnam War. The papers made liars out of the Johnson administration.

When Ellsberg admitted he leaked the documents the government charged him with treason. Evidence would be found of illegal wiretapping perpetrated against Ellsberg for two years prior to the release of the papers.

By July 1973, because of gross misconduct by the government, the charges would be dismissed.

Separated from Marx (papers would continue to list her as his wife) and living in Cambridge, Massachusetts, Barbara (still going as Idella) possibly helped her stepson stash incriminating documents. Her son Spencer was also thought to have helped Ellsberg.[898]

BARBARA WAS CALLED TO TESTIFY ABOUT ILLEGAL WIRETAPS arranged against her (the government denied it). She refused to answer. It was believed she was well aware of the distribution of the documents, if not actually involved in the Xeroxing of them. The judge ordered the forty-five-year-old mother of five thrown in jail if she would not testify. She was out on $100,000 bail. On

November 10, 1971, Barbara appealed. Her defense was "that the questions are the product of information obtained by the government as the result of an illegal electronic surveillance."[899] She was granted immunity and eventually did testify before the Boston grand jury. In December she answered questions. Emerging, she said to reporters, "I told the truth."[900]

Barbara was spent after her ordeal. She wasn't one to stand up to anyone—let alone the courts. She and Marx argued. He was vehemently anti communist and did not like what Ellsberg had done. Barbara's refusal to testify must have angered him greatly. Marx would have considered her standing by Ellsberg a betrayal. And Marx was not a forgiving man.

By all accounts Marx was "apoplectic," "ranting and raving," furious at his son-in-law's disloyalty, as he saw it, against the country.[901] "Marx never spoke to Ellsberg again but his anger caused him to spew "his rage mainly towards others." He became more critical of the wife he had once been so proud of.[902]

Barbara turned from Louis and found comfort in another. She had an affair and Marx found out. Dardy thought it might have been with a priest she was particularly close with, or he was a cover for another man. And there might have been more affairs. According to author Tom Wells in *Wild Man,* Marx threw Barbara out after she was caught in some "adulteries."[903]

Barbara moved to Stanford, according to stepdaughter Jacqueline Barnett, who lived nearby with her family. Adrift from her life without Marx, Barbara was bereft. The young woman who had learned what songs were being played on the radio before she went on dates so she could recite them back now had no one to please. For so many years Barbara had "put on a good front."[904]

"He got mean," admitted daughter Barbara Marx Hubbard. He divorced Barbara. Marx became distressed by the struggles of his five sons, who experimented with drugs."[905] "It ruined the last years of his life."[906] No longer able to "boss it [life] around," the last years of his life were difficult for Louis Marx.[907]

It was a bitter end to a self-made man who had achieved so much. He lived out his final unhappy days in his *Gone with the Wind* mansion with a dozen dogs and nurses to attend to his needs. He died at eighty-six in 1982, broken. In Marx's New York obituary there would be no mention of Barbara.[908]

FOR THE FIRST TIME IN DECADES BARBARA WAS ALONE. SHE REACHED out to Dardy. Barbara's voice sounded fragile over the phone line. Twenty years of pain and separation from her family.

Dardy insisted Barbara come out to "stay as long as you like." She was imagining her once-sunny blonde sister, filled with laughter, sharing martinis and good times.

1 Mrs. LOUIS MARX
2 Gen. OMAR BRADLEY
3 Gen. EMMETT O'DONNELL
4 LOUIS MARX
5 LOUIS MARX ,Jr.
6 PRESIDENT EISENHOWER
7 SPENCER BEDELL MARX
8 Gen. WALTER BEDELL SMITH
9 EMMETT DWIGHT MARX
10 Gen. GEO. C. MARSHALL
11 BRADLEY MARSHALL MARX
12 JACQUELINE MARX BARNETT
13 BARBARA MARX HUBBARD
14 PATRICIA MARX

The Marx family and several prominent generals

"I can stay two weeks," Barbara told Dardy when she showed up in California. She stayed a year and a half.

Whatever had happened, it was a very changed Barbara. She was like someone going though "post war syndrome because she was lost trying to find her place in the world again," Dardy said.

"I will forever hate that bastard," Dardy said. "He sucked the life, everything out of her. She didn't have any money. She had been watched and badgered and brow beaten for twenty years by Louis Marx. She was stone broke when she left him. She just couldn't take it anymore."

It was a thin, terribly insecure Barbara, going by the name of Idella Ruth Marx, that huddled in a guest room at Dardy's apartment.

BARBARA SPENT MOST OF THE FIRST YEAR WITH DARDY IN BED CRYING. She would allow herself to be dragged to the Hollywood Bowl to listen to music, or to a museum or movie, but there was no joy. She was frightened for her future. Older, frail, and miserable. "She would have high moments but then low, depressing moments. I lived at the "Villa Madrid," a beautiful place with a big terrace overlooking L.A.," Dardy said. The 1929 U-shaped apartment complex at 1338 Miller Drive was built around a courtyard with arched windows and sweeping views of the city. "And Barbara would sit in bed and cry and cry."

It began to wear on Dardy. No matter how hard she tried to lighten Barbara's mood nothing helped. Dardy would work all day, come home, try to cheer up her sister, make food, cajole her out of bed and into a shower. She did all the errands and cleaning and worrying. But after a time, "It brings you down."

Dardy found Barbara a doctor at UCLA. She was diagnosed manic-depressive. She began shock treatments.[909]

The doctor "would prescribe a medicine and it would start working after a few weeks," Dardy explained. "Then after about thirty days the medicine would stop. And we would go back, and she'd get another prescription and the same thing kept happening over and over. It would take weeks to work. Then it would stop working after a month. Then another drug." And Barbara didn't do anything or go anywhere or see anyone except Dardy.

Dardy tried to be there for her sister but it got tough. "I didn't want to come home. It's hard to be around someone so down all the time." Barbara's sons visited and it was "stressful" for Dardy. She didn't like her nephews, whom she considered spoilt, "going through the inheritance," and even one son "stole her jewelry, valued at a half million dollars."

Eventually a little apartment opened up in the same complex and Dardy suggested Barbara take it. Barbara bravely moved out.

"I would come home from work and she'd come over every night and I'd make her dinner." Barbara wasn't getting better and Dardy didn't know what to do. It was like taking care of a helpless child. Where had Barbara's light, her glow, her *joie de vivre* gone? She was a hollow shell. Dardy, always the one to pull herself up from her bootstraps and get on with things, didn't understand it. Like Lili, Barbara was unable to cope with certain changes, certain realities. Without Marx she was adrift.

Barbara possibly had always struggled with emotional issues and depression, whether she masked it or not. Perhaps it only surfaced later in life. Those around her remembered her as vivacious, caring, generous, and gracious, but "extreme." Had her family's propensity toward mental illness surfaced with pregnancy as some cases of bipolar disorder do? Had too many years of being spirited and pleasing and dealing with troubled children she couldn't fix finally unseated her emotional stability? Whatever the case, Barbara was very ill.

Lili was nowhere in the picture at the time, so the sole burden of propping up Barbara fell to Dardy.

On March 25, 1986, Barbara found her way down to the police station not

Idella Ruth ("Barbara") Blackadder Marx

five minutes from Dardy's apartment at San Vicente and Santa Monica Boulevard in West Hollywood. In the parking lot, sixty-two-year old Barbara put a revolver in her mouth and pulled the trigger. Her son Emmett, living in Tiburon, was notified. Two days later Barbara was cremated.[910]

"It was very hard," Dardy said. "It took days for her sons, who I guess the police called, to even call and tell me." Barbara's ashes were scattered out to sea. "The same we did with Mother."

BARBARA'S SUICIDE WOULD ECHO AN EARLIER TRAGEDY IN 1977 related to John Alfred "Ian" Blackadder.

"We were all used to his migraines," Dardy said. He had had them ever since he was a kid and broke a vertebrae in his neck after a motorcycle accident in Scotland." As time went on the frequency of the migraines grew. It was so bad Ian couldn't stand to be touched.

It is conceivable that Ian, like his two siblings, Rosemary and Frederika, and his daughter and his grandchildren, suffered from a mental illness, possibly manic-depressive or bipolar disease that is genetic.[911] Ian was taking Percodan for migraines in large doses, sometimes as much as fifteen a day.

Since at least 1962 Ian and his second wife, Marguerite Green from Illinois, had been living in Monrovia. He owned a trailer park, the Walnut Grove Mobile Park on Peck Road.

One day in September of 1977, Ian telephoned Dardy. "I miss you. I want to see you."

"How are you, Dad? You okay?"

"I'm good. Can you bring your camera out and take picture of the neighbor's wall? It's collapsing on my property."

She said she could and arranged to go out the following weekend.

He looked tired when she saw him. Not usually one who wanted his picture taken, he asked Dardy to snap photos of him holding his beloved cat.

"Take care, Dad," Dardy held his hand a little longer before getting in her car. She had a weird feeling.

He smiled.

The next day, September 28, Ian drove the nearly four miles from the trailer park and checked into a modest motel. Always the considerate gentleman, he probably did not want his wife to discover his body. Then Ian Blackadder took a pistol and shot himself in the head.

IT IS THOUGHT THAT SIGNIFICANT DEATHS COME IN THREES, AND that would prove true for Lili and her family. Dardy's son Danny had moved to France and married a French woman with whom he had a daughter. Seven or eight years later, and struggling with a serious alcohol problem, Danny was back in the states, comatose and hospitalized at UCLA, listed for six months as a John Doe. When he awoke, the hospital needed to release him into the care of someone; when contacted, Dardy referred them to Ava in New Jersey. But before Ava could arrange for help, Danny found someone to sign him out and headed straight to a liquor store.

He fell off a dock in Marina del Rey. Fifty-seven-year-old Robert Scott Minsky's body was found floating in the cold November water.

CHAPTER SIX

During the early eighties Lili developed a series of blood infections. Septicemia is a common occurrence with intravenous drug users, either by sharing a needle or reusing the same. It is also sometimes caused from frequently injecting into an inflamed spot. Septicemia is life-threatening and could have caused Lili's organs to shut down.

"I need help," Lili called Dardy in the middle of the night. "I think I'm really sick, sweetie."

Dardy sighed, wanted to say, *Where's Lorenzo? Where's your soul mate?* But why start that old argument?

Dardy dressed with no real urgency. She did wonder what she'd find as she pulled her car in front of Lili's apartment building and sat looking at the walkway to her door. It was quiet. There was a cat or two outside on the step.

Dardy knocked.

It was well after midnight and Lili hadn't bothered to lock her door. Dardy shook her head.

"Lil?" The apartment was dark, which wasn't unusual for her sister. There was a bed in the front room, piles of letters and junk around. The place smelled as if it had been locked tight.

"Oh my God," Dardy said, looking at her sister's arm.

The top of her arm was swollen, "the size of a small melon." Lili's pale, scarred skin held a brilliant blood-red streak from her wrist to her shoulder.

"We've got to get you to the hospital."

Though she didn't like hospitals, Lili couldn't put up a fight. It was that serious.

Dardy took her to the emergency room. "It exploded when they lanced it." Lili was in denial. "She kept saying it was a cat scratch." Dardy was furious. Lili stayed in the hospital for two days. "Lili and I didn't talk for three, four, five years. She was giving Lorenzo cash to buy drugs. He was taking her down the road of destruction."

Lili would write, apologizing for being a "drain" on Teedle's bank account. She was trying to sell videos of *I, Mobster* and some color negatives she had. In the meantime could Dardy pay some bills?

Though she rarely saw others, believing her beauty gone, her 1983 California ID shows Lili to still be a striking woman. Certainly the leanness of youth was gone, her face had settled into gravity. She had brown chin-length hair, her face wider, still strong, but certainly not unattractive.

"Her bone structure. The skin. Her beauty isn't even captured in pictures," Lillian Hunt's granddaughter Pearl had said. "She was so beautiful."[912]

Lili wouldn't visit salons, preferring to cut her own hair. She spent her days stringing together beads making cheap jewelry. It occupied her and was an inexpensive pastime. The years continued to roll on for Lili, aimless, drugged, and frightened.

Neighbors testified to seeing her leave the apartment completely covered up, wearing a long skirt and top. She made trips to the post office (to mail fans pictures) and to Al's Liquor a couple of blocks away to cash checks and buy booze for her and Lorenzo. And she could make it to the pawnshop just a block farther on Melrose when she was in need of cash. Eventually her excursions out would be only at night, and then not at all.

Lili began to make a *serious* business of corresponding with a smattering of fans. Since at least the seventies—and before, if one counts photos and films sold in her mail-order lingerie business—Lili had been making cash selling glossies to fans, advertising in *Movie Collector's World*. "It's my mail that I find most enjoyable today." The last decades of her life would see her most intimate relationships deepen with strangers, usually young men who had no concept of the woman they were writing. Perhaps they believed she still looked as she did in the photos she sent.[913]

Thank you for being in touch, began most of her letters.[914]

CHAPTER SEVEN

Lili called Dardy, "I have the most beautiful china bowl here." Dardy knew what
that meant: Lili had a list of things she needed. "I need a toaster" or, "Could you
get me some fresh peanut butter at the farmer's market?" Dardy bought her white
Chinese-style blouses and men's ballet shoes because her feet had grown wide. Lili
always gave her something in return even if it was only a trinket left on her doorstep.
Small things, a flower, a ribbon, or an angel she'd hang on the door. She seldom
opened the door unless absolutely necessary.

Dardy had assumed Lorenzo was gone by the very fact Lili needed her to
deliver so many things to the apartment on a regular basis. Lorenzo made himself conveniently absent during Dardy's visits. But there also came a time when
Lili wouldn't open the door for Dardy so Lorenzo might have been lurking inside,
unable to leave.

"Just leave it on the step, Tweedle," Lili would call from behind the closed door.

Every week Dardy would leave $100 worth of groceries at her front door.
"And cigarettes, I'd buy her two different brands. Occasionally gin *and* vodka.
Then I found out *he* was still living there. I was furious. Not only was I spending
my money on her, but on him. Buying *him* cigarettes and vodka. I wouldn't speak
to her for a few months. Then we'd have lunch. Eventually, I couldn't see her anymore." Lili had always been adept at keeping those in her life separate from each
other. She couldn't tell Dardy what a mess Lorenzo was, high, nearly crippled.

Lili knew Dardy would disapprove if she was caught stoned. "She *hid* in
that place."

Lili knew she was a burden and apologized, but she was so damn "terrified."

"Oh, for Christ sake's, Lili." Dardy would stand outside her sister's apartment,
staring at the dark wooden door she refused to open. "It's me."

"No. I'm not feeling good," Lili would say. Dardy hadn't seen Lili since the last crisis with her arm.

Lili relied on an early love. She sent letters and he in turn sent money. Six hundred cash. The return address was his restaurant, not his home. In one letter he sent her $2,000, which "was not so easy" to come by but the thought of her living "with roaches and everything" he could not bear. He was trying to give her much-needed "peace of mind" and begged her to spend it carefully, knowing she was "hopeless with money." He sympathized with her hard time, himself having his own health issues. He told her it was not "so bad to be alone with oneself."[915] Of course Armando had no idea she wasn't living alone.

Occasionally Lili's name surfaced. In 1985 Bob Dylan gave an interview for *Spin* magazine where he said, "Lily [*sic*] St. Cyr . . . that's my definition of hot." When she was read the quote she merely said, "That's nice." She probably didn't know who Dylan was. She wouldn't have liked his music.[916]

LIFE OUTSIDE HER DOOR WAS SCARY. SHE WOULD HIDE INSIDE WITH pen, paper, and the phone, doling out advice, telling stories, witty always, usually upbeat. Strangers became her friends. For once she *needed* others. If only to survive.

When she felt she knew a fan well enough she would tear a page from her scrapbook and send it to him. Why not give her past to her friends? Maybe by giving them to someone it would be remembered Lili St. Cyr had been someone.

In 1986 she sent a picture of her first car to Don Barreca in Elmwood Park, Illinois; another at seventeen, posing in an overgrown yard, her long curly blonde hair trailing down her back. She was wearing a short skirt that showed the gams that had made her famous.

She was conscientious to answer letters usually within a few days of receiving them. When delayed because of an "accident," she apologized. To another she mailed a jewel case that he could purchase for $20. If her luggage could talk, she joked, they would certainly have stories to tell. She was thrilled when she learned some of her items were displayed at a party. She envisioned just how the audience would view it. She had a lifetime of catering to an audience's point of view. She sent a teacup used as a prop from a photo shoot in which she'd dressed as a geisha. Little by little Lili was giving away her past.

AROUND 1987 LILI BEGAN A CASUAL CORRESPONDENCE WITH ONE OF the last men that would play a significant role in her life. His name was Pat Carroll. The young man would become an anchor, a support, and eventually the guardian of some of her history. To him she would give not only her stories but also her luggage, jewelry she made, photos, scrapbooks, and a plethora of documents that do—and don't—tell who she was.[917]

Like the others, Pat had seen a small advertisement in the back of a men's magazine. He didn't know who the barely clothed blonde was. His mother told him she had been a "stripper." Pat's father winked. "She was the greatest. Class. She was one classy lady." He decided to write her.

Lili wrote back as she typically did:

Dear Pat –
Thank you for purchasing these old photos of a bygone era. Should you wish
others, I'm not sure why you would, please write again and I can send more.
Different ones. Some are real collectors' items.
Lili

After enough correspondence she enclosed her phone number; *why don't you call sometime?* He did after working up his courage.

Pat wanted to know about her show business past.

She deflected. That was "another life," she laughed. All the privileges of her great beauty were gone. They spoke about his apartment, Lili giving advice on furnishings and décor. After just thirty minutes she told him she felt as if she'd known him her entire life.

They talked of little things, like when she shopped how tellers thought she was "crazy" because she brought her own bags. But she believed there were far too many plastic bags cluttering up the environment and she didn't want to contribute any more trash.

As was her habit, she let slip that her circumstances were tough. She didn't have stamps to mail photos. She wasn't feeling well. She was alone.

Though hardly "flush," Pat began sending little gifts. Sometimes a book, sometimes $5 and stamps. The calls became more frequent. She liked hearing about his travails working in a record store. Long hours, a shit job, really, but he could be around the music he loved, he could feel the 33s in his hands. He appreciated things and people from another era.

He called her weekly. Then daily. Months turned into years. She swore occasionally, laughed often. He could hear her smoking, drawing deeply on a cigarette. Sometimes she sounded more—tired?—a little *off* maybe. He took it for depression. She could be down and worried often.

Pat built her up as she did for him. She gave him encouragement. He assuaged her loneliness. She grew to rely on his calls.

Toward the end of her life they would talk nearly every day. Sometimes for hours, always signing off "the light bulb over my shoulder is getting hot so I have to hang up now."[918] (He would learn that quite literally the floor lamp next to her bed had no shade and the bulb would start to heat her up.) When she could no longer care for herself, Pat arranged for a buddy to look after her.

Lili became hooked on a weekly television program, *Beauty and the Beast* starring Ron Perlman and Linda Hamilton. The series was about a romance between a hairy-faced beast and an assistant district attorney who discovers a community of misfits living beneath New York City. She cried with the characters and declared it a "lucky day" when two episodes aired in the same evening. The woman who had thrilled thousands looked forward to sitting in the dark alone watching a show about outcasts.

CHAPTER EIGHT

Lili was sent low by the coming holidays. (Both Idella and Alice passed around Christmas.) It was the fall of 1987. She predictably fell into a funk around Thanksgiving, as she explained in a letter, "[I] am usually glad when it's over. Things just get too hectic with all the traffic and disruptions."

After decades of life on the road, few performers were sentimental about holidays. Lili rarely spent it with family. "Holidays were our busiest time," Dardy explained about burlesque shows.

Lili's days and nights were barren; no more packing, traveling, sipping champagne. How lonely and quiet her apartment must have felt during the holidays with the noise of families gathered nearby drifting through her windows.

At Christmas a few fans remembered her with small tokens of their affection.

After divorcing Lili, the handsome Armando did what all serious playboys of the time did: He became an avid tennis player in summer and skier in winter. He developed tendinitis in his knees. He flew to Los Angeles to see a "guru." "I called Lili to have lunch with her. She said, 'I'm not going to see you.' 'Why?' I asked. 'Armando, you'll never see me again. I want you to remember me as I was when I was beautiful.'"

Lili complained to Armando that her apartment was "like living on 125th Street in New York." Tough and dangerous. She was "petrified to go out at night." Lies. Regardless of whether she believed her neighborhood was dangerous, or if she was continuing to manipulate Armando, as she did most everyone, her final days were lived in a nice middle-class neighborhood. Hardly the "125th Street" she compared it to.

LORENZO CONTINUED ON HIS PATH OF DRUGS, LIVING IN THE BED-room, out of sight of everyone in her life. It would be years before Pat found out Lili lived with a man—and then only accidentally. Dardy too thought Lorenzo had finally gone.

Pat sent Lili Christmas music. He waited for a reply.

She wrote weeks later, apologizing; she had to go out of town for two weeks. She kept the details to herself.

Her apartment building had been tented for bugs. Lili, along with the other tenants, had to suffer the inconvenience of moving into a motel paid for by the landlords. She must have hated the exposure. And what cats she had left she couldn't bring with her.

"Dardy," Lili called her sister in a panic. "I need your help."

"What is it, Lil?" Though they hadn't spoken for a while they would pick up again as if it had been yesterday. The disagreements forgotten.

"I'm getting some papers from the government and I don't understand them." Lili never had a head for paperwork or keeping track of money.

Dardy drove the short distance to Lili's apartment. They poured over the official-looking letter.

"They have questions about mail fraud, Lili." Dardy was shocked. "Someone complained they sent you money for a picture and they never got it."

"Oh, dear." Lili pressed a hand to her forehead.

Lili showed her a stack of envelopes from fans.

"How do you keep track of what comes in and what goes out?"

"If I write on the envelope," Lili explained, "the amount they sent, that means I've sent them a picture. If I don't write on the envelope, I haven't sent them anything." It made sense to her.

"Oh, Lil," Dardy shook her head. No wonder it was all a mess. Lili easily got confused about whom she had sent—or not sent—what. Thus the mail fraud complaint.

"Well, I don't have a secretary or anything," Lili joked. They both laughed.

Dardy explained to Lili that because this involved money being sent through the mail it was a serious allegation. Lili had to keep better records.

Dardy got Lili a lined legal yellow pad and she brought pencils and paper clips and envelopes. "Here. You're going to write *everything* down. The amount you get and from who. Every name. Then make a note on your pad the amount of money they send you. All in one place. I'll make copies and send it to the Postmaster and see if we can clear this up."[919]

Dardy was able to straighten out the misunderstanding and keep Lili out of jail. Now wouldn't those headlines have been something? *Seventy-Year-Old Former Stripper in Jail for Mail Fraud*. Lili would never have survived the publicity—the photographs. She would have been humiliated to have been found out. Aging was a fault she had succumbed to. Fans would be so disappointed to know she wasn't the beauty in her photos. She was through with tabloids and publicity. No more pictures would be taken of Lili St. Cyr.

CHAPTER NINE

For Christmas of 1989 Lili asked Pat for a phone call. She would like to hear a voice on Christmas morning from a friend. Oh, and a calendar. Her calendar was practically a secretary at this point. She warned, this year she was not sending cards out.

Her apartment was stacked with her old photos, and Lorenzo's stuff. She complained about the lack of space. Bedrooms, closets, fireplaces in Canyon Drive, all gone. A yard. A fenced courtyard. Privacy. All gone. Looking on the bright side, she had Pat. She thanked him for "saving her neck more times than maybe you realize."

Lili probably liked to fantasize about Pat. Her last prince. Handsome? Tall? Did he look like Armando or Paul? She wanted to send him some marvelous gold watch or something, have a cute car delivered. But, "Alas, we met too late for all that, my dear." Instead she would just have to send her best wishes and prayers.

Incredibly, Dardy managed to drag Lili to a matinee of *Pretty Woman*. "Once we went to the Beverly Center and she refused to get in the elevator, instead walking up stairs. During the middle of the movie she got up and said 'I've had enough.' And left." If a movie didn't meet her expectation, she left. She had no patience for anything. Dardy thought either she didn't like it or maybe her back was hurting. "She would just get up and go. She didn't feel like she had to explain anything to anyone."[920] Some things about Lili never changed.

That same year, 1990, Dixie Evans started the first "Miss Exotic World Pageant" at her goat farm in the desert. She sent out a press release announcing that Lili St. Cyr would attend. Dixie had fallen on hard times; deep into alcoholism she was living out in the desert with a friend, another exotic, Jennie Lee, known as the Bazoom Girl.[921]

Jennie had moved to Helendale, California, with her husband, Charlie. It was her retreat of sorts. Like so many of the strippers who had nowhere to go when burlesque died, they found themselves adrift, scrapping by. No one cared about their former type of entertainment.

Jennie casually started collecting stripper memorabilia. Stuff no one wanted. It would grow into a passion that Dixie would share, eventually taking over for Jennie when she passed away in 1990. It had been both women's hopes to start a museum, which they did—to a degree—in their home in the Mojave Desert. It was called "Exotic World." Dixie, who was sixty-four, wore sequined gowns and long gloves when she gave the odd interview.

Lili had rung out to the desert. "Dixie, it's Lili."

Dixie, in her usual enthusiastic voice, said, "Lili! How are you?"

"I'm fine. You're getting as much attention now as I did when I was at my heights."

"Yes. Exotic World's been in the news."

Dixie said she missed the old days.

"I need the address of Marta Becket," Lili requested.[922] Becket was an older former ballerina living in Death Valley Junction, continuing to dance for anyone who showed up in the abandoned theatre she had adopted.

Lili explained, "Marta once sent me a check for $25."

"Are you okay, Lili? Need any help?"

Lili would take help wherever she could get it. "It's tough. I have no money. No help."

"I'll see what I can do," Dixie promised.[923] In the coming weeks Dixie would rally her forces and her formidable contacts. One such benefactor was Dusty Sage, a former stripper who ran an animal refuge. She began sending Lili care packages of food and stationery. Charles Tlucek, a prominent Vegas accountant (according to Dixie) for the casinos, would send Lili a check. "For $10,000. He was from New Jersey and had always admired her. I tried to get her to come out here and live in the desert," Dixie told me. "But she wouldn't. She was always a recluse. She never mingled with the girls. All the exotics admired her. They looked up to Lili. They just worshiped her."

Why do you think that was?

"She was such a presence!" Dixie exclaimed. "I saw her at the Follies. It is indelible in my mind. The curtain opened. She was at the top of the stairs. There was a solid glass tub at the bottom. There were pink and lavender bubbles blowing. She told a story. Lili always told a regular story. She had gorgeous gowns that she twirled across the stage. At a particular show, the phone rang onstage. Actually rang. And the music went down low. Lili picked up the phone, shook her head no. She smiled and laid back down on bed and you just knew that was the guy she loved. Then she'd get up, spray on perfume. Try on a different gown. This particular night it was champagne colored and slinky satin. Real gorgeous! And a mink coat. Well, we all had coats back then. Soon a man's hand would poke through the curtains with roses. She would reach for it and be lead off stage. Every teeny thing she did. The details! It was mesmerizing! She didn't look at the audience. And the audience was absolutely quiet."

Why don't you think she became a big Hollywood star?

"Oh, she got offers. But she told me she couldn't remember lines. She had a memory problem. Always had. Didn't do very well in school. She lost her memory in Canada, I think she said. Got beat up. And she had problems with this preacher. There was some trauma and some man actually found her. Had to take her in. He found her wandering around or she had no money or something dramatic like that."[924]

Did you like her?

"Oh, I adored her! She made it big."

Made what big?

"Burlesque! She made it big! Lillian Hunt, who ran the Follies, told this great story about Lili working at the Follies and this guy sees the show. Lillian told Lili some men, studio executives, wanted to see her. Lili was backstage, half-nude, her hands in two crystal bowls of lotion, leaning back as cool as could be. She says, 'Tell them to make an appointment.'

"Lillian Hunt says, 'Now Lili, put on some clothes. We've never had studio executives here. Go out and talk to them.' Lili just says, 'Have them make an appointment.' Well, an appointment for Lili at the studio was arranged. She arrived but left because no one had left an order for her to be driven onto the lot. When Lillian Hunt heard about it she exploded. 'Well, I would have had to park a couple blocks away and gotten my shoes dirty walking,' Lili says. So the meeting was rescheduled. When Lili arrived at the studio the executives were lined up with bouquets of roses. There was just no one like Lili!"

CHAPTER TEN

Sometime in 1992 Lili again went into the hospital. She was growing more dependent on Pat Carroll. One afternoon he called Lili, who was back at home. She was audibly distraught. She asked him to call back.

He did a half hour later. All she would say was she had things "to regret."

He didn't realize until he hung up that it was Mother's Day. Was she missing hers or regretting she had never been a mother? Pat didn't know.

"I'm paying for my sins," was all she would tell him.

By 1993, Lili, at seventy-six, was almost a total recluse. She was in ill health. She still smoked, drank occasionally, and was shooting heroin, to what degree was anyone's guess. Heroin was her only fantasy world now that *Beauty and the Beast* was off the air.

She surprised Pat during one conversation. "Guess who called me today?"

"Who?"

"Artie Shaw."

"What did he call about?" Pat asked.

"He's having a party and wants me to come."

"Are you going?"

"Of course not. I haven't talked to him in a million years and he calls me out of the blue," Lili marveled, clearly pleased.

"How come you're not going?"

"I don't go to parties anymore. We talked for about five minutes and exhausted every point of interest and that was it. It was nice of him to think of me."[925]

IN 1996 AT THE AGE OF SEVENTY-NINE, LILI KICKED HER HEROIN HABIT. Though hardly by choice.

Lili was desperately ill and went into the hospital. To recover she was sent to a rehabilitation facility under the name Willis Van Schaack, sharing a room with a stranger. Dardy had dropped out of the picture, pushed out by the presence of Lorenzo and Lili's willingness to continue down the path with him.

Unable to obtain drugs, Lili's body would have gone into withdrawal. It must have been awful, nerve-shattering, for the frail old lady she had become.

Her stomach would cramp, her bowels would empty. The ever-present pain in her legs and back would return. She would sweat. Her anxiety would double. Depression would crush her. She would *crave* more drugs. The occasional gin or vodka wouldn't bring the same numbing relief.

Pat called and worried when there was no answer.

Finally she picked up. She explained that she had had some trouble but was back now.

She was so mysterious. He didn't push it.

It was a cold January and she had no heat—maybe she couldn't afford it—in the apartment. *I turn the stove on to stay warm.*

"I'll send you money for a space heater," Pat offered.

As nice as it might have sounded, as necessary as it might have been, how would she get to a store and buy it?

"I've just about run out of my perfume." White Shoulders, he knew. She'd been wearing it for decades.[926]

He gathered her requests and stuck in some money, hoping it would get her through a little longer.

Between August and November of 1997 Lorenzo was in and out of the VA hospital five times. Dardy thought it might have been gangrene.

Lili panicked, worried something was going to happen to Lorenzo. They had tumbled together for so long down the rabbit's hole she knew she would never climb out with anyone else even though it was hard—if not outright impossible—for her to care for him. Only occasionally did she even make the difficult foray out, bundled in scarf and hat and a long skirt.

Selling her photos remained her major source of income. Chump change. Nothing compared to what she used to toss away on a beautiful fur. She still had some designer gowns stuffed in the little closet in the hall.

Finally, old worn curtains were thrown out and in their place she taped magazine pages to her windows. She did have fans who occasionally showed up trying to get her to open the door. She would out-Garbo Garbo. There would be no pictures of her ducking down the street, a man's jacket pulled up to her neck, gray hair blowing across her panicked eyes. Lili found it interesting how both were reclusive and seeking peace that escaped them both.[927]

IT WAS 1998. PAT MADE HIS DAILY FOUR P.M. CALL TO CHECK IN ON LILI. She told him she had a spider bite, apparently quite painful. They talked for a little bit, with Pat promising to call the next night.

The next evening a man answered, saying he was Lili's neighbor and that she had been bitten by a spider and had to be hospitalized at Cedars-Sinai. The two chatted for a few minutes; the man [Lorenzo, unbeknownst to Pat] was "friendly and funny."

Concerned, Pat tracked Lili down in the hospital. She had checked in as Willis Van Schaack. As she had become again.

Pat told her about the call. "Someone answered the phone. He said he was your neighbor."

She paused. She launched into an explanation as best she could.

Pat found Lili "paranoid." She liked neither hospitals nor doctors and wanted to go home. Another evening he found her distressed, "suspicious about her entire situation."

When she recovered they transferred her to a nursing home. Two elderly ladies shared a room with the notoriously private Lili. She hated it.

The only way she could talk to Pat was to have someone wheel her out to the pay phone in the hall. Lili retained her unique sense of humor. She relayed that most of the nurses' aides were Filipino and she told Pat she was looking for one to be his wife. Pat paid to have a phone in her room. It is intriguing to think of whom else she might have called.

While Lili recuperated Lorenzo returned to the VA hospital. Pat thought it was the Long Beach Medical Center. His symptoms were serious, lower extremity weakness, incontinence, and epidural abscess (pus between the brain and spinal cord). He was diagnosed with pneumonia and hypertension, septic shock. They would stabilize him and he checked out in February. Released, Lorenzo was transferred to some home, possibly in the San Fernando Valley.

Somehow Lili managed to make a brief trip back to her apartment. Bill, a friend of Lorenzo's, was apparently camping out in her apartment surrounded by all of his possessions.

Lili told him to get out. He did.

Lili had had enough of the nursing home. She claimed to pay an orderly $2,000 to "spring her."[928]

Lorenzo wasn't at the apartment. He was gone. The two would continue to speak but never see each other again. Her longest relationship had ended. Lili was finally truly alone.

PAT WORRIED ABOUT LILI. HIS FRIEND WAS ALONE. DARDY WAS OUT OF the picture. He offered to fly out to California to help her organize the mess Lorenzo and/or Bill had made of her place. Lili must have been desperate because she finally agreed. So in May of 1998 Pat flew to California. His friend Ian Macdonald had moved to Los Angeles and Pat stayed at Ian's fiancée's apartment, borrowing one of his cars.[929] After fourteen years of a phone friendship he was going to see Lili St. Cyr face to face.

Barely taking time to clean up and change clothes Pat headed over to Lili's after his flight landed.

"It was late afternoon . . . and I could smell a mixture of Salem cigarettes and incense as I walked through the little courtyard," he remembered. "There were mourning doves cooing in the bushes as I knocked on her door for the first time."

He heard a woman's voice tell someone to open the door.

Surprising Pat, a "Latin-looking" man in black pants and a white shirt opened the door.

A cloth screen stood directly behind him. He wasted no time in directing Pat around the screen. And there sat his friend.

Lili was on her bed in men's pajama bottoms and a man's T-shirt, smoking and watching her little portable TV with rabbit ears.

Pat held out his hand and introduced himself awkwardly.

The walls were beige and looked as if it had been a while since anyone had painted. By now Lili had lived on Plymouth for over two decades. The ceiling was peeling in spots. She was a frail, sickly old woman.

Lili eyed Pat up and down. Whomever she had envisioned in her mind, "She wasn't impressed. Victor Mature I'm not."

It was a painful meeting. "After the daily phone conversations over the many years, I guess she was disappointed that I didn't look like a knight in shining armor."

Abruptly she dismissed the "orderly." "I dine alone and don't like to be watched while I eat."

He was surprised at her "officious" angry manner.

Like many older people in her circumstances, Lili was frustrated at her need for help, the betrayal of her body.

Pat found her to be "pretty cantankerous most of the time and it was hard to get a read on exactly what she needed done." It was heart-breakingly obvious she was utterly unable to take care of herself any longer.

But she was determined not to go back into a hospital or nursing home ever again. She was not going to leave her apartment.

Lili told Pat how he would enter her apartment. She claimed there was no key, so he would need to slide a credit card over the lock and pop it. Pat tentatively made some suggestions regarding cleaning and painting and moving some of the sparse furniture, but Lili wasn't interested.

"I like things as they are," she told him.

After the first day he never saw the orderly again. With thoughts of leaving in a few days, he gently mentioned that his friend Ian and his fiancée, Kathleen, lived nearby. Ian could easily could come by and bring her food, help her. Lili didn't want someone she didn't know around. Lili acted embarrassed at what she had become—how she looked—and it made her unpleasant.

"I visited her every day and spoke with her on the phone but she remained distant," Pat said. "I was completely flummoxed and tried to figure out how I could best assist her while I was there."

After a week of awkwardness, where she grew angrier and acted as if she didn't want him around at all, Pat left to return to Silver Springs. "Just before I flew home, I called her from a pay phone in LAX and she was very indignant."

Lili accused him of coming only to visit Ian and Kathleen and not her. She said his trip had been a mistake. "It would be best if I didn't call anymore."

Pat apologized for not being more helpful. "She hung up on me."

Deflated but not undaunted, Pat called when he returned home.

Lili was a little friendlier but kept the conversation brief. "By the next day she seemed to have forgotten that she was mad at me and everything was back to normal. I think she was so used to knowing me as a voice on the phone that finally meeting me might have seemed weird to her. I also think that she was starting to experience mild dementia so that made things more difficult."[930]

It must have been torment for her to reveal her current face and body.

Lili fell back into a pattern of requests of Pat, which frustrated him, as many things could have been taken care of when he had been there.

One night she called Pat. The French doors leading to the lawn out front were open. Earlier in the day she had managed to open them, but now she couldn't get out of bed and she was cold.

Not knowing what else to do, Pat called her local Thai restaurant that delivered her nightly dinner. "The restaurant sent the delivery guy over to close the doors." It was at this point Pat became more insistent she let Ian help.

So Lili called Ian. His fiancée, Kathleen, answered. Not pleased, Lili left her number.

When Ian Macdonald called back he said he could come that afternoon. She asked him if he was a "hep cat."

He said he thought so.

"Can you pick a lock?"

Lili in the garden

"I don't know."

"You know, with a credit card like you see on TV," she said, and hung up.

Ian showed up with a small bag of groceries. He was dismayed by the apartment, not exactly clean, sparsely furnished with nicotine-stained walls. It had the "air of a junky's den." The place needed a good airing out. "It looked like it had been that way for years if not decades." He was startled to see an old woman with white hair sitting on her bed in the middle of the living room.

He paused in the doorway, credit card in hand after jimmying the simple lock. "Hello."

"Close the door," she commanded in a shaky voice, and looked away. He did.

Later she would tell him he looked like her first husband, Cordy. Possibly that allowed him entry. He would never leave her life. Neither would she really leave his.

Ian began coming over on a daily basis, armed with groceries and cigarettes. The only thing in her refrigerator was what he put there: "milk, oranges, vodka, sometimes bread, and ready-to-eat meals . . . her favorite was Crab Louie salad from Vons."

For being so dependent on him she never asked for anything nicely. He wasn't "enamored of her like Pat." But he could feel her fear and he felt sorry for her.

She hated having him there. Hated the fact she needed him. She prided herself on her independence and to have that taken from her by age and ill health brought out a beast in her. She didn't feel the need to charm.

"She was scared," he said, "and bitter. She didn't want to be seen in the shape she was in. I mean she looked nothing, *nothing* like she used to." He sympathized with her anger and fear of aging and all the endless betrayals her body played on her. He didn't fawn over her; instead he treated her both "sweet and sour," which she seemed to like.

She didn't leave her bed.

He tackled the job of cleaning out the back bedroom, which was a mess. A twin bed, walker, food wrappers. He also found evidence of drug use and bottles of pills. "I took the valium." He threw everything else out in a couple of large trash bags.[931]

What was Lili doing when he visited?

"She talked, and talked, and yelled at me, and bossed me around . . . stuff like that. I would like to say she was a sweet old lady, but she wasn't."

"I can only recall two times she walked to the bathroom, once she needed my help. It was weird because she needed me to pull down her underwear but wouldn't let me. So I remained a gentleman and helped her get back to her bed after she was done." He said, "I am not sure what she did other than lay there and complain. She kept her cards close to her chest. Remember, I didn't even know she had a sister or that she ever had other visitors. She was a professional . . . on many levels."

Lili was bent and her face was shockingly decompressed. From the drugs, from the neglect. She no longer had teeth. Nor did she have false ones. Time indeed had been cruel to one of the most beautiful women of her time.

CHAPTER ELEVEN

Lili St. Cyr, the Contessa of Las Vegas, the Queen of the Sunset Strip, the sexiest, most celebrated, highest-paid stripteaser in the world, had shrunk to a slip of paper taped on the wall near her phone. In shaky big block letters she had written less than a dozen numbers including "Pat Carroll, Elio, Mike market, Ian, St. Cyr Lingerie . . ."

She was the type of lady, despite her grouching, that would always need a man. She needed Ian.

When she wasn't bragging about seducing men, she spoke about her cat Teeny and the lot next to her house. She was feeling nostalgic for Canyon Drive. She constantly asked him if he could score for her. *You sure you don't have anything? You can't get me something? Don't you know anyone in the army? They always have morphine.* She confessed to Ian "that her lifestyle choice got her to 'this place.'" To the walls of the three-room apartment. Then Lili did the unexpected. She began to cry. "One of a few times she cried about her past, leading me to assume there was some shame involved," Ian said. "I never would push her further during those times. She had a sharp mind, which would often seem like a curse to her."

Pat and Lili continued their daily phone calls. Once she woke him in the middle of the night, confused. She thought he was in Los Angeles. She was anxious. He assured her to hang tight, Ian would be over in a few hours.

Ian believed she knew she was dying and she was scared. It contributed to her wild moods. Because of her rapid deterioration, he brought a nurse friend over to take her blood pressure. She must have been in bad shape to allow another person to see her. Especially a woman.

"Cancer," the nurse told Ian when they left.

THE LAST TWO MONTHS OF LILI'S LIFE WERE DIFFICULT. SHE WAS "FRAIL, scared. Terrified of dying." She had come to regret losing contact with her family.

She said they were all dead. She was never out of her men's pajamas and "old lady slippers."In fact, she wore her men's undershirts until they were dirty and then tossed them away.

Pat made another trip in December and found her to be a "pussycat."[932] One morning she was sitting in bed mending. Though her eyes were covered with cataracts she expertly threaded a needle. She asked him to tear off a small piece of her bed sheet so she could use it to mend her clothes. Was she sure she wanted him to do that?

"It doesn't matter," she shrugged.

Lili was easier on Pat, perhaps resigned to the reality of her knight. He did so much for her. He helped her mail a letter and some papers to Lorenzo.

Lili and Lorenzo hadn't seen each other in months—since his hospitalization.[933] He might as well have been an ocean away. They couldn't get to each other, if they even wanted to. They kept in contact via the phone.

On Christmas morning Pat called. Lili was in tears. Her first Christmas truly alone in decades.

In January she surprised Pat one day. "I wish I could talk to a priest."

He could hear in her voice the distress, the honest desire to *talk* to someone. It was impossible to find a priest, to convince them to respond to a stranger calling halfway across the country to pay a home visit to someone the priest had never met and wasn't even a member of his church. Or any church. Lili had never been religious. She had never attended church. However, on the bookcase near her bed was a cheap statute of St. Francis, her favorite saint. The patron saint of animals.

A crucifix hung over her bed next to a large picture of an Italian villa.

IAN TOLD LILI HE WOULD FIND SOMEONE TO LOOK IN ON HER WHEN he and Kathleen went on their honeymoon. Lili seemed crushed. Betrayed.

When Ian returned he called Lili. "We want to show you photos of the honeymoon. Is it okay if Kathleen and I come over?"

He was surprised that Lili agreed. In all the months she had never been nice to Kathleen on the phone. But she was perfectly sweet and lovely in person.

They brought her dinner. Kathleen, utterly aglow, showed Lili the wedding album.

Kathleen thought she was interested, maybe even happy for them. Kathleen, young, excited, and proud of her new life, was unaware of Lili's reactions but Ian, who knew her better, observed Lili as she seemed to "deflate." Maybe she recognized the sort of happiness that had eluded her.

They left Lili alone. Ian smiled as he closed the door. "See you in the morning, Lili."

"'Night."

Pat called a few minutes later. They chatted for three and a half minutes. Just long enough for Pat to reassure Lili he was thinking of her.

Lili said the two had brought her an early dinner. "What was it?" Lili laughed. She couldn't remember. She sounded weak, but seemed happy and had enjoyed seeing the wedding pictures. "You know the art of photography is very important," she said. She mentioned how important it had been in her career.

She told Pat he was probably the best friend she ever had. She seemed to come to no small conclusion—realizing that no matter how important romances and marriages were, they could not compare to friendship. Did she realize what she had missed in life?

She seemed at peace.

Her voice was getting weaker as she talked. Pat wanted to let her go rest.

"I love you, Lili."

"I know you do, baby." Most likely those were Lili St. Cyr's last words.

CHAPTER TWELVE

Sometime in the night a spotlight hit the silver curtains as they began to open. She was young again. As she stepped through the curtains, the music soared.

It had started with a dance.

And now it must end with one.

We will never know who her last dance partner was that night. But we can be sure she was grace personified. *La Belle Lili* would have aroused her audience. *The Able-Bodied Dancing Enchantress* would have bent her body in ways that hadn't moved in years. Graceful. Dynamic. Sensuous.

Perhaps "Fascination" was playing. *Languid Lili* had used it in so many of her acts.

For the first time in decades she could rotate her hips freely, she could swivel back and forth minus any discomfort. She could grind. She could do all the things she had been accused of. She had freedom. Her torso swayed. Her legs were light and lifted, kicking above her head. Her arms were lean and strong.

The Body Beautiful emerged from the curtain, a sparkling tiara on her blonde hair, and the audience applauded. They were waiting for her. She feared them. She hated them. She needed them. She loved them. And they loved her.

One arm, then the other, twirled above her platinum curls. Amazing, there was no stiffness. The arms were tanned and free of scars and needle marks and decades of abuse.

She smiled. *Montreal's Sweetheart* held a secret. Her head bent backward. She leaned over, her legs split apart. Her heart felt light.

Her partner took her in his arms. Strong. Protecting. He would never leave her. He was strong enough for both of them. He loved her. *The American Venus*.

Off came some clothing. *The Ample Anatomy's* form was perfection. No longer thick, no longer hunched. She didn't shuffle. She soared. Diamonds adorned her like feathers.

Tonight she would stuff her garter belt with hundreds, kiss Sadie good night, and rush home into the arms of her lover. They were dance partners on and off the stage, which is how she had always wanted it. A partner forever.

One more turn across the stage. *The High Priestess of Sex* was hot. Her brow bathed in sweat. Euphoric. Dancing. Her head lead the way as she turned and turned and turned again.

It was the need to dance, whether on a porch on a frosty arid morning or in a smoky, steamy nightclub.

It started with a dance.

Cordy tried to grasp her hand to hold her to him. She managed to leap away. Dick looked at her with resignation, knowing she had to jeté beyond what he could offer. Paul held her too tightly, suffocating her. She kicked her legs, arched her back; the audience sighed.

Armando looked at her with brilliant blue eyes. Sad. Misunderstood. Ted laughed as she twirled in his arms. Mistrustful. He wanted to absorb her fame. Murphy disappointed. Jimmy made her heart race with his smile. She couldn't have him. Frankie bemused. Hurt. Jimmy again. Others. She twirls and splits away. She fights with her body arched. She is breathtaking. She feels so lonely. She searches for another partner as hers leaves the stage. For a moment Joe is there, but his movements are awkward and he leaves. Lorenzo is too hazy. He disappears in vapor like one of his magic tricks, his arm reaching out to her.

Her body trembles as the violin strings vibrate through her. Her wrists circle over her head. She is on point. She then crouches down. She is free of the pain that has racked her body. She is happy. She is on her back. Her legs kick, she can feel the Catholic church condemning. She laughs, her skin is tanned and slick and smooth. She knows all eyes are on her and she is in her power.

It is her dance. It is in her blood. It is her. She arches forward. She reaches for the curtain. She takes a last look back at the audience—her life—all that has been. A finger to her full blood-red lips as if she's eaten all of life she can. There is no more. A knowing smile. They will forget. But it is enough. She once was. She once was there. Knowing it started with a dance.

Lili?

Yes.

Lili? He was calling her. It was time to answer.

It was time to take a bow.

IAN SLICED HIS CREDIT CARD THROUGH THE SEAMS OF HER DOOR. LILI lay on her bed, her arms by her side. "Her eyes and mouth were open . . . it seemed like she saw something and gasped one last and final breath," Ian recalled. "A surprise perhaps. It always made me wonder what she saw."[934]

IN THE DAYS FOLLOWING LILI'S DEATH, DARDY WOULD "TEAR" through the apartment, ripping the backs of pictures. "Looking for something," possibly anything of that might have remained.[935] Lili had no hidden money or jewelry or anything of value stashed.

There were old dresses crammed into the tiny hallway closet. Dardy took them and gave them to a "Spanish speaking" woman at a bus stop, then gave the woman a ride home. Shades of Alice.[936] Dardy doled out things to Pat and Ian. There wasn't much from a life that had been lived so spectacularly.

It wouldn't be until June when Pat could come to California. He and Dardy planned a memorial.

Dardy drove up Bronson Canyon. They found a spot in the hills across from 2639 Canyon Drive. They could see her house. It was June 2.

The next day was hot and sunny on what would have been Lili's eighty-second birthday.

Dardy hung a little bracelet around the oleander and little brass bells on the trees around the hills across from Lili's house. "She loved the sound of bells. She had them hanging all over her house."[937]

The four perched on the hillside. Dardy, Ian, Kathleen, and Pat. A sister, a fan, a student, and his wife. A small contingent for someone who had thrilled so many.

They planted the oleander bush. Ian read a poem Pat had selected and a couple of Bible verses as well as "Jesus Christ the Apple Tree":

> *For happiness I long have sought*
> *And pleasure dearly I have bought*
> *For happiness I long have sought*
> *And pleasure dearly I have bought*
> *I missed of all but now I see*
> *'Tis found in Christ the apple tree.*

Dardy had brought a tape deck and they listened to Lili's favorite song, "Fascination."

> *It was fascination*
> *I know*

And it might have ended
Right then, at the start

As the song spread over the canyon, around Lili's sanctuary and beyond the white heat of the day, Dardy opened a small urn, hardly big enough to hold the force once known as the "Anatomic Bomb." Pat and Ian each lifted some ashes as a breeze stirred though the trees, sending the bells tinkling.

Lili?

Dardy uncorked a bottle of champagne. The four drank the champagne, then tossed their glasses down the hill. The fifth glass was for Armando, who was grieving in his own way across the country.

The tiny group of mourners looked down at Lili's house and up at the sky.

And so they said good-bye to Lili St. Cyr.

PART SIX

APHRODITE

*"My experience with men has brought me
many disappointments"*

—LILI ST. CYR

EPILOGUE

Lili St. Cyr made headlines for the last time. Obituaries mentioned suicide attempts, troubled marriages; they marveled over the bathtubs, whispered about drugs and poverty. Ted Jordan got another fifteen minutes when they dug up his scurrilous charge of an affair with Marilyn.

The end was not how she would have written it. She would have remained cloistered with a handsome prince in her beloved home with her luxuries: a chauffeur on hand, help in the kitchen, a hand-carved Italian bed to recline on.

"The end was so sad," niece Ava Minsky Foxman said. "So sad."[938]

"Tragic story," Armando summed up Lili's life. "Such a waste."

But does her end nullify all that came before?

As a young girl, painfully aware that she didn't come from a "good family" with money and a fancy house, she began dancing away from Marie Van Schaack toward the glittery Lili St. Cyr of her imagination. She dreamed big, wishing and wanting and working toward a better life.[939] She vowed to live and work "on a lavish scale."[940] And she accomplished it, with a string of lovers and all the accoutrements of success that she desired. She hadn't wanted success by playing the marriage game. She would obtain it on her own.

In the end she was "cut off from the world, as women who have lived only for love" were.[941] Had Lili lived only for love? She claimed to. Her actions led us to believe so. Yet, after Ted Jordan she never tried to kill herself again in a fit of passion. Perhaps the histrionics were over. Perhaps the heart-pounding love also.

Lili's romances were the strength and weakness of her life. They gave her impetus to live large, to lavish care on another whether they were worthy or not.

For Lili, being in love was like being "sick."[942] Love knocked her out. But she was hardly indiscriminate in who she gave herself to. Despite the man-eater reputation she had never been partial to one-night stands. All her relationships had potential to last. She needed to get to know a man. She never intended for her affairs to be quick weekends tossed off with abandon. Some of her affairs lasted months, some years.

Relationships for Lili held certain responsibilities that she took seriously, but, "When I'm expected to do anything, the fun goes out of it for me."[943] She fell out of love easily. Her varied love life kept gossips' tongues wagging but she was far from nymphomaniac in her pursuit of *romance.*

Relationships were a complex spider web for Lili. She hadn't been taught how to cultivate friendships or develop intimacy or the necessary sustaining give and take of marriage.

"Those sisters were on their own," Ava Minsky Foxman said about Lili and her sisters, who were forced to survive, thrive, or fail on their own. Their relationships with each other were fluid, dipping in and out of each other's lives. They all had the ability to simply move on.

In the end Lili would regret she let family drift away.

A woman of contradictions, she lived in the spotlight but revealed nothing of herself. "Very few ever penetrated the iron curtain."[944] She was a performer who didn't want to work, yet performed tirelessly. It was the ceaseless working that caused her marriages to fail. "She never had two weeks off."[945]

It wasn't the arrests and headlines that sustained her. "I do not wish to thrive on scandal but on art."[946] Work gave her something relationships did not. "As long as I have that I won't have to be dependent on anybody."[947]

She lived her life independently, fiercely, stubbornly. She made her own sometimes-fatal decisions. She made the best of most situations.

Independence and freedom were of life-sustaining importance for Lili. She would not be bound by the conventions of her time or the expectations society placed on a stripper.

"I try and give it dignity,"[948] she said about stripping.

She succeeded brilliantly. "She does things," it was noted, "to her audience that no one in the early days of burlesque dreamed could be done." But Lili had dreamed. She created Lili St. Cyr and knew how to convey "her personality across the footlights." And during her height she became "a blonde blowtorch . . . she is the atomic age version of the stripper."[949]

Lili slipped easily into burlesque. It was "a first step" she said, and she "quickly wanted out," which would prove to not be so easy.[950] It was important that she bring her imagination to the stage. Her act made her "defiant," doing what she was not supposed to. She reveled in the "bad woman" image.[951] Yet she invented her little stories, her pantomimes, so stripping was palatable.

Lili was a determined woman of supreme self-control who lost herself in drugs, the ultimate letting go of control.

She was the typical Gemini, traditional, witty, yet elusive. She sought new stimulus to hold her attention. Self-interest was the key to her survival.

She had "no great connection" with people.[952] She was neurotically introverted. Shy with a boiling anger underneath. Confident onstage, plagued by doubts off.

"Eccentric, brilliant, and complicated."[953] She was a dazzling light others sought to pull into their orbit. She abhorred prejudice, hypocrisy, censorship, and prudish thinking. She didn't judge others yet she was so often unfairly condemned.

She was labeled, belatedly and incorrectly, a feminist. Lili was simply making the best of what she could do. She wasn't a feminist cheerleader. In fact, she made fun of feminists, saying they "looked like cows."[954] She wasn't interested in fighting for others' rights. She was never political, wasn't interested in causes. She wasn't a joiner of groups or organizations. She didn't speak up.

Lili was more than her measurements, 34-24-35. She was more than her photos. She was artist, icon, and inspiration.

Lili was the first—and probably only—exotic to travel with truckloads of antique furniture, hiring her own classically trained violinist. As she stated, she "was the first stripper to get dressed onstage, the first to take a bath onstage, and the first to pantomime the great charmers of history."[955]

She performed "with a complete obliviousness of her audience—as though she were dancing to and for herself."[956] She rarely acknowledged the audience, who salivated over her beauty, because they terrified her. If they were there, she would have to please them. The responsibility was great. She explained, "If you put the best ingredients into anything, you're bound to come out with a good product." That is why her gowns and sets and music were all first-class. "I think my ideas have paid off."[957]

A great part of Lili's appeal was that "she looks cool and controlled, so expensively unattainable."[958]

What she offered was "a subtle air of intelligence and good breeding"[959] in an atmosphere that was usually far from that.

Lili was not an actress, singer, or even a spectacular dancer. Beyond pirouettes, she rarely did much true dancing. She floated and drifted. She learned what worked for her, slow and languid. She was elegance personified.

"I like to live gracefully" she told a reporter.[960] So she bought a home and decorated it with exquisite things. She wore expensive clothes and adorned herself in jewels.

She might have thought she accomplished little, but in her field and in her time she achieved much. She "raised burlesque from an all-time low—low in box-office receipts as well as in quality of presentation."[961] Lili St. Cyr was the first stripper to infiltrate Hollywood nightclubs. She was the first to conquer Las Vegas as the "resident Stripper on the Strip," making enormous sums of money and ushering in the glitzy nude era we know Las Vegas to be today.

"I don't approve of myself as a person," she said because she was conflicted by her role as stripper. Yet she remained at the top of her profession for most of her career. And though she often pretended to be indolent, she admitted that "ambition is the most important qualification" for a stripper. [962]

Lili didn't fade away after scrambling for jobs like her idol Faith Bacon, though drugs would doom them both. Lili exited gracefully when she thought it was time and with enough money to live comfortably.

Was it just money she was after? She loved money and how it could change her life but "wasn't attached to it." Money was a by-product of success. It gave her freedom. She was proud of her house, yet easily gave it up for Lorenzo. She bought lovers and husbands cars, engraved gold lighters, and expensive watches, settled apartments on them, doled out alimony. She paid for limousines and taxis and travel.

Lili St. Cyr was a self-manufactured creature. Like a girl named Norma Jean. Both women presented glamorous packages to the world to protect the vulnerable creatures behind the masks. But the similarities ended there. Lili wasn't resentful of her "character," as Monroe claimed to be. Lili thrived off of being Lili. She wasn't tormented by being called a sex symbol or a "bad" woman. She played it up. She relished the fuss it garnered. Maybe that's why she survived her demons and Monroe did not.

"Narcissistic," her niece described her. Indeed, Lili was in love with the image she crafted.

A characteristic of the narcissist is self-focus. Not discounting any help she received, she was largely her own producer, director, and publicist for over thirty years. A narcissist has a problem sustaining a relationship. Difficult for any performer on the road. They are hypersensitive to insult. As we've seen, Lili would attempt suicide numerous times when a relationship "went south." [963] She would be devastated and her self-worth eradicated.

Narcissists have haughty body language. Lili made a career of it. She used people without considering the cost to them—Dardy, Armando, Lorenzo, Pat.

She kept those in her life separate from one another so she would appear more vulnerable, more helpless. She took money and loans of cars, and sent bills to lovers, while maintaining other relationships, exploiting some for what they could do for her. She would feel twinges of "guilt." [964]

Shame is a major characteristic of narcissism. Lili grew up with shame, for a family that wasn't what it said it was, for the way her marriages and love affairs faltered, for the profession she was in.

With little education Lili had a desire to improve herself. She became a voracious reader. Her mind was nimble and quick—beset by her own doubts but smart nonetheless and slyly witty.

It is easy to trace the influences that shaped her. As a young girl she was star struck by Garbo, who taught her about the allure of mystery and withholding. She would emulate much about this Swedish sphinx.

Tom Douglas told Lili that Garbo's behavior was "specific. She lived her life exactly as she pleased."[965] That resonated with Lili. As Tom didn't intrude upon Garbo, he wouldn't with Lili, understanding the great beauties' need for privacy. Lili would emulate not only Tom's style of décor in her home and on the stage, but also the way he lived his life with Filipino servants and gilded furnishings. She ordered monogrammed towels like Douglas; they exchanged extravagant gifts of jewelry.

From Virginia Burroughs Lili cultivated society manners, "kindness, humor."[966]

Photographer Bruno Bernard was a friend and a collaborator. He transformed Lili from burlesque stripper to "goddess." Many of her most famous shots they created together. *Variety* claimed that Bruno had taken over five thousand photos of her by 1957.[967]

Offstage Lili led a surprisingly simple life, reading or hosting quiet dinner parties. She wasn't in the tabloids for drunken behavior or outrageous dress. She didn't attend premieres or galas.

In her Canadian biography Lili said she enjoyed playing the role of a dominating woman who punished men, but it was they who often punished her. Men offered Lili different things at different times in her evolution.

Cordy gave her the first taste of fame and travel; Dick Hubert provided attention when she was desperate to break from an anonymous chorus. Paul Valentine perfected her act. Armando was the man who made her forget Jimmy Orlando; he brought class and European sensibility, reflected in her choice of designer gowns. Ted Jordan was a handsome braggart but she felt protected on his arm.[968]

Joe Zomar was reliable; he had a job. Lorenzo might have been an attempt to recapture her youth. His free spirit certainly resonated with her. He was nonjudgmental and content to share a fantasy world beside her, offering her the final respite from pain.

Jimmy Orlando was Lili's first true love. He died in 1992 at age seventy-six. He had married the daughter of Lili's former lover, Eddie Quinn, when she was in her early forties, though she had known him for years. It was presumably his second marriage. They had a daughter and he remained in Canada for the rest of his life.[969]

Paul Valentine's second marriage to Flevur Ali Khan lasted until his death in 2006 at ninety-four. He largely never received credit for all he did for Lili: the bathtub act, pushing her, the inclusion of classical music in her repertoire. She was grateful for his faith in her and never denied the importance he played in her success.

Armando died in 2011 during the writing of this book. Dardy thought part of Lili's and Armando's problem was his jealousy. "He was very European." Lili liked the manners and way of dressing, but she didn't care for his Mediterranean machismo.[970]

After their divorce Ted Jordan continued to act in films and television, sometimes billed as Eddie Friedman. A nine-year stint on *Gunsmoke* in the seventies filled up most of his resume, with minor parts on *Dallas* and *The Waltons.*

When he wasn't trying to gain limelight off Marilyn, claiming they had been lovers and intimates for twenty years, he claimed the same about Lili. When neither worked he wrote they were lesbian lovers. His biography about Norma Jean was a self-serving vehicle, a trashy, gossipy account of no substance. He claimed Lili had affairs with other women, an accusation she laughed at. Didn't he know she didn't like women?

Jordan claimed strange things in the book: That Marilyn imitated Lili's "French-Canadian accent." When he asked Lili, "Don't you read the papers?" She replied "yes." She *never* read the papers. Ted, the poor little boy who chased fame and his father's approval, never achieved either. He never earned the celebrity he craved, sulking in the shadow of his famous uncle, his infamous marriage to Lili, and lastly in his modest acquaintance with a sex symbol. He died in 2005 in Palm Desert at age eighty, having lived with his mother for years.

Donald Markick was despised by many, hidden from most. Like Lili he played fast with the truth. A lost soul. Besides the drugs, ultimately insignificant for Lili. Not a grand love but her last one, one who knew how to tie her to him so she would never leave.

Donald continued in and out of the ER. In 2000 he was admitted with abdominal pain and lower-extremity pain. He was diagnosed with a urinary tract infection. He died a day after his sixty-ninth birthday on February 12, 2003, of chronic obstructive pulmonary disease. He had been living at a nursing home, the Vermont Care Center in Torrance.

On his death certificate his profession was listed as a cabdriver for five years. He was cremated and his ashes scattered off the coast of Los Angeles.

DID LILI RETREAT FROM THE WORLD? OR DID SHE INCREMENTALLY SLIP out of sight? At the end confined as much by her vanity as her physical limitations, each year a little further in the shadows?

Many floundered with the death of burlesque. They found themselves becoming, as Dixie Evans said, "old, fat . . . something's gone wrong in our lives" to do nothing but sit "in a room with our pictures."[971]

Lili certainly wasn't the first to preserve the image she had meticulously crafted. Marlene Dietrich did it. Ava Gardner too. Both great beauties who became recluses. But, like Dietrich, it wasn't until the last wretched, ailment-filled decade that Lili

Lili as Aphrodite

truly closed the door. Because "she looked *nothing* like who she had been."[972]

Lili believed her value—in her own and other's eyes—was her beauty. She knew she would lose everything when her looks went. And that was the tragedy of Lili St. Cyr. "Her attitude about her looks shaped her life."[973] And when she was no longer the kind of beauty she had been, Lili St. Cyr crumbled into nothing.

It wasn't phobia that made Lili hide like former employer Howard Hughes. And it wasn't until she was in her seventies that she stopped seeing people. Prior to that she had worked and been photographed and enjoyed making headlines for almost thirty years, including her quiet appearances at the Undie World at least into the 1980s. Greta Garbo's career encompassed two decades, but she lived another *fifty* years blocking her image with coats, collars, glasses, and an upheld hand.

Lili did not pull a Bettie Page, who vanished from the public for nearly sixty years, in and out of mental institutions.

Lili concluded, "I don't disillusion myself. If there is any art in my performance, it's simply in creating an atmosphere in a short time, telling a story and leaving an impression of beauty."[974]

Dardy wanted to recall the happy times—"We had such fun,—when three beautiful sisters stunned a room into silence. "She had such a good life. She enjoyed it. Most people didn't do a tenth of what she did."

Back in 1953 Lili claimed, "All my life my real ambition has been to play Aphrodite."[975]

Lili's "lucky photo" of herself was Aphrodite, the goddess of beauty, pleasure, and love.[976]

Perhaps that's all Lili had ever wanted. Beauty. Pleasure. Love.

NOTES

INTRODUCTION

1. Jordan, *Norma Jean.*
2. "a certain stand-offishness" Peter Diome, "Lili St. Cyr—Art Plays Minor Role In World of Burlesque," *The Gazette,* n.d.
3. Guild, *And Men My Fuel* (hereafter MMF).
4. "vulgar" St. Cyr, *Ma Vie de Stripteuse* (hereafter MVS).
5. "her sexy beauty" James Bacon, unknown newspaper article, n.d.
6. "necessary" MVS.
7. "obsessed with a man" Dawson, "The Durability of Lili."
8. "responsible" MVS.
9. "People bowed down to her" Dardy to author.

PART ONE
CHAPTER ONE

10. "I'm a northern girl," Letter from Lili to her friend Pat Carroll. She made this reference often.
11. "Lili people are going to think" Pat Carroll to author.
12. "women past their prime" Colette, *Chéri.*
13. "touches" Dardy to author.
14. You could hear a pin drop" Dawson, "The Durability of Lili
15. "With the fretful anticipation" "Lili St. Cyr's Royal Wedding Night," *Man Magazine,* August 1956.
16. "Lili is always the heroine" Dawson, "The Durability of Lili."
17. "anyone who doesn't understand the story" *Los Angeles Times,* April 15, 1948.
18. "she had the wonderful haughtiness" Lili's obituary, *Los Angeles Times,* February 4, 1999.

CHAPTER TWO

19. Lili's first cousin Ellie Hiatt insisted Lili's grandmother (later called Alice) told them Lili was named Willis at birth (and that Alice was named Marie). I believe both are Alice's inventions. No documentation supports either claim and is another example of both Alice and Lili rewriting their histories.
20. According to the 1930 census.
21. "for those not slender" Pasadena directories. Maud's death certificate would state she worked nine years for Peterson.
22. I am going off the 1880 Wisconsin census and records of the family where she is listed as six-year-old

Mariah. By 1900 her name would be Marie, her birth date given as 1877, and her birthplace South Dakota. By the 1920 census she would be listed as having been born in Minnesota. Other records indicate she was born in Tennessee or Louisiana. Her family is quite adamant she was born in Wisconsin, though I could locate no records.

23. Paul V. Coates, Well, Medium and Rare, *The Los Angeles Mirror,* September 5, 1951.
24. Francis "Frank" Peeso seems to have remained in Hennepin, dying in 1950 at the age of seventy-three of coronary disease. Amusingly, as to the sloppiness of records in my possession, on the death certificate Peeso's birth date is listed as September 1976, twenty-seven years after his passing.
25. Van Schaack is also listed as a travel agent and living in a hotel in 1916.
26. "black Scottsman" and "aristocratic manners" Dardy to author.
27. Minneapolis City Directories.
28. William's daughter Ellie Hiatt relayed to me that William worked for Boeing in Seattle, eventually moving to Cheyenne and Oakland. When Ellie was seventeen he deserted his wife and four children, eventually remarrying and starting a new family.
29. It was in Seattle that first cousin Ellie Hiatt would get to know Lili and always referred to her as "Marie," saying that's what everyone in the family called her.
30. "three-time" Unknown author, "Barbara Moffett and Her Horses Get the Bits," unknown newspaper, n.d.
31. Dardy's daughter Ava Minsky Foxman to author.
32. "grueling" All quotations in this section are from MVS.
33. "not let it affect her" Ibid.
34. "But I knew I was loved" Ibid.
35. In the days before invasive databases, Lili would sign many legal documents as Lili St. Cyr—though that person did not legally exist. Her Social Security card and California ID would bear the name Willis Van Schaack. Alice's sister Katherine, who the Klarquists, including Lili, lived with or near in Seattle, had the middle name of Willis.
36. Cousin Ellie Hiatt swears that Marie was given the name Willis at birth, but this is related by Alice, clearly after the name change anyway. Ellie knew

Lili when she was Marie in Seattle.

37. Various documents, including birth records, census documents, and obituaries for Lili's mother, would show the spelling of her name as Peasu, Pescav, Pezo, and Peeza, also listing her name differently for each of her children. Cousin Hiatt swears the family name was originally Peeso.

CHAPTER THREE

38. "No, no" Dardy, unpublished memoirs.
39. "You look like a queen" Ibid.
40. "I never remember her" Ibid.
41. "the biggest money making" Paris, *Garbo*.
42. As Harlow was the biggest star at the time, along with Garbo, it can be assumed that Lili, a movie nut, saw *Dinner at Eight*. In a short time her brows would mimic Harlow's. Lili admired the vamp, the "bad girl" that Harlow portrayed.
43. "I wanted to have money" Lydia Lane, *Los Angeles Times*, June 21,1953.
44. Lili's former husband Armando Orsini to author. I assume it was her profile she didn't care for, as she mostly posed facing the camera square on.
45. "Daddy doesn't feel well" Dardy to author.

CHAPTER FOUR

46. "It gives me an opportunity" MVS.
47. "to look into a mirror" Stuart, *Empress of Fashion*.
48. "Alice" Dardy to author.
49. "couldn't stand the noise" MMF.
50. Ibid.
51. "Vicious tongue" Ibid.
52. "car loads of suitors" Ibid.
53. "adventure" MVS.
54. Ibid.
55. "you should have told me" Ibid.
56. "value" Ibid.

CHAPTER FIVE

57. Various ship manifests would list his birth date from 1911 to 1914. He was probably born 1914, according to the 1930 census.
59. "flat track races" *Oakland Tribune*, July 24, 1933.
59. "deliberately attempted) *Oakland Tribune*, September 26, 1934.
60. MVS.
61. "financial stability" Ibid.

CHAPTER SIX

62. "expressive purple eyes" Smith, *Women Remember*.
63. "degrading" School records from Girton.
64. Her sister would claim that Rosemary had been kicked out. Not true. Erica, who had her own set of problems, claimed the same about Ian, though there is no evidence to support the accusation.
65. "over Europe" Ibid.
66. "go away little girls" Ibid.
67. "terrified" Peck, *Mariga*. Mariga would have her own tragic life, marrying into the wealthy Guinness family, ultimately becoming an alcoholic, divorcing, losing her money, and dying young of a heart attack. When asked, she would not speak about her past or her mother.
68. It is not known who performed her lobotomy. Most likely Lili never knew any of this history.
69. Sue K., *psychosurgery.org*.
70. "incarcerated" Peck, *Mariga*.
71. Rosemary's and Ian's sister Erica would have her own colorful past. In 1923 Erica married a minister thirty years older than herself. They lived in Jamaica and had a couple of children. Returning to Chirnside, Scotland, Erica became sexually involved with a man thirty years younger. Like her maligned sister, Erica would have a nervous breakdown and attempt suicide, spending months—compared to her sister's decades-long incarceration—in a psychiatric hospital where she underwent electric shock treatments. Described as exhibiting "reckless indiscretion," she was said to have "acted a part" instead of revealing her true self (Smith, *Women Remember*). She spoke compulsively about sex.

CHAPTER SEVEN

72. "rich people" MVS.
73. "a passion for the joy of life" Ibid.
74. "surly" Ibid.
75. "with compliments" Ibid.
76. He possibly had two stores, as he is also listed on Regent Street.
77. He might have been twenty-three. The passenger lists have him born in 1919. Though Lili claimed in her bio he was twenty-eight, she was never good with datesor remembering numbers.
78. "star giving" MVS.
79. "easily" Ibid.
80. "romance" Ibid.
81. "Tomorrow's my birthday" Ibid.
82. "Special dinner given" Menu and names of guests from Lili's scrapbooks, courtesy of Lili's friend Pat Carroll.
83. "Beautiful Cheri" MVS.
84. "old loyalty" Ibid.

CHAPTER EIGHT

85. "Willis van Schaack" Unknown newspaper from Lili's scrapbook, courtesy of Lili's friend Pat Carroll.
86. "to be different" MMF.
87. Some reports have the date as July 27.
88. Unidentified newspaper from Lili's scrapbook, courtesy of Pat Carroll.
89. "mysterious" MVS.
90. "Some tea?" Dardy to author.
91. "I've got just the spot for you" Dawson, "The Durability of Lili." Amusing to note there is one photo of stripper Lilly Christine mistaken for Lili.
92. "it was immaturity" MMF.
93. "had gypsy soul" and "for the first" MVS.

94. "You are supposed to be" MVS.10. Ibid.

95. "for the first" Ibid.

96. Various ship manifests show Lili and Maxwell sailing together.

97. Lili and Maxwell at the very least sailed together in February of 1939 and April of 1939 twice.

98. "Good morning" Lili's scrapbooks, courtesy of Pat Carroll.

99. "Can't live without you" MVS.

100. Maxwell would marry in 1946 and for a second time in 1971.

CHAPTER NINE

101. "enchanted" MVS.

102. "causes" Ibid.

103. Marriage certificate from a relative of Lili's (who asked to remain anonymous) shared with author.

104. "Girls!" MVS.

105. Dressage is likened to a ballet for horses. It is a form of training where the rider minimally guides the horse through walking and trotting.

106. "bible" Letter from Lili to fan Bob Bethia.

107. "bible" Dardy to author.

108. "Rosemary" Ibid.

109. Smith, *Women Remember.*

110. "How tall are you?" Dardy to author.

111. "creator of modern" Slide, *Encyclopedia of Vaudeville.*

112. "stripped of" *Variety*, December 18, 1940.

113. And still yet another version, NTG's: He claims to have hired Dardy and Barbara (fourteen and sixteen), which isn't possible. He claimed the two showed up at the Paramount Theatre and he had them report to the Florentine. He also claims to have given Lili her stage name, though advertisements at the time show her dancing as Marie Van Schaack.

114. "necessary" MVS.

115. In 1957 NTG came into the Dunes in Las Vegas where Dardy was living with her husband, producer Harold Minsky. NTG was out of work and broke and asked Harold for help. When he died a few months later Harold paid for his funeral. (Dardy to author.)

116. built around NTG" *Billboard*, May 16, 1942.

117. Movie stars were often listed in *Variety*, December 5, 1941.

118. The 2 million figure from the *Los Angeles Times*, April 22, 1957.

119. During an interview at Granny's house in 1946 the reporter claimed to have seen the most "immense bed" he ever saw. And when asked if they all slept together—the girls and Granny—he said yes. Bob Raines, *Los Angeles Times.*

120. "society songstress" *Palm Beach Daily News*, 1940. Coincidentally, Adelaide Brook's father's first wife would fall to her death from her New York apartment.

121. "The 'bookends'" Dardy to author.

122. "as long as her dates didn't" *Eureka Humboldt Standard*, September 11, 1959.

123. Barbara's stepdaughter Barbara Hubbard Marx to author.

124. "rodeo performer of note" *Billboard*, March 14, 1942. They also noted she was seventeen years old and had just been signed by RKO.

125. "Belgian descent" MMF.

126. "nuts about each other" Dardy to author.

127. "cobra dance" *Billboard*, December 26, 1942.

128. "favorites" *Billboard*, June 3, 1944.

129. "near nude" *Billboard*, December 26, 1942.

130. "Taking off your clothes" Roberts, "Strip for Action."

131. "Always the lady" 32. Ibid.

132. "indefinite" *Variety*, July 8, August 16, and August 21, 1940.

133. ". . . if I was going to do" Roberts, "Strip for Action."

134. "Faith bacon was" Dawson, "The Durability of Lili."

135. For Lili's star-making debut in Montreal a few years later, she would appropriate this dance and make it one of her more popular pieces "Leda and the Swan".

136. "This is the kind of thing" Dawson, "The Durability of Lili."

137. "the stage was haunted" MVS.

138. "big moment" Ibid.

139. "aggressive" Ibid.

140. "inventor of the fan dance" De Lafayette, *Showbiz.*

141. "this is how we push" Ibid.

142. If indeed it was *Scheherazade* she saw, it was January of 1936.

143. "sensuously skimpy" Dunning, *Alvin Alley.*

CHAPTER TEN

144. Dardy to author.

145. "hang out with" Ibid.

146. "Who is Rex St. Cyr?" *Variety*, February 28, 1941.

147. "dwarfed by the table" MVS.

148. "someone wants to meet you" Ibid.

149. "Why do you wear that Lili" This and the following conversation with Orson from MVS.

150. "mean-looking man" Jordan, *Norma Jean.*

151. "tomorrow" MVS.

152. "I am at the pool." Ibid.

153. "great" Dardy to author.

154. *Billboard*, May 16, 1942.

155. "a lot" MMF.

156. "We were strangers" Ibid.

157. "waiting for men" MVS.

158. "dapper, slim" Nick Paumgarten, *The New Yorker*, May 8, 2006 .

159. Walters, a gambler, was fabulously successful, making a lot of money but, according to his famous daughter Barbara, would lose everything before he died.

160. "to be discreet" MVS.

CHAPTER ELEVEN

161. "different world" All quotations and italicized passages are from various letters from Lili to her friend Pat Carroll in 1987.

162. "pigeon breast" Dardy to author.

163. "As a school girl" Letter from Lili to fan Bob Bethia, April 15, 1991.

CHAPTER TWELVE

164. "ideal location for a club" *Variety*, October 22, 1941, and September 3, 1941.

165. "riot of success" *Variety*, October 22, 1941.

166. "rude" MVS.

167. "seemed tired" *Variety*, October 22, 1941.

168. "untouchable beauty" MVS.

169. "clothes were unimportant" Granlund, *Blondes, Brunettes, and Bullets.*

170. *Variety*, November 26, 1941.

171. ". . . she had absolutely nothing" Sullivan, *Va Va Voom!.*

172. It was a good thing she worked only a few months in the highly toxic G-string, as radium would be proved to deposit itself in the bones, causing radio activity that degraded the marrow and mutated bone cells. Perhaps it contributed to the pain she later suffered in her spine.

173. "It was the presence" Roberts, "Strip for Action."

174. "pleasure in tantalizing" Ibid.

175. "I hate the audiences" Dawson, "The Durability of Lili."

176. "I walked her until" "Peeress of the Peeleries," *Cabaret Quarterly* 4, Winter.

177. "intrinsically graceful" Sullivan, *Va Va Voom!.*

178. *Variety*, December 10, 1941.

179. "one of the strongest" *Billboard*, October 24, 1942.

180. "Their varied sets" *Billboard*, March 2, 1944.

181. *Billboard*, November 25, 1944.

182. "infatuated" MVS.

183. "long friendship" Ibid.

184. *Titusville Herald*, October 8, 1945; *Madison Wisconsin State Journal*, October 12, 1945.

185. Though many shows were called "vaudeville," it was a fine line between vaudeville and burlesque. Vaudeville was dying out. Harry Howard was also the impresario who, according to Dardy, first hired Lili and Barbara at the Florentine Gardens.

186. "What's this?" Dardy to author.

187. "we had to look our best." Dardy, unpublished memoirs.

188. "loved gangsters" Ibid.

189. "Capone of Los Angeles." 194. "how dare you" MVS.

190. "How Dare you?' MVS

CHAPTER THIRTEEN

191. Years later Lili would return to the Hollywood and the Johnston's at a much lower fee than her $3,500 weekly, so loyal did she feel toward him. *Variety* February 25, 1970.

192. "local creditors" *Variety*, August 12, 1942..

193. "couldn't get a seat" *Behind the Burly Q*.

194. "gave it life" MVS.

195. Ibid. She once called him from Boston while performing at the legendary Old Howard Theatre. A

former church, the Old Howard had seen every noteworthy stripper from Ann Corio to Gypsy Rose on its boards. A burlesque theatre of some renown, well-attended by the notorious, popular, and convicted felon Mayor Curley and a young John F. Kennedy, it was said, "You couldn't graduate from Harvard until you've see Ann Corio." (Corio's husband, Mike Iannucci, to author.)

196. "experience" MVS.

197. "your strip teacher" Photo at the San Diego Historical Society.

198. "have a sense of spectacle" MVS.

199. "shabby office backstage" Author interview with Hunt's granddaughter Pepper Aarvold (formerly Pearl).

200. Lillian Hunt would go on to a long career at the Follies, mentoring other star strippers such as Tempest Storm and Blaze Starr, nearly to her death in April of 1964.

201. It was at the Follies where Lili saw star stripper Rose la Rose perform. Known to "flash," Rose was a popular headliner. Though Lili thought her "vulgar" (MVS), she did admire her professionalism.

202. It is all rather confusing. Either Idella or Lili wanted others to believe Edward Van Schaack had deserted Idella.

203. "I don't want to talk about it" *Spokane Daily Chronicle*, n.d.

204. I was unable to find a marriage certificate for Cornett and Idella, which does not mean they were never married.

205. "Lili Finova" *Eureka Humboldt Standard*, September 11, 1959.

206. *Variety*, July 9, 1943.

207. "I didn't have money to waste" Dardy to author.

CHAPTER FOURTEEN

208. Lou Walters, journalist Barbara Walters's father, opened his first club in New York in 1942. There would be Latin Quarters in New York, Boston, and Miami.

209. "state-of-the-art kitchen" Walters, *Audition.*

210. *Billboard*, May 15, 1943.

211. "sixty-three cents" Walters, *Audition.*

212. "murals of Parisian" Ibid.

213. "murals" Ibid.

214. "the brassy blare" Roberts, "Strip for Action."

215. "nothing to the imagination" *Billboard*, January 12, 1944.

216. "helpers" Dardy to author.

217. "sophisticated women" "Lili St. Cyr Co-Stars in State Hit," *Union Town Evening Standard*, August 23, 1958.

218. Sullivan, *Va Va Voom!.*

CHAPTER FIFTEEN

219. "it bores me" MMF.

220. *Variety*, January 12, 1944.

221. *Variety*, June 14, 1944.

222. "outstanding stripteuse" *Famous Models Magazine*, September-October 1951.

223. One newspaper (unknown) claimed her debut was in *Ziegfeld Girl* for MGM and *Shanghai Gesture* for RKO.

224. "Glamazons" Unknown newspaper, from Dardy's scrapbooks, author's collection.

225. "cool, emotionless" Sullivan, *Va Va Voom!*.

226. "that dump" Dardy to author.

227. "I've got us tickets" This and subsequent night out conversation relayed by Dardy to author.

228. "Irishman"Lili's friend Pat Carroll to author.

229. Lili's colleague stripper Sherry Britton to author. Britton stripped for the "families."

230. "bartenders, actors" Dardy to author.

231. "I always knew when she had" Ibid.

CHAPTER SIXTEEN

232. Jordan did claim this, though the diary never appeared.

CHAPTER SEVENTEEN

233. "She needs an office," Both MVS and Dardy to author.

234. "gentle loving submissive" Hubbard, *The Hunger of Eve*.

235. "Do your best" Ibid.

236. "material security" Ibid.

237. Dardy to author.

238. "was in love" Wells, *Wild Man*.

239. Dardy to author.

240. "sable coat" Lili explains she didn't "like having that little girl, helpless feeling" asking for money. Dawson, "The Durability of Lili."

241. "good friend" Barbara's stepdaughter Barbara Marx Hubbard to author.

242. Ibid.

243. Ibid.

244. She admits this herself in MVS.

245. "Gone with the Wind" Hubbard, *The Hunger of Eve*.

246. Wells, *Wild Man*.

247. "children stood on chairs" Historylink.org re Jacqueline Marx Barnett.

248. "work, work, work" Ibid.

249. "the best" Hubbard, *The Hunger of Eve*.

250. "brilliant" Barbara's stepdaughter Jacqueline Marx Barnett to author.

251. "night after night" Hubbard, *The Hunger of Eve*.

252. Five-star generals Eisenhower, Omar Bradley, George C. Marshall, Walter Bedell Smith, and Hunter Harris along with Prince Bernhard would be godfathers to Barbara's and Marx's five sons.

253. "Flighty" "gold digger" "dubious background" Wells, *Wild Man*.

CHAPTER EIGHTEEN

254. "population, economy" Linteau, *The History of Montréal*.

255. "two hundred major" Weintraub, *City Unique*.

256. "wide-open town" Ibid.

257. "fast moving" Al Palmer, Man About Montreal, *The Herald*, September 1948.

258. Montreal took its name from Mont-Royal.

259. "Conway here" MVS.

260. "weird demands" Weintraub, *City Unique*.

261. Strictly speaking, though burlesque houses had strippers and vaudeville did not, the Gayety advertised its entertainment as a vaudeville review.

262. "languorous and melancholy" Weintraub, *City Unique*.

263. "you could hear a pin drop" Dawson, "The Durability of Lili."

264. "mysterious" MVS.

265. Being in a career where the performer was virtually in charge of her performance, acting as her own boss, creating her own acts, putting it together, oftentimes doing her own agenting and publicity, the girls in burlesque—Lili included—were very self-sufficient.

266. Blind pigs proliferated in the city. One newspaper surmised that there were fifty blind pigs in operation (*Edmonton Journal*, November 13, 1945). They were a result of curfews put on legitimate bars and operated without a proper liquor license, and so the police turned a blind eye to them.

267. Not unlike the first hit of heroin. Euphoric, elusive, the sense of indestructible confidence and well-being, a sense never to be repeated, though the search was on.

PART TWO
CHAPTER ONE

268. Maurice's sister Maria was married to Mafia criminal Vic Cotroni (1911–1984) after Cotroni was charged with raping her. The charges would be dropped.

269. "Maurice" MVS.

270. "someone like her" Ibid.

271. Ibid.

272. Ibid.

273. Palmer, *Montreal Confidential*.

274. "disheveled" MVS.

275. "wealthy and fabulous" *Billboard*, September 28, 1946.

276. "the King of the Montreal" Schneider, *Iced*.

277. The rumors of her being badly beaten up and left wandering the street had reached (stripper Dixie Evans to author). It was physically traumatic. Maurice Bresciano died in 1988.

278. "If you buy men a drink" MVS.

279. Mike Wallace interview, 1957.

280. "If one has morals" Ibid.

281. LZ research

282. "high hat" *San Antonio Express*, August 2, 1953.

283. "no performers could leave the stage" "Strip-Teaser Now Dresses for Her Work," *Brandon Daily Sun*, May 23, 1953.

284. "I don't just take off" *LA Herald*, March 24, 1955.

285. "come to the belief" "Do Women Hate or Envy Lili?" *Screenland TV*, February 1954.

286. "cosmopolitan" MVS.

CHAPTER TWO

287. "romping" Roberts, "Strip for Action."
288. *"There was one time"* "Do Women Hate or Envy Lili?" *Screenland TV*, February 1954.
289. "They were mad" Dardy to author.
290. "enforcer" Greenland, *Wings of Fire*.
291. "major team sport" Alex Capstick, *BBC News Magazine*, 2012.
292. "working-class super heros" John Branch, "Punched Out," *The New York Times*, 2011.
293. "easy-going" Greenland, *Wings of Fire*.
294. "lived furiously" MMF.
295. "essential war effort" *Pittsburgh Press*, April 1943
296. *Ottawa Citizen*, July 1943.
297. As late as 1967 Orlando was trying to appeal his conviction and a prison sentence conviction. He could not enter the United States, despite being married to a US citizen, as he would be immediately arrested.
298. Dardy to author.
299. "good looking peeler" *Billboard*, April 15, 1944. Sherry's official biography has her born in 1918, putting her at twenty-two in 1941.
300. This according to the book *The Secret Life of a Satanist* by Blanche Barton (Feral House, 1990).
301. "Her smoldering gaze" 15. Roberts, "Strip for Action."
302. "You'll be the greatest" MMF.
303. "spoiled by the mechanical movements." Roberts, "Strip for Action."
304. "Just show me what to do" Ibid.
305. "taught her how to dramatize" *Behind the Scenes Magazine*, September 1957.
306. "sponsors" MMF.
307. "overlong" *Billboard*, May 4, 1946.
308. "Lili St. Cyr's dancing" *Jet Age Airlines*.
309. "earned her money" MVS.
310. Ibid.
311. "It's another bright sunny day" Ibid.
312. "it was such a drag" MMF.

CHAPTER FOUR

313. The manager and bouncer Toots Shore would open his Toots Shore restaurant in the same place that the boys retired, in 1953, running it until 1971.
314. "prudish" Shaw, *52nd Street*.
315. "men's seed" Lili's colleague stripper Sherry Britton to author (for *Behind the Burly Q*).
316. "the blood temperature" *Billboard*, February 9, 1946.
317. "most 'artistic'" *Billboard*, October 9, 1948.
318. The current owners were listed renting elsewhere.
319. "demanding and vain" MVS.
320. "Before I spent a night" Dawson, "The Durability of Lili."

CHAPTER FIVE

321. "bubbles" MMF.

322. "modern looking bathtub" Ibid.
323. MVS.
324. Lili had a cavalier attitude toward marriage, neither liking it, believing it was necessary, nor caring if her marriages lasted. (MVS)
325. "best dancer since" *Dancer's Magazine*.
326. Server, *Robert Mitchum*.
327. Roger Ebert, www.RogerEbert.com, July 18, 2004.
328. Various sources list the date as December 25.
329. "social secretary" Pizzitola, *Hearst over Hollywood*.
330. "artistic inspiration" Roberts, "Strip for Action."

CHAPTER SIX

331. "was no fun" MMF.
332. *New Liberty Magazine*, 1947.
333. Unknown newspaper from Dardy's scrapbook.
334. Crocker would die at age sixty-four in 1958.
335. Lili told reporters that Barbara would be marrying Harry Crocker, maybe to goad Marx into setting a wedding date. (MVS)
336. "the man who is going to" *Olean Times Herald*, June 21, 1946.
337. "throngs" *Los Angeles Times*, November 29, 1947.
338. "unreal" Lillian Hunt's granddaughter Pepper Aarvold, formerly Pearl, to author.
339. "White brocade" "Barbara Moffett and Toy King Wed in Florida," unknown newspaper, n.d., from Ellie Hiatt's scrapbook.
340. *Belle Isle* (blog) and *Miami Daily News*, March 30, 1947.
341. "Lillian St. Cyr" *Miami Daily News*, March 30, 1947.
342. "grande dame of Miami Beach Bramson, *Miami Beach*.
343. "had to rush back" *Port Arthur*, May 20, 1947.
344. "always wanted a husband" Dardy to author.
345. "tyrannically" Hubbard, *The Hunger of Eve*.
346. "Aunt Lili" Barbara's stepdaughter Barbara Marx Hubbard to author.
347. Ibid.

CHAPTER SEVEN

348. "unusual dance routines" "Lili St Cyr Review Star," *Los Angeles Times*, October 15, 1948.
349. "abbreviated" "Lili St. Cyr Set for Zucca Duty," *Los Angeles Times*, October 14, 1948.
350. "must learn to grow" MMF.
351. Dardy to author.
352. "the fun goes out of it" *"The Durability of Lili."*
353. Jean Harlow, whose color Lili imitated, would wear a wig at the end of her career, so damaged and thin was her hair from peroxide. Lili amazingly never had the problem and said she oiled before washing her hair.
354. "You are my friend" MVS.
355. "not good enough" Ibid.
356. "refused to allow" "Mate Sheds Strip Teaser," *Los Angeles Herald & Express*, n.d.

357. "of course there is" *Teese.*

358. "Take it off" *Billboard*, July 10, 1948.

359. "you're under arrest." MVS.

360. The late hour would cause confusion as to her actual arrest. Her mug shot shows the seventeenth; various papers would relate it as being on the eighteenth.

361. The Follies was owned by Mr. Robert D. Biggs Sr. and his son Robert E. Biggs Jr. According to Follies manager/producer Lillian Hunt's granddaughter Pepper Aarvold (formerly Pearl), who was often backstage at the theatre, she thought Mr. Biggs Sr. owned the theatre so his son could "have access to the girls." It is assumed Anna Biggs was the wife of Biggs Sr. The previous owners, the Daltons, three brothers, were somehow still involved, as one brother was noted as the producer on a show in 1948.

362. "carried on a table" "Follies Dance Film in Court," *Los Angeles Examiner*, April 1948.

363. "shed practically" *Los Angeles Times*, April 15, 1948.

364. Apparently the young officer had snuck a camera into the Follies. It was the same sort of thing that would happen to Rose la Rose at the Old Howard in Boston when film was taken to show her, along with Irma the Body and Marino Russell to be "gross lewdness." Boston Crimson, 1953, no author attributed. Rose and the other two strippers would indeed be arrested and fined five hundred dollars in 1953.

365. "except for shoes" *Indiana Eve Gazette*, April 16, 1948;, "Strip-teaser Fined $350," *Long Beach Press Telegram*, April 16, 1948.

366. "then maybe it's" "Strip-teaser Fined $350," *Long Beach Press Telegram*, April 16, 1948.

367. "surprised" MVS.

368. "corrupted public morals" "Scheherazade Dance Act Ruled Immoral," *Oakland Tribune*, April 16, 1948.

CHAPTER EIGHT

369. "interpret independently" "Lili St.Cyr 'Interprets' at Garden," *Los Angeles Times*, March 3, 1948.

370. "what to do with it" *Los Angeles Times*, March 3, 1948.

371. "the easy work" *Billboard*, March 13, 1948.

372. "she dallies" "Vaudeville Sneaks Back," *Oakland Tribune*, March 30, 1948.

373. Dardy's daughter Ava Minsky Foxman to author.

374. Author emails with Cathy Tennant.

375. "I you want to get married in white" "The Little King," *Time*, December 12, 1955.

376. Valentine was billed above Monroe.

377. "white-haired" Anderson, *Beverly Hills Is My Beat*.

378. "Rounders" I could find no reference to a "Rounders" bar in any directory; it may have been called something else.

379. When I asked Dardy why so many got married in Tijuana at the time, she said it was because California had a three-day waiting period.

380. "night club owner" "Actress Quits Wedded Life," *Los Angeles Times*, July (day illegible) 1948.

381. "month-old Robert" "Beauty Wins Child Support," *Los Angeles Examiner*, "n.d.

382. "coo over him" Ibid.

383. "Trouble in paradise?" MVS.

384. "perpetual lover" MMF.

385. "You are a star" MVS.

386. "blue headdress" "Raund Town," *Miami Daily News*, October 14, 1950.

387. "blue mink" Al Palmer, Montreal Man About Town, *The Herald*, April 27, 1948.

388. "hair dressers reporting" 20. Al Palmer, Montreal Man About Town, *The Herald*, May 4, 1948.

389. Al Palmer, Montreal Man About Town, *The Herald*, September 21, 1948.

390. The film was never made.

391. "a fairly good idea" Al Palmer, "'New' Lili Surprises Old Gayety Regulars," Montreal Man About Town, *The Herald*, June 29, 1948.

392. "her entire collection" Al Palmer, Montreal Man About Town, *The Herald*, July 2, 1948.

393. Al Palmer, "Gayety Closes Season with Popular Program," Montreal Man About Town, *The Herald*, July 6, 1948.

394. "How are we going?" All the conversations between Dardy and Lili were retold by Dardy to author.

395. "I always need to pay for things," Mike Wallace TV interview, 1957.

396. I myself had a several white-knuckle moments as a passenger in Dardy's car. Dardy, in her eighth decade, insisted on driving to lunch.

397. "tricky finale" Partial newspaper, it's assumed to be Al Palmer's Montreal Man About Town column from *The Herald.*

CHAPTER TEN

398. "sister Lili's" Al Palmer, Montreal Man About Town, *The Herald*, October 1948.

399. "hours to open them" MMF.

400. "adds to her unattainability" *Rogue Magazine*, June 1956.

401. "anti-climax" Al Palmer, "'New' Lili Surprises Old Gayety Regulars," Montreal Man About Town, *The Herald* June 29, 1948.

402. "Paul I'm sorry" MVS.

403. In her bio, she claims Bellevue Hospital, but it might have been a different overdose.

404. "You saved me" Roberts "Strip for Action."

405. Dawson, "The Durability of Lili."

406. "speed-dial" I assume figuratively, not literally, as there weren't speed-dials yet. Dardy's daughter Ava Minsky Foxman to author.

CHAPTER ELEVEN

407. On Sunset Boulevard, the apartment was actually Hughes's, located above the studio of photographer Paul A. Hesse. Hesse was a famous photographer who

shot many of Hollywood's brightest stars. (Brown, *Howard Hughes*.) Kane lived nearby on Doheny.

408. Kane had been married for four years to B actress Lynn Bari. Kane would die in 1983 after a thirty-two-year career serving Hughes. Though he was listed as being a talent agent, some say he was Hughes's pimp for a never-ending parade of starlets, and lastly an entertainment director of Summa Corp., supposedly largely responsible for Wayne Newton's Las Vegas success. According to one biography, Kane had been a former vaudeville performer with Fatty Arbuckle and ran a talent agency with Zeppo Marx. It is intriguing to think that if Hughes had arranged the meeting with Kane why nothing came of it. Perhaps Lili declined an offer of a contract. She was independent and would not want to be "kept" dangling on call for Hughes. She also didn't appear to have any real movie star ambitions. Most likely she struck up a friendship and brief romantic relationship with Kane. Later Hughes would use Lili in a film.

409. "dapper" James, *Jeanne Carmen*.

410. "Lili turned on her charm" Roberts, "Strip for Action."

411. "I have to call you back" MMF.

412. "You must really have wanted to leave" MVS.

413. "It's not like you" Ibid.

414. Al Palmer cited her as "terrific" in the role. Montreal Man About Town, *The Herald*, September 28, 1948.

415. "would lock herself" "Mate Sheds Strip Teaser," *Los Angeles Herald & Express*, September 27, 1949.

416. He would stay only a year.

417. "title to the couple's" "Strip Artiste Stripped of Mate by Court Decree," *Los Angeles Times*, September 27, 1949.

418. Lili did return to her house and became his roommate when she performed at the Follies, as she often would (May 1950). Kilgallen also wrote that their friends hoped for a reconciliation, which was hogwash; Lili's friends never liked Paul nor his friends her.

419. "She didn't have bitter divorces" Dardy to author.

420. "divorce boosted her fame" Dorothy Kilgallen, November 1949.

CHAPTER TWELVE

421. "tasteful strips" *Variety*, August 9, 1950.

422. "I like to spoil men" Dawson, "The Durability of Lili."

423. "uninhibited and exotic" Dee Phillips, "Famous Models," *Screenland TV*.

424. "exotic, svelte charming" Ibid.

425. "Hello" Conversation relayed by Dardy to author.

426. "a million dollars" Zemeckis, *Behind the Burly Q*.

427. Jane Feehan, *Fort Lauderdale Daily News*, June 9, 1945 .

428. $200,000 was reported in *Billboard*, November 20, 1948.

429. "hoighty toighty" *Billboard*, January 15, 1949.

430. "Harold's in the hospital doll." All conversations in this section relayed by Dardy to author.

431. "Friends are trying to reconcile" *Olean Times*, May 6, 1950.

432. "raising him" Paul V. Coates, Well, Medium and Rare, *The Los Angeles Mirror*, September 5, 1951. Alice gave an interesting interview to Coates, in which she clearly calls the boy Danny.

433. Dardy's daughter and Danny's half-sister Ava Minsky Foxman thought Danny renamed himself.

CHAPTER THIRTEEN

434. "I suffer when you're away" MVS.

435. "relief" Ibid.

436. "Why my younger brother" Ibid.

437. "Where's Jimmy?" Ibid.

438. "How many shows do you want Harold?" Dardy to author.

CHAPTER FOURTEEN

439. He also asked me to make no reference to it. I didn't promise I wouldn't and in his New York obituary his real name is cited. Early in his relationship with Lili, one gossip columnist used his real name . Travel manifests show Armando using Cocchi well into the fifties. When he traveled with Lili to Rome he was listed as Cocchi and her name underneath is Marie van Schaack. Interestingly, on the ship's manifest for 1927, when Armando is four years old, the passenger listed underneath his mother's name is Ilario Orlandi.

440. Presumably the Orsini family was no relation. Armando's *New York Times* obituary states he was "the son of a cruise ship captain" or "the son of a deckhand." But his wife would deny it.

441. An ex-lover of Armando Orsini, who asked to remain nameless, to author on how Armando was in bed.

442. *Sandusky Register*, September 14, 1950.

443. "but on the installment plan" *Greenville Delta Democratic Times*, November 7, 1950. Armando told me they met her at the club.

444. "We didn't communicate." Armando to author.

445. Not only did he put his career on hold for her, but an avid sportsman, tennis player, and skier, he also "stopped it for her." Ibid.

446. "I never saw the show" Ibid.

447. By the time *And Men My Fuel* published, she would claim to have bought ten cars for her men.

448. "forbidden to talk to Lili" Armando to author.

449. "I will give you" Ibid. Armando related a story where years later one of Marx's sons dined at Armando's New York restaurant. "He hollered, 'He's my in-law,' or something, 'He was married to my Aunt Lili.' Strange family," Armando said.

450. In MVS she would tell an alternative story. Fearful of losing his money if she remained in the picture, Marx gave her an ultimatum. Lili was not to see or

communicate with his wife ever again. To ensure her cooperation Marx sent Lili a check. (Maybe it was easier for Lili to believe she had control over whether she was in Barbara's life or not.)

451. "Lili loved Barbara" Armando to author.

452. "shuttering" *Billboard*, May 5, 1951.

453. "designed to resemble" "When the Cops Said 'Sunset for Lili's Strip!'" unknown magazine, n.d.

454. The reference is to the Follies on Main Street in Los Angeles, strictly a burlesque house. *Variety*, February 28.

455. "seek the new" *Los Angeles Times*, February 26, 1951.

456. "bringing out many of our" *Los Angeles Times*, March 7, 1951.

457. "Mayor Fletcher" "Ban Strips but They Like 'Em," *Billboard*, April 7, 1951.

458. "Strip-Tease Ends Tonight," *Los Angeles Examiner*, May (day illegible) 1951.

459. Gay Dawn would take advantage of Hunt, who didn't sign contracts, going off oral agreements with the talent. As her manager, Hunt booked Dawn in several places and the stripper was making good money. But Dawn's boyfriend thought he could do better and took over the booking, thus depriving Hunt of her commission. After that, Hunt wrote contracts for the strippers. Gay Dawn was, ironically, billed as "Miss Opportunity." (*Variety*, July 6, 1950.)

460. "The perfumed water" *Billboard*, March 24, 1951.

461. "dreadfully ill" Entire retelling is Dardy to author.

462. "She didn't know how" Armando to author.

463. "Oh you know Mr. Conway" MVS.

464. "Lili, you're a star" Ibid.

465. "came as a shock" Al Palmer, "'New' Lili Surprises Old Gayety Regulars," *Montreal Man About Town*, *The Herald*, June 29,1948.

466. Linteau, *The History of Montréal*.

467. Though burlesque was banned in New York, it didn't mean burlesque wasn't alive and thriving, it had simply been renamed "follies" or "revue." But gone was the name "Minsky" in New York, LaGuardia blaming the family for the corruption of his city. Many of the strippers simply moved into nightclubs, which LaGuardia left alone.

468. "discreet" MVS.

469. "behaviour that was" Weintraub, *City Unique*.

470. "being nasty to her" Dardy to author.

471. "have confidence in me" MVS.

472. "I don't like" *San Antonio Express*, August 2, 1953.

473. *Billboard* reported one patron killed (July 28, 1951).

474. "Bitch" MVS.

CHAPTER FIFTEEN

475. "gorgeous" Tom Douglas, unpublished autobiography.

476. "bright young people" .Ibid.

477. "Lili St. Cyr Ring Is 'Only a Gift,'" *Los Angeles Examiner*, August 31, 195? (year is illegible).

478. "nothing can ever change" Open letter to Beldon Katleman from Tom Douglas, University of Nevada at Las Vegas, December 20, 1952.

479. One report maintained the El Rancho used ten million gallons of water a month to keep everything green.

480. Weatherford, *Cult Vegas*.

481. "the millionaire interior decorator" Lili St. Cyr, "My 10 Favorite Men," *Top Secret*, summer 1954.

482. "asexual" Richard Ogden's nephew Peter Ogden to author.

483. "*permit Negro artists*" Best, *Las Vegas*.

484. "I was shocked" Armando to author.

485. "Westside" Best, *Las Vegas*.

486. Dick would go on to marry a Suzanne, Miss Poland of 1959, and they would have one child. Ogden died January 2011 at age eighty-five.

487. Foley, son of a district court judge, would go on to be a United States federal judge named to the bench by JFK. The prominent Foley family was often in the news. In 2012, sixty-three-year-old Roger T. Foley II was arrested for shooting two at a senior citizens' center.

488. *Reno Evening Gazette*, September 17, 1951.

489. "insecurity" Armando to author.

490. "I can't get pregnant" Ibid.

491. "all the lies" Ibid.

CHAPTER SIXTEEN

492. "touches" Dardy to author.

493. Elio would die in Miami Beach at age seventy-seven in 2006, long after Lili died and before Armando, who was said to be devastated by the loss.

PART THREE
CHAPTER ONE

494. "We went shopping for beautiful gowns" Armando to author.

495. In 1958 Hover would be arrested for the attempted murder of his brother-in-law, whom he tried choking to "death on the streets of Beverly Hills" after he had an affair with Hover's wife. Hover's wife and brother-in-law would go on to marry (Zemeckis, *Behind the Burly Q*). It wasn't Hover's first violent outburst. In 1950 he was involved in a $20,000 assault and battery suit"(*Billboard*, January 12, 1952). Hover's bad luck continued, his own daughter Ellen Jane would be murdered in 1977 by a serial killer and her bones found buried on a Rockefeller estate in New York. Hover son's Ian would take a gun to his own head and kill himself after the tragic death of his seventeen-year-old son, who threw himself off a high-rise. Hover ended up broke, living in an apartment in Hollywood and banging out his (unpublished) memoirs about when he had been the king of the Strip.

496. *Variety*, December 4, 1942.

497. "character" MVS.

498. "book her as" *Los Angeles Examiner*, October 23, 1951.

499. Sometimes the painting would be on the wall. The same painting was used often in her act and hung on her bedroom wall and now is in my possession.

500. "going to the moon" MVS.

501. "She had never worked so hard" Armando to author.

502. Most likely the maid was Sadie, as she would remain with Lili till about 1957 or '58. However, in some photos, re-created for *Life* magazine, it is clearly another maid attending to Lili.

503. Lili's Ciro's act was relayed by Armando to author.

504. "poodle haircut" Figes, *The Big Fat Bitch Book*.

505. "proving herself" MVS.

CHAPTER TWO

506 "the stripper on the strip" *Ciro's Monthly*, spring 1952.

507. This is her reported income, though it would vary from $1,250 to many thousands per week, depending on how much cash she demanded and received.

508. "elegant" Armando to author.

509. "worn a similar costume" "Motions in Stripper's Act Create Problem When Put into Words, Witness Discovers," *Los Angeles Times*, December 6, 1951.

510. Other reports claimed she was hit by a ricocheting bullet. (Paul Lieberman, *Los Angeles Times*, October 27, 2008) It was nearly four in the morning and Muir had been hanging tight with the mobster, hoping someone would take a crack at him and she'd get the scoop. Someone did take a shot. One of Cohen's crew died.

511. "special relationship" Zemeckis, *Behind the Burly Q.*

512. Sheila Weller, Hover's niece, would write *in Dancing at Ciro's* (New York: St. Martin's, 2003), "Everybody on the Strip knew everybody in the sheriff's department. . . . They knew what was going on."

513. "terrified" MVS.

514. "Hire Giesler" Ibid.

515. "Money is not an obstacle" Ibid.

516. Lili would mention a Beverly Hills office; other sources say he had an office at Broadway and Fifth in downtown LA.

517. "formal relationship" MVS.

518. "follow his orders" Ibid.

519. "original idea" Giesler, *The Jerry Giesler Story.*

520. The phrase was used in 1950 during the Ingrid Bergman-Lindstrom divorce (Gladstone, *The Man Who Seduced Hollywood*).

521. "guinea pig" Giesler, *The Jerry Giesler Story.*

522. "When I'm finished" "How to Tame a Wolf," *Cabaret*, September 1955.

523. *Los Angeles Times*, October 21, 1951.

524. "her act . . ." 19. Ibid.

525. "upright position" *The Los Angeles Mirror*, February 15, 1952.

526. "A performer was not permitted" Paul V. Coates, "Rules Regulating Strip Tease in the City of Los Angeles," *The Los Angeles Mirror*, February 8, 1952.

527. "breezed" *Los Angeles Times*, October 23.

528. All quotes regarding Lili's trial, unless noted, are from the *Los Angeles Examiner*, the *Los Angeles Times*, *Variety*, and *Billboard.*

529. "his wife's new bathing suit" *Variety*, December 3, 1951.

530. "If I have to perform"25. Roberts, "Strip for Action."

531. "some of her appeal" *Variety*, December 5, 1951.

532. Jon Bruce, "The Stripper on the Strip," *Ciro's Monthly*, spring 1952.

533. "bad woman" MVS.

534. Armando to author.

CHAPTER THREE

535. "Appears in mink" *Variety*, December 5, 1951.

536. *Herald Express*, December 4, 1951.

537. "demonstrate the decency" Ibid.

538. "He was known to appear" Zemeckis, *Behind the Burly Q.*

539. "artistic performance" Giesler, *The Jerry Giesler Story.*

540. "Nudity is essential" *The Independent Long Beach*, December 5, 1951.

541. "a couple of times" Unknown magazine, "Those Fabulous Sisters," unknown magazine, n.d., from Ellie Hiatt scrapbooks.

542. "serious offence" Giesler, *The Jerry Giesler Story.*

543. *Variety*, December 6, 1951.

544. Lili's act was twelve minutes according to some, fourteen to others.

545. "peeled down to a couple" *Berkley Daily Gazette*, December 6,1951.

546. In Tom Douglas's unpublished memoirs he claimed the tub was made out of Lucite.

547. "massive" Dardy to author.

CHAPTER FOUR

548. "Lured by the thought" *Variety*, December 7, 1951.

549. "A bump" *Los Angeles Examiner*, December 7, 1951.

550. "grew into a row" Giesler, *The Jerry Giesler Story.*

551. "No further questions" Ibid.

552. "conservatively garbed" *Los Angeles Examiner*, December 8, 1951.

553. "grinds to close" *Variety*, December 10, 1951.

554. "ten tired women" 7. Ibid.

555. "Oh boy" *The Independent Long Beach*, December 12, 1951.

556. "having that case" Giesler, *The Jerry Giesler Story.*

557. "shifted her mink coat" Dorothy Cuthbertson, *The Daily Review*, December 20, 1951.

558. "celebrating" *Variety*, December 13, 1951.

559. "hacked" *Variety*, December 22, 1951.

560. "She liked the attention" Armando to author.

561. MVS.

562. Lang would go on to produce *Airport 1975* and *Earthquake*, dying at age eighty-one in Palm Desert in 1996.

563. Out of jail, Wanger showed up at a dinner party at Lili's home but they never worked together.

CHAPTER FIVE

564. "scanty panties" *Herald Examiner*, December 4, 1951.

565. "I sort of directed it myself." Schaefer, *Bold! Daring! Shocking!*

566. "a fast look" *Variety*, January 30, 1952.

567. "dress and undress" Ibid.

568. *Variety*, February 4, 1952.

569. "to be known as" *Stare Magazine*, 1952.

570. The Follies had shuttered, and the Burbank Theatre, another burlesque house also on Main Street, had been renamed the "New Follies."

571. "lewd" *Variety*, November 17, 19, and December 10, 1952.

572. Or at least a portion of her pay. Spade Cooley was a handsome part–Cherokee Indian bandleader. A hugely popular western star with a swing band as well sought after as Dorsey. He would become a heavy drinker and was convicted of killing his second wife, blonde Ella May Cooley in 1961, after torturing and stomping on her stomach and crushing her head repeatedly against the floor, all in front of his fourteen-year-old daughter, whom he had forced himself on sexually. On a seventy-two-hour furlough from prison in 1969, Spade suffered a fatal heart attack after performing a set and died just offstage.

573. "There was a certain seediness" Stripper Dixie Evans to author.

574. "I knew I was a part of that" Lili's colleague stripper Sherry Britton to author.

575. It was Wilson's secretary Phyllis Gates who would marry Hudson in 1954.

576. Tab Hunter to author.

577. "powerful" Ibid.

578. "Are you tired of taking off your clothes" Earl Wilson, "On Broadway With," It Happened Last Night, *New York Post,* June 7, 1952.

579. "It's a heck of a nuisance" Weatherford, *Cult Vegas.*

580. "There are a thousand girls" *San Antonio Express,* June 1952.

CHAPTER SIX

581. An interesting note: In those days airlines offered insurance policies purchased for a minimal amount from vending machines at the airport. George Schlatter, Lili's friend and the general manager of Ciro's, listed Lili as a beneficiary on his policy. It's not known if Lili reciprocated. Schlatter would go on to produce the very burlesque-type television hit *Rowman & Martin's Laugh-In.*

582. Armando told me that he rented an apartment in an old part of Rome.

583. "normal" MVS.

584. Vilelmina (on the 1927 ship's manifest spelling from Ancestry.com).

585. Technically "New" Follies. In 1952 the Follies at 337 South Main Street closed. Owner Robert S. Biggs took over the Burbank at 548 South Main Street, moved Lillian Hunt, her husband, and straight man Leon DeVoe in, and renamed it the New Follies.

586. "The largest sum" *Los Angeles Examiner*, December 10, 1952.

587. "I am a lady" *Chicago Herald*, March 18, 1951.

588. Many photos from the time show Dardy in similar costume, poses, and settings as Lili.

589. "sister Lili's tutelage" Al Palmer, Montreal Man About Town, *The Herald*, October 5, 1948.

590. "one of the most" "Lili Dresses for Art," *Los Angeles Times*, n.d.

591. Sometimes the painting would be on the wall. The same painting was used often in her act and hung on her bedroom wall and now is in my possession.

592. Wilson story retold to by Armando to author.

593. "I didn't realize how much" MMF.

594. "woke up" Ibid.

PART FOUR
CHAPTER ONE

595. "We used to get these" Ibid.

596. *Cabaret Magazine*, n.d.

597. "fun guy" Ibid.

598. The Fischetti brothers, Rocco, Charles, and Joseph, were first cousins to Al Capone and on the FBI's most wanted list.

599. "she froze" Dardy to author.

600. "fashion show" Weatherford, *Cult Vegas.*

601. "chichi" *Variety*, October 29, 1952.

602. ". . . gone are the days" 8. Ibid.

603. "reception is mild" *Variety*, August 19, 1953.

604. Dardy to author.

605. Dardy's daughter Ava Minsky Foxman to author.

606. "no closing date" *Variety*, January 27, 1954.

CHAPTER TWO

607. "stole into her life" MVS.

608. "royal boxes" Ibid. All conversation with Murphy is from MVS.

609. "nearly across the alley" Dardy to author.

610. MMF.

611. "feel frivolous" MVS.

612. In a conversation with me in 2011, Armando said he had no idea the home hadn't been hers when he lived there with Lili. It is entirely possible he thought because of the divorce he had to sign a quit claim deed, not knowing she had only just purchased the home. They were not living together and had not been for some time. Dardy would insist that Lili used the money Barbara gave her from Marx, $10,000, to buy the home, but the dates don't match. Barbara was married in 1947 and Lili didn't purchase the house until 1954. Also Lili's friend Ian Macdonald would remember being told that someone bought her the house.

613. She would repay the loan in 1958.

614. "owed" MVS.

615. "But maybe neither" Ibid.

616. "his side" Dardy to author.

617. Approximately four feet by eight feet, enough to keep a fire lit for many cold nights.

618. "It's always so cold up here" Ibid.

CHAPTER THREE

619. "black broadcloth Balenciaga" *Los Angeles Times,* May 10, 1953.

620. "every time I pass him on the lot" MMF. It's possible she started her affair with Mature as early as this since Mature was filming at RKO the same time Lili was shooting *Son of Sinbad.*

621. "I was used to doing my own hair" Sullivan, *Va Va Voom!*

622. "I don't like the hours" *Winnipeg Free Press,* May 13, 1953.

623. "there is not enough room" "Do Women Hate or Envy Lili?" *Screenland TV,* February 1954.

624. "small egos" MVS.

625. "simple gray" "St. Cyr Dresses for Women," *Los Angeles Times,* June 21, 1953.

626. I was continually astounded at Dardy's recall. In the 1950s there was indeed a nail varnish called Sky-Blue Pink, just as she described it. It sold for $1.

627. Marusia's obituary called her a couturier whose "designs were worn by Rosaline Russell, Greer Garson and Doris Day" when she died of cancer at age sixty-seven (March 17, 1982). Marusia had formerly been married to Russian Prince Nicholas Toumanoff of the last royal family (Wilson, *Harold Robbins*). She had a distinguished career and worked with celebrated Hollywood costume designer Travis Banton.

628. "I guess we just drifted" *Los Angeles Examiner,* July 1, 1953.

629. "looking for trouble" *Uncensored,* February 1957.

630. "shapely figure" *Police Gazette,* March 1961.

631. *Variety,* May 6, 1953.

632. "unhappy woman" Hush-Hush, "Lili St. Cyr's Fantastic Flirt with Suicide," *Hush-Hush,* May 1959.

CHAPTER FOUR

633. "capricious demands" MVS.

634. Dardy recalled the bar had several carousel horses in place of traditional stools.

635. "your home should always be" Letter from Lili to her friend Pat Carroll.

636. "It will give us a chance" Conversations with Murphy from MVS.

637. "Lili St. Cyr would cease to exist" Ibid.

638. "Get in" Dardy to author.

CHAPTER FIVE

639. "a little devilish" *Los Angeles Times,* May 10, 1953.

640. "different than run of the mill" Oakland Tribune, "Lili St. Cyr Opens at Oakland's El Rey," *Oakland Tribune,* July 10, 1954.

641. "the most fabulous girl in the world" Weatherford, *Cult Vegas.*

642. If I want something" "Lili Is Not Ready to Retire," unknown newspaper, n.d., from the scrapbooks of Ellie Hiatt.

643. Lili's friend Pat Carroll to author.

644. "Fucking slut" 5. Ibid.

645. "I always seem to be a year behind" Mike Wallace TV interview, 1957.

646. Pat Carroll to author.

647. Ibid.

648. "skid row joints" *Variety,* August 6, 1954.

649. "she couldn't write" Armando to authr.

650. "My 10 Favorite Men" and following quotations from Lili St. Cyr, "My 10 Favorite Men," *Top Secret,* summer 1954.

651. A friend of Armando's told me that coincidentally Yul's son Rocky ended up working for Armando years later.

652. Army Archerd, *Variety,* September 22, 1953.

653. "tonier" *Variety,* February 24 ,1954.

654. "an essential party" Ibid.

655. "all night for her" Jordan, *Norma Jean.*

656. "What does he look like?" MVS.

657. "uncouth" Dardy to author.

658. "like a duck out of water" Jordan, *Norma Jean.*

659. "percentage deal" *Variety,* February 24, 1954.

660. "the actor" Dardy to author.

661. "cage act" *Variety,* April 20, 1954.

662. "the diners shriek" *Variety,* April 26, 1954.

663. *Los Angeles Herald,* March 24, 1955.

664. Actually, a Herbert F. Greenberg did not trademark the name "Undie-World" until 1970. The first recorded date of commerce was in 1955.

665. "setting new attendance records" *Variety,* April 29, 1954.

666. "Many great things" Harry Ingrham, "What's Doin' Downtown," May 1, 1945.

667. "bed reclining contortions" *Variety,* April 27, 1954.

668. *Variety,* 6, 1954.

669. *Variety,* July 28, 1954.

670. "swan song" *Variety,* April 29, 1954.

671. He stayed in Vegas, as he would for decades longer. His immediate job was redesigning the former Red Rooster into the Patio. Lili would dine there frequently. And he wasn't entirely through with Beldon. Throughout 1958 and 1959 Douglas was winging into Vegas, once from Paris, to produce shows at the El Rancho. In September of 1959 the show featured "nude models," perhaps to compete with the now de rigueur topless showgirls on the Strip (*Variety,* April 9, 1959, and September 23, 1959). Coincidentally Zsa Zsa, a demanding diva, would perform in a show for Harold Minsky. Unlike Lili, Dardy considered Zsa Zsa to be supremely untalented and very demanding. Harold finally had to throw her out of the show because she was so "impossible" (Dardy to author).

CHAPTER SIX

672. "merely a convenience" *Behind the Scenes*, September 1957.
673. "intrigued her" MVS.
674. "worn a bit thin" *Variety*, April 2, 1955.
675. "too forward" Lili's friend Pat Carroll to author.
676. *Variety*, August 20, 1954.
677. "*surprise*" *Los Angeles Examiner*, October 1, 1954.
678. "friends said it was permanent" *Los Angeles Examiner*, October 4, 1954.
679. "the marriage is postponed" "Lili St. Cyr's Wedding Off Indefinitely," *Los Angeles Times*, October 4, 1954.
680. "marital woes" *Variety*, September 23, 1954.
681. "soon" *Variety*, December 8, 1954.
682. "constant at her side" *Variety*, March 2, 1955.
683. Some later blamed the testing for the cause of widespread cancers among those who had been there. *Conqueror* (1953), starring John Wayne and Susan Hayward, was filmed in the Utah desert during testing. Hayward, Wayne, director Dick Powell, actors Pedro Armendari and Agnes Moorehead, and various visiting relatives were later diagnosed with cancer.
684. "national media would be in town" Weatherford, *Cult Vegas*.
685. "good" MVS.

CHAPTER SEVEN

686. "Stripper with imagination" *Billboard*, April 9, 1955.
687. "plumber" Email from Lili's friend Pat Carroll to author.
688. "Goddamn it" Author interviews with strippers Tempest Storm and Dixie Evans.
689. "mother's little helper" Tone, *The Age of Anxiety*.
690. "Uncle Miltown" Ibid.
691. "America's Long Love Affair with Anti-Anxiety Drugs," *Newsweek*, 2009.
692. "loved it" Dardy to author.
693. "that's gonna hurt" Lillian Hunt's granddaughter Pepper Aarvold (formerly Pearl) to author.
694. "agitated" MVS.
695. "sensuous interpretation" *Variety*, September 9, 1955.
696. "Bolero" *Variety*, September 9 and 14, 1955.
697. "at her trade" *Variety*, April 22, 1955.
698. "for about thirty-six minutes" MVS.
699. "good enough" Ibid.
700. "perfectionist" Ibid.
701. IMDB shows a series of "uncredited" roles and unconfirmed parts in films in 1953, then nothing until 1958.
702. "went through their routines" Jordan, *Norma Jean*.
703. "stuck to it." Ibid.
704. "gilded within an inch of itself" Tom Douglas's unpublished memoirs.
705. In 1954 Webb would discover his friend fabulously wealthy friend Countess di Frasso (former girlfriend of Bugsy Siegel) dead in her Pullman car, wearing mink coat and loaded with jewels. She had apparently suffered a heart attack (Anderson, *Beverly Hills Is My Beat*).
706. "having breakfast served to her" Jordan, *Norma Jean*.
707. "If I want to throw it away" Ibid.
708. "gorgeous" Ibid.
709. "brief" *Variety*, April 25, 1956.
710. *Variety*, April 25, 1956. Ironically, Ted Jordan claimed—but this author has been unable to substantiate—to have doubled for William Holden as he was shot in *Sunset Blvd*.
711. "I think Lili rented it" Kevin Thomas to author, including following
712. "she rummages" Modern Man, "Lili St. Cyr's Royal Wedding Night," *Modern Man*, August 1956.
713. "inept" *Variety*, May 16, 1958.
714. "Lili called him back" *Variety*, August 29, 1956.
715. "normalcy which Harold and I" From Dardy's unpublished memoirs.
716. *Cult Vegas*.
717. "Don't you remember" Dardy to author.
718. "bare-bosomed" *Variety*, January 2, 1957.
719. Oftentimes Klaw would reuse the same pieces in different films. Lili claimed, "The one I did he put into several other movies that I heard about later." (Schaefer, *Bold! Daring! Shocking!*)
720. "Whore" Lili's friend Ian Macdonald to author.
721. "Why do you stay with these men Lili?" Dardy to author.
722. "Who is he?" MVS.
723. "hood" Armando to author.
724. "Hey nobody talks" *Suppressed*, February 1957.
725. "Perhaps you're right" Ibid.
726. "Salad Battle Ends," *Holland Evening Sentinel*, August 24, 1956.
727. Though strangely by September Derek was once again quoted in papers saying he was going to propose to Zsa Zsa.
728. "I was forever known" Lili's friend Pat Carroll to author.
729. "mystery and elegance" MVS.
730. "younger members" Jordan, *Norma Jean*.
731. "French steward" MMF.
732. According to Dardy she would pay for a beautiful apartment for him in Los Angeles on Fountain Avenue.
733. "stripper by night" Taffey O'Neil to author.
734. William Overend, "When the Sun Set on the Strip," *Los Angeles Times*,1981.
735. "sparse turnout" *Variety*, October 9, 1957.
736. "Tonight we go after" Mike Wallace TV interview, 1957 (and all following quotes).
737. Years later, old and in ill health, Wallace, himself a semirecluse, after a career interviewing statesmen, presidents, and dictators, would mention Lili over the others. She was the one who had made the biggest impression. She might have taken

some satisfaction if she had known. (A member of Wallace's staff to author.)

738. "I was more interested in getting the real story" Stars Dodge the Mike Wallace Interview to Avoid Being Tagged 'It' in Public," *Los Angeles Times*, December 1, 1957.

739. "flirting with disaster" Dorothy Kilgallen, "Show Times," *Charleston Gazette*, February 27, 1952.

740. "vain" Dardy to author (and following recollection of her operation).

741. Lili wasn't the only burlesque dancer terrified of being operated on. Scars could cost a career. Margie Hart said she would rather have wrinkles than a scar. Lilly Christine would end up dying due to peritonitis. She didn't believe in having her gorgeous torso cut.

CHAPTER EIGHT

742. Ted Jordan would allege he called Marilyn the night she died. He would claim the same thing when Lili died. (John Gilmore to author.)

743. "She called me" Ibid. (And following conversation.)

744. "stable of strippers" "Stripper St. Cyr Says She Plans Stable of Strippers," *The Progress-Index*, April 25, 1957. *Show Magazine* mentioned Sharon Knight.

745. "reach the end of a rock" *Lowell Sun*, August 10, 1957; "due to some other woman" *Hamilton News Journal*, August 8–10, 1957.

746. *Raleigh Register*, October 7, 1958.

747. "A strange place" *Albuquerque Tribune*, May 23, 1958.

748. "exhausted" MVS.

749. "indestructible beauty" *Escapade*, April 1958.

750. "implication of Lili's name" *Variety*, October 29, 1951.

751. She claimed that's how her reverse strip started.

752. Dell Gordan, *Inside Story*, February 1958. Lili asserted in MVS that Sadie had gotten tired of life on the road and told Lili, "I'm not going on road with you again, Miss St. Cyr."

753. "filled in for her" *Variety*, November 3, 1958.

754. "she takes a lot of knocks" "Lili St. Cyr's Fantastic Flirt with Suicide," *Hush-Hush*, May 1959.

755. "such regularity" Dardy's daughter Ava Minsky Foxman to author. Ava thought it was a Dr. Starr and a Dr. Klifegan (she was unsure of the spelling).

756. "admiring glance" *Variety*, October 8, 1958.

757. "most expensive staged act." *Billboard*, May 8, 1954.

CHAPTER NINE

758. "bathing suit" *Farmington Daily News*, February 19, 1958.

759. "too much mental effort" *Oxnard Press Courier*, February 20, 1959.

760. Sadly Nichols would die at forty-six from complications following a car accident.

761. "I went to Warner Brothers" "Paul Gregory on: Making of the Naked and the Dead," interview, American Legends Interviews, http://www.americanlegends.com/interviews/paul_gregory_natd.html.

762. "excel in next to nothing" *The New Yorker*.

763. "engaged a dietician" *Star News*, July 1, 1958.

764. "Lili" Beldon conversation related to author by Dardy.

765. Mature sent Lili a postcard, misspelling her name, which angered her enough that she kept it for the rest of her life. She told others as far as his fidelity was concerned she trusted him as far as she could throw him.

766. Mildred Halbreich and Beldon were married in 1953 and lived at the El Rancho in a six-room bungalow. They were divorced in 1970. Beldon would be caught rigging an illegal card game at the Friars Club in July of 1967 and die in 1988.

767. "appeared with well worn bathrobe" Frank Scully, *Variety*, September 3, 1958.

768. "well-turned" *Variety*, December 29, 1958.

769. "I've never disrobed" *Tucson Daily Citizen*, August 23, 1958.

770. "films from France" *Bakersfield California*, August 15, 1958.

771. "an hour" Lili's friend Pat Carroll to author.

772. "I don't think anyone" Bill Kennedy, "An Evening with Lili," Mr. L.A., *Los Angeles Herald-Examiner*, June 8, 1965.

773. "conventional" Corman, *How I Made a Hundred Movies in Hollywood and Never Lost a Dime*.

774. "censorship is holding back" *Oxnard Press Courier*, February 20, 1959.

775. "No one church" "Lili St. Cyr Wins Church Battle on Strip," *Los Angeles Herald*, August 18, 1958.

776. "movieland mansion" *Los Angeles Herald-Examiner*, October 2, 1954.

777. "The dancer is separated from" *Tucson Daily Citizen*, October 31, 1958.

778. "sealed court order" "Lili St. Cyr Hopes to Shed Spouse in Reno," *Nevada State Journal*, November 18, 1958.

779. "doesn't know the whereabouts" *Los Angeles Examiner*, November 18, 1953.

780. "will wed singer" *Variety*, December 30, 1958.

781. "hold an audience" *Chicago Tribune*, May 17, 1959.

782. "managed to retain her reputation," "Lili St. Cyr's Fantastic Flirt with Suicide," *Hush-Hush*, May 1959.

783. "desperate despondency" MVS.

784. *Los Angeles Examiner*, October 29, 1959.

785. Armando's wife Georginna to author. In 1979 Armando made the best-dressed list (as did Yul Brynner). *Indianan Evening Gazette*, January 13, 1971.

786. Interestingly, Ted Jordan would continue to sing with Lili in Mapes around the same time Marilyn was filming *The Misfits* in Reno.

787. "didn't want him around" MVS.

788. *Los Angeles Examiner*, December 11, 1959.

789. Joe Zomar's wife Gloriato author.

790. "but that was supposed to have happened" Anonymous source to author.

791. Beldon and Mildred would have their own tax troubles, as Lili had. They appealed and won the tax penalties for the years 1962 through 1970. Dardy claimed Beldon "bought parking lots in Los Angeles, and raked in more money.

792. Warren "Doc" Bailey had also owned the Hacienda with his wife, Judy. Catering to families they installed a miniature golf course. He also owned a small fleet of airplanes and offered customers a package deal including a flight and a stay at the Hacienda.

CHAPTER TEN

793. "cold storage fur closet" Lili's second cousin Kris Plasch to author.

794. This was another bit of Lili fiction. She claimed to her friend Pat Carroll that she didn't purchase a TV until the 1960s, but she shows invoices from Douglas that she bought her first one in 1954. So both Ted and Paul complaining all she would do was watch TV was correct. Lili was not behind the times; she was ahead of times.

795. "giant bed" Joe Zomar Jr. to author.

796. "lynx-like" *Variety*, July 7, 1960.

797. Barbara's stepdaughter Jacqueline remembered that once one was on her father Louis Marx's list , he didn't supervise the list of gifts, he just went out with all regularity.

798. "possessive and dominant" MMF.

799. Ironically she and Jordan had dined there in June of 1954 so Lili could meet her future in-laws.

800. Tom Douglas claimed in his unpublished memoirs to have decorated the Mapes and it being the first high-rise casino/hotel.

801. In his late sixties, hawking his book, Ted was still living in LA with his eightysomething mother.

802. "supply" Jordan, Norma Jean.

803. "you couldn't graduate" Zemeckis, *Behind the Burly Q*.

804. "not only what they were offering" Hearings Before the Committee on Post Office and Civil Service House of Representatives, June 25, 26, 27, and July 10, 24, 1963.

805. "became abusive" Galveston Daily News, "Lili St. Cyr Wins Divorce on Charge of Hubby Cruelty," *Galveston Daily News*, July 11, 1964.

806. She had a nonconsecutive forty-seven-week contract with the Silver Slipper, *Variety*, April 2, 1964.

807. "drank to excess" "Lili St. Cyr Sheds No. 6 Husband," *Citizen-News*, July 7, 1964.

808. "He'd call me nasty names" "Strip Queen Lili Sheds Number 6," *Los Angeles Herald-Examiner*, July 6, 1964.

809. "No . . ." Ibid.

810. "But I would have to be" *Los Angeles Times*, July 9, 1964.

811. "Cashing in his Motion Picture Fund" Ibid.

812. "annoyance" *Variety*, August 31, 1964.

CHAPTER ELEVEN

813. A sixteen-year marriage was claimed in the article "Divorce Parts MinskysAfter Long Marriage," *Bakersfield California*, May 10, 1963.

814. "He carried a briefcase full" Minsky, "A View from the Runway," from unpublished memoirs.

815. "over $300,000" Ibid. (*Nevada State Journal* reported there was $100,000 in back taxes. May 11, 1963.)

816. "Thank God" *Cullman Times*, May 10, 1963.

817. "forced to sell" "Warrant Issued for Producer," *Reno Evening Gazette*, March 22, 1963.

818. "dare attempt suicide" VFB and Dardy to author.

819. "struggling" McGilligan, *Robert Altman* .

820. "romantic"Ibid

821. Lili told her friend Pat Carroll this. Coincidentally, Colette, a former dancer, suffered crippling arthritis, as would Lili.

822. Colette, *Chéri*.

CHAPTER TWELVE

823. The circus" MVS.

824. "hyperactive grown" Weatherford, *Cult Vegas*.

825. "fascination" Ibid.

826. "different kind of improbable" *Variety*, November 6, 1966.

827. "She had them lined up" *Lili St. Cyr*, documentary.

828. "La Belle Lili"; "as close to the rules" *Variety*, April 14, 1965.

829. Ibid.

830. She also wrote the book when she was living with Lorenzo, who presumably would be not too happy if she was dallying with a long-ago dalliance.

831. "quality of the entertainers" *Montreal Gazette*, November 26, 1965.

832. Palmer would die in 1971 at age fifty-seven of lung cancer.

833. "I hardly recognize" MVS.

834. "enclosed patio" Bill Kennedy, "An Evening with Lili," Mr. L.A., *Los Angeles Herald-Examiner*, June 8, 1965.

CHAPTER THIRTEEN

835. "coming to end" MVS.

836. Guild, *Ecstasy and Me*.

837. "the greatest hack ever" Paul Collins, "The Worst Pulp Novelist Ever," *The Stranger*, March 14, 2007.

838. "Every girl would like to marry"Guild, *Ecstasy and Me*.

839. "Fill fifty one-hour" Paul Collins, "The Worst Pulp Novelist Ever," *The Stranger*, March 14, 2007. 845. "I pride myself about doing an" MMF.

840. "I pride myself about an" MMF

841. Lili had at least two, doubtfully ten or eleven.

842. "too strong" MMF.

843. Lili's friend Pat Carroll to author.

844. "The World's Greatest Tabloid" Advertisement for *Midnight Magazine*, showing Lili on the cover, but I've found no copies.

845. "there this week" From Lili's scrapbook.
846. "handicapped" Variety, October 19, 1966.
847. "about a half a dozen" "Lili St. Cyr Adv. Nudes Not Fit to Print, Rules New York Times," Variety, September 7, 1966.
848. She would default on a loan for "delinquent unsecured property taxes" for the tax year of 1971. Interestingly, it was not recorded until 1979—two years after the property was transferred to a new buyer. There is no explanation on record as to why these taxes were not paid in 1971 (oversight, error, etc.) or whether the delinquency was paid by the buyer after recording the lien.
849. "I bought the bra" Cassandra Peterson to author, August 8, 2013.

CHAPTER FOURTEEN

850. "Harold told them" Stripper Dixie Evans to author.
851. "full of life" Lili's cousin Ellie Hiatt to author.
852. "instigator" Ibid.
853. His obituaries state he had heart problems and died in his sleep at seventy-five, the same year as Marilyn Monroe, 1962.
854. "test case" "Montreal Police Arrest Lili St. Cyr in Test Case," European Stars & Stripes, February 24, 1967.
855. "blah chorus line" Los Angeles Times critic Kevin Thomas to author.
856. "fantastic shape" Delaware County Daily Times, July 25, 1967.

PART FIVE
CHAPTER ONE

857. "I'm terrified of old age" Inside Story, February 1957.
858. "La Belle Lili" Al Palmer, "Gayety Closes Season with Popular Program," Montreal Man About Town, The Herald, July 6, 1948.
859. "A woman" Colette, Chéri.
860. His death certificate would say his father was from Croatia.
861. "prefers the company" "Lili Is Not Ready to Retire," unknown newspaper, n.d., from Ellie Hiatt's scrapbooks.
862. "proved to be tumultuous" DiNardo, Gilded Lili.
863. Ted Barker to author (Korean War Project).
864. When I asked one of his relatives—previously friendly—about the information provided under the Freedom of Information Act, she was highly indignant that his records had been obtained and she was no longer "interested in providing" any information to me.
865. "shaggy" Dardy's daughter Ava Minsky Foxman to author.
866. "They both adamantly believed" Ibid.
867. "more theatrical" Lorenzo/Donald Markick's sister to author.
868. She did bring Lorenzo/Donald Markick to Montreal and he was spotted at Champ's with her

in September of 1966.
869. Variety, November 25, 1964.
870. His mother would be a witness at the marriage on March 24, 1958, at the Independent Lutheran Church. The marriage certificate shows they were both from Burbank. I could find no divorce record, which doesn't mean there wasn't one.
871. "That's not of my people" Email from Lili's friend Ian Macdonald to author.
872. "writer" Galveston Daily News, January 11, 1966; "actor" Naugatuck Daily News, September 30, 1965.
873. "looks about 27" Advocate, March 21, 1965.

CHAPTER TWO

874. "a scumball" Ava Minsky Foxman to author.
875. Delaware County Daily Times, July 25, 1967.
876. "a premise, as always" Variety, March 11, 1970.
877. "autoerotic" Variety, March 12, 1970.
878. Harold Minsky would die in Las Vegas after struggling with cancer for six months. He died Christmas morning 1977.
879. "doesn't sing" Van Nuys Valley News, September 15, 1970.
880. Technically it was a cardiac tamponade due to an aneurysm.
881. According to Dardy at one point, either before or after her last husband's death, Idella had been living in a large Victorian house, taking in boarders from the nearby air force base for income. She also lived next door to her mother, Alice.
882. "crabby" Ibid.
883. "not too friendly" Lili's cousin Ellie Hiatt to author.
884. Phone interview with author, 2013.
885. "aches and discomforts" Ibid.

CHAPTER THREE

886. "Don't you know anyone" Lili's friend Ian Macdonald to author.
887. "women past their prime" Colette, Chéri.
888. "took the role" Dardy's daughter Ava Minsky Foxman to author.
889. "weird fat old woman" Ibid.
890. It is assuming Charles B. Murphy was still alive, which is the only thing that makes sense. He possibly died in 1972 or 1977. It's likely he was doing Lili one last favor.

CHAPTER FOUR

891. "adolescence was swamped" Email from Richard O'Brien to author.
892. Ibid.
893. January 16 letter from Lili to Dardy, author's collection.
894. At least by 1975 the owners were Dorothy White and Lana Henderson and the shop catered to a "show-business clientele," Los Angeles Times, February 14, 1975. The shop was in business at least until 1983.
895. "Lili's husband" Author interview with Brett Carlisle, Lili's upstairs neighbor.

896. "aimed at the Quebec market" Weintraub, *City Unique.*

897. Interestingly, the preface misspells her name as "Lily."

CHAPTER FIVE

898. Spencer, it was reputed, was a heroin user and "bad" according to several of the Marx daughters. It was told to me that he stole from both his father and mother.

899. "a claim that the questions" United States of America v. John Doe, United States Court of Appeals.

900. "I told the truth" "Relative of Ellsberg to Testify," *Newport Daily News,* December 3, 1971.

901. "apoplectic" Wells, *Wild Man.*

902. "He couldn't control" Ibid.

903. "adulteries" Wild ManIbid.

904. Dardy to author.

905. Ibid.

906. Barbara's stepdaughter Barbara Marx Hubbard to author.

907. Hubbard, *The Hunger of Eve.*

908. Barbara's stepdaughter Barbara Marx Hubbard to author.

909. In hindsight both Marx's daughters, Jacqueline and Barbara Marx Hubbard, would say they thought Barbara was bipolar.

910. Barbara's death certificate.

911. Rosemary died in 1975, Frederika in 1989.

CHAPTER SIX

912. "Her bone structure" Lillian Hunt's granddaughter Pepper Aarvold (formerly Pearl) to author.

913. Serious. Lili's correspondences.

914. Ibid.

CHAPTER SEVEN

915. "was not so easy" Letter from Armando to Lili.

916. Email from Lili's friend Pat Carroll to author.

917. And which Pat Carroll generously shared with this grateful author.

918. "the light bulb" Pat Carroll to author.

CHAPTER EIGHT

919. "Dardy, I need your help" This and following conversation retold by Dardy to author.

CHAPTER NINE

920. "Once we went to the Beverly Center" Dardy to author.

921. Dixie's reported "alcoholism" was relayed by ex-stripper April March to author.

922. Dixie Evans to author

923. "I think anyone who does what she does" Ibid.

924. A story Lili related in MMF—certainly not a reliable source—was a time in Pasadena when a boyfriend had bloodied and beaten her. "He threatened to kill me for loving someone else." Trauma of some kind did come up with other people when speaking of Lili. She would claim she was hospitalized for weeks.

CHAPTER TEN

925. "Guess who called me today?" Ibid.TK

926. Ibid.

927. She remarked on their similarity in MVS.

928. "spring her" Ibid.

929. The same Ian Macdonald that had lived in Silver Springs had moved to Los Angeles.

930. "It was late afternoon" Email from Lili's friend Pat Carroll to author (and the source of subsequent quotes involving Pat).

931. "frail, scared" Lili's friend Ian Macdonald to author.

CHAPTER ELEVEN

932. "pussycat" Lili's friend Pat Carroll to author.

933. Ibid.

CHAPTER TWELVE

934. "surprise" Lili's friend Ian Macdonald to author.

935. "tear" Ibid.

936. "Spanish speaking" Lili's friend Pat Carroll to author.

937. "She loved the sound of bells" Dardy to author.

PART SIX
EPILOGUE

938. "The end was so sad" Dardy's daughter Ava Minsky Foxman to author.

939. "good family" MVS.

940. "on a lavish scale" *Union Town Morning Herald,* August 23, 1958.

941. Colette, *Chéri.*

942. "sick" MVS.

943. "When I'm expected to do anything" Dawson, "The Durability of Lili."

944. "few ever penetrated the iron curtain". "Mate Sheds Strip Teaser," *Los Angeles Herald,* September 27, 1949.

945. "She never had two weeks off" Armando to author.

946. "I do not wish" "How to Tame a Wolf," *Cabaret,* September 1955.

947. "dependent on anybody." "Lili Sincere, Wanting It Clear She Doesn't Strip, She Dresses," *Los Angeles Times,* May 10, 1953.

948. "I try and give it dignity" *Los Angeles Herald,* March 24, 1955.

949. "She does things" Milton Schuster, *Cabaret,* January 1957 (from Sullivan, *Va Va Voom!*).

950. "first step" MVS.

951. "defiant" Ibid.

952. "no great connection" Armando to author.

953. "Eccentric, brilliant and complicated" Dardy's daughter Ava Minsky Foxman to author.

954. "looked like cows" Lili's friend Pat Carroll to author.

955. "Was the first stripper" "Do Women Hate or Envy Lili?" *Screenland TV,* February 1954.

956. "with a complete obliviousness" Kenneth Johnson, Wolf Gal brochure from Montreal Standard, n.d.

957. "if you put the best ingredients." "The Stripper on the Strip," *Ciro's Monthly,* spring 1952.

958. "she looks cool and controlled" *Rogue for Men*, June 1956.

959. "subtle air" "Do Women Hate or Envy Lili?" *Screenland TV*, February 1954.965. *"I like to live gracefully" Monroe News Star*, February 20, 1958.

960. LZ research

961. "raised burlesque" "Do Women Hate or Envy Lili?" *Screenland TV*, February 1954.

962. "ambition is the most" *The Progress-Index*, April 25, 1957.

963. "went south" Dardy to author.

964. "guilt" MVS.

965. "specific" Ibid.

966. "kindness, humor" MMF.

967. "goddess" *Art Photography*, October 1952; "5,000 photos of her by 1957"*Variety*, June 24, 1957. Bruno would die of cancer in 1987 at seventy-five, not having seen his muse for decades.

968. Cordy died in 1978.

969. Eddie Quinn would die in 1965 in Hobb Nursing Home in New Hampton, New Hampshire, which he owned.

970. Armando in turn said he never liked Dardy. Lili was so "warm, never a critical person. Never nasty. Dardy had that side." Armando to author.

971. "old fat" Stripper Dixie Evans to author.

972. "she looked nothing" Lili's friend Ian Macdonald to author.

973. "her attitude" Dardy's daughter Ava Minsky Foxman to author.

974. "I don't disillusion myself" Peter Diome, "Lili St. Cyr—Art Plays Minor Role in World of Burlesque," *The Gazette*, n.d.

975. "all my life" "Lili Sincere, Wanting It Clear She Doesn't Strip, She Dresses," *Los Angeles Times*, May 10, 1953.

976. "lucky photo" Letter from Lili to her friend Pat Carroll.

BIBLIOGRAPHY

Acton, Harold. *Memoirs of an Aesthete*. London: Methuen, 1948.

Allen, Jane. *Pier Angeli: A Fragile Life*. Jefferson, NC: McFarland, 2002.

Anderson, Clinton H. *Beverly Hills Is My Beat*. Engelwood Cliffs, (NJ): Prentice-Hall, 1960.

Apcar, Frederick. *Vive Les Girls*. n.p.: Circle Theatre, 1966.

Best, Katharine, and Katharine Hillyer. *Las Vegas Playtown USA*. New York: David McKay, 1955.

Best, Katharine. *Las Vegas: Playtown USA*. New York: David McKay, 1955.

Bloom, Ken. *Broadway: Its History, People, and Places*. New York: Routledge, 2003.

Bramson, Seth. *Miami Beach*. Charleston, SC: Arcadia Pub., 2005.

Brown, Peter Harry. *Howard Hughes: The Untold Story*. Cambridge, MA: Da Capo, 2004.

Cédilot, André, André Noël, and Michael Gilson. *Mafia Inc.: The Long, Bloody Reign of Canada's Sicilian Clan*. Toronto: Random House Canada, 2011.

Colette, and Roger Senhouse. *Chéri*. London: Folio Society, 1963.

Collyer, Martin. *Burlesque: The Baubles . . . Bangles . . . Babes*. New York: Lancer, 1964.

Corio, Ann, and Joseph DiMona. *This Was Burlesque*. New York: Madison Square, 1968.

Corman, Roger, and Jim Jerome. *How I Made a Hundred Movies in Hollywood and Never Lost a Dime*. New York: Random House, 1990.

Dawson, Mike. "The Durability of Lili." *Adam Magazine*, 1996.

De Lafayette, Maximillien. *Showbiz, Entertainment, Cabaret Music and Superstars Around the World*. Self-published, 2010.

DiNardo, Kelly. *Gilded Lili: Lili St. Cyr and the Striptease Mystique*. New York: Argo-Navis, 2013.

Dunning, Jennifer. *Alvin Ailey: A Life in Dance*. Reading, MA: Addison-Wesley, 1996.

Figes, Kate. *The Big Fat Bitch Book*. London: Virago, 2007.

Ford, Henry. "My Trip to San Francisco in 1940." Snopes.com, accessed February 5, 2015, www.snopes.com/photos/automobiles/mytriptosf.asp.

Giesler, Jerry, and Pete Martin. *Hollywood Lawyer: The Jerry Giesler Story*. New York: Perma, 1962.

Giesler, Jerry, and Pete Martin. *The Jerry Giesler Story*. New York: Simon and Schuster, 1960.

Gifford, John Charles. *Last Tram on Dorchester Street: A Montral Murder Mystery*. Bloomington, IN: Universe, 2013.

Gladstone, B. James. *The Man Who Seduced Hollywood: The Life and Loves of Greg Bautzer, Tinseltown's Most Powerful Lawyer*. Chicago: Chicago Review Press, 2013.

Goldstein, Richard. *Helluva Town: The Story of New York City During World War II*. New York: Free Press, 2010.

Granlund, N. T. *Blondes, Brunettes, and Bullets*. New York: D. McKay, 1957.

Greenland, Paul R. *Wings of Fire: The History of the Detroit Red Wings*. Rockford, IL: Turning Leaf Publications, 1997.

Grossman, Joanna L., and Lawrence M. Friedman. *Inside the Castle: Law and the Family in 20th Century America*. Princeton: Princeton UP, 2011.

Guild, Leo (for Hedy Lamarr). *Ecstacy and Me: My Life as a Woman*. N.p.: Fawcett Crest, 1967.

Guild, Leo (for Lili St. Cyr). *And Men My Fuel*. Chicago: Novel, 1965.

Hale, Georgia, and Heather Kiernan. *Charlie Chaplin: Intimate Close-ups*. Metuchen, NJ: Scarecrow, 1995.

HistoryLink.org: The Free Online Encyclopedia of Washington State History, accessed February 2, 2015.

Hubbard, Barbara Marx. *The Hunger of Eve*. Harrisburg, PA: Stackpole, 1976.

Humphreys, Adrian. *The Weasel: A Double Life in the Mob*. Mississauga, Ont.: J. Wiley & Sons Canada, 2012.

K, Sue. "Sir Wylie McKissock: Part I: The Surgeon." *Psychosurgery.org*. (blog), September 30, 2006, psych.surgeryorg.blogspot.it/2006/09/sir-wylie-mckissock.html

Jacobson, Mark. *Teenage Hipster in the Modern World: From the Birth of Punk to the Land of Bush: Thirty Years of Millenial Journalism*. New York: Grove, 2005.

James, Brandon. *Jeanne Carmen: My Wild, Wild Life as a New York Pin Up Queen, Trick Shot Golfer & Hollywood Actress*. Bloomington, IN: Universe, 2008.

Jarrett, Lucinda. *Stripping in Time: A History of Erotic Dancing*. London: Pandora, 1997.

Jordan, Ted. *Norma Jean: My Secret Life with Marilyn Monroe*. New York: W. Morrow, 1989.

Korean War Project, accessed December 22, 2014. www.koreanwarproject.org.

Leaming, Barbara. *Orson Welles: A Biography*. New York: Viking, 1985.

Linteau, Paul-André. *The History of Montréal: The Story of a Great North American City*. Montreal: Baraka, 2013.

Manning, Susan. *Modern Dance, Negro Dance: Race in Motion*. Minneapolis: U of Minnesota, 2004.

Marlowe, Ann. *How to Stop Time: Heroin from A to Z*. New York: Basic, 1999.

McGilligan, Patrick. *Robert Altman: Jumping Off the Cliff*. New York: St. Martin's, 1991.

Moss, Jeremiah. *Jeremiah's Vanishing New York* (blog), accessed January 2, 2015, http://vanishingnewyork.blogspot.com.

Palmer, Al. *Montreal Confidential*. Montreal: Véhicule, 2009.

Paris, Barry. *Garbo: A Biography*. New York: Knopf, 1995. Print.

Peck, Carola. *Mariga, and Her Friends*. Ballivor, Co. Meath: Hannon, 1997.

Pink, Sidney. *So You Want to Make Movies: My Life as an Independent Film Producer*. Sarasota, FL: Pineapple, 1989.

Pizzitola, Louis. *Hearst over Hollywood: Power, Passion, and Propaganda in the Movies*. New York: Columbia UP, 2002.

Roberts, Luke. "Strip for Action." *Inside Story* 1958: n.p.

Ross, Becki. *Burlesque West: Showgirls, Sex, and Sin in Postwar Vancouver.* U of Toronto, 2009.

Russo, Gus. *The Outfit: The Role of Chicago's Underworld in the Shaping of Modern America.* New York: Bloomsbury, 2001.

Schaefer, Eric. *Bold! Daring! Shocking! True!: A History of Exploitation Films, 1919–1959.* Durham: Duke UP, 1999.

Schneider, Stephen. *Iced: The Story of Organized Crime in Canada.* Mississauga, Ont.: Wiley, 2009.

Schrag, Peter. *Test of Loyalty: Daniel Ellsberg and the Rituals of Secret Government.* New York: Simon and Schuster, 1974.

Server, Lee. *Robert Mitchum: Baby I Don't Care.* New York: St. Martin's, 2001.

Shaw, Arnold. *52nd Street: The Street of Jazz.* New York: Da Capo, 2009.

Shteir, Rachel. *Striptease: The Untold History of the Girlie Show.* Oxford UP, 2004.

Slide, Anthony. *The Encyclopedia of Vaudeville.* Jackson: UP of Mississippi, 2012.

Smith, Anne. *Women Remember: An Oral History.* London: Routledge, 2012.

St. Cyr, Lili. *Ma Vie de Stripteaseuse.* Montreal: Editions Quebecor, 1982.

Stuart, Amanda Mackenzie. *Empress of Fashion: A Life of Diana Vreeland.* New York: HarperCollins, 2012.

Sullivan, Steve. *Va Va Voom!: Bombshells, Pin-ups, Sexpots, and Glamour Girls.* L.A.: General Pub. Group, 1995.

Summers, Anthony, and Swan Robbyn. *Sinatra: The Life.* New York: Random House, 2005.

Tone, Andrea. *The Age of Anxiety: A History of America's Turbulent Affair with Tranquilizers.* New York: Basic, 2009.

Walters, Barbara. *Audition: A Memoir.* New York: Alfred A. Knopf, 2008.

Wanamaker, Marc, and Robert W. Nudelman. *Early Hollywood.* Charleston, SC: Arcadia Pub., 2007.

Wanamaker, Marc. *San Fernando Valley.* Charleston, SC: Arcadia Pub., 2011.

Weatherford, Mike. *Cult Vegas: The Weirdest! The Wildest! The Swingin'est Town on Earth!* Las Vegas: Huntington, 2001.

Weintraub, William. *City Unique: Montreal Days and Nights in the 1940s and '50s.* Toronto: McClelland & Stewart, 1996.

Wells, Tom. *Wild Man: The Life and Times of Daniel Ellsberg.* New York: Palgrave, 2001.

Wilson, Andrew. *Harold Robbins: The Man Who Invented Sex.* New York: Bloomsbury, 2007.

Zemeckis, Leslie. *Behind the Burly Q: The Story of Burlesque in America.* New York: Skyhorse Publishing, 2013.

ACKNOWLEDGEMENTS

I was helped in part by many who had known Lili, some briefly and some for decades. To all of them I am greatly indebted.

First, I thank Lili's sister Dardy, for her generosity with her stories, documents, and photos and patience answering endless questions. She was right, it is a hell of a story. Without Dardy there would be no book.

Next, I thank Lili's biggest fan—and, ultimately, friend—Pat Carroll, who was more than munificent with Lili's personal photos and letters. Pat shared personal conversations and answered repeat questions with much good humor. I truly believed he brought comfort to Lili in her final years, both spiritual and physical. Lili wrote Pat thanking him for *every penny* he sent. I spent a lovely evening in Pat's apartment while he shared some of Lili's memorabilia. She would be glad to know he cherishes it.

Through Pat I met the (now ordained) Reverend Ian Macdonald and his lovely wife, Kathleen. Ian, Kathleen, and Pat are the only firsthand accounts of Lili's last months. I am indebted to them and cherish our friendship.

It was a great pleasure to get to know Mr. Armando Orsini, who I can attest was charming until the end. He clearly adored *Leelee*. And I laugh about—but won't share—his flirtatious conversations with me over many months before he died. I could see why he was a notorious playboy. We even spoke in his native language. Me, admittedly badly. He clarified many things about Lili. He was tickled to know I had stood on the very same spot where he and Lili honeymooned over the waters of Capri. I recognized the statute in the background of a photo of the two of them sitting on the terrace, both looking radiant.

Armando loved talking about Lili, and though his health and his spirit were deteriorating we enjoyed some laughs. Armando encouraged me to write her story. "It's a tremendous story."

I was devastated to learn, within mere hours, of Armando's destruction of handfuls of love letters, some from Lili, that he had kept for fifty years but was finally getting rid of out of respect for his wife. In hindsight I believe he was preparing for his end. He took a turn for the worse not long afterward and died. I thank his wife, Georginna, for speaking with me several times about Armando and his background.

I thank my dear friend Linda Cody who knew Armando and Elio in their heyday and relayed more Armando and Lili stories. It was through Linda that I was able to reach Lili's Italian "prince."

Many fans were generous. Bob Bethia imparted many conversations, showed me Lili's clothes from the store, and shared pictures. Larry Marshall shared his correspondence with Lili. Jim Norcross was generous with hunting down photos and answering questions, especially as pertained to Lili in Montreal, and continues with his own Lili project, which I hope comes to fruition.

The late Dixie Evans spent hours discussing burlesque and Lili. I miss Dixie and her enthusiasm for all things burlesque.

My dear friend Betty Rowland, former stripper, the Ball of Fire, shared her stories about Lili and burlesque in general.

Peter Ogden was a most generous soul, recounting his Uncle Dick's life with Tom Douglas in "sunny California." I was thunderstruck when he gave me "Uncle Dick's" painting. "Uncle Dick always wanted to go back to California. You should have the painting." I am beyond grateful.

Author Tom Gilmore's stories brought me closer to discovering who Tom Douglas was to Lili.

Pepper Aarvold recalled her backstage memories of Lili, the Follies, and her grandmother Lillian Hunt.

Thank you Ms. Ellie Hiatt, Lili's first cousin. We spent a pleasant morning attempting, once again, to untangle names—chosen and taken—from Alice to Lili, and for the generous use of her scrapbook photos. Thank you also to her daughter Kris Plasch, who is a dead ringer for Lili.

It was important for me to tell the Marx family side of the story and for that I enjoyed conversations with Louis Marx's daughters, Barbara Marx Hubbard and Jacqueline Barnett, both gracious women. I felt an instant kinship with the extraordinary artist Jacqueline, an inspiration if there ever was one.

Glenn Ridenour of the Marx Museum shared an extraordinary home movie of Barbara and three of her sons. For the first time it really brought Barbara to life for me.

I talked and emailed with Ava Minsky Foxman, Lili's niece. I felt as if I'd known Ava forever. She was honest and generous with stories, some which might have once been painful.

Another distant relative of Lili's who wished to remain anonymous did much to clarify Alice's family tree and share records and photos. She knows I thank her as loudly as she permits.

I am most grateful to Ted Barker of the Korean War Project and his help explaining what Donald Markick did—and more importantly, did not do—in the army.

Thank you goes to author Patrick McGilligan for his remembrances of Lili and the rare photo he allowed me to include.

I thank actor Spencer Garrett for allowing me into Lili's apartment. He told me he still occasionally receives fan mail for Lili and feels her presence, and the overly large poster he gifted me of Lili resides proudly among my ever-bursting burlesque collection.

Friend Blake Boyd helped with many introductions and behind-the-scenes-photos in Lili's apartment. Thank you for knowing and using Photoshop.

I reached out to former colleges of Lili's and though many were helpful, others, amusingly were not; Joel Grey—thought his agent—denied he had ever met Lili, though he was on the bill with her at the El Rancho. Roger Corman had no recollections of Lili to share.

Former Ciro's general manager, George Schlatter (who still believed the jury was bussed to Ciro's) was "thrilled" I was doing a story on Lili. He kept saying—as so many did—"she had such humor."

I thank Melisa Cinarli, a French Canadian who enthusiastically translated, not only line by line, but also the meaning of Lili's French biography, not always to be taken literally. Thank you Marine Revel for additional translations.

I thank former college Valerie Wisot, Esq. and my attorney Nancy Boxwell and her team, including Leslie Stevens, who helped untangle the mystery of Lili's Canyon Drive home. Thank you also to Wendy Hamilton for searching the title of Lili's home, which was more than insightful and brought up the name Charles B. Murphy. I traced his family down and spoke with someone who asked me "Is this about one of his mistresses?" When I said yes, no further information was forthcoming.

Thank you goes to the rest of the "gang" at Gang, Tyre, Ramer & Brown, especially Danny Passman, Barbara Silberbush, Harold Brown, and Bruce Ramer. You all go above and beyond and I consider you my warriors.

Thank you, Ted Gerdes, for continuing to untangle rights in all my projects.

Thank you to Matthew Richards and Morgan William for help researching, tracking, logging and finding documents never before uncovered. Monique Perez is the voice of calm and organization, getting me where I need to go to find Lili. Derek Hogue kept me and Lili from disappearing into the ethers of the Internet, thank you so much.

Evan Finn, my film editor extraordinaire, did a fab job with Lili's promo videos and trailer. You rock!

Ironically Lili's last husband, Joe Zomar, worked on my husband's film *Used Cars*, though he could not recall Zomar. I did email Joe's son Joe Jr., who was most helpful with descriptions of Lili's house. And thank you to Zomar's last wife, Gloria, for sharing her stories.

Thank you, Cassandra Peterson, Elvira, for sharing recollections of Lili's store still open in 1981; and to the talented Richard O'Brien for his explanation of why Lili was in his classic *The Rocky Horror Picture Show*.

Author Noel Riley Fitch's beginning research into Lili's story at the behest of Dardy was a starting point for me. A special thank-you for giving me your blessing to continue when you could not.

I believe librarians must be the most wonderful people in the world and I thank many and apologize if I overlooked any; Jacqueline Morin, processing archivist at the USC Library Special Collections, for her clippings on Lili St. Cyr, especially in regards to Ciro's, Nena Couch at Ohio State University, Orville, Martin, Amy Schwegel at the Jerome Robbins Dance Division of the NY Performing Arts Library for information on David Lichine and Ballet Russes; Por Hsyu at the Monrovia Public Library in tracking Ian Blackadder; archivist Renee Jackaman at the Devon County Council for all things related to Lili's brief shipboard romance with Otto Struller; Emma Sinclair at the Lorettonian Society; Martin Gostanian at the Paley Center.

The librarians in Hennepin tracked down what little records remain of numerous Klarquist and Cornett and Peeso relatives; the librarian at Stanford University, Phyllis Kayten, did much to uncover the hearing regarding Lili's mail-order lingerie business and the complaint Protecting Postal Patrons.

A huge glass of wine and many thanks to my agent, Eileen Cope and her undaunting belief in Lili and her story and me. You are a champion and I love having you in my corner.

My editor, Dan Smetanka, and the team at Counterpoint Press for their enthusiasm and smarts. Thank you for letting me have almost everything Lili needed to be in the book. It goes beyond my expectations.

Kelly Cutrone at People's Revolution for her brilliance and good humor getting the extraordinary Lili's story to a wider audience and diving way further into burlesque than she ever imagined. Pop Tart!

Not least of all, I thank my friends, fans, and strangers even, who encouraged me to tell Lili's story. Love and kisses, and thank you lastly to my husband and our three beautiful children, Zane, Rhys, and Zsa Zsa, who give me space to write, knowing they can always interrupt Mommy. I love you all.

INDEX